Working with Children and Families

Working with Children and Families

Knowledge and Contexts for Practice

Edited by

Robert Adams

palgrave
macmillan

First published 2012 by
PALGRAVE MACMILLAN

Palgrave Macmillan in the UK is an imprint of Macmillan Publishers Limited,
registered in England, company number 785998, of Houndmills, Basingstoke,
Hampshire RG21 6XS.

Palgrave Macmillan in the US is a division of St Martin's Press LLC,
175 Fifth Avenue, New York, NY 10010.

Palgrave Macmillan is the global academic imprint of the above companies
and has companies and representatives throughout the world.

Palgrave® and Macmillan® are registered trademarks in the United States,
the United Kingdom, Europe and other countries.

ISBN: 978–0–230–55307–1

This book is printed on paper suitable for recycling and made from fully
managed and sustained forest sources. Logging, pulping and manufacturing processes
are expected to conform to the environmental regulations of the country of origin.

A catalogue record for this book is available from the British Library.

A catalog record for this book is available from the Library of Congress.

10 9 8 7 6 5 4 3 2 1
21 20 19 18 17 16 15 14 13 12

Printed and bound in Great Britain by MPG Books Group, Bodmin and King's Lynn

Contents

List of Boxes, Figures and Tables

Boxes

Figures

Tables

Notes on Contributors

Robert Adams is Emeritus Professor at the School of Health and Social Care, Teesside University. He has researched and written extensively about social work and social policy, including bestselling books translated into several languages. His social work experience includes directing a community-based centre for Barnardo's, working multiprofessionally with children and families.

Elizabeth A. Boyle is a lecturer in psychology at the University of the West of Scotland where she teaches courses in child development, lifespan development, psychology and education and psychological theory. Her research interests lie in the area of thinking, learning, communication and motivation. She has published papers in the areas of learning styles, motivation and the use of computer games in learning.

Alison Cocks began work in social care in the early 1990s, in a centre for physically disabled adults. Once qualified as a social worker, she discovered the challenges and excitement to be gained from working with children with disabilities and their families. Since joining academia, her research interests have primarily been concerned with how disabled children experience the provision of social services. She is also interested in social work values and the ethics of research and methods that promote inclusion in research. Alison is currently working as an independent consultant and researcher.

Liz Davies has many years of practice experience as a child protection manager and now teaches social work at undergraduate, postgraduate and post-qualifying levels. She has a particular interest in training police and social workers in joint investigation and interview skills and has developed an online multiagency child protection training resource with Akamas Publishing. Liz writes widely on the subject and contributed to a *Real Story* BBC television documentary *Saving Becky* on the subject of the sexual exploitation of children.

Patricia Higham is an independent consultant for social work and social care education and training. She is professor of social work and social care emeritus at Nottingham Trent University, visiting professor at the University of Northampton, and a non-executive director of NHS Nottinghamshire.

Sandy Hobbs, senior research fellow in the School of Social Sciences in the University of the West of Scotland, was previously reader in psychology. His main fields of research are child employment and the social psychology of knowledge.

Jan Horwath is professor of child welfare at the University of Sheffield. She has a social work background. Jan has particular research interests in assessment practice, factors that influence parenting and multidisciplinary practice. Jan is the author of a number of publications on childcare practice, her most recent book is *The Child's World: The Comprehensive Guide to Assessing Children in Need* (2009).

Maggie Jackson is a senior lecturer at Teesside University and has previously worked for the county psychological service in Redcar, where she worked with children, schools and families on issues of loss and bereavement. She was a also a member of their critical incident debriefing team. She has written a number of articles and books about loss and death, including *The Teacher's Handbook of Death* (2001), which she co-wrote with her colleague Jim Colwell.

Lesley Jessiman completed her PhD in the psychology department at the University of Dundee. This was followed by a postdoctoral research fellowship in the same department, researching the effects of typical and pathological ageing on language and communication. Lesley currently has a lecturing post at the University of the West of Scotland, where her primary teaching is in developmental psychology. Lesley's research interests are quite broad, her principal interest being the neuropsychology of language. She is particularly interested in the relationship between language development in children and language degeneration in older adults.

Janet Lees is a speech and language therapist and an ordained minister of the United Reformed Church. She has published a wide range of work in both fields. Her PhD was about parental knowledge of learning to talk in a multicultural, multifaith community. Her research interests include parenting in multicultural urban UK contexts. She is an honorary research fellow of the Department of Human Communication Sciences of the University of Sheffield.

Jim McKechnie is a professor of psychology at the University of the West of Scotland. His primary research area is developmental psychology and his early research investigated infant's problem-solving abilities. He has published extensively in the area of young people's transitions into employment.

Jennifer Newton is currently director of postgraduate programmes in the Department of Applied Social Sciences at London Metropolitan University, and teaches on social work, policy and management programmes. Her background is in research and service evaluation, and her published work includes *Care Management: Is It Working?* (1996, co-authored) and *Preventing Mental Illness* (1988).

Terence O'Sullivan is principal lecturer in social work at the University of Lincoln. He has written a number of articles with particular regard to practice. He is the author of *Decision Making in Social Work* (1999).

Terry Thomas is professor of criminal justice studies at Leeds Metropolitan University. He was a social worker and team leader in a local authority social services department.

David Thompson is a graduate of the University of Teesside and University of York. Dave now works as a part-time lecturer at Leeds Metropolitan University and Teesside University, with research interests in policing, criminal justice and young people's involvement in crime.

Neil Thompson is the managing director of Avenue Consulting Ltd (www. avenuecon sulting.co.uk), a company offering training and consultancy across the people professions. He is a well-established and highly respected author. His latest book is *Theorizing Social Work Practice* (2010). Neil has held full or honorary professorships at four UK universities and has been a speaker at conferences and seminars worldwide. He is the editor-in-chief of the online community Social Work Focus (www.socialworkfocus.com). His personal website is www.neilthompson.info.

Wade Tovey is the director of Enhancing Practice and Innovation Centre for Care and assistant dean at the School of Health and Social Care, Teesside University. He was formerly head of social work. He has led over 50 projects, including national projects around participation for people who use services and carers and has interests in personalization, partnership working and workforce development. He edited the successful *The Post-Qualifying Handbook for Social Workers* (2007) and has a number of other publications. He plays a leading role in various regional activities, is a member of the executive of Skills for Care, North East, and is on the board of the Open Learning Foundation and Darlington Children's Trust.

Pat Watson is an experienced researcher with a particular interest in participatory research and evaluation techniques with both adults and children. Her key areas of expertise include participation, user involvement, regeneration, organizational change, community safety, antisocial behaviour, drugs, social exclusion, youth empowerment and delivering training. She has a strong commitment to the participation of harder to reach groups, particularly children and young people in the research and evaluation process.

Michael Wyness is associate professor in childhood studies at the Institute of Education, the University of Warwick. His research interests are in the sociologies of childhood and education. His current book *Childhood and Society* (2006) is going into a second edition. His previous books were *Contesting Childhood* (2000) and *Schooling Welfare and Parental Responsibility* (1995). He is currently working on projects in relation to primary-secondary transitions and social trust in schools.

Acknowledgements

I should like to acknowledge the help given to me by Catherine Gray at Palgrave Macmillan in the preparation of this book. I am also grateful for the careful and detailed editorial attention provided by Kate Llewellyn at Palgrave Macmillan.

The editor, contributors and publishers would also like to thank United Nations Children's Funds (UNICEF) for permission to use the ladder of participation in Chapter 17, adapted from R.A. Hart (1992) *Children's Participation: From Tokenism to Citizenship*, Innocenti Essays No. 4, UNICEF International Child Development Centre, Florence.

Every effort has been made to trace the copyright-holders, but if any have been inadvertently overlooked the publishers will be pleased to make the necessary arrangements at the first opportunity.

Abbreviations

CAF	Common Assessment Framework
CAMHS	child and adolescent mental health services
CEHR	Commission for Equality and Human Rights
CPAG	Child Poverty Action Group
CPD	continuing professional development
CRB	Criminal Records Bureau
CWDC	Children's Workforce Development Council
DCSF	Department for Children, Schools and Families
DfE	Department for Education
DfEE	Department for Education and Employment
DfES	Department for Education and Skills
DH	Department of Health
DHSS	Department of Health and Social Security
DHSSPS	Department of Health, Social Services and Public Safety (Northern Ireland)
DWP	Department for Work and Pensions
ECHR	European Convention on Human Rights
ECM	Every Child Matters
ECRI	European Commission against Racism and Intolerance
EDCM	Every Disabled Child Matters
ESRC	Economic and Social Research Council
EU	European Union
EYFS	Early Years Foundation Stage
GP	general practitioner
HIV	human immunodeficiency virus
IRR	Institute of Race Relations
MBPS	Munchausen by proxy syndrome
NACRO	National Association for the Care and Resettlement of Offenders
NCB	National Children's Bureau
NGO	nongovernmental organization
NSPCC	National Society for the Prevention of Cruelty to Children
ODPM	Office of the Deputy Prime Minister
Ofsted	Office for Standards in Education

ONS	Office for National Statistics
QCA	Qualifications and Curriculum Authority
SCIE	Social Care Institute for Excellence
SEU	Social Exclusion Unit
ToM	theory of mind
TSO	The Stationery Office
UN	United Nations
UNCRC	United Nations Convention for the Rights of the Child
UNHCR	United Nations High Commission for Refugees
UNICEF	United Nations Children's Fund
WHO	World Health Organization

Introduction

Robert Adams

This book aims to provide practitioners working with children and their families with a broad range of material to underpin their practice. The intended readers of the book include the very varied workforce of children's services, including managers and practitioners; social workers, teachers and children's and nursery nurses; childminders; healthcare, nursery and teaching assistants; children's activity coordinators and workers, in the statutory, private, independent and voluntary sectors.

The content of the earlier contextual chapters of the book contributes to the requirement that students and new entrants to the children's services workforce not only have expertise in their particular professional and vocational area but also possess an understanding of the social factors affecting childhood and the world of children, policy and legislation, procedures and standards for practice. The later chapters in the book aim to help practitioners respond confidently and appropriately to the challenges represented by the range of experiences, problems and needs of children, their families and carers.

The future priorities for services for children in need and their families continue to attract high-profile professional, political and public debates. The history of child education and care has established a rich tapestry of national and local provision throughout the UK. However, partly because of this richness and partly because issues surrounding children's development and childcare continue to generate controversy, there is great complexity and – in Scotland, Wales, Northern Ireland and England in the wake of devolution in the 1990s – significant national, regional and local variety in policies, legislation and practice concerning these services for children and their families. It is true that over the past decade policy initiatives such as Sure Start have aimed to put in place national and local resources and services that are more joined up than ever. At the same time, however, enormous challenges remain, one of which this book aims to tackle – namely, to provide material for practitioners to use in critically debating and developing more informed practice in work with children and their families.

Structure of the book

This book sets out to provide an introduction for practitioners across the field of work with children and families to the 'social' aspects of the knowledge required. **Part 1**, comprising Chapters 1 and 2, introduces the major policy themes that have preoccupied policy makers, managers and practitioners, concerning work with children and families. It is important for practitioners to appreciate the wider context of perspectives on this work (**Parts 2** and **3**). This entails debating the nature of childhood (Chapter 3) and the changing character of the family in society (Chapter 8), as well as appreciating key aspects of children's development and learning (Chapters 4–7 and 9). It is important also to appreciate perspectives on parenting (Chapter 10) and to develop a grasp of available knowledge and research evidence on particular areas of practice (Chapters 11–15).

Work with children and families is rooted in values and principles, tackled in different ways in **Part 4**. The ethical basis for practice is discussed in Chapter 16 and the importance of participation by children in Chapter 17. The evidence justifying equality-based practice is examined in Chapter 18. Finally, Chapter 19 discusses a pertinent professional issue of working with children regarded as challenging.

Part 5 deals with aspects of children's welfare in connection with their health (Chapter 20), mental health (Chapter 21), the mental health of their parents (Chapter 22) and their safeguarding (Chapter 23). These areas all need considering when children are being assessed and services are planned and developed with them and their families (Chapter 24).

Work with children and their families needs to take account of their particular needs and circumstances and part of this responsibility is exercised by practitioners having due regard for their uniqueness and diversity. **Part 6** highlights particular aspects of this diversity, beginning in Chapter 25 with consideration of differences of faith. Chapter 26 deals with some practice implications of the development of children's identities. Chapter 27 discusses aspects of physical impairments and Chapter 28 explores learning disabilities. Finally, policy and practice concerning asylum seekers, refugees and Travellers are examined in Chapter 29.

Features of the book

The chapters in the book use the following features to maximize their clarity and relevance to the busy reader:

■ *Learning outcomes:* a list of bullet points at the start of each chapter, specifying what you should achieve by reading it.

■ *Points for reflection:* these are inserted at key points in the text, inviting you to think about a topic of particular importance.

■ *Practice studies and examples:* these are threaded through each chapter, to give you illustrations of particular ideas, concepts or approaches in practice.

Towards the end of each chapter, you will find the following:

■ *Review questions:* a short list of questions to stimulate you to reflect on the material you have read in the chapter and, hopefully, the additional study this has stimulated you to undertake.

■ *Chapter links:* a brief indication of connections you can make with material in other chapters.

■ *Further reading:* a short list of relevant articles, chapters or books, which you can use to follow up particular areas in more detail.

■ *Websites:* an indication of some relevant websites that provide information and may enable you to undertake further study.

It only remains to express the hope that you find the material in this book stimulating and that it leads you to further study and helps you to practise with greater confidence and expertise.

Part 1

Introducing Working with Children and Families

Working Together with Children and Families

Robert Adams

LEARNING OUTCOMES

By the end of this chapter, you should be able to:

- understand the structure of children's services across the UK
- understand key aspects of policy and law for children and families, including Every Child Matters and the Children Act 2004
- identify key themes of working with children and families

This chapter provides a critical context for the study of children and the practice of working with them, whether in education or social services. It offers a general introduction to services for children and their families, as well as the main policies and legal contexts. The practice of work with children, their parents, carers and families is shaped by the major policy and legal changes of the early 21st century, and particularly by the services and provisions put in place by past and present governments.

Services for children and their families

The policy and legislative basis for children's services in the 21st century in England and Wales is expressed in the Children Act 1989 and the Children Act 2004, the latter stimulated by the inquiry report into the death of Victoria Climbié (Laming, 2003), which led to the Green Paper *Every Child Matters* (DfES, 2003a). In England, the Children Act 2004 led to:

- the creation of children's trusts, bodies responsible for setting the strategic policy for services and delivering these services through a partnership board of participating agencies, organizations and groups

■ new children's services departments being formed from the merger of local authority education and social services departments.

The aim of this was to bring about more integrated, that is, 'joined-up', services than formerly.

In Wales, similar functions are still carried out by education and social services. In Scotland, most of the social work services for children and families are commissioned directly by the 32 local authority social work departments, whereas education services, including schooling, are provided separately by local authorities. In Northern Ireland, the Department for Education is responsible for children's education services and the Department of Health, Social Services and Public Safety (DHSSPS) for social services.

The policy on children's trusts is changing as this book is being written. The coalition government (2010 onwards) announced in July 2010 that a forthcoming Education Bill would downgrade the importance of children's trusts, remove the obligation on local authorities to set up a children's trust board and withdraw statutory guidance on the Children and Young People's Plan (the blueprint for children's services).

A symbol of the increasing importance to policy makers and practitioners of children's rights in the UK is the creation of children's commissioners, responsible for promoting awareness of children's views, interests and rights. The first of these children's commissioners was appointed in Wales in 2001, the second in Scotland in 2002 and the third in Northern Ireland in 2003. In England, the first children's commissioner was not appointed until 2004, under the Children Act 2004.

Let us take a closer snapshot of the way children's services are organized in the UK. A complex array of services for children and families is maintained by national and local government in the four countries of the UK. Since the general election of May 2010, when the coalition government replaced the Labour government (1997–2010), responsibility for children's services in England rests with the Department of Education.

Services in England

Since 2009, the director of children's services, who also directs children's social services, has taken over from the former local education authorities the responsibility for administering local education in the state sector. Figure 1.1 illustrates the different functions of children's services in a typical local authority. These are carried out by trusts, agencies, departments and groups in health, education, social services, youth justice, housing, community and environment and providers in the third sector, that is, private, voluntary and independent bodies and groups. Details of the typical practitioners employed in these different sectors are shown in Table 1.1.

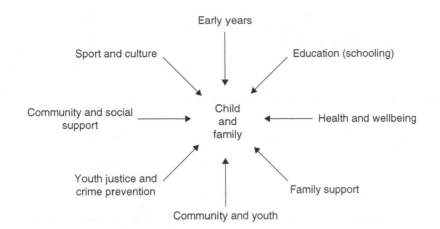

Figure 1.1 Functions of children's services in an English local authority

Table 1.1 Examples of practitioners in different sectors

Sector	Examples
Health	Nurses, midwives, health visitors, general practitioners (GPs), paediatricians, dentists, ophthalmologists, clinical psychologists, mental health workers, dieticians, occupational therapists, physiotherapists, speech therapists
Education	Teachers, educational psychologists, education welfare officers, learning mentors, support workers
Social services	Social workers, care workers, childminders, foster carers, early years staff, home carers, substance abuse workers
Youth justice	Youth offending team staff, probation officers, police officers, community support officers, domestic violence staff, juvenile home staff
Housing, community and environment	Housing officers, benefits staff, community workers, workers in different faiths, leisure and sporting workers
Third sector	Care workers, support workers, volunteers

The Care Standards Act 2000 established the framework for the registration of practitioners in social services. The Commission for Social Care Inspection established under the 2003 Health and Social Care (Community Health and Standards) Act and the Commission for Healthcare Audit and Inspection set up in 2004 (later known as the Healthcare Commission) were replaced in 2009 by the Care Quality Commission (CQC). The CQC is responsible for registering, inspecting and reporting on adult social care services in England. The Office for Standards in Education (Ofsted), which was set up in 1992, inspects children's services, under the Children Act 2004 (Box 1.1), which amended some of the arrangements made under the Care Standards Act 2000 (Box 1.2).

Box 1.1 Children Act 2004

- Put in place a single children's services department in each local authority
- Ensured that by 2006 each local authority had a Children and Young People's Plan
- Generated mechanisms to create children's trusts to allocate funding to children's services by 2008

Box 1.2 Care Standards Act 2000

- Created mechanisms for regulating private and voluntary healthcare in England
- Set up systems for regulating and inspecting healthcare and social care in Wales
- Established independent councils and registers for practitioners in social care, including social work

---

Services in Wales

In Wales, the DHSS is responsible for the children's commissioners, the Healthcare Inspectorate Wales and the Care and Social Services Inspectorate Wales, which regulates adult and children's services and works directly to the National Assembly of Wales, independent from the Welsh Assembly Government. Through these mechanisms, the governance of Wales in less independent from England than Scotland, but more independent than Northern Ireland. In social services in general and children's and families' services in particular, the direction of policy in Wales puts a greater emphasis than in England on promoting the rights of children and young people.

Services in Northern Ireland

In Northern Ireland, health and social care are provided as integrated services through the central Department for Health, Social Services and Public Safety (DHSSPS) and the Health and Social Care Board. There are five Education and Library Boards responsible for education provision within the local council areas. There are six Health and Social Care Trusts, five of which provide integrated health and social care services across Northern Ireland, the sixth being the Northern Ireland Ambulance Service. The Regulation and Quality Improvement

Authority regulates health and social care services, including social services for children and adults, inspected by the Office of Social Services in the DHSSPS.

Services in Scotland

In Scotland, the councils in each council area retain responsibility for local government services; for instance, there are generic departments for adult and children's services. So health and social care services include criminal justice as well as adult services and services for children and young people. Figure 1.2 provides an example of how provision is organized in a Scottish city setting.

In Scotland, the Care Commission regulates standards of social care services under the Regulation of Care (Scotland) Act 2001, through the Social Work Inspection Agency, which is responsible for regulating and inspecting social care in general. On 1 April 2011, the work of the Social Work Inspection Agency passed to a new body, Social Care and Social Work Improvement Scotland. The HM Inspectorate of Education (Scotland) participates in joint inspections of children's services.

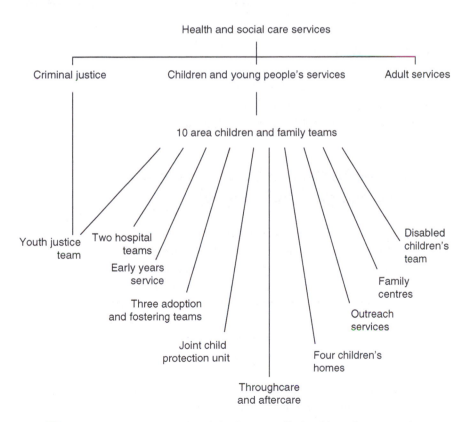

Figure 1.2 Example of a Scottish city council's health and care service

Point for reflection

In your opinion, to what extent should the government be involved with the upbringing of a child in modern society?

Policy and legal developments leading to 21st-century children's services

In 2000, the *Framework for the Assessment of Children in Need and their Families* (DH/DfEE/Home Office, 2000) made it clear that services and work with children must take place in the context of work with the family. This was followed by the Green Paper *Every Child Matters* (DfES, 2003a) and the Children Act 2004. Meanwhile, service standards for children, young people and maternity services were published (DH/DfES, 2004a) (Box 1.3).

Box 1.3 *National Service Framework for Children, Young People and Maternity Services* (DH/DfES, 2004a)

Aims to improve the delivery of five main aspects of health and social care:

1. Health and wellbeing
2. Child-centred services
3. Safeguarding and promoting welfare
4. Supporting disabled children and those with complex health needs
5. Promoting mental health and psychological wellbeing

Birth to Three Matters (DfES, 2002) and *Every Child Matters* (DfES, 2003a)

The two main policy statements that set the direction of travel for policy and practice in the early 21st century are *Birth to Three Matters* (DfES, 2002) and *Every Child Matters* (DfES, 2003a). The publication of the *Birth to Three Matters* framework marks the official recognition that the upbringing of infants and small children should be a matter of public and professional responsibility, rather than being left to the private concerns of parents, carers and other family members. This shift is a stage in a longer and deeper rooted historical process of change (see also Chapter 2), but in the 21st century it is clearly given a boost by three main factors:

■ The accumulating weight of research evidence on the importance to children's later development of their experiences in the early years.
■ The aftermath and outcomes of a continuing series of major scandals attributed to failures of the state to safeguard infants and younger children

from serious abuse, neglect and death at the hands of those adults primarily responsible for their care.

■ Since the 1970s, there has been awareness of the positive value of joint working between different professions engaged in practice with children and their families. Repeatedly, the message from the failings of childcare services has been that the major education, health and social services agencies, in local authority and voluntary and independent sectors, need to work more closely and effectively together.

The direction of present-day policy and practice regarding services for children is towards holistic provision and practice. *Holistic approaches* are those that view the person and the person's needs and personal fulfilment as a whole, physically, mentally, emotionally and spiritually, as individuals and in their relationships with other people, their family and the wider environment.

The principles of the government Green Paper *Every Child Matters* (DfES, 2003a) are largely holistic, in the sense that the purpose is to meet the needs of the whole child and aim at complete health and wellbeing. The Green Paper set out five main goals to achieve for children and young people, as shown in Box 1.4. In order to achieve health and wellbeing, services need to be delivered in an integrated way, that is, there should be a high level of collaboration between the different agencies and professionals.

Box 1.4 *Every Child Matters* (DfES, 2003a)

---

1. *To be healthy:* Promoting their mental and emotional health
2. *To stay safe:* Safeguarding them from having to be looked after, so as to protect them against abuse and exploitation
3. *To enjoy and achieve:* Ensuring they are treated inclusively and can enjoy high-quality facilities provided not only by statutory but also by voluntary and independent agencies in their play, social and leisure time
4. *To achieve economic wellbeing:* Ensuring looked after and disabled children can progress through education
5. *To make a positive contribution:* Ensuring children are not bullied, are listened to and are able to take part in significant decisions affecting their lives

---

Early Years Foundation Stage

The Early Years Foundation Stage (EYFS) was published by the government in 2008 (DfE, 2008) to form the basis for the learning and development of children in their early years. The EYFS is the mandatory quality framework for all providers of early years services, including maintained schools, non-maintained schools, independent schools and childcare on the early years register and inspected by Ofsted. The EYFS combines the publications *Birth to Three Matters* (DfES, 2002), *Curriculum Guidance for the Foundation Stage* (QCA, 2000) and aspects of the *National Standards for Under 8s Day Care and Childminding* (DfES, 2003b). Four principles of the EYFS express the values on which they are based, each principle being linked with a commitment indicating how it can be implemented:

1. *A unique child:* Each child has the ability from birth to learn and the capacity to be resilient and confident.
2. *Positive relationships:* A foundation of loving and secure relationships enables each child to develop strength and independence.
3. *Enabling environments:* Children's development and learning are furthered by their environment.
4. *Learning and development:* Children have unique patterns of learning and development, all aspects of which are equally important and are connected with each other.

The Foundation Stage Profile was renamed the EYFS Profile and is a summative assessment of the progress of each child towards the early learning goals. The EYFS links with Key Stage 1 (DfES, 2003c), which forms the basis for primary education. The aim of the EYFS is to introduce a flexible approach to care and learning through inclusive practice with children, their parents and carers. The EYFS is intended to empower children to make their own decisions, as is appropriate to their age and maturity, and to promote their participation in partnership with their parents and carers (Kirby et al., 2003a).

Ofsted

Childminders, playgroups, nurseries and other similar early years services must register with Ofsted in England, the Care Standards Inspectorate for Wales, the local Health and Social Care Trusts in Northern Ireland, or the Scottish Commission for Regulation of Care (known as the Care Commission).

In England, Ofsted monitors, registers and inspects services for children and families, including looked after children and early education and child-care. *Looked after children*, apart from those looked after in informal arrange-ments, includes children fostered out, adopted or in residential care. Informal arrangements include the increasingly common kinship care, entailing a rela-tive or friend, which is positively viewed by a significant proportion of children and young people (Broad et al., 2001). Foster care – by far the commonest arrangement – is a temporary way in which the local authority ensures that the child is looked after, while the child's birth parents still remain firmly in the picture. Adoption is permanent, with the new, adoptive parents assuming full legal parental responsibility. The Labour government introduced arrangements to speed the process of adoption (see DH Adoption and Permanence Taskforce, 2001).

There are five main forms of early education and childcare: childminding, full day care, out of school care, sessional daycare and crèches (Ofsted, 2005):

- *Early education* is the term used to cover childminding (often referred to under group daycare) and other daycare such as nurseries for children under eight years. *Childminder* is the term used for a person, other than a foster carer, who, on domestic premises and for more than two hours a day, looks after one or more children under eight, unrelated to them and on a paid basis.
- *Full daycare* is continuous care exceeding four hours a day in a nursery, children's centre or family centre.
- *Out of school care* is daycare before or after school for more than two hours a day and five days per year, for children aged three to eight.
- *Sessional daycare* is up to four hours of care for up to five sessions a week for children up to eight years old. A *playgroup* is a non-daycare setting where children attend either the morning or the afternoon session but are not present during the lunch break.
- A *crèche* provides temporary or occasional daycare for children up to eight years old.

Children's trusts

Government policy has led to the creation of a market for services for children, young people and their families, which means that services are provided by many different agencies, organizations and groups. Local authorities are expected by government to encourage the development of these providers, through investing in them, building their capacity and developing an infrastructure to support them. Children's trusts play a central coordinating role in these developments. They contribute to the government's goal of developing services provided by a variety of private, voluntary and independent agencies, organizations and groups, rather than through a single public sector provider.

In the wake of the government's aspiration to transform children's services, expressed in the publication of the Green Paper *Every Child Matters* in 2003, the Children Act 2004 (s. 10) placed a duty to cooperate on relevant partners, such as local authorities, strategic health authorities, primary care trusts, probation service, police, youth offending teams, Connexions, the Skills Funding Agency and the Young People's Learning Agency. Local authorities are expected to produce a Children and Young People's Plan. The purposes of children's trusts are to ensure joint planning and commissioning of services and to deliver better outcomes for children, organized around the needs of children and families, through effective joint working and integrated frontline delivery. Children's trusts are very diverse in different localities of England and comprise the total array of partnership arrangements between different local organizations to deliver better outcomes for children and young people. Each trust is governed by a children's trust board, intended to be strongly integrated and responsible for ensuring that interagency working, Sure Start and other comparable services as well as the Common Assessment Framework are all working together.

In 2004, the DfES published the *Common Core of Skills, Knowledge and Competence for the Children's Workforce* (DfES, 2004a). The aims of the six components of this common core are:

- to provide a shared basis of understanding, values and skills for the greatest possible range of workers in children's services
- to promote more flexible development and career progression in the children's workforce.

Under the Apprenticeships, Skills, Children and Learning Act 2009, children's trusts have been extended to include as statutory partners maintained schools, non-maintained special schools, academies, sixth-form and further education colleges, among other services. Children's trusts also are intended to work with providers in the third sector, many of whom – such as voluntary childcare charities like Barnardo's and The Children's Society – are major providers of children's and families' services.

The third sector

The third sector is the term used to refer to the variety of nongovernmental organizations whose activities are based on values, are not primarily motivated by profit and involve reinvesting any surpluses in resources with a social purpose. The third sector comprises charities, voluntary organizations, community organizations, cooperatives, mutual organizations and social enterprises.

Organizations in the third sector can be distinguished from public sector healthcare authorities and local authorities in three main ways:

- they are set up independently of the state
- they run themselves, that is, their governance is independent of the state
- they rely, at least to some extent, on volunteers.

Some social enterprises blur this distinction between state agencies and the third sector, since they share some characteristics of both the voluntary and private sectors. At its simplest, the voluntary organization in the third sector does not distribute profits, whereas some social enterprises that straddle the boundary and possess some features of third sector organizations do distribute profits. In some parts of the UK, especially rural districts and communities that are isolated and dispersed as in Scotland, the term the 'social economy' is used and measured (Scottish Government, 2011).

Working with children and families: integrated qualifications and integrated working

The Integrated Qualifications Framework, embodying a common core of skills, knowledge and understanding, was implemented in 2008 and entails a progressive procedure for reviewing new and existing qualifications so as to develop a single children's workforce and a culture of integrated working.

The professionalization of early years work does not of itself solve all the problems of previous generations. It creates new challenges of its own. As part of this, a new balance has to be struck between the nurturing of parents and other primary carers for children in the privacy of their homes and the professionals, including new professions, in children's services. The Commission on Families and the Wellbeing of Children (Rutter, 2005) was established in 2004 to consider the relationship between the state and the family in bringing up children. The commission examined how far the state should intervene in children's care and upbringing; how far parents should be held responsible for what their children do; how far the state should support, and at the same time intervene in, families. It recommended that restrictions should be placed on the criminal sanctions against parents on account of their children's misbehaviour and that parents should be given the right to participate at every level in the development and implementation of family services (Rutter, 2005: xxiii).

A new balance also has to be struck between the education, health and 'social' professions. The main point to note is that in England, for instance, where in the first decade of the 21st century local authority education departments and social services departments have merged into new departments of children's services, this has not just brought 'care' and 'education' together but, as important, the 'social' in social work. The 'social' perspective is as much of a challenge as the integrating of 'care' and 'education', since the 'social' brings the family and the wider social environment into the consideration of the needs of the child. Despite the aspiration of policy towards a seamless service, authoritative commentators (Langston and Abbott, 2005) maintain that there remains a disparity between what in a shorthand way we may call the education and the childcare components:

> In daycare settings inspectors are largely interested in care and health and safety issues, as outlined in the *National Standards for Under 8s Day Care and Childminding* (DfES, 2003), and only Standard 3 focuses fully on play and learning. On the other hand, it could be argued that there is an overemphasis on the curriculum, as opposed to the child, in require-ments for the inspection of Nursery Education (s. 122), and that the wider issues which lead to children becoming strong and emotionally healthy can sometimes be overlooked. The philosophy and ethos of *Birth to Three Matters* (DfES, 2002) and the *Curriculum Guidance for the Foundation Stage* (QCA, 2000) purport to be the same, yet there are clear differences in priorities. Although in theory, it should be easier for settings providing for babies and children from birth to 5 years to offer experiences that are 'seamless', in practice a different regime often exists for children over the age of 3 years. Similarly, there are two distinct purposes of inspection and each makes assessments of quality in relation to very different criteria. It is not surprising that, to the uninitiated, their ratings can give rise to some confusion. (Langston and Abbott, 2005, p. 74)

The lesson to central and local government that emerges from repeated inquiries into the shortcomings of children's services is the challenging nature of the goal of developing and delivering integrated services.

Tensions between nurturing children, attending to their rights and controlling them

The twin themes of reform and rescue have been recast over the last century and a half, in the different incarnations of policy and legislation for children and young people. From the last quarter of the 20th century, they have been most clearly visible in the tension between the goals of meeting the welfare needs of children and young people, attending to their rights, or meting out justice to them (Table 1.2). We shall consider these in turn.

Table 1.2 Nurture, rights and control in work with children

Nurture	Rights	Control
Caring for children	Preserving the rights of children	Prevention of harm to children
Therapeutic services to children	Promoting participation by children	Intervening to stop abuse and minimize risks

---

Point for Reflection

In which order of priority, in terms of the relative importance of each to the upbringing of children, would you place these notions of nurture, rights and control?

The reality is that, as they grow up, all children require nurturing, as well as attention to their rights and a measure of control:

1. *Nurturing approaches* in the public services prioritize care for children, which, where there are problems, requires therapeutic services. This includes approaches to caring for children and therapeutic services. A range of caring and therapeutic services respond to children's nurturing – that is, emotional, physical, moral and social needs – at different points in their development. Direct therapeutic or care work with some children will be more necessary and urgent than with others, depending on the extent to which they have been affected by various problems, perhaps arising in the family or perhaps on a wider basis. The most probable difficulties are likely to arise in four main areas (Table 1.3).

2. *A rights-based approach* is based on the principle that children have the right to be consulted about, and involved significantly in, decisions about them. This is laid down in Article 12 of the UN Convention on the Rights of the Child (UNCRC) (UN, 1989). The importance of direct work that engages children in participation is emphasized in the Children Act 1989, the Children (Scotland) Act 1995 and the Children (Northern Ireland) Order 1995. Article 26 of the Universal Declaration of Human Rights (UN, 1948) asserts the right of every child to free elementary education. Box 1.5 gives some key rights contained in the UNCRC.

Table 1.3 Main areas where additional care or therapeutic work needed

Nature of problem	Examples
Development delayed temporarily	Accident and broken leg preventing child learning to walk; illness leading to other physical impairments; short-term emotional and psychological difficulties
Development disrupted	Family disturbances due to separations, divorce, other losses including grieving through death; traumas through violence or other forms of abuse
Development misperceived	Problems arising from different views about, and difficulties in communicating about, developmental needs
Development slowed	Chronic factors affecting child development such as learning disability

---

Box 1.5 UN Convention on the Rights of the Child 1989

One of half a dozen major instruments of human rights published by the UN as part of its framework of international human rights. It contains 54 Articles, or statements, including:

Article 1:	Definition of the child
Article 3:	Child's best interests
Article 8:	Preservation of identity
Article 10:	Family reunification
Article 12:	Respect for views of the child
Article 13:	Freedom of expression
Article 16:	Right to privacy
Article 19:	Protection from violence
Article 23:	Rights of disabled children
Article 42:	Right to knowledge of rights

Children's rights are often talked about but are seldom granted. This may be an exaggeration, but only marginally so. Lansdown (1995) demonstrates that the law does not routinely grant children the right to express their wishes. Hendrick (2005, p. 60) notes that: 'Children are nearly always excluded from power – they meet it in circumstances not of their own choosing and then they have to work on it accordingly.'

Acknowledging the rights of children, including very young children, to be heard and to have their wishes taken into account, alongside their right to have their needs met, introduces a further layer of complexity to the already complicated process of assessing, planning and meeting their needs.

3. *A control-based approach* prioritizes preventive work, or intervening in the lives of children and families, depending on their needs. It relies on the power of the law. Through the law, children's services exercise statutory duties, powers and responsibilities to intervene in the lives of children and families.

The term 'prevention' is commonly used in childcare to refer to work done to lessen the likelihood of children being removed from their families and looked after by the local authority. In the 1970s, the scope of 'prevention' was widened to include not just the behaviour of children from so-called 'problem families', who were considered 'at risk' and 'in trouble', but also a range of social and environmental factors, such as poverty, long-term unemployment of parents and poor housing and schooling, which contributed to their difficulties. The twin elements of prevention and intervention, including the balance of resources between them so as to improve prevention, assumed greater importance after the conviction in 1993 of two 11-year-old children for the murder of 2-year-old James Bulger. Another outcome included lowering of the age of criminal responsibility, so that in England and Northern Ireland it is 10. In the wake of the Bulger case, there was increased emphasis on the need to develop preventive work with children and their families, so that early intervention would identify children and disrupt and hopefully extinguish intergenerational dysfunction of the kind that it was assumed led to the Bulger murder. Family intervention partnerships began. There was even an interest in intervening pre-birth, through family–nurse partnerships. There was greater debate about what children should be learning preschool and in primary and secondary schooling. There was controversy, for instance, over whether too much attention was paid to children achieving literacy and mathematics and other targets, while too little was paid to social and emotional learning at primary school.

Key themes for working with children and families

Let us pick up now some of the main social policy themes of working with children and families and link them with the current direction of services for children in need and their families. This is by no means a complete list, but the way it is presented introduces the material discussed in more detail in the chapters in the rest of this book. While it helps to highlight the themes individually, it is important to be aware that quite commonly they are interwoven and embedded in different areas of policy and practice.

Point for Reflection

At the start, it is worth considering the themes you would identify from what you have read and understood so far. Make a list of these and relate them to the discussion below as it proceeds.

Combating social exclusion

The Labour government linked policy and practice on children and families in need with the wider policy goal of reducing child and family poverty and combating social exclusion. Children and young people in need, especially those looked after by local authorities, tend to be most likely to be socially excluded. *Social exclusion* is the umbrella term used to refer to a range of factors – poverty, family breakdown, abuse and neglect, lack of family support, poor performance at school and a high level of special educational needs – related to the marginalization and material disadvantage experienced by children and young people (see Chapter 18).

Preventive work and early intervention

A particular aim of the Labour government was the strengthening of services for children and their families, particularly through programmes such as Sure Start (Box 1.6), so that over time many problems could be prevented or receive early intervention. The Children Act 1989 – the basis of contemporary children's services – was rooted in the assumption that, where possible, families would be left to bring up their own children. Subsequent policies, as illustrated in *Every Child Matters* (DfES, 2003a) and the Children Act 2004, reinforced the emphasis on prevention.

Box 1.6 Sure Start

A 1999 UK government initiative, which aims to:

- Reduce the impact of social exclusion on young children and families
- Provide additional family support

Ensuring secure attachment

Much work with children and families is concerned with minimizing disruptions and discontinuities in their lives. It is vital that children experience secure attachments to carers who can nurture them throughout childhood. There is far more involved in attachment than stability, which can be a feature of indifferent or even poor care. *Secure attachment* is the term used to refer to the consistency, stability, continuity and quality of permanent or substitute nurture and care that children and young people receive from their parents or carers, sufficient to ensure their health and wellbeing (see Chapter 4 for a discussion of attachment).

Safeguarding

Sadly, it is the case that many services for children, as well as policies and Acts, exist to protect children from harm and abuse. The abuse of children can take many forms – it may be physical, emotional or sexual, or a combination of these. Children may be abused not only through various forms of harm, but also through neglect. Child abuse is not a problem solely for individuals and families but is a social problem as well. Beckett (2007) argues that the maltreatment of children takes place in a social context, and child abuse and neglect are linked with issues of social class, poverty and social exclusion. It is important that children are protected not just from abuse but also from neglect. Safeguarding is not just about protecting children, but extends to maximizing their health and wellbeing. We can define *safeguarding* as the range of measures taken to prevent abuse, harm or neglect of children and young people, protect them and promote their health and welfare.

A scandalous history of shortcomings of services associated with the deaths of children in the care of local authorities has led safeguarding children to be a paramount policy priority in the early 21st century. Children have been harmed not only by individuals whom they knew – close relatives, foster parents and carers – but also by people who had access to them in institutions such as children's homes. Some notable instances of institutionalized abusive childcare establishments and systems have emerged in shocking detail through inquiries since the early 1990s, for instance in Staffordshire, England (Levy and Kahan, 1991) and Clwyd, Wales (Waterhouse et al., 2000).

This history points to the persistent failure of social services agencies to protect more than 30 children between the 1970s and 2010, including Maria Colwell (DHSS, 1974), Jasmine Beckford (Blom-Cooper, 1985), Kimberley Carlile (London Borough of Greenwich, 1987), Tyra Henry (London Borough of Lambeth, 1987), Victoria Climbié in 2000 (Laming, 2003), children receiving complex heart surgery at Bristol Royal Infirmary (Kennedy, 2001) and Baby Peter.

The deaths of 8-year-old Victoria Climbié (on 25 February 2000, with 128 injuries to her body) and 17-month-old Baby Peter (on 3 August 2007) have led to two important reports (Laming, 2003, 2009), which are milestones in the policy and organization of children's services.

The Laming Report (Laming, 2003) was the main stimulus for the Green Paper *Every Child Matters* (DfES, 2003a), the *National Service Framework for Children, Young People and Maternity Services* (DH/DfES, 2004a) and the action plan for carrying forward policies for children's services (DfES, 2004c). The Childcare Act 2006 requires compulsory registration of providers who care for children aged five to seven. Laming (2003) was the immediate spur for the creation of the Commission on Families and the Wellbeing of Children, led by Sir Michael Rutter. Other starting points for the commission were general concerns that some families appeared to be disintegrating; youth crime, drug taking, emotional problems and behavioural difficulties were increasing; and family support and nurturing of some children were inadequate, 'putting the future of the nation's children at risk' and leading to 'pleas both for more support for stressed families and for greater pressure to be placed on families to take responsibility for their children (Rutter, 2005: vii). United Nations and European conventions and laws, plus campaigns by organizations such as the Children's Legal Centre, are concerned with defending and promoting the rights of children. Laming's (2009) review of systems for safeguarding children was the wake-up call that the previously identified failings in child protection had not been rectified and the report recommended further major reforms to improve central government policy and local agencies' procedures and practice for safeguarding children.

Safeguarding children against risks from staff

There have been concerns since the late 20th century over the ease with which some people later convicted of abuse were able to apply for and secure responsible positions working with children or adults. Increasing efforts were made to use data recorded about people – notably records of criminal convictions – to improve measures to safeguard children against abuse by those working with them. For instance, under the Protection of Children Act 1999, a register was introduced, listing people deemed unsuitable to work with children, although the Rehabilitation of Offenders Act 1974 gave people the right not to reveal information about their criminal convictions. However, under the Rehabilitation of Offenders (Exceptions Order) 1975, people applying for posts working with children or vulnerable adults had to reveal both unspent and spent convictions. After the conviction in 2003 for the murder of two children in Soham, the *Bichard Inquiry Report* (Bichard, 2004) recommended that a national IT system should be set up urgently to support police intelligence, which ensured that a code of practice on the management of information was put in place under the Police Reform Act 2002.

The Criminal Records Bureau (CRB) (Box 1.7) was set up under the Police Act 1997 because of longstanding concerns about the need to improve the gatekeeping of people's suitability for work with people. The CRB began work in 2002. As a consequence of shortcomings identified in the Baby Peter case and other cases of adult and child abuse, it was decided in 2009 that, in future, the Independent Safeguarding Authority (ISA) would be engaged in applying the CRB policy.

Box 1.7 Criminal Records Bureau (CRB)

- Aims to identify people unsuitable for certain work, for example with children or vulnerable adults
- Covers England and Wales
- Equivalent in Scotland is Disclosure Scotland and in Northern Ireland is Access Northern Ireland

The requirement to have a CRB check will be extended to include anybody working intensively and frequently with children and vulnerable adults. It is estimated that it will cover more than 11 million adults. The CRB has already carried out over 20 million checks on people. There is debate about whether this policy reflects a moral panic, undue caution and a loss of perspective, given the fact that most abuse of children is carried out not by professionals or strangers but by family members and people already known to them (see Chapter 23 for further discussion on safeguarding). A vetting and barring scheme providing enhanced checks was introduced by the Labour government and began work in 2010, but was suspended by the coalition government later that year, pending the introduction of less stringent, time- and resource-intensive measures.

Family support

A growing policy commitment to family support is evident in services for children and families in the early 21st century. Family support is predicated on a neoliberal view of the good citizen, as a child, young person or adult, whose rights are conditional on them exercising responsibility and making an active contribution, which during the years of economic activity means working to earn a living.

In the area of work with young children, the National Childcare Strategy (DfEE, 1998) was launched in 1998 by the Labour government, with the aim of strengthening childcare services, linked with the aim of encouraging women back to work. This was a key aspect of the neoliberal agenda, making support for families with childcare conditional on enabling parents to work, that is, reassuring parents that they could go to work knowing their children were safe and being looked after.

There has been an increasing trend in the early 21st century towards social policy comprising not just the carrot but also the stick. By this is meant the double concern of welfare legislation with the benefits of services being conditional on young people leaving school and college as well as adults, including lone parents, unemployed and disabled people, demonstrating an active commitment to seeking work, as reflected in the Welfare Reform Act 2007. This Act followed the Green Paper *A New Deal for Welfare* (DWP, 2006), which directly associated the Labour government's Pathways to Work programme with the reformed Incapacity Benefit by introducing a qualifying threshold for higher benefits for ill and disabled people. Those unwilling to proceed to work-focused interviews would remain on a basic level of benefits and only those willing to be considered for work would be eligible for enhanced benefits.

Good parenting

Social policy since the early 21st century has increasingly emphasized the responsibility of parents as a condition of their entitlement to recognition and support as citizens – an idea often referred to as the *conditionality of citizenship*. A key component of the conditionality of citizenship is the notion of good parenting. The neoliberal assumption is that the family is the foundation of the good society and the quality of parenting makes a unique contribution to the health and wellbeing of children and young people. Parents hold responsibility under the Children Act 1989 in England and Wales and, with minor differences, the Children (Scotland) Act 1995, for the upbringing of their children, while local authorities are responsible for the welfare and nurture of 'looked after' children. Conditionality means that, on the one hand, parents are offered resources as an aspect of family support measures, while on the other hand, where the child's situation is held to be the responsibility of parents who have fallen short, punitive sanctions are applied through the courts. The clearest example is in non-school attendance. Under section 444(1) of the Education and Inspections Act 2006, parents can be fined, or in extreme cases imprisoned, for failing to ensure that their children attend school.

Partnership and empowerment and personalized services in work with children and parents

Contemporary policy and practice incorporate an increased emphasis on partnership between children, parents and carers and other family members and agencies providing services. This is worked out in the different, but overlapping, notions of involvement, participation and empowerment. The term *involvement* is used to refer to the continuum from tokenism, ad hoc consultation, junior partnership, equal partnership, senior partnership and exercising full control. Participation is that part of the continuum of involvement where children exercise greater power, more choice and make a significant contribution to changing practice and policy. *Participation* by children refers to a level of direct or indirect taking part in, and affecting, decisions affecting them, in ways appropriate to their age, capacity and wishes (see also Chapter 17). Arguments supporting the empowerment of children and their families are rooted in democratic and egalitarian notions of their rights. Some children, particularly looked after children and children in need, benefit from advocacy services aiming to put children's views across to professionals and others. Unfortunately, research by Ofsted (2008) indicates that there is a wide variation in the availability in different geographical areas of advocacy services for children.

In the first decade of the 21st century, there has been a growing emphasis on developing personalized health and social services. *Personalization* is an important feature of the public services, which entails the person having control over the planning and delivery of their own services, emphasizing the value of building on personal strengths and achieving empowerment.

Multiprofessional working and integrated services

Successive governments since the 1970s have espoused the principle of improved collaboration between professionals. The findings of inquiry reports since the 1990s – notably Laming (2003, 2009) – have emphasized the vital necessity for improved multiprofessional working and this is enshrined in government guidance, updated since 2006 (DfES, 2006) on safeguarding children (DfE, 2010a).

Policy may aim at integration but the complexity of organizations and agencies makes it difficult to achieve this. The aim of the Labour government was the development of joined-up services for children, exemplified by Sure Start centres in the 500 most disadvantaged localities of England, where all children under four and their families would be offered a full range of services to promote their health and wellbeing. A further goal was to create 3,500 children's centres, largely modelled on the lines of the Sure Start centres and reflecting what had been learned from the early experience of running them, by 2010, thereby providing the means for delivering a range of integrated services.

Different models of understanding

At the level of practice, as the excellent critical review of the literature by Brown and White (2006) demonstrates, it is extremely difficult to achieve integration in children's services, in the sense of creating a single system of service commissioning, procurement and delivery. Brown and White (2006, p. 6) show that the term 'integration' has no single, agreed meaning and is often used interchangeably with 'terms such as partnership working, joint-working, joined-up working, inter-agency working, multi-agency working, multi-professional working, inter-agency communication, intra and inter-organizational collaboration and collaborative working'. Building on their discussion, we can define *integrated services* as a single set of arrangements to manage and run services, with contributing partners who retain their legal independence from each other. Anning et al. (2010) show how different models of understanding predominate in different professional settings. While the aim of government was full integration of former education and social services, it is clear that in many circumstances, this is an aspiration rather than achieved reality. The reasons are partly to do with the complexity of people's lives, the variety of services and agencies to which they relate, and the range of different professions delivering services. As we focus on these different professions in more detail, we become aware that there is no final, essential truth about their professional reference points and the nature of what they do. It will be apparent (see Chapter 3) that just as childhood is socially constructed, so different professions involved in working with children and families construct their practice differently, according to different discourses (see Chapter 4 for discussion of discourse). Research by Anning et al. (2010) illustrates the variety of models of understanding relied on by different groups of professionals in five teams:

- *Young people's team:* family-focused or systemic model
- *Child development team:* medical model, based on medical diagnosis
- *Youth offending team:* social model, identifying social factors
- *Nursery team:* needs model, focusing on individual needs
- *Head injury team:* medical model, as in the child development team.

It is important to recognize that despite the complexity of legislation, policies, agencies and professionals, the goal of attending to the voices of children, promoting children's rights and meeting their needs has remained a consistent goal shared between them. This chapter has set out the major constituents of these policies and indicated the major contours of the work of agencies and professionals. Hopefully, it provides some initial stepping stones for the more detailed coverage of these different areas in the remaining chapters of this book.

Conclusion

This chapter has opened up for detailed exploration in this book the main features of the professionalization of children's upbringing, care and protection that have contributed to present-day policy and practice. To date, while successive governments have aspired to closer collaboration between the different agencies and professionals engaged in delivering services to children and families, the goal of developing integrated provision for children from birth to adulthood remains work in progress rather than an achieved reality. Governments in the late 20th century and early 21st century are concerned with how to improve the quality of childcare, through supporting parents and families, early education and the school system and additional and specialist childcare services for children with particular needs. These services are provided not only by children and families themselves in the process of child development, but also, through legislation and policies, by a range of agencies and professionals in the public sector and by voluntary, private and independent organizations and groups in the third sector. Not surprisingly, there is a need for procedures to be developed to ensure that these arrangements are well coordinated and children and their parents and carers receive the services they need.

It is vital not to accept the surface rhetoric of government aspirations, but to view this in the context of a critical perspective on social policy. Undoubtedly, there are important areas of significance, in terms of the allocation of enhanced resources to support children and their families. It is important to appreciate the complexity of the human problems tackled by agencies working with children in need and the inevitability that a minority of regrettable shortcomings in services will continue to occur.

REVIEW QUESTIONS

1. What are the main goals for children set out in the Green Paper *Every Child Matters* (DfES, 2003a)?
2. What do the initials EYFS stand for and what is the importance of the policy initiative they represent?
3. Outline the basic features of the Children Act 2004.

Chapter Links

For further discussion of the history of policy aspects, see Chapter 2.

Further Reading

Davis, L. (2008) *The Social Worker's Guide to Children and Families Law*, London, Jessica Kingsley. Clearly written handbook covering the main aspects of the law relevant to practice with children and families.

DCSF (2005) *Engaging the Voluntary and Community Sectors in Children's Trusts*, London, DCSF. Advice for agencies on how to involve the third sector in children's trusts.

Hendrick, H. (ed.) (2005) *Child Welfare and Social Policy: An Essential Reader*, Bristol, Policy Press. Stimulating and in-depth series of essays on aspects of welfare theory and policy relating to children and families.

Langston, A. and Abbott, L. (2005) Quality matters, in L. Abbott and A. Langston (eds) *Birth to Three Matters: Supporting the Framework of Effective Practice*, Maidenhead, Open University Press. An important, authoritative and readable survey of key aspects of policy and practice in work with young children.

Stein, M. (2009) *Quality Matters in Children's Services*, London, Jessica Kingsley. Authoritative review of the lessons from research into key aspects of children's services.

Tunstill, J. and Aldgate, J. (2000) *Children in Need: Policy into Practice*, London, HMSO. Authoritative review of relevant research and practice concerning children, young people and their families.

Websites

www.ofsted.gov.uk Information about the inspection of children's services
http://www.cabinetoffice.gov.uk/ The government's information sources on the development of public services beyond public agencies. Click on 'Big Society' on the top row of items

History and Traditions in Education and Care

Robert Adams

LEARNING OUTCOMES

By the end of this chapter, you should be able to:

- understand the historical roots of current services for children and families
- identify some key figures in history responsible for developments in education and child welfare
- examine the significant themes of child reform and rescue

The conditions in which many children live and are brought up, as well as the parenting they receive in the context of their family and environment, have provoked concern and remedial action by philanthropists and governments from the mid-19th century to the present day. Late Victorian founders of charities, such as Dr Barnardo, were moved by the condition of pauper children. In a different vein, but no less important, are the campaigns against child labour by Victorian activists, such as the Rev. Charles Kingsley, reflected in his book *The Water Babies*, which was inspired by the appalling conditions endured by child chimney sweeps, forced to climb inside chimneys to clean them. Twentieth and 21st-century counterparts are UN and European conventions and laws, plus campaigns by organizations such as the Children's Legal Centre, defending and promoting the rights of children. Finally, we have the many thinkers and practitioners who have contributed to the development of services – from playgroups and nurseries to elementary and primary schools – to educate and care for children and encourage their health development.

These strands of belief and action capture the complexity of children's circumstances, with question marks not only over their problems but how they have arisen, the extent to which they may relate to what goes on in families, and how far it is appropriate for the state and professionals to support families, intervene in them or simply expect them to exercise more responsibility for the upbringing of their children.

Point for Reflection

From your own knowledge of history, what do you consider to be the main differences between how children are educated and provided for by the government today versus in the 19th century? Are there any similarities?

Contemporary policies reflect historical trends

Despite appearances, today's responses by the state and professionals to the problems of children and families are not creations of the 21st century. Present-day policies in the UK bear the imprint of generations of beliefs about what is best for children, how they should be brought up and, not least, the 19th-century tendency for philanthropists and reformers to undertake moral crusades to rescue those children viewed as vulnerable, poor, helpless victims and, in some cases, potentially dangerous. Therefore, the image of the child is not one dimensional.

Assumptions about what is best for babies, infants, young children, older children, their parents, carers and other family members tend to be rooted not only in our own experiences, but in the legacies of what our own parents, their parents and grandparents believed and how they were brought up. We cannot escape the imprint of our own upbringing and so, collectively, policy in the UK inherits what has gone before.

Values and personal experiences shape the views of politicians, policy makers, practitioners and campaigners about what is best for children. Work with children and families in the 21st century is shaped by the complex mix of policy responses to children, reflected in the array of agencies responsible for delivering services. These services are diverse and their interrelationships are complex, as befits their multiple organizational bases, in education, health and social services, in public (local authority), private and voluntary agencies (such as Barnardo's, the NSPCC and The Children's Society) and in the disciplines supplying the knowledge (such as psychology and sociology) in which professional practice is rooted.

Contemporary practice has grown out of the responses of policy makers and philanthropists to the rapid growth of towns with their overcrowded slums and unsanitary housing. Poverty and sickness grew during the rapid industrialization of Britain in the 19th century, which saw the huge growth of towns such as Birmingham, Leeds, Manchester and London. The Census Act 1800 (Box 2.1) made it possible to ascertain that the population of England increased from about 5.7 million in 1750 to 8.3 million in the 1801 census, doubling in 1851

Box 2.1 Census Act 1800

Required the government, every 10 years from 1801, to gather data about the population of England, Wales, Scotland and, from 1821, Northern Ireland as well. The information included the number of people, their occupations, families and houses. Early census information included only summaries of these aspects, whereas more detail was added in successive censuses.

---

to 16.8 million and almost doubling again in 1901 to 30.5 million, reaching 49.1 million in 2001. Scotland's population, meanwhile, was 1.6 million in 1801 and multiplied to 4.5 million by 1901, while Wales increased more modestly from 0.6 million in 1801 to 2 million in 1901. The overall population of the UK in 2010 is estimated to be just over 60 million. The situation in Wales, Scotland and Northern Ireland is more complicated than in England, because they have at times experienced periods of population decline (Jeffries, 2005).

These huge increases in the population, particularly in urban areas, to led to overcrowding and poor housing for the majority of people in the lower classes, high rates of chronic childhood conditions and premature deaths, as well as many children being left without parents, or working and caring for parents unable to work through disability. The distress of children and families in rural settings should not be forgotten. The migration of people to the towns has often been motivated by economic conditions.

The Victorians relied on the care of children and families who fell on hard times to be provided by two means:

1. private charity through voluntary children's organizations and the good deeds of individual philanthropists
2. public charity through the workhouse and outdoor relief through the Poor Law Amendment Act 1834 (Box 2.2).

Box 2.2 Poor Law Amendment Act 1834

- Reformed the Act for the Relief of the Poor 1601
- Attempted to distinguish 'deserving' from 'undeserving' paupers
- Discouraged giving outdoor relief (a small payment to people in their own homes)
- Provided workhouses as a refuge of last resort for paupers, again on the principle of 'less eligibility', making them less appealing than the lowest level of paid labouring

Present-day policy and practice are rooted in the enduring themes of nurturing all children through childcare and education and recovering those perceived as casualties through child reform and rescue.

Childcare and education

Until the late 19th century, many British children endured long hours working in harsh conditions in factories or on farms, to supplement their families' meagre income. Compulsory schooling for children of primary school age did not begin in England and Wales until after the passing of the Education Act 1870 (Box 2.3), when board schools began to be built, many of which are still evident in towns and villages, some of which are still used as schools.

Box 2.3 Education Act 1870

- Established a system of elementary education in England and Wales for children aged 5–13
- Attendance was not made compulsory until 1880

The 1870 Education Act ensured that newly created school boards in each area of England and Wales, wherever existing voluntary arrangements were not adequate to ensure that children aged 5–13 years received elementary schooling, would fund new elementary schools from the local rates to do this. However, the roots of the elementary school system lay in much earlier provision, such as public schools (many predating the state schools by several centuries) and, from the early 19th century, charity schools, church or 'dame' schools and ragged schools. There were also Sunday schools or local schools sponsored by particular religious groups or philanthropists. The division between rich and poor meant that public schools catered for a relatively small, elite group of children from better off families, while the remaining schools catered for children from poorer families.

Four-fifths of families in the mid-19th century lived in poverty, and lack of sanitation and poor housing among them meant that mortality among infants and small children remained high, often as high as 50%. Children were often treated harshly by adults, and many poorer children spent their early years in hard labour, on the land or in factories, where they were prone to suffering terrible accidents – maiming or even death – as they crawled about the floor cleaning between machinery or undertook even more dangerous work beyond the reach of adults, on account of their larger size. Children of better off parents who died prematurely tended to go into orphanages, whereas their poorer counterparts tended to be sent to the relatively harsh workhouses.

Conditions in the early primary schools were invariably basic and discipline varied from merely strict to harsh and punitive. Corporal punishment was the common means of first resort in controlling children.

Conditions were also harsh in public schools attended by children of the wealthy. While it was common that daughters were kept at home, as future wives and mothers, the sons were sent to public boarding schools and prepared for a career in the law, the armed services or the Church. Abuses of the boys were common in many of these schools.

Development of schooling for younger children

In contrast with the condition of most schools, ideas about socializing younger children and ideas about children's development, learning and schooling developed rapidly in the 19th century. The following figures are notable in the history of education:

■ *Robert Owen* (1771–1858), a philanthropic Scottish entrepreneur who can be regarded as one of the pioneers of social reform and a founder of the cooperative movement, opened one of the first infant schools in Britain in 1816 at New Lanark, Scotland. This catered for the social as well as educational needs of children and was an integral part of the community – a model community he created for his employees and their families around the mills he owned in New Lanark (still open as a museum).
■ *Margaret McMillan* (1860–1931), a Scot, carried out pioneering work in nursery education in Bradford and London. She developed socialist ideas about the link between the emotional development of children and their physical conditions (McMillan, [1911]2008). She wrote about the development of nursery education (McMillan, [1919]2009) for young children rooted in the linked notions of the health-giving qualities of fresh air, emotional support and nurture. With her sister Rachel, Margaret McMillan established a school clinic in Bow, London in 1908 and by 1914 had opened an open-air nursery school in Peckham (Steedman, 1990).
■ There was resonance between these ideas and the work of *Maria Montessori* (1870–1952), who was born in Italy and had an influence on schooling not only in Italy but in many other countries including Britain and the USA. Montessori developed educational methods based on:
  ■ the child-centred environment, including, for instance, child-sized equipment such as chairs
  ■ the emphasis on the classroom being beautiful and orderly
  ■ the importance of children having time, space and freedom to engage in interesting activities around them
  ■ a curriculum that included large blocks of open-ended time.

■ Margaret McMillan was also influenced by the ideas of *Johann Heinrich Pestalozzi* (1746–1827), who was born in Zurich, Switzerland. He developed the principle of holistically educating the head, heart and hands of the child and created schools in Germany and Switzerland emphasizing education as a social experience. He believed children should learn through exploring and doing themselves, rather than being given knowledge. In 1836, the Pestalozzian Home and Colonial Infant School Society began training infant teachers in London and began influencing thinking towards children needing specific education geared to their age.

■ *Rudolf Steiner* (1861–1925), born in Croatia, founded the independent Waldorf schools (the first Waldorf school was founded in 1919 to serve the children of employees at the Waldorf-Astoria cigarette factory in Stuttgart, Germany), of which there are now about 1000, plus more than 1,000 Waldorf kindergartens, in more than 60 countries. Steiner set out a holistic and anthroposophical view of childhood following three major developmental stages. Early childhood learning was based on experiences and the senses, mid-childhood was a period when the artistic and imaginative aspects emerged, while intellectual powers and the capacity to think about ethics and social responsibility develop during the teenage years. Space for free play formed an important part of Steiner's early years curriculum. Guided free play in the classroom gave the child opportunities of homelike experiences and outdoor play offered experiences of nature and different weathers.

■ The ideas of *John Dewey* (1859–1952), who was born in the USA, were increasingly influential in many parts of the world, including Britain, from the late 19th century. He believed that education should:

■ be based on children's interests and grow from their experience
■ help children understand the world around them
■ encourage child development
■ enable children to develop skills
■ enable children to live a fuller life.

Enhanced emphasis on education for younger children

In the second half of the 20th century, a new impetus was given to the development of services for children under five and their families, with increasing numbers of women going into full- or part-time work, or being driven into work through financial circumstances. There was an increasing demand for childminders, daycare, residential care and extended school services outside normal school hours, including childcare before and after school and parental support.

The most notable early progress was made by women themselves, as Crowe's (1977) history of the Pre-school Playgroups Association (PPA) illustrates, creating the playgroup movement from the 1960s when there was little provision for older preschool children. These groups grew rapidly because they filled a desperate need, from the point of view of parents and, in those days, mothers in particular. In 1960, there were 179,000 children under five in schools in England, representing 14% of children aged three to four, over half of whom were not in nursery schools or classes but were in reception classes in infant schools (Statham et al., 1990). The PPA was founded in 1962 and, for the next two decades, the voluntary playgroup movement led developments in preschool learning and partnerships with parents. The significance of this lay in the impetus towards social policy change in preschool provision coming from mothers themselves in the voluntary and informal sector, rather than from government, public services or professionals.

There were moves by government to develop services for young children, but despite this, government targets set out in 1972 for free nursery education to be provided within a decade for 50% of three-year-olds and 90% of children aged four had still not been met 20 years later (Moss, 1991). Schedule 2 of the Children Act 1989 lists family centres as a service that local authorities are required to provide. Without recognition of weaknesses in the system, provision would become increasingly 'incoherent, fragmented, inequitable and under-resourced' (Moss, 1991, p. 99). Services for children in need and their families took another leap forward in the early 21st century as symbolized by the introduction of family centres on a countrywide basis under the Children Act 2004 and the introduction in 2008 of the Early Years Foundation Stage (see Chapter 1).

Child reform and rescue

There has been growing concern in Britain since the early 19th century about the need to improve the health and welfare of children who are neglected, homeless and subjected to abuse. Nineteenth-century initiatives aiming to socialize children who had lost their foothold in regular family life focused on the contrasting goals of reforming children and rescuing them from the social and family factors, which, on occasions, were identified as responsible for many being paupers and not surviving into adulthood. The pauper children and families entering the workhouses were almost as badly off in some institutions as those denied help. Conditions were deliberately made unpleasant, on the principle of 'less eligibility', which meant keeping payments in the form of poor relief, food and accommodation to a level below the minimum earned by a labourer, so that people would be encouraged to fend for themselves, seek work and thus not become dependent on charity.

In the UK, the expression 'tough love' has particular significance in relation to the ambivalence of adults towards children, as expressed in policy and provision. Responses to children perceived as in need have traditionally been Janus-faced – that is, partly sympathetic and concerned with providing welfare, and partly preoccupied with controlling them, reforming and bringing them back into law-abiding ways through the different aspects of the justice system. In the mid-19th century, the goal of reforming children was exemplified in the campaigning of Mary Carpenter to segregate children from adults, which was largely responsible for the Reformatory Schools (Youthful Offenders) Act 1854. This paved the way for the creation of a system of schools and similar institutions that under the Children and Young Persons Act 1933 became Home Office approved schools and under the Children and Young Persons Act 1969 became community homes with education. Alongside this, a network of orphanages grew up, many of which were better known for their tough regimes than for any notion of loving upbringing.

Rescuing children was illustrated in the work of several charities and their founders to 'save' children by removing them from their home environment. These include:

- the National Children's Homes (now Action for Children) founded by the Reverend Stephenson in 1869
- Dr Barnardo's (now Barnardo's) founded by Dr Barnardo, who opened the first orphanage in Mile End in 1870
- the Church of England Children's Society (now The Children's Society) founded in 1881
- the National Society for the Prevention of Cruelty to Children (NSPCC) founded in 1889.

The usual equation was made between urban squalor and childhood problems and the curative effects of a move to the countryside, or, in Dr Barnardo's scheme, out of Britain altogether, to a farm school in Manitoba, or opportunities in service in African colonies or in Australia. Barnardo's policy of child emigration was finally exposed (Bean and Melville, 1989) and led to attempts over the succeeding decades to lessen the harm done to children in more recent generations.

In the 20th century, there was a move towards the state taking responsibility for the provision of a range of residential and community-based services for children. The gatekeeping of such services, today carried out through a process of assessment by practitioners from children's services, was carried out in the 19th and early 20th century by the Poor Law guardians and forerunners of today's social workers: the workers for the Charity Organisation Society, founded in 1869. Essentially, they assessed people according to whether they seemed to be 'deserving' or 'undeserving' paupers. In general, people were judged to be deserving if they made efforts to pull themselves up by their own bootstraps, in other words showed the capacity for self-help. If not, they were judged as beyond help, part of the underclass or 'residuum', on whom resources would be wasted.

Point for Reflection

Consider whether you would place more faith in a young child's financially poor close-knit family or a residential orphanage as the best place for them to be brought up and educated.

Policy and legal developments

A succession of legal measures reformed services for children, beginning with:

- the Prevention of Crime Act 1908, which created the young offenders' institutions known as borstals (abolished in 1982)
- the Children and Young Persons Act 1932, which introduced supervision orders for children deemed at risk
- the Children and Young Persons Act 1933, which raised the age of criminal responsibility from seven to eight
- the National Assistance Act 1948, which abolished the Poor Law and the widely hated workhouses that had stigmatized many children and families for almost a century
- the landmark Children Act 1948 (Box 2.4), which in the same year set up children's departments in local authorities, symbolizing the government's recognition that local authorities had a duty to undertake the care of children in need.

Box 2.4 Children Act 1948

- Set up children's departments
- Established a more professionalized childcare service
- Introduced duty of local authorities to receive abused or neglected children into care

---

Children's legislation progressed, with the Children and Young Persons Act 1963 (Box 2.5), dealing with the care and control of children, and the Children and Young Persons Act 1969 (Box 2.6), promoting positive measures for supervising children deemed 'at risk' or 'in trouble'. Further major reorganization of services for children came when the Seebohm Report (1968) was followed by the reorganization of local government welfare, including childcare services, in the Local Authority Social Services Act 1970, which led to the creation of social services departments in England and Wales. In Scotland, the Social Work (Scotland) Act 1968 led to similar reorganizations, in which local authority social work departments were set up. During subsequent decades, much legislation was passed to try to back up attempts by governments to reduce youth offending. Critics produced evidence of increased punitiveness (Thorpe et al., 1980), illustrating the increasing numbers of children sent to detention centres, borstals and, after the early 1980s, the new youth custody centres that replaced them.

Box 2.5 Children and Young Persons Act 1963

- Established service for families and children regarded as in need
- Introduced powers and duties of local authorities to provide services to meet children's welfare needs
- Aimed to reduce the necessity for children to be taken into the care of the local authority

---

Box 2.6 Children and Young Persons Act 1969

- Distinguished between children assessed as in need and children in trouble
- Developed community-based services to support children in need and their families
- Attempted to divert children in trouble who otherwise would have gone into custody to intermediate treatment schemes in the community

---

Box 2.7 Children Act 1989

- Consolidated previous childcare legislation
- Emphasized the principle that the interests of the child are paramount in any decisions made about children and families in need
- Promoted parental responsibility and, where possible, parents looking after their own children
- Required childcare decisions to be made without court orders where possible and without delays
- Advanced the notion of children in care being helped in the transition from care
- Advocated that the child's cultural, ethnic and faith should be considered in any childcare decision

---

The most notable children's legislation after the Children and Young Persons Act 1969 was the Children Act 1989 (Box 2.7). This is still used as the legal basis for many interventions by local authorities to meet the needs of children and safeguard them from harm.

Conclusion

This chapter has provided a broad historical and legal context for policy and practice that has led to the development of children's services in the 21st century. It has identified key themes of childcare and education and child reform and rescue, embedded in the history of policy and practice. The preoccupations of policy and practice in the 21st century identified in Chapter 1 are embedded in this wider history and it is helpful to bear this in mind when proceeding to examine ideas about how childhood, families and social conditions have changed. It is to these that we turn in the next few chapters.

REVIEW QUESTIONS

1. What important piece of legislation affecting the situation of children was passed in 1870?
2. What was the particular contribution of Margaret McMillan to the development of provision for children?
3. What key aspects of the Children Act 1989 would you identify as most important?

Chapter Links

For further discussion of changing ideas about childhood, see Chapter 3.

Further Reading

Baldock, P., Fitzgerald, D. and Kay, J. (2009) *Understanding Early Years Policy* (2nd edn), London, Sage. Good introduction to the historical context of early years policy, especially since the mid-20th century.

Frost, N. and Stein, M. (2003) *Child Welfare: From Policy to Practice*, Abingdon, Routledge. Helpful critical treatment of child welfare from a policy perspective.

Harris, J. (2003) *The Social Work Business,* Abingdon, Routledge. Chapter 1 provides a useful critical and historical context for the 'social' aspects of work with children and families.

Nutbrown, K., Clough, P. and Selbie, P. (2008) *Early Childhood Education: History, Philosophy and Experience*, London, Sage. Wide-ranging treatment of topics relevant to the past and present of early education of children. Chapter 2 focuses on many of the pioneers referred to in this chapter.

Payne, M. (2003) *The Origins of Social Work: Continuity and Change*, Basingstoke, Palgrave Macmillan. Wide-ranging survey of the past and present of social work, with useful material on the historical context.

Websites

www.steinerwaldorf.org.uk; www.whywaldorfworks.org; www.ecswe.org Websites related to
   the Steiner Waldorf organization and Waldorf Schools in North America and Europe
www.montessori.org.uk Information about the Montessori organization and its work
www.camphillschools.org.uk A business name for some of the work of Camphill Rudolf Steiner
   schools
www.pestalozzi.org.uk Information about the Pestalozzi International Village Trust

Part 2

Social and Psychological Perspectives on Childhood and Child Development

The Social Construction of Childhood
Sociological Approaches to the Study of Children and Childhood

3

Michael Wyness

LEARNING OUTCOMES

By the end of this chapter, you should be able to:

- understand the contested character of childhood
- appreciate how childhood is a socially constructed and changing concept
- discuss how this perspective on childhood affects approaches to research and practice

In recent years, childhood has become a far more contested phenomenon, with public commentary shifting between the reporting of its terminal decline through to the promotion of a new pluralized and culturally embedded version of the child. Arguably, it is clear now that policy makers and professionals have embraced the latter view, working alongside children and their families in providing them with the support needed to take more control of their lives (Mayall, 2002). In this chapter, the sociological basis of this approach, the social construction of childhood, is outlined. First, I discuss the importance of the cultural and social dimensions of childhood and go on to explore the implications this has for understanding children's lives. I then discuss the social construction of childhood in terms of the different ways that we might view children's lives. Here we can start to talk about the diversity of childhoods. Finally, I explain why an emphasis on the cultural and social realms can lead to insights on children's identities as relatively independent, rights-bearing members of society. In the final section, by way of a critique of social constructionism, I briefly explore alternative ways of researching children and childhood.

Culture rather than biology

The work of Aries (1961) provides the early impetus for social constructionism, in that he challenges the orthodox view that childhood was a universal and ever-present feature of all societies. His often referenced argument is that childhood simply did not exist until around the 16th century. Beyond their physiological immaturity, children in the medieval period were rarely treated differently from adults. There was next to no awareness that children had to be nurtured and guided through a period called 'childhood' by responsible adults in order for them to become full members of their communities. While his thesis has been subject to numerous critical reviews, his work clearly establishes a distinction between 'biological immaturity' and the ways that this has been understood within specific societies and historical periods (Archard, 2004; Gittins, 1998). Childhood in modern Western societies is viewed as a set of powerful sentiments and ideas that have fundamental consequences for the way we view, treat and relate to children.

One radical version of this argument is put forward by Stainton-Rogers and Stainton-Rogers (1992). They argue that modern childhood has a 'disembodied' character. The title of their book *Stories of Childhood* nicely summarizes their argument, in that powerful groups of adults have constructed accounts and narratives of children as physiologically immature humans that generate dominant representations or ways of seeing children. These 'discourses' of childhood have come to appear as natural, inevitable and universal. Social constructionists challenge the taken-for-granted nature of childhood and argue that there is no material essence or physical reality that can be called 'childhood'.

Others have taken a less radical line in generating a new programme, or 'emergent paradigm', emphasizing childhood as an 'interpretive frame' for understanding the biologically immature (James and Prout, 1997). Children's lack of biological maturity is often a self-evident feature that differentiates them from adult populations. However, this biological state is often a poor guide to understanding children. It is this 'understanding' that is critical in defining childhood, and shapes the way that adults relate to children. Moreover, this interpretive frame structured by adults within specific social and political contexts becomes the dominant guiding force through which children themselves grow up and take on the roles and responsibilities within their families, communities and societies.

Diversity of childhoods

As societies are different in the way they are organized and in the values, roles and responsibilities that characterize social relations, children are also different in the ways they inhabit their families, communities and societies. Researchers have identified a diversity of roles for children. If we explore the nature of children's roles and experiences within and across countries, we become more aware of quite significant differences between the way that children's lives are understood. Rather than talking about a single universal model of childhood with a strong emphasis on children's biological and psychological underdevelopment, there is an emphasis on the *diversity of childhoods.*

Let us take the example of child labour. The child labour debate focuses on a comparison between a positive preferred model of the 'schooled' child found in more affluent, developed countries and a more negative conception of exploited child labourers found in poorer, less developed countries. The former has often been used as a universal standard with which children from the developing world are measured against (Boyden, 1997). Thus 'labour' is construed as an unnatural imposition on children, which compromises their social, emotional and educational development (Article 32, Convention on the Rights of the Child, UN, 1989). Children who work in factories in India or on the streets of Paraguay have had their childhoods compromised because they do not conform to an idealized image of the happy carefree child who regularly attends school and has limited involvement in the adult world of work and responsibility.

To take a social constructionist view is to explore the contexts within which children are expected to assume the status of 'child'. A more pluralist view on childhood is to emphasize the distinctiveness of the two models of childhood rather than making judgements about one model being superior to the other. Thus the schooled child is different from the labouring child, the societies within which they are found generate different conceptions of childhood. A more nuanced comparison of child labouring in an Indian carpet factory and secondary school pupil in London might uncover a different balance of child-related activities. The child labourer juggles paid work, schooling and play. Economic necessity and cultural values might dictate that the former is prioritized rather than the latter, with children's labour constituting an important family responsibility. The schooled child, on the other hand, juggles their time between the school, their family and playing with their friends. While increasing priorities are placed on school work, their time is still relatively free of family responsibilities (Wyness, 2006, Ch. 7). They are not expected to have the same economic responsibilities as their Indian counterparts.

A more nuanced view of child labour is also apparent when we examine international policy. The norm has been to promote the abolition of child labour, with governments in affluent societies attempting to penalize companies who employ children (see Bissell's 2003 discussion of the USA's Harkin Bill). However, an emphasis on childhood diversity is also evident in the way that particular 'hazardous' forms of child labour are banned rather than child labour per se. Thus the International Labour Organization's (1999) Convention No.182 on the Worst Forms of Child Labour targets children who are involved in the sex industry, drug trafficking and armed conflict. There is an implicit sense here that children whose paid work is carefully regulated by the family, the community or the local government constitute a rather different state of affairs for children. Here children are relatively safe and less likely to be exploited. While this regulated and protected form of child labour still poses difficulties for children who want to regularly attend school, it does suggest that a comparison between child labour in developing countries and children in school in more affluent settings is more difficult to make. An awareness of the differences between these distinctive forms of childhood cannot simply be made in moral terms.

Point for Reflection

Is childhood a universal feature of all societies?

Children as social actors

Hendrick (1997, p. 34) has argued that 'during our period "childhood" – both the institution and the construction of – was composed by adults; usually those of the professional middle class'. Thus children were absent from any 'constructing': images, representations and assumptions about children, what have been referred to as 'discourses of childhood', were generated by powerful adults and imposed on populations of children (Stainton-Rogers and Stainton-Rogers, 1992). However, James and Prout (1997) argue that if the character of childhood is conditional on the culture and society within which children are found, then children themselves, as constituent members of their communities and societies, may play an integral part in their social construction.

Social constructionism thus opens up the possibility of seeing children differently as *social actors* and *social agents*. As social actors, children take part in social events and are recognized as full members of their communities. As agents, children can make a difference: their actions can make a significant difference to the way we see the world (Mayall, 2002). This view of childhood also importantly underpins the notion of children's rights to participate (Wyness, 2006). The stumbling block here has been the unwillingness of powerful sectors within society, including those within the academic world, to recognize children as full members of their societies. Childhood is characterized in many affluent societies as a period of time through which children learn about the world, prepare for their entry into society, and are largely excluded from decision-making processes. Moreover, this has been endorsed by social science research on children and childhood, in that the main focus has been the role that adults play in these processes through the concept of socialization. Children as social learners and apprentices are in a sense incomplete members of society, relying on the powers of adults to guide them through childhood into society (Wyness, 2006, Ch. 6). Children are thus viewed as 'human becomings', with childhood a transitional phase ending in the completed status of adulthood or 'human being' (Lee, 2001).

Research now identifies a range of contexts within which both the 'becoming' and 'agency' views of childhood come into view. Let us take the example of the children's hospital ward. Alderson's (1994) research on children with life-threatening diseases explores the relations that child patients have with their parents and the hospital's professional staff. The desire by doctors and parents to protect children from knowledge about their conditions sometimes brings them into conflict with the child patients, particularly where the latter have been 'growing up' with their diseases. Despite their lengthy experiences living with their conditions, child patients under the age of 16 were often felt to be too young to consent to treatment. Discussions about treatment were often routinely conducted between parents and medical professionals, with decisions taken by the adults on the basis of their knowledge of the child and the disease. The issue of consent was critical here: the desire to protect children often excluded them from decisions that affected the course of their treatment.

There are two issues here with respect to children's inclusion:

1. the extent to which children are involved in decision-making processes that affect their lives
2. the issue of who actually consents to children's medical treatment.

A recent case in the UK is instructive here. In 2008, a 13-year-old English girl was granted the right to decide on whether to have a life-saving heart transplant (BBC News, 2008). The girl had been in and out of hospital since the age of 5 with leukaemia and a heart condition and eventually turned down the offer of surgery. The issue achieved national prominence when the local medical authority threatened to take her family to court to force the girl to receive the heart transplant. The threat was rescinded when it became clear that there was no national professional consensus over the issue and it was apparent that the girl's consent to refuse treatment was negotiated with her parents. The girl has since consented to having the surgery. The point being made here is that she was fully involved in decisions with regards to her treatment.

For some, the girl was recognized as being 'Gillick competent', that is, irrespective of her age, having the capacity to make an informed judgement on issues that directly affect her. There were two schools of thought here: on the one hand, there were those who felt that her status as a child excluded her from important life-saving decisions. On the other hand, there were those who recognized her agency. Her life experiences, which shaped her ability to make sense of the chronic illness from an early age, and the parents' recognition of these abilities endorsed her 'being' status and what Alderson (1994) calls her 'human rights to integrity'.

Social constructionism: some critical commentary

While social constructionism has become the dominant theoretical approach within childhood studies, it has generated a range of critical commentary from those who challenge the view that childhood is something that can be constructed as a set of powerful ideas or a cluster of social meanings. There are a number of 'essentialist' approaches that emphasize the fixed, permanent and material nature of childhood. Qvortrup (1994, 2008) is a leading exponent of the 'structuralist' school of thinking. He concurs with the proponents of social constructionism that until recently the social presence of 'childhood' has been 'invisible' and children as a sector of the population have been largely absent from the consideration of social scientists. However, structuralists also argue that childhood is an ever-present feature of social structures. In the mid-1990s, Qvortrup and his colleagues (1994) committed themselves to establishing childhood as a permanent and highly visible presence within social structures. This permanence is often countered by the argument that as childhood is a transitional phase because children 'grow up', they never stay children for long. Qvortrup's response is that childhood is a pre-existing social category that many children embody, while different children inhabit this social space at different times, the category of childhood remains. The key claim that structuralists make about childhood is that children inhabit a subordinate social category: in all societies, childhood is a concept that denotes that the young are systematically disadvantaged in terms of access to resources, rights and decision-making processes.

Other challenges to social constructionism emphasize its overly abstract approach to childhood. Childhood becomes a set of ideas or representations that are imposed on the biologically immature. Gittens (1998), on the other hand, brings biological immaturity back into play. Notions of children's vulnerability and innocence are not simply products of historical and social change, they are built into the concept of childhood. Thus child abuse and child poverty not only reflect particular categories of problems defined by adults, they also in some respects reflect the material aspects of being a child. They tell us something about the lived experiences of children, if you like, the problems of children's embodiment. Thus in historical terms, 'child abuse' may be a relatively recent social problem, but it is also a category of problem that tells us something about the way children are physically and emotionally violated because of their inferior social and political status.

A third challenge to the social constructionist approach takes us back to the conventional universalist view of childhood. The material and psychological differences between children and adults necessitate the former being subject to constant supervision and regulation from the latter. Notions of child development, socialization and, in more commonsense terms, the process of growing up are controlled by adults invested with responsibilities and authority (Archard, 2004). What is particularly interesting about this critical view of social constructionism is that there is no simple return to some halcyon period in the past where adults always knew best, and where children were seen but not heard. We have a synthesis of ideas that corresponds to Archard's (2004) crucial distinction between a 'concept' and a 'conception' of childhood. There is the focus on the universalist notion that children are dependent on adults for their growing up. This implies that in all societies, there are clear differences between the *concepts* of childhood and adulthood, with adults underwriting the integrity of childhood and thus the wellbeing and welfare of children. At the same time, the ways in which these differences manifest themselves, and the ways in which the concept of childhood is viewed, are dependent on the nature and structure of the societies within which they are found. *Conceptions* of childhood imply different ways of relating to children and different methods for supporting children as they grow and mature. This would clearly allow for historical and social circumstances where children have greater degrees of involvement.

Conclusion

Critical commentaries on social constructionism emphasize the material and fixed nature of childhood, which clearly differentiates children from adults. In some respects, there has been a return to more embodied notions of childhood, where children's biological and psychological development are important focal points for researchers. One of the weaknesses of social constructionism is that it tells us very little about the process of growing up, particularly in the early stages of development (Lee, 2001). In recent years, social context and biological development have become equally significant in influencing the direction of social scientific agendas on children and childhood (Prout, 2005). Moreover, they have helped to support a more integrated and holistic approach for professionals working with children and their families. Those with an interest in child development are able to explore complex dynamic processes within the child. At the same time, the social constructionist approach has shaped policy and professional practice with respect to understanding the complex ways in which children interact with their social environment and the ways in which powerful adults shape these environments.

REVIEW QUESTIONS

1. When discussing the ways childhood is constructed, we may talk about a pluralist approach to understanding different childhoods. What does 'pluralist approach' mean in this context?
2. What does the expression 'children as social agents' mean?

Further Reading

Archard, D. (2004) *Children: Rights and Childhood* (2nd edn), London, Routledge. Offers a more philosophical reading of the social constructionist approach, with a particular emphasis on children's rights.

Christensen, P. and James A. (eds) (2008) *Research with Children: Perspectives and Practices* (2nd edn), London, Falmer. Offers up-to-date articles on the implications that the 'children as social agents' theme has for researching children and childhood.

James, A. and Prout, A. (eds) (1997) *Constructing and Reconstructing Childhood* (2nd edn), London, Falmer. A key text containing a number of articles that explore the various facets of social constructionism.

Wyness, M. (2006) *Childhood and Society: An Introduction to the Sociology of Childhood*, Basingstoke, Palgrave Macmillan. Introduces the undergraduate to the sociology of childhood and examines a number of different approaches to researching children and childhood.

Social and Emotional Development
Entering the Social World

Sandy Hobbs and Jim McKechnie

LEARNING OUTCOMES

By the end of this chapter, you should be able to:

- describe the complex set of factors that may influence the social development of the child
- understand the significance of attachment in the child's emotional development
- recognize the significance of the different ways in which children may interact with their peers

Complexity of factors influencing the child's social development

Most psychologists believe that both biological and social influences have an impact on how we develop. However, it is more of a problem to decide just how important various factors are and how they interact with each other.

One writer who has offered a model to help us picture the different influences at work is Uri Bronfenbrenner (1917–2005). His approach is termed 'bioecological'. Bronfenbrenner (1979) conceives of the environment in which an individual develops as being part of five different systems:

1. The most basic he refers to as the *microsystem*. This includes the direct relationships a child has, at any given moment, with, for example, parents, school and the local community. Bronfenbrenner regards the relationships as reciprocal. The child is affected by others, but also affects them too.

2. The second level is the *mesosystem*. This refers to relationships between elements in the microsystem, for example between the child's parents and teachers.
3. The third level, termed the *exosystem*, contains elements in wider society which the child does not interact with directly, but which, nevertheless, may influence the child's development. For example, the hours a parent is required to spend at work may affect the time the child spends with that parent and the quality of care the parent provides.
4. The widest layer is the *macrosystem*, which includes the customs, laws and values of society at large.
5. Finally, there is what Bronfenbrenner terms the *chronosystem*, in which he includes the changes which take place over time, not only the changes in the child's body that come about through maturation but also changes in the child's environment.

While it is possible to accept that all these systems have an impact on the child, one important question that a description of systems does not itself answer is: Which are the most important influences?

Bronfenbrenner himself believed that, other things being equal, we should pay particular attention to what happens in the early years of life. He expressed anxieties that too little attention is paid to the effects that changes in modern advanced economies like Britain and the USA may have on children. He was involved in the Head Start programme in America (Bronfenbrenner, 2005), which aimed to help young children whose upbringing might leave them disadvantaged at school. Head Start concentrated on the development of cognitive skills. However, many psychologists believe that we need to look carefully at the early stages of a child's emotional development too.

Attachment

John Bowlby (1907–90) has exerted great influence on our thinking about early emotional development. Initially, on the basis of his work in a child guidance clinic and a study he made of juvenile delinquents, he produced a theory of 'maternal deprivation' (see Bowlby, 1953). He argued that any mother who had been separated from her child for a substantial period could tell from the child's behaviour when they were reunited that this had been emotionally disturbing. For a time, the child appears 'emotionally frozen'. Prolonged separation could have serious long-term effects. He argued that for normal healthy emotional development, a child needs a steady loving relationship with the mother. He found that many teenage delinquents had been separated from their mothers in the critical early years of life. He argued that separation from the mother meant that the child failed to develop a strong emotional bond with her. As a result, the child was emotionally unprepared for the complex social interactions they would face in later life. This emotional unpreparedness could display itself in an inability to form warm relationships and in various sorts of antisocial behaviour.

His theories exerted a good deal of positive influence. Hospitals saw the need for children in hospital to have regular contact with their parents. Traditionally, hospitals had discouraged too many parental visits because of the need to avoid infection. Bowlby's view was that a child's time in hospital would be less traumatic if there were regular contact with the parents. It also became appreciated that orphaned and other children being brought up in institutions had needs other than food, clothing and formal education. In line with Bowlby's views, they should be given the opportunity to bond with caring adults.

However, Bowlby's theories also came under criticism from a variety of sources. Feminists argued that his theories implied that the mothers of young children should not take outside jobs, although Bowlby denied he had suggested this (see Riley, 1983). More telling were the findings of fellow researchers, such as Michael Rutter (1981), who claimed that Bowlby's theories were oversimplified. Bowlby himself came to accept that matters were more complicated than had first appeared. The adult with whom a young child bonds need not be the mother. Cross-cultural studies (see Lamb et al., 1992) suggest that children may develop quite normally even if they are brought up by a number of different adults. Also significant is the research that the harmful effects of the sort Bowlby identified will not necessarily be the same for every individual. Furthermore, even when the child is disadvantaged by the lack of opportunity to bond with a caring adult, the effects need not be permanent.

Experimental research employing a method called the Strange Situation shows that babies may adopt quite different approaches to potentially stressful events (Ainsworth et al., 1978). The experiment arranges for an infant to face eight situations involving the presence and absence of their mother and a stranger. These include time spent with the mother alone, the mother and stranger together, the stranger alone and with both mother and stranger absent. The child's behaviour is closely observed when reunited with the mother. Three characteristic patterns were observed in different children: type A, avoidance of the mother, type B, close proximity and interaction with the mother, and type C, ambivalence. A few children are categorized as showing type D behaviour, because they appear to be disorganized or disorientated. How such patterns emerge and their significance for later development are the subject of much debate.

In later years, Bowlby presented his work in a more subtle and complex manner. He came to use the broader term 'attachment' rather than 'maternal deprivation' (Bowlby, 1969). This concept has the merit that it reminds us of the emotional needs of the young child, without making unjustified assumptions about the likely outcome of particular types of experience. He also saw merit in reminding us that human beings share many characteristics with other animals. He believed that we may learn from research by 'ethologists', that is, those biologists who study the behaviour of animals in their natural settings. The behaviour of the young of some other species has features in common with human children. He ultimately described his own approach as 'ethological' (Ainsworth and Bowlby, 1991). In doing so, he was recognizing, like Bronfenbrenner, the complex interaction of biological and social influences.

Beyond the nuclear family: relationships with peers

As a child grows older, more time is spent with people other than the parents. Of particular importance is the time spent with other children. An older brother or sister may act as a significance attachment figure. There may also be strains and rivalries among siblings. Here, however, we shall concentrate on relationships with others of around the same age outside the family, the child's peers.

Studies of children as young as one year old suggest that other children are an important part of the child's environment. For example, observations of infants spending time together with other infants have found that although each child typically spends much of the time in close proximity to their own mother, they also spend a lot of time looking at the other infant, but not at the other infant's mother (Lewis and Rosenblum, 1975). Thus although there is virtually no observable interaction with the other child, their presence is meaningful.

Once children begin to spend time together in nurseries or playgroups, it is possible for psychologists to study the social aspects of their play. Different sorts of relationship may be found. The behaviour of children in playschools has been classified as 'unoccupied', 'onlooker', 'solitary', 'parallel play' and 'cooperative play' (Smith, 1978). At first, it may be common for a child placed with other children to do nothing, to watch others or simply play on their own. Then parallel play may emerge, in which two children may engage simultaneously in the same activity but not interact with each other. More fully social, cooperative play involves the children acting together and influencing each other. Typically, the percentage of time spent in group play increases as the child gets older. Of course, the development of cooperative play is seen as an important aspect of learning to live effectively in society. It is to encourage the social skills of playing with other children that is often seen as the main justification for playschools.

Once the child has grown to beyond the playschool age, the patterns of relationship with peers will become more complex. Children will spend time with their peers in the classroom, in school-directed play and also in free time play. These situations are particularly important in the development of relatively stable relationships, both positive and negative, with peers.

So-called 'peer groups' have been the subject of study by psychologists and sociologists. In some ways, the way in which peers function will be familiar to anyone who reflects on their own childhood. One may have been a member of a formal 'class' in a school, but within that class there exist informal groups. One spends more time with some classmates than others. One may feel friendlier to some of them than to others. Beyond such commonsense awareness, however, it is possible to gather information about how peer groups function.

One technique is referred to as *sociometry* (from the Latin *socius* meaning companion, and *metrum* meaning measure, a quantitative method for measuring social relationships). Researchers can attempt to build systematic evidence of relationships among children. Evidence may be collected by asking them questions such as: With whom do you spend most time? Who are your closest friends? It is also possible to ask: Who do you dislike?, but some believe that this is an unethical and potentially dangerous question. Evidence can also be collected by observing the children, recording how much time each spends interacting with others.

These methods may establish which children belong to which group. They may also establish the relationship between groups, which are friendly towards each other, which are hostile and which simply coexist. This type of evidence may help us distinguish between the different positions an individual may hold, for example which members of a group may be regarded as central figures, 'leaders', who seem to exert most influence over others. Detailed studies of group relationships have led to the suggestion that individuals may be classified as popular, controversial, rejected, neglected or simply 'average' (Coie et al., 1982). Naturally, when such distinctions are made, the question arises of why an individual falls into a particular role. One way of explaining why a child becomes popular is by seeing that child as more skilful in interacting with others, being better able to interpret another child's actions and better able to react appropriately.

However, it is not surprising that most attention is paid to children who are in some form of isolation from their peers through rejection. To remain in such a position might have serious long-term consequences for such children, which means they merit particular attention.

Research suggests that children who appear to be rejected do not form a single homogeneous group. One Dutch study of boys of infant school age (Cillessen et al., 1992) gathered a variety of different sorts of information from observation by researchers, teachers' reports and the children themselves. Just over 1 in 10 of the boys seemed to be rejected by their peers. Almost half of the rejected children were what could be termed 'rejected-aggressive'. They were seen to be not only aggressive but also impulsive, dishonest and relatively unsuccessful at school work. It is not difficult to understand why boys with these characteristics might not be readily accepted by their peers. However, not all rejected boys fitted this pattern. There was a small group whom the researchers called 'rejected-submissive'. They were shy rather than aggressive and did not have any particular problems with school work. Finally, about 4 out of 10 of the rejected boys did not fit readily into either of these sub-groups, so the reasons for their being rejected are less easy to understand. One significant fact emerged when the researchers went back to look at the boys a year later. Many of the boys originally seen to be rejected had come to be accepted by their peers. However, this was much less likely to be the case for the rejected-aggressive boys than the others. The majority of them remained rejected, whereas the majority of the non-aggressive groups were no longer isolated. This suggests that, although aggressiveness is not the sole cause of rejection, it is those rejected children who are aggressive that give most cause for concern.

Aggressive behaviour generally is an important and well-researched aspect of children's social behaviour. Many possible factors have been explored as possible causes. For example, there is some evidence that there may be genetically influenced factors at work (Mason and Frick, 1994). However, much more importance seems to be attributed to the child's experience. In particular, certain types of child-rearing practices seem to increase the propensity for aggression. Parents who fail to display warmth, fail to monitor conduct and are ineffective at imposing discipline may thereby contribute to a child's aggressive tendencies (Patterson et al., 1989).

Example: bullying

Social interactions between children may not always run smoothly. In recent years, researchers have drawn attention to the extent of bullying that is experienced by children. Studies across a range of countries indicate that up to 20–25% of children experience bullying at school (for example Whitney and Smith, 1993).

There is debate over how to define bullying but there is now some acceptance that it can take two forms, direct and indirect (Farrington, 1993). Direct bullying refers to behaviour such as pushing and hitting, whereas indirect bullying can involve teasing, spreading rumours or socially excluding someone. The distinction between direct and indirect bullying has been linked to gender differences. Males are more likely to display direct forms, while females tend to use indirect forms. Bullying may be carried out by one person or a group but does involve some repetition of the actions against another person.

Research findings have identified characteristics linked to bullies and their victims. Bullies tend to be aggressive in responding to others, children and adults. They tend to display antisocial behaviour patterns, with rule-breaking a common pattern. Bullies aim to dominate others and it has been suggested that they lack empathy (Olweus, 1993). However, we should not assume that they lack social skills. Recent work suggests that they are skilled at interpreting social information but that they then use this knowledge to support their antisocial behaviour (Sutton et al., 1999).

In contrast, victims are typically unassertive, quiet and lack social confidence. They are also low in self-esteem, can be anxious and rarely initiate social contact. Research evidence shows that these behaviours precede their victim status and can be viewed as a cause of their experiences (Schwartz et al., 1993).

Bullying has long-term consequences for both bullies and their victims. Victims can experience psychological problems that may last for a long time, for example lack of confidence and poor self-worth, which then impact on their adult relationships. Those who bully have been found to be more likely to have criminal records and alcohol-related problems in later life (Olweus, 1993). These individuals often rely on power-assertive approaches in social relationships and this can create problems in adult settings, for example the workplace.

The extent, and consequences, of bullying has meant that schools have developed anti-bullying policies. There is some evidence that these strategies can be effective in reducing the extent of these dysfunctional social relationships (Smith and Sharp, 1994).

Conclusion

If you go back to the beginning of this chapter and look again at the various possible influences Bronfenbrenner suggested might influence a child's social development, you will realize that we have touched on only a tiny proportion of them. However, Bronfenbrenner would probably agree with us that, other things being equal, the early direct influences are those that deserve most attention. To understand the development of a child experiencing war, famine or a tsunami would require us to take account of factors not dealt with in this chapter. However, when free from such extreme circumstances, a child's relationships with their parents and other children are likely to be crucial forces moulding the individual that child turns out to be. In order to understand children growing up in British society today, these are the influences that most justify careful study.

REVIEW QUESTIONS

1. What is the Strange Situation and what does it claim to assess?
2. How do children come to form relationships with other children?
3. Why are some children rejected by their peers?

_____*Further Reading* _____

Ainsworth, M.D. and Bowlby, J. (1991) An ethological approach to personality development, *American Psychologist*, 46, 331–41. Provides a summary of the authors work on attachment.

Berk, L.E. (2006) *Child Development* (7th edn), Boston, Pearson. Chapter 15 gives an overview of research and issues relating to peers and their social world.

Bronfenbrenner, U. (ed.) (2005) *Making Human Beings Human: Bioecological Perspectives on Human Development*, London, Sage. Reviews the author's work on social development.

Monks, C.P. and Smith, P.K. (2006) Definitions of bullying: age differences in understanding the term, and the role of experience, *British Journal of Developmental Psychology*, 24, 801–22. Provides an example of some recent research in this area.

Understanding Right and Wrong
Moral Development

Jim McKechnie and Sandy Hobbs

LEARNING OUTCOMES

By the end of this chapter, you should be able to:

- understand cognitive explanations of moral development
- show an awareness of the range of factors that influence moral development
- understand the debates surrounding the link between moral reasoning and action

Imagine a nursery where two three-year-old children are playing at the sandpit. Suddenly, one of them starts to pull on the other child's bucket and to hit the other child. Two adults quickly move in; one seeks to comfort the 'victim', while the other pulls away the 'attacking' child, saying that the behaviour is 'bad' and you are 'not allowed to hit other people', because 'it's wrong'.

Such scenes are played out in one form or another in numerous settings. They raise the key question for this chapter: How do we come to understand what is right and wrong? The capacity to make this distinction lies at the heart of our ability to become moral agents.

To participate in any society, children must learn the rules and expectations of that culture. For example, we have rules about eating with a knife and fork, about queuing and about appropriate dress in various social settings. Such conventions enhance social organization, setting parameters for our behaviour and interactions with others. However, they may change over time. In contrast, moral considerations are much more stable. Moral rules underpin the principles of social relationships. As such, they relate to issues of justice, violations of rights and concerns about the welfare of others.

In this chapter our focus is on the factors that may influence the development of the understanding of moral rules.

> **Point for Reflection**
>
> Make one list of social conventions that vary between societies or between groups within a society, and another list of the key moral rules that extend across all groups within society.

The influence of cognitive development

Our nursery example demonstrates that in early childhood, our compliance with moral rules is imposed by external forces. However, our ability to distinguish right and wrong and behave accordingly is ultimately internalized, that is, we control our own sense of morality. Children interpret the world around them and seek to make sense of their experiences. Researchers have made interpretation a primary focus and they have linked moral development to changes in reasoning ability.

Cognitive development and moral understanding

Jean Piaget's *The Moral Judgement of the Child* (1932) set out many of the questions that researchers are still addressing today. Piaget (1896–1980) was primarily interested in cognitive development and his ideas on moral understanding emphasize the role of the child's ability to reason and think about rules. His ideas about moral reasoning were based on his study of the use of rules within the games that children played.

For Piaget, our ability to understand moral rules progresses through three stages:

1. In the *premoral stage* (approximately up to 4 years), children have no understanding of rules and they make arbitrary judgements about what is right and wrong.
2. In the *moral realism stage* (around 4–10 years), children are aware of rules but view them as emanating from adult authority figures. In judging responses to 'bad behaviour', children at this stage focus on the amount of damage caused by the behaviour and pay little attention to the intentions of the individual.
3. In the *moral subjectivism stage* (around 10 years and above), the focus changes. Here the child's views change to acknowledge that many rules are arbitrary, based on convention and agreement, for example the rules of a game. Furthermore, at this stage, the individual starts to consider the intention behind behaviour and to judge right and wrong on the basis of moral principles.

How does the child progress from one stage to the next? For Piaget, there were two important factors, cognitive ability and social experience. His work on moral development has been criticized for lacking detail and failing to look beyond mid-childhood. Nevertheless, he is acknowledged to have drawn attention to key issues that must be examined.

Lawrence Kohlberg (1927–87) produced a more detailed and coherent cognitive development theory of moral understanding. His work has also opened debates about how we can assess moral reasoning. He devised a set of stories where people are faced with a moral dilemma, as for example the story of 'Heinz':

> In Europe, a woman was near death from a special kind of cancer. There was one drug that the doctor thought might save her. It was a form of radium that a druggist in the same town had recently discovered. The drug was expensive to make, but the druggist was charging ten times what the drug cost him to make. He paid $200 for the radium but charged $2,000 for a small dose of the drug. The sick woman's husband, Heinz, went to everyone he knew to borrow the money, but he could only get together about $1,000, which is half what it cost. He told the druggist that his wife was dying, and asked him to sell it cheaper or let him pay later. But the druggist said 'No, I discovered the drug and I'm going to make money from it'. So Heinz got desperate and broke into the man's store to steal the drug for his wife. (Kohlberg, 1963, pp. 18–19)

Should Heinz have done this? Why? Why not? Kohlberg's primary interest was in the justification offered in response to the second question.

Using these moral dilemma stories, Kohlberg carried out longitudinal research, following the same participants over time. He concluded that moral development progresses through three levels (pre-conventional, conventional and post-conventional). Within each level, he posited two stages, but in this short chapter we focus on the three levels:

- At the first level, Kohlberg argued, like Piaget, that *pre-conventional morality* is what others tell us to do. The individual has still to understand rules and expectations.
- Progression to level two, *conventional morality*, results in moral judgements that are based on the importance of conforming to the rules and conventions of society.
- *Post-conventional morality*, the third level, emerges when an individual demonstrates awareness of the moral principles that underlie societal rules. Where there is a clash between social conventions and moral rules, judgements are based on the moral rule and not the social convention.

An individual's level of moral reasoning emerges from their responses to moral dilemmas. Kohlberg believed that pre-conventional moral judgements dominate throughout early and mid-childhood; conventional morality emerges in mid-adolescence and post-conventional morality is associated with adulthood. However, he also argued that the highest stage in the final level is rarely attained.

As was the case with Piaget, Kohlberg believed that progression through the levels and stages in his model was linked to cognitive development. For Kohlberg, individuals progress through his levels in the same sequence and there is no stage jumping. Given the view that cognitive development patterns are universal, the corollary is that moral development sequence is also universal.

Kohlberg's theory has dominated debates in this area and has been subject to criticism. The reliability and scoring of the responses to the moral dilemmas has been questioned (Kurtines and Gewirtz, 1984; Siegal, 1982), while others have felt that the dilemmas do not relate to real-life situations. For others, the concern is that the dilemmas focus on only some aspects of morality, namely justice and fairness (Gilligan, 1982). Carol Gilligan (1982) has argued that there was a male bias in Kohlberg's theory. According to Gilligan, males resolve moral dilemmas by adopting a justice orientation, while females, due to their different experiences in society, adopt a care orientation. The different orientation of females, according to Gilligan, is not captured in Kohlberg's approach. It should be noted, however, that subsequent research has failed to find any consistent sex differences in moral reasoning (see Walker et al., 1995).

Kohlberg's theory has also been criticized for its focus on moral rules and its neglect of the development of children's understanding of social conventions. Research has shown that children are able to distinguish between social conventions and moral rules at young ages (Turiel, 1998). These findings question the link between cognitive development and moral development, since children appear to be able to make this distinction at younger ages than Piaget and Kohlberg would predict.

Kohlberg's claim that moral development is universal has received mixed support. A review of cross-cultural studies by Snarey (1985) concluded that there was evidence of progression through the first two levels of Kohlberg's theory in a wide range of cultures. Beyond this level, there was more cultural diversity.

Other critics argue that, by focusing on our ability to reason about moral issues, Kohlberg has neglected both our emotional responses to moral decisions and the relationship between our reasoning and our overt behaviour (Blasi, 1980). These deserve further exploration.

Emotions and morality

As adults, when we behave in a way that we know is wrong, we experience guilt and possibly remorse. In contrast, when we do something that we know to be right, we experience a sense of positive self-regard, a feeling of wellbeing. This indicates that there may be some association between our emotions and our understanding of right and wrong. We will consider two examples, empathy and conscience.

Empathy

Behaviour such as helping others, comforting them or sharing what we have with others is referred to as *prosocial behaviour*. Such behaviours entail a 'cost' for the individual, so why do we exhibit these behaviours or experience a sense of outrage when exposed to the sufferings of others?

Underpinning our emotional reactions in these cases is our capacity to empathize with others, our awareness that others feel pain, happiness, grief. The capacity to empathize is based on the ability to take the perspectives of others, to put ourselves in their shoes. Some researchers believe that empathy is at the root of the actions that we refer to as prosocial behaviour. Furthermore, empathy may have some biological basis. Even very young infants respond to the distress of another infant. We can see this in so-called 'sympathy crying' by other infants in response to the crying of a distressed infant (Eisenberg and Fabes, 1998).

However, true empathy requires the ability to take another person's perspective. This emerges during childhood. In later childhood, the ability to understand another's perspective broadens, allowing us to judge another's intentions by putting ourselves in their place. At approximately 8–10 years of age, we start to be concerned about the general conditions that other people face, such as poverty and oppression. Such awareness will play an important role in prosocial behaviour, since it adds an emotional aspect to our perception of what is right or wrong.

Conscience

The idea of conscience tends to be associated with the production of feelings of guilt. Erik Erikson (1902–94) suggests that the conscience can be thought of as an inner voice that comments on our behaviour, providing 'self-guidance' and 'self-punishment'. This inner voice appears to emerge in the preschool years (see Kochanska et al., 1994) and is thought to be important, in that it will inhibit immoral actions and punish us through the creation of guilt if inhibition fails (Erikson, 1968).

Conscience and empathy do not develop in a social vacuum. Significant others, for example parents and peers, have an impact on the child's development of moral understanding.

The wider context

During childhood, adults have the capacity to monitor and maintain acceptable standards. In the early stages of childhood, they have a dual role, in that they act as the external control of moral rules and influence the child's attainment of behaviour. Adults are in the position to reward or punish their child for displaying certain behaviours. Learning theory (O'Donahue and Ferguson, 2001) tells us that reward strengthens the behaviour rewarded. It also tells us that punishment is not the most effective way to influence a child. Punishment may only suppress the negative behaviour temporarily. A more positive approach is to reward the alternative behaviours that you wish to see displayed more often, for example helping others. Over time, the child will show more of the rewarded behaviour, thus reducing or eliminating the negative behaviour.

Adults are also models for the child (Bandura, 1977). As children seek to make sense of the world around them, they attend to what others do and the outcomes of their actions. The most obvious models for young children are their parents and their peers. The impact of learning from observing others is potentially an important influence.

Parents may also aid their child's understanding and reasoning about moral issues. Research has shown a link between parenting styles and developmental outcomes (Baumrind, 1989). The use by parents of 'inductive techniques' has been linked to the child's moral maturity (Hoffman, 1988). These involve the parent explaining to the child the implications of their behaviour, and emphasizing the impact that the child is having on others. By adopting this approach, the child is encouraged to think about how others feel and develop feelings of empathy. Induction may also play a role in generating feelings of guilt.

Research suggests two important points about such inductive interactions:

1. The parent needs to tailor explanations to the child's level of cognitive development.
2. Parents' negative emotional reaction to unacceptable behaviour can facilitate the understanding of moral rules.

Combining inductive explanations with a show of distress at the child's behaviour is an effective way to raise the child's awareness. Parents need to balance the emotional reaction and explanation, since overreacting emotionally may be counterproductive.

Delinquency and moral development

Many of the problems associated with young people in society revolve around their delinquent acts. Kohlberg argued that this is the very area to consider the link between moral reasoning and behaviour. In one of his studies (Kohlberg, 1975), he found that adolescents who had a record of delinquent or antisocial behaviour were shown, via the moral dilemmas, to be reasoning at lower levels. Subsequent research has supported this finding (Blasi, 1980).

These findings suggest that delinquent behaviour may be tackled by improving the delinquents' reasoning in the moral domain, in effect a form of moral education. This strategy has had mixed results. A major issue is that this approach ignores the other factors that may influence the delinquent's actions. For some, delinquency is the result not of poor moral reasoning but of the social conditions that the individual finds themselves in. Kohlberg acknowledged this in part when he suggested that, in his study, delinquents' lower moral reasoning reflected poor child-rearing or parental practices.

Recently, Tarry and Emler (2007) have argued that delinquency is at best weakly associated with moral reasoning. They argue that it is the link between attitudes and authority that is of importance in understanding antisocial behaviour. If they are correct, education programmes that focus solely on this element will at best be of limited use.

The gap between moral understanding and behaviour

Kohlberg acknowledged that, in some circumstances, we may be able to understand what is right but not behave in a way that matched this understanding. How consistent are our reasoning and our action?

In one set of studies (Kohlberg, 1975), adolescents who were functioning at higher stages of moral reasoning were less likely to cheat in school when given the opportunity. They were also less likely to come into contact with the police and display higher levels of prosocial behaviour. However, the degree of consistency between reasoning and action does vary. In one classic study, Hartshorne and May (1928) showed that whether a child cheated or not was in part dependent on the situation they were in, for example in school or at home. This led to the conclusion that honesty is influenced by situational and motivational factors.

Consistency between reasoning and behaviour may be dependent on factors such as the influence of those around us, the perceived costs to ourselves, and personality. Recently, the idea has emerged that the level of consistency between our reasoning and action will depend on how important we view this to be to the image we have of ourselves. Augusto Blasi (1980) has argued that we all have a moral identity, and for those with a strong identity, consistency will be important. Inconsistency or behaving in a manner that is known to be 'bad' will result in guilt. The more important our moral identity is to us, the greater the negative reaction to our own wrongdoing will be. This approach expands our idea of moral development. While acknowledging the role of reasoning and cognitive development, Blasi argues that we need to examine how we develop a moral character or identity. For some, this means that we need to look more closely at moral education and its link to character formation.

Conclusion

Acquiring an understanding of right and wrong is clearly a complex process. Explanations drawing on cognitive development have dominated the field and this has obscured the other factors that influence our understanding in this area. We need to acknowledge that our awareness of morality takes place within a social context and against a background emotional development. We need to attend to the influence of those around us, since they, in part, provide the information that we use to decide what is right or wrong.

The complexity of the area is added to by our knowledge that our behaviour is not always consistent with our moral reasoning. One explanation for this gap may be found in the idea of our moral identity.

Developing our understanding of moral development is important since it has many practical implications. These range from discussions about how to enhance young people's moral awareness or how to react to immoral behaviour through to debates about the legal age of responsibility.

REVIEW QUESTIONS

1. What is the link between cognitive development and moral reasoning?
2. What do you consider to be the key influences on moral development?
3. Outline the relationship between moral reasoning and moral action.

_____*Further Reading*_____

Bee, H. and Boyd, D. (2004) *The Developing Child* (10th edn), Boston, Pearson. Chapter 12 considers moral development within the wider context of our emotional relationships with others.

Bergman, R. (2002) Why be moral? A conceptual model from developmental psychology, *Human Development*, 45, 104–24. Considers theoretical explanations for our moral behaviour.

Schaffer, H.R. (1996) *Social Development*, Oxford, Blackwell. Chapter 6 explores the development of moral behaviour within the context of the development of self-control.

Tarry, H. and Emler, N. (2007) Attitudes, values and moral reasoning as predictors of delinquency, *British Journal of Developmental Psychology*, 25, 169–83. Explores the link between reasoning and behaviour.

Developing through Play

Robert Adams and Lesley Jessiman

LEARNING OUTCOMES

By the end of this chapter, you should be able to:

- understand what we mean by play
- appreciate the contribution of play to children's development
- describe the functions of play
- understand how play contributes to professional work with children

---

The many roles of play

Play makes a vital contribution to the cognitive and linguistic development of the child, and is instrumental in the formation of friendships. Play and peer interactions also allow children to develop important skills such as conflict resolution, empathy and moral understanding (see Chapter 5), and these important cognitive skills in turn facilitate the development of more sophisticated play activities (Eisenberg and Fabes, 1990, 1998; Harris, 2003; Kavale and Forness, 1996; Ricaud-Droisy and Zaouche-Gaudron, 2003). In this chapter, we will discuss the different types of play, examine the role of play in child development, and identify the importance of play in educational and therapeutic settings. We will begin our discussions with a brief historical account of play.

'Play' in history

The painting *Children's Games* by Pieter Bruegel (1560) beautifully depicts the many different types of play children engaged in during the 1500s. Looking at Bruegel's depiction of children playing, we can draw some similarities with how children played 450 years ago and how they play today. Thus even with all the technology our children find themselves surrounded by, free play still often involves simple contact games such as 'tag' and 'hide and seek'.

Great philosophical writers such as Locke (1632–1704) and Kant (1724–1804) also wrote of play as integral to the learning process. Similarly, Schiller (1759–1805) proposed that play is part of mental, symbolic and physical forms, which opens gateways to creativity and higher spiritual thought. He also regarded play as extending 'enjoyment beyond necessity'.

Motivated by great thinkers and writers such as Locke, Kant and Schiller, educationalists in the early 20th century began to integrate play into the child's curriculum. Almost a century ago, space for free and guided free play in the classroom and outdoors formed an important part of the early years curriculum; a curriculum envisaged by people such as Rudolf Steiner (1861–1925). Steiner's pedagogical model thus emphasizes the importance of supporting the physical, emotional and intellectual growth of the child, and time and space to play is pertinent to achieving all these things (see Chapter 2).

Maria Montessori (1870–1952) also developed educational principles on which today's Montessori school curricula are still based. Montessori schools offer a child-oriented programme with space, time and freedom for children to play and engage in activities that interest them (see Chapter 2). However, even today, we find play still occupies a somewhat ambiguous position in the curriculum, which is reflected in its two major functions:

- As a central aspect of children's experiences and pleasure and the culture of childhood that they own
- As a contributor to the early years curriculum and children's health and development, as defined and governed by professionals.

Defining play

Play is, without question, a multifaceted activity. It can involve children having spontaneous fun, letting off steam, engaging in creative arts, self-discovery and getting to know others. Play can thus can be defined as activities in which children engage that have no purpose beyond pleasure and entertainment. Despite this, play contributes considerably to the learning and development of children. This is, of course, the very reason practitioners incorporate play into their practice, through the professional activities of planning, implementing, reviewing and evaluating a sequence of appropriate sessions identifying children's needs and promoting their development and learning. Play clearly is a powerful medium through which practitioners achieve the goals of assessment, family support or therapeutic change (see Chapter 4).

Point for Reflection

Is play simply something children do when they are not learning and developing, or is play integral to learning and development?

Functions of play

Play has multiple and important functions such as contributing to children's physical, intellectual and emotional development. Play also enables children to engage in physical exercise, it provides children with mental stimulus, provides the child with an emotional outlet, encourages children to enjoy themselves, provides children with opportunities for social interaction and enables children to tackle and resolve problems.

Table 6.1 illustrates the interest that developmental psychologists have in children's play activities and how, through empirical research, developmental psychologists have managed to categorize the different stages and types of play.

The reasons such different play behaviours emerge at specific ages is the result of the child's physical and cognitive development. For example, when the child learns to walk, run and jump, the range of play behaviours widen somewhat. The younger child who can only shuffle around on their bottom or crawl along the

Table 6.1 The developmental stages of play

Age	Stages of play and description
6–12 months	*Parallel play:* Children play in close proximity with each other but without paying attention to each other
By 1 year old	*Parallel aware play:* As above, but children are more aware of each other, occasionally looking at the other child to see what they are doing
1–1.5 years	*Simple pretend play:* Children engage in similar activities, like playing in the sandpit, but engage in some level of interaction such as talking and/or sharing toys
1.5–2 years	*Complementary and reciprocal play:* Action-based role reversals, such as 'I'll run and you chase me', or 'you hide and I'll find you'
2.5–3 years	*Cooperative social pretend play:* Children play out pretend roles such as 'you be mummy, I'll be daddy and they can be baby', but with little discussion and planning of the roles, for example what they will do when in their roles
3.5–4 years	*Complex social pretend play* (also known as *sociodramatic play*): As above, but the children put more thought into the roles they will play and how they will each execute the roles assigned

Source: Adapted from Howes and Matheson (1992)

floor is more constrained to static, less interactive types of play. The younger child thus engages in solitary exploration more than actual social play (Howes and Matheson, 1992; Parten, 1932). All children of all ages do, however, engage in some level of solitary play and exploration. For example, the older, more cognitively mature child engaging in social pretend play, such as acting out the role of the family, may engage in their role away from the other children because their role as 'mummy' demands more solitary activity. Thus, less mature play activities such as solitary play don't necessarily disappear as the child gets older, instead they might simply change in function (Moore et al., 1974; Rubin, 1982).

Understanding play and exploratory behaviours is important for people working with children for many reasons. For example, the toddler entering a nursery for the first time will spend time exploring their physical and social environments. During this time, the child is unlikely to engage in play behaviours and instead might seem apprehensive of their new environment. Once the child has assessed the possible dangers and familiarized themselves with the environment, the other children and the adults, they will begin to engage in more social play activities. It is thus not until the child has gone through this period of observation that more social play will emerge. Withdrawal from normal play activities can simply reflect the child's attempts to make sense of their new environment and is therefore quite normal behaviour (Pellegrini et al., 2007). However, if withdrawal from play activities continues, it is then that carers should look for the cause of the child's social withdrawal.

Play and language

Play is not only dependent on the child's physical development but also on their cognitive development. The development of language seems to be particularly important for play between the ages of two and three years where social pretend play emerges. For example, for social pretend play to happen, the child has to communicate their wishes and feelings with their friends, such as 'you chase me and I'll hide'. They will also engage in play that is motivated by a specific narrative, such as acting out roles, for example 'you be mum and I'll be dad', or 'I'll be the policeman and you be the bad man'. Thus, research shows that social pretend play and language form a symbiotic relationship and the interplay between language and play can be observed in children as young as two years of age (Illgaz and Aksu-Coç, 2005; McCune-Nicholich, 1981; Paley, 1990).

It is also important to note here that we are not suggesting that the development of language is solely dependent on play but rather that play facilitates language development and vice versa. By the time the child is 18 months of age, they have already acquired some level of language ability. Our proposal is that children's language skills clearly develop within the context of meaningful social interaction, and social interactions become more meaningful with the development of language. As argued by Vygotsky (1962, 1978), cognitive and linguistic development is the result of learning, and learning occurs through social interaction, such as play.

Play and theory of mind

Theory of mind (ToM) can be defined as one's knowledge and understanding that other people have beliefs, feelings, perspectives and memories separate from our own (see also Chapter 10). In other words, just because I know or see something, it does not necessarily mean another person will also know it or be able to see it. The child's understanding of self is an integral component of ToM development and both are important for the development of more complex play behaviours (Rogers and Pennington, 1991; for a review, see Symons, 2004). By the time the child is two years old, they will have internalized representations of *self*, that is, 'I know what I know', or 'I feel what I feel'; these are known as *metarepresentations* (Leslie, 1994). In this sense, the child has some understanding of who they are and also knows something about 'what is in their head'. An understanding of self thus also leads to understanding of others. During play activities, we will hear children say things like 'look at me', 'what is this?', or 'what are you doing?' Children's language can thus tell us something about their understanding of others, such that children after the age of two years begin to grasp that other people have intentions, beliefs and desires that can be separate from their own intentions, beliefs and desires. This level of understanding becomes integrated within their play, such that we might hear them say: 'no, don't play like that, that isn't the way to do it, do it like this!' Without ToM and language, one can readily identify how play activities could not develop into more complex interactions, as we see with social pretend play, for example.

We might therefore reasonably assume that much of what developmental psychology has discovered about the importance of play activities, and also our identification of play as a child-specific activity, is why, at the very least, play activities have made their way into formal educational and therapeutic settings. For example, if play activity does indeed facilitate the development of ToM, language and social competence, then it stands to reason that educators would want play as a formal part of the education curriculum, as indeed will the parents of young children.

The formal roles of play

Since the late 20th century, policy has shifted towards play making a more structured contribution to the early learning curriculum. Tina Bruce (2005), a leading advocate of the essential function of play in the development, health and wellbeing of children, proposes that the government's *Birth to Three Matters* (DfES, 2002) framework underpins and supports play, and also that play supports the framework.

The central paradox of play is that it can be purposeful work without losing the fun element of play. In a real sense, although play with children can be fun, we are not being 'killjoys' to suggest that when staff play with children they are working. They need to manage the tension between enjoying the activity and maintaining their sense of this as resonating with the practitioner's purpose. Play clearly has the potential to be purposeful as well as pleasant.

The most longstanding settings where young children can play are playgroups. The word is made up of the two important words 'play' and 'group', which informs us about the function and purpose of playgroups. It is also common for care workers in nurseries and family centres to work with children in groups rather than individuals and to recognize the importance of workers becoming involved in various play-type activities.

Another formal setting for play is child and family therapy. There are many different ways in which play makes a contribution to professional work with children and their families, and we explore some of these below.

The role of play in a therapeutic setting

Anna Freud (1895–1982) and Melanie Klein (1882–1960) were two of the first therapists to use play as a means of assessing childhood trauma, by adopting play into their psychoanalytical therapy. They saw play as providing therapists/ practitioners with the ideal medium with which to observe and assess children. Thus, because children naturally engage in play activities and seek out environments that support these play activities, therapy that adopts and permits these natural behaviours will clearly provide the therapist with a more reliable and effective therapeutic resource (Landreth, 2002).

In the therapeutic setting, it is suggested that play can be used as a means of developing the therapeutic relationship between the practitioner and the child and it also enables the child to express views and feelings nonverbally, which is particularly useful for children who have not yet developed the necessary communication skills or when trauma has affected the child's ability to verbally communicate (Gil, 1991). Clearly, play contributes to a broader, more comprehensive and neighbourhood-based approach to practice, which can be readily identified in a range of play-specific therapies.

Imaginative, pretend play

In Table 6.1, we illustrated how play activities can help us to identify the typical development of the child. For example, between 12 and 18 months of age, children begin to engage in *simple pretend play*, for example playing in the sandpit but engaging in some level of interaction such as talking and/or sharing toys, and by three and a half and four years of age, we begin to see more *complex social pretend play* (also known as *sociodramatic play*), where children put more thought into roles they will play and how they will each execute the roles.

These developmental stages of play therefore provide therapists with a means of identifying typical and atypical development. For example, young infants' play activities usually involve making noises with objects, stacking and manipulating objects in place and although some older children might still engage in some of these play activities, when they do so in the absence of more pretend-type play, it may indicate some form of problem. For example, atypical play behaviours may indicate:

- delayed cognitive development
- the child has been deprived of a setting where they can play
- the child has experienced some form of trauma
- they may be shy about risk taking in play.

Geldard and Geldard (1997) note that in situations where a child has experienced any of these problems, play therapy can enable them to:

- verbally and nonverbally express their wishes, fears, and ideas
- gain some relief from emotional pain
- gain some control
- develop their understanding of events
- practise new ways of behaving
- build on their self-esteem
- improve communication skills.

Play therapies thus use of a wide range of everyday objects to encourage the child to engage in imaginative play, for example clothing, household objects, toys and dolls. Providing these types of object allows the child's make-believe world to coexist alongside the immediate setting. In using toys and objects, the practitioner also provides the child with the opportunity to express their 'story' without the need for words (Carmichael, 2006). The practitioner may also adopt different roles in parallel play, co-play and play tutoring.

Parallel play in therapy

Parallel play involves the practitioner sitting next to the child, imitating the child's play activities and making comments about what they (the practitioner) are doing. This is done in such a way so as not to intrude on the child's play, but to illustrate to the child possible ways of behaving. This type of play therapy is designed in such a way as to help the child see that their play activities are valued. For instance, the practitioner may show appreciation of the child making a pretend cup of tea and add a suggestion, by saying: 'Thank you for making a cup of tea. Let's give mummy the teacup on a saucer so it won't spill.'

Co-play in therapy

Co-play involves the practitioner joining in the child's play and asking the child to help them (the practitioner) in the play activity. For example, they might ask the child for help by saying: 'Baby hasn't drunk her milk. I'm her mummy. What shall I do?' This helps the child to identify that the practitioner values their role in the play activity and also helps the child to identify that they are valued as a person. It also facilitates verbal communication, which is particularly important when communication has been affected by trauma.

Play tutoring

Play tutoring differs from co-play in that the practitioner can introduce a play idea rather than simply joining in with what the child is playing. The practitioner may ask questions, which, in effect, are much more directive: 'Baby is crying. He wants you to take him out in the pram, so you can rock him to sleep.' Geldard and Geldard (1997) do point out, however, that play tutoring is more intrusive and it should be used as little as possible, with the practitioner falling back into observing as soon as the play activity has been established.

We should also note here that it is extremely important that play does not lose its natural association with being fun and spontaneous, even though this is somewhat in tension with its function in a therapeutic setting. It is important to manage this tension judiciously, with reference to the goals of the setting and the needs of the child.

Although there are varied opinions about whether play provides a means of bringing about change, or whether it is insufficiently structured to be effective, there are many who support play therapy as a reliable and effective means of helping the child overcome a wide range of problems. Bishop and Curtis (2001), for example, argue that play has a positive and creative relationship with structured arrangements for socializing children, such as found in school settings. Others see play therapy as an effective means of facilitating the important and necessary relationship between the therapist and the child; believing that play therapy promotes notable and positive change for children

(Carmichael, 2006; Landreth, 2002; Leblanc and Ritchie, 2001; Shaefer and Kaduson, 2007).

Whether play therapy is effective or not will perhaps always remain a contentious issue. As Sue Jennings, a leading creative therapist and a pioneer of dramatherapy in the UK, acknowledges (2010, p. 367):

> play therapy is still an emergent profession and is finding its own identity within the plethora of child-centred practices that include play, for example play worker, therapeutic play worker, paediatric occupational therapist, social worker, special needs teacher, as well as the arts therapists who also use play within their practice.

What is also important is that the therapy adopted meets the needs of the child. As Gil (2006) points out, the needs of the child are our greatest concern and it is indeed the child's needs that should determine the type of therapy employed. There is no simple 'off-the-shelf' prescription for this. What is required is a careful matching by the practitioner of needs to available resources in which the learning and experience of the practitioner are a vital ingredient.

Conclusion

This chapter has discussed the way in which play activities develop in concert with other important cognitive functions such as self-awareness and theory of mind. It has also discussed the importance of language in the development of more sophisticated play activities such as social pretend play. It is also clear that educational and therapeutic settings have greatly benefited from developmental psychology's discoveries that play activities contribute to the child's social, emotional, cognitive and linguistic development. Without question, play is an integral part of the human experience and is much, much more than whimsical or pointless activity.

REVIEW QUESTIONS

1. What are the different types of play and why does more complex play develop as the child gets older?
2. Does language facilitate the development of play or does play facilitate the development of language?
3. In what ways can the stages of play, as identified by developmental psychology, help in assessing developmental delay or possible trauma in children?

Chapter Links

For a discussion of social perspectives on children's socialization, see Chapter 3.

Further Reading

Bruce, T. (2005) Play matters, in L. Abbott and A. Langston (eds) *Birth to Three Matters: Supporting the Framework of Effective Practice*, Maidenhead, Open University Press. Useful summary of the most important features of play, of relevance to work with young children.

Pugh, G., De'Ath, E. and Smith, C. (1994) *Confident Parents, Confident Children: Policy and Practice in Parent Education and Support*, London, National Children's Bureau. Helpful source of practical guidance.

Shaefer, C.E. and Kaduson, H.G. (2007) *Contemporary Play Therapy: Theory, Research and Practice*, New York, Guilford Press. Up-to-date reference for students, researchers and practitioners interested in play therapy.

Tyler, S., Hutt, J., Hutt, C. and Christopherson, C. (1990) *Play, Exploration and Learning: Natural History of the Pre-school*, London, Routledge. Useful reference book on the development of preschool services.

Websites

www.playtherapy.org.uk   Play Therapy UK   Source of resources for therapeutic play and creative play therapies

www.bapt.info   British Association of Play Therapists   Major association for play therapists in the UK

Perspectives on How Children Develop and Learn

Elizabeth A. Boyle

LEARNING OUTCOMES

By the end of this chapter, you should be able to:

- provide a definition of learning
- understand the claims underlying different theories of learning
- know how these theories might be applied in the classroom to help children become more effective learners
- have an understanding of formal and informal ways in which children might learn differently at different stages in development

What is learning?

There are many different definitions of learning but generally when we say that an individual has learned something, we mean that they have acquired some factual knowledge, skills or both, which they did not have before. However, we can also learn behaviours and emotional responses to objects, people and events, such as agoraphobia, a learned fear of public spaces.

Point for Reflection

Are people born with particular aptitudes or do they need to learn them?

A longstanding philosophical debate in learning concerns whether human beings are born with knowledge, skills and abilities 'hardwired' at birth, as nativists suggest, or whether everything has to be learned through experience, as empiricists suggest. Bernstein et al. (2008, p. 194) define learning as 'the modification through experience of pre-existing behaviours and understanding'. This definition allows for both possibilities, that there is some pre-existing knowledge but that experience modifies it. In early infancy, many of the perceptual and motor advances, which are primarily biologically determined by massive increases in interconnections between neurons, also depend on experience. This experience-expectant neural system expects to receive a particular kind of experience at a particular point in time; for example, if the child were deprived of early visual input, the visual cortex would not develop normally.

A very basic kind of learning that is evident even in very young babies is *habituation*. Habituation reflects our preference for new stimuli. When we repeatedly see the same stimulus over and over again, we become bored with it and stop looking at it, that is, we habituate to it. When a new stimulus is introduced, we start to look at this new stimulus, that is, we dishabituate to the novel stimulus.

Theories of learning

There is no grand overarching theory of learning. Instead, a number of theories have been proposed about how children learn and these different theories highlight different aspects of learning as being important (see Table 7.1). These theories differ on fundamental issues, such as:

- whether the individual is regarded as playing an active or a more passive role in learning
- whether there are qualitative differences in learning at different stages (a stage-like model) or whether learning is best described as the gradual and incremental accumulation of facts or skills (a continuous model)
- what the theory focuses on
- how learning occurs
- whether learning is viewed more as an individual or social activity.

Behaviourism/learning theory

Behaviourist accounts of learning (also called learning theory) propose that everything a child knows is learned through the fundamental mechanisms of conditioning. Two different kinds of conditioning are proposed, classical conditioning and operant conditioning.

In classical conditioning, a neutral stimulus (such as a bell) is repeatedly presented alongside a 'natural' stimulus (such as food), which already elicits a specific response (salivation). After several such pairings of the two stimuli, the neutral stimulus begins to elicit a response when presented alone. This is called the 'conditioned response'. Pavlov famously demonstrated a conditioned

Table 7.1 Theories of learning

Theory	Child's role in learning	Is learning stage-like or continuous?	Focus	The reason learning occurs
Behaviourism/ learning theory	Passive	Continuous	Classical and instrumental conditioning	Strengthening of associations between stimuli and responses, that is, children's acquisition of new learning through a range of stimulus materials, activities and other learning resources
Piaget's cognitive account	Active	Stage-like	Assimilation and accommodation underlie organization into more complex, increasingly logical structures	Increasingly complex cognitive schemas developed through children's growing ability to recognize, understand, differentiate, manipulate and do things with objects
Vygotsky's social constructivism	Active	Stage-like	Scaffolding: more able individuals provide support for the child until they are able to tackle tasks on their own	Social interactions with more able individuals in the zone of proximal development, which is the difference between what a learner can do with, or without, help
Information processing	Active	Continuous	Computer metaphor for cognition: perception, attention, memory, strategies	Faster processing, increases in capacity of working memory, more complex organization of information, wider range of strategies to tackle problems

response to a tuning fork in dogs when the tuning fork was sounded just before the dogs were fed. After a while, just on hearing the tuning fork, the dogs would salivate, even without the presence of food. Classical conditioning explains how physiological or emotional responses can be elicited to 'unnatural' stimuli, but does not apply well to explaining how we learn facts and skills.

Operant conditioning also regards learning in terms of the strengthening of stimulus-response connections, but emphasizes how connections can be strengthened by the provision of a reward or weakened by a punishment. Positive behaviour management techniques capitalize on this kind of learning, such as praising a child for producing desired behaviours like dressing themselves or brushing their teeth.

Cognitive accounts of learning: Piaget

Piaget (1954) claimed that children are biologically programmed to understand the world in different ways at different stages in development. He argued that children of different ages have different *schemas*, that is, they have different ways of representing and organizing knowledge mentally. The stages are as follows:

- *Sensorimotor period* (between birth and 2 years): Children learn about their world through sensory exploration of and actions on objects. Children find out about the properties of objects by turning them over, dropping them, putting them in their mouths and so on.
- *Preoperational stage* (ages 2–6 years): Children start to attend to features of objects other than their sensory properties, due to the acquisition of the 'symbolic function'. This refers to the child's ability to use words, mental images and objects to represent other objects mentally. For example, the child can understand and use words such as *mummy* to refer to a person and *dog* to refer to a class of objects. He can also use objects to represent other objects in play, for example imagining that a cardboard box is a space rocket. However, there are still serious limitations in the child's thinking at this stage; in particular, children are egocentric, unable to take another person's point of view.
- *Concrete operational stage* (7–11 years): Children begin to impose a more logical structure on their understanding, using the cognitive operations of classification, seriation and conservation. Piaget developed a series of tasks to test for these more advanced forms of logical thinking, such as the conservation of volume and conservation of quantity tasks.
- *Formal operational stage* (11 years and up): The final stage of understanding is reached when the child is able to think in more abstract logical structures and can reason about objects without their actual physical presence. At this stage, the child should be able to think scientifically, using principles of deduction, proportionality, isolation and testing of variables and so on.

Another important feature of Piaget's theory concerns his claims about the processes of assimilation and accommodation, which are used in learning. In learning about a new object, the child will assimilate new information into an existing schema. So, for example, in learning about a tiger, they will assimilate, that is, interpret, the tiger in terms of their existing mental schema for mammals. However, when confronted with a duck-billed platypus, they cannot understand this new animal as a mammal, as it has too many characteristics that will not fit their mammal schema and they will need to accommodate or reorganize their schema to include such an example.

Piaget's theory has been important in highlighting the child's active exploration of their environment and the increasingly logical organization of knowledge as the child gets older. However, his account of stages has been strongly criticized for underestimating the logical capacities of younger children (Donaldson, 1986).

Cognitive accounts of learning: information processing

Information-processing accounts of learning are based on an analogy between how the human mind works and how a computer works. Learning is described in terms of the flow of information about a stimulus into the perceptual system, the allocation of attention to relevant features of the stimulus, the transfer of information about the stimulus into long-term memory, and the use of a variety of problem-solving and decision-making strategies in deciding what to do with this information. Increases in skills and abilities as the child gets older are explained in terms of faster processing of information, increases in the capacity of working memory, more effective organization of information and a wider variety of strategies for organizing, structuring, processing and remembering information.

Information-processing accounts of learning make a useful distinction between declarative knowledge and procedural knowledge. Declarative knowledge refers to factual or semantic knowledge such as 'Edinburgh is the capital of Scotland'. Procedural knowledge is knowledge of skills such as reading or riding a bike. Many skills that require considerable attention and concentration to learn when a child is younger become automated, allowing the older child to direct their attention to other features of the stimulus. For example, when the child is learning to read, most of their attention is allocated to identifying letters and words. Once these recognition processes have become automated, the child is able to direct their attention more to understanding the meaning of the text.

Vygotsky's social constructivism

Piaget was a cognitive constructivist who emphasized how children's understanding of the world develops through their actions upon objects in the environment. In contrast, social constructivists, such as Vygotsky, propose that language and social interactions with other people play a key role in learning. The child's knowledge originates in the social world but is subsequently internalized to become their own knowledge.

Vygotsky (1986) argued that children learn best when they are tackling problems that are just beyond their current level of understanding and when they have a more experienced and able adult or peer on hand to provide hints and guide their attempts at solution. The difference between the child's attempts to solve a problem on their own and their attempts to solve the problem with the help of a more able adviser is called the *zone of proximal development*. Learning in the zone of proximal development emphasizes the collaborative nature of learning. The support provided by adults or more able peers is called 'scaffolding', since it provides a framework of support for the child until they are ready to carry out the task on their own. While Vygotsky's ideas were originally developed in the context of language acquisition, he was also interested in other cultural tools and symbol systems as supports for learning. Recently, his ideas have been applied in trying to understand the impact of computers and other learning technologies as tools in learning.

Vygotsky's ideas have been influential in encouraging children to work in groups to solve problems. Working in groups can benefit both more and less able pupils. More able children benefit from being able to explicitly articulate their ideas about how they would tackle a problem to another child, while less able pupils benefit from the explanations provided by their better informed peer. Both benefit from trying to reconcile their differing points of view.

Metacognition and self-regulation of learning

Metacognition and self-regulation are not theories but rather are recent ideas about what is important in learning effectively. *Metacognition* refers to the idea that learners who are more aware of what learning is and how they go about learning will be more effective learners. Metacognitive learners will not just regurgitate facts but will plan, monitor and evaluate their learning. The use of metacognitive strategies should help with the difficult issue of transfer, where a strategy that was used to solve a problem successfully in one domain can be applied to a similar problem in a new domain.

Self-regulation is related to metacognition but focuses on who is in control of learning. The suggestion is that learners are most effective when they, rather than a teacher or a tutor, take responsibility for their own learning and are able to select and deploy effective processes and strategies independently.

Formal and informal learning

Children learn an enormous amount before they go to school. They have acquired impressive motor skills, developed a remarkable grasp of language, learned how to interact socially and play together, and have developed a basic moral understanding.

Play makes a vital contribution to the learning of preschool children (see also Chapter 6). Many of the activities that preschool children take part in involve play with objects and other people. They might pretend, for example, that a chair is a bus or that they and their friends are pirates. Play helps young children to learn about the properties of and constraints upon objects, the roles and responsibilities of different individuals, and it allows them to practise and explore social rules within a safe environment. Many children today go to playgroup, nursery or reception class where there is a strong emphasis on learning through play. Research suggests that preschool learning is a positive experience for children and enhances their all-round development, particularly for disadvantaged children.

Compulsory schooling for children under 14 was introduced into the UK in 1870 to teach children the formal skills of literacy and numeracy, which could not be learned at home. Today, children in England and Wales start school in the September following their fourth birthday. However, there is a continuing debate about the right age of entry to school: some have argued that children of this age are too young to cope with the more formal learning required in school, pointing to other European countries such as France, Germany and Italy where children don't go to school until they are 6 and Scandinavia where children start school at 7. These children nevertheless fare well on reading tests at the age of 9.

Once they are at school, there is a clear specification of what children should be taught, through the national curriculum (QCDA, n.d.). While reading, writing and numeracy are still important, the curriculum is now much broader and paradoxically includes many things that used to be learned at home. Through the national curriculum, the government spells out the knowledge, skills and understanding that every child in England and Wales should learn at different key stages in development to allow each child to achieve their potential. The national curriculum also specifies core areas of learning and expected levels of attainment at each stage of development. For example, the core areas for the foundation stage (preschool) are personal and social development, language and literacy, maths, knowledge and understanding of the world, physical development and creative development. Formal assessments are carried out at the ages of 4, 7 and 11 to ensure that children have learned these core skills. The national curriculum attempts to ensure consistency of learning experiences and opportunity for all children. However, it has been criticized for being over-prescriptive in what children should learn, leaving little room for following up children's interests, and stifling their creativity.

Disengaged learners

In the UK, the USA and other countries, concern has grown in recent years that a sizeable minority of children and young people, especially boys, fail to engage with school (McLean, 2003). These disengaged learners seem to lack any academic aspirations, regarding school as uninteresting and irrelevant. A pressing issue that many schools need to face is how to re-engage these young people in learning.

School marks the entry into a more formal learning environment, in contrast with the informal learning that happens naturally at home through play and less structured activities. A key issue that schools face is how to keep their pupils engaged and encourage them to be lifelong learners.

With respect to theories, it is not really a case of which is right and which is wrong; rather the theories offer different perspectives focusing on different aspects of learning. Classical conditioning provides an explanation of how we learn unnatural emotional or behavioural responses to stimuli, such as the fear of spiders. The other theories are more concerned with learning in the traditional sense of knowledge acquisition. Both Piaget and Vygotsky claimed that learners play an active role in constructing their own understanding of the world, but Piaget focused on how children learn through their actions upon objects, while Vygotsky focused on learning through interactions with other people. Both Piaget and information-processing theory emphasize the importance of the representation of information, but information-processing theory is a more contemporary theory, which tries to specify more clearly the mental operations and strategies used in solving specific tasks.

Implications for practice: Adey and Shayer's Cognitive Acceleration through Science Education (CASE) intervention

An important aim for professionals, including teachers, and parents is to try and extract from the vast literature on learning some useful tips for helping children to learn more effectively. Different theoretical approaches to learning have differing implications for classroom practice.

Adey and Shayer (1994) reported an impressive and effective attempt to help secondary school children learn concepts in science more effectively. Adey and Shayer's study was an eclectic approach to helping children learn more effectively using a range of theories and ideas about effective learning. Their large-scale intervention programme was grounded in Piaget's ideas that around the age of 12 children should be able to understand a number of logico-mathematical concepts or schema, such as proportionality, isolation and testing of variables, ratio and proportion, correlation and probability. Children typically have difficulties in acquiring these concepts.

The intervention also used Vygotsky's ideas that knowledge is socially constructed. In tackling the problems, the children worked in small groups talking around different ideas, listening to others' views, asking for explanations, offering justifications for their views, evaluating discrepant explanations of the problem and trying to resolve contradictory points of view. Cognitive conflict emerged as children with different levels of understanding of the task voiced differing predictions. To resolve the contradictory opinions, the teacher guided the children through different explanations, pushing them to understand why incorrect explanations were wrong and finding support for the correct explanation. Children were also encouraged to take a meta-cognitive approach by articulating strategies they had applied successfully to help promote the transfer of thinking from skills learned in one domain into another domain.

Adey and Shayer's carefully planned intervention was a relatively long duration project, lasting for two years prior to GCSEs. Some of the science timetable was given over to skills intervention. It was successful in showing gains of one grade in GCSEs not only in science but also in maths and English. Importantly, this suggested that general thinking strategies taught in one domain did transfer to other domains. Adey et al. (2002) applied a similar cognitive acceleration approach in a programme for five- to six-year-olds, where it was also found to improve performance on age-appropriate Piagetian conservation tasks.

Conclusion

This chapter has recognized that there is no single definition of learning and no single theory of what learning entails and how it takes place. It is possible, nonetheless, to use different approaches to understanding learning so as to help children to learn. Children learn informally throughout their lives, as well as formally in the classroom and the experienced practitioner capitalizes on the richness of all these opportunities for learning.

REVIEW QUESTIONS

1. What are the main claims of the different theories about how children learn?
2. What are the main points of comparison and contrast between Piaget's cognitive constructivist theory and Vygotsky's social constructivist theory?
3. How would you use ideas from theories of learning in the classroom to try and help children become more effective learners.
4. What kinds of things do you think children might learn through play?

Further Reading

Adey, P., Robertson, A. and Venville, G. (2002) Effects of a cognitive acceleration programme on Year 1 pupils, _British Journal of Educational Psychology_, 72, 1–25. Following the success of their CASE project with year 7 and 8 pupils, this paper shows how Piagetian and Vygotskian approaches to learning were both used in the design of an intervention programme to help 5–6-year-olds learn about conservation.

Long, M. (2000) _The Psychology of Education_, London, Taylor Francis. An online book that provides a detailed account of the different theories of learning.

Websites

http://curriculum.qcda.gov.uk/index.aspx The website of the national curriculum for England and Wales; contains useful information about what children should learn at school in the primary and secondary curricula

The Child and Family Life

The Family in Social Context

Neil Thompson

LEARNING OUTCOMES

By the end of this chapter, you should be able to:

- ◼ understand why it is important to understand family life in relation to the wider social context
- ◼ appreciate how our understanding of 'the family' changes over time and from culture to culture
- ◼ identify ways in which the social context of the family is relevant to working with children and families

Why study the family?

The family is something that most of us grow up in and which forms an important part of our society – it is what sociologists refer to as a 'social institution'. It is therefore easy to take it for granted and not give it a further thought. However, to study children and work with them in an *informed* way, we need to look more closely at the family: what we mean by the term; how it changes over time; and how different cultures have different conceptions of family. If we are unclear about these important issues, we may be basing practice on an oversimplified understanding of the issues involved when studying children or understanding a child, and that can be dangerous.

This chapter therefore aims to give readers an overview of some key issues relating to the family and their relevance to understanding working with children and their families. We begin by trying to clarify what we mean by the family – an undertaking that is actually more complex than it might initially appear.

What do we mean by the family?

For a word that we use quite a lot, it is surprising just how ambiguous a term family is. Think about the following different ways in which it is commonly used:

■ *Immediate family:* This refers to the way we use the term 'family' to mean the people who share our household who we are related to. An example of this usage would be: 'In my family, we take it in turns to do the dusting and polishing.'

■ *Family of origin:* For children growing up with their parents, this will generally be the same as their immediate family. However, for most adults, there will be a difference as a result of leaving their family of origin and either living alone or starting their own family. An example of this usage would be: 'In my family, we used to take it in turns to do cleaning tasks, but in my partner's family, they all had their own allocated roles and never varied what they did.'

■ *Offspring:* Family can also be used to mean specifically children, as in: 'We have been married for nearly two years, but we don't have any family yet.'

Despite this ambiguity, family is an important concept because, for most people, they will have been brought up in a family that will have had a significant set of influences on their sense of self, their values and their overall worldview. In this respect, the family acts as a mediating factor between the individual and wider society. For example, the family is an important part of the process known as 'socialization', that is, the way in which we learn to be part of our society and, equally, our society becomes part of us, in the sense that we internalize certain norms and values.

Points for Reflection

Consider your own family context and jot down a few notes in response to the following questions:

1. Can you identify three things that you learned from your family of origin about life and society?
2. How might different people in other families have learned different things from their family experiences? Can you give examples?
3. Does this tell us anything about working with children and families?

Of course, there are no right answers to an exercise like this. However, what should be apparent is that:

■ we tend to learn a great deal about life from our families
■ different families teach their members different lessons about life
■ we need to bear such differences in mind when working with children and families.

We shall explore this third point in more detail below.

What do we mean by 'social context'?

The point has already been made that the family is an important part of socialization. However, this is not the only way in which the family links in with wider society. The family therefore needs to be understood in its social context, that is, we need to be able to see family issues as reflections of the society in which the particular family is located. This can be seen to apply in a number of ways:

- *Class:* There are well-established differences across families that relate to class. For example, even basic things like timings of meals, what people eat in those meals and what the meals are called will vary from class setting to class setting ('tea' at 5pm or 'dinner' at 8pm, for instance). There will also be a wide range of other class-related differences, some of which are quite obvious, while others are more subtle.
- *Gender:* The family is significant when it comes to learning gender roles. Indeed, much of our understanding of such matters derives from how such roles were practised in our families of origin. What is particularly important in terms of the family is how motherhood and fatherhood are understood and what expectations this creates in relation to how parenting is carried out.
- *Race and ethnicity:* There are (at least) two main issues here. The first is that family forms differ from culture to culture. There is a wealth of anthropological literature relating to how family (or 'kinship' relationships) vary across cultures. For example, in some cultures, aunts and uncles have a much more significant role than in others. The second is that racism is a significant factor to consider in relation to families from ethnic minorities. For black children, how their family responds to racism in the wider community will be significant for how they learn to deal with such discrimination.
- *Sexuality:* The introduction of civil partnerships for same-sex couples shows that families do not need to fit in with the traditional stereotype of married, heterosexual parents living with their biological children. As we shall see below, families come in various shapes and sizes.

What is also significant about the social context of the family is that as society changes, so too does the family. Allen (2007, p. 326) captures the point well when he argues that:

Confusion often arises within popular discourses because change in family organization is frequently viewed as inherently negative. Romantic visions of the past are glorified, so that almost any change gets defined as damaging. Yet precisely because family relationships are both personally and socially significant, family organization cannot be expected to remain static. Any social institution which is central to the workings of a society is necessarily integrated with other key aspects of economic and social structure.

The family can be seen to have been changing in the following ways:

- *Marriage:* While marriage continues to be a popular institution, the number of marriages has been dropping over the past three decades or so. The average age at which people marry is also now significantly higher compared with the 1970s.
- *Divorce:* The divorce rate has also risen significantly during that time, bringing with it a rise in the number of remarriages.
- *Lone parenthood:* This too has been characterized by a significant rise, partly as a result of the increased divorce rate and partly because some parents never marry or cohabit in the first place.

What is particularly interesting is the fact that not only have the patterns of family composition been changing, but so too have *attitudes* towards family composition. For example, cohabiting without being married was previously stigmatized and looked down upon, whereas now it is generally seen as quite 'normal' in both senses of the word, that is, statistically quite usual and ideologically acceptable.

From the point of view of the social context of the family, then, what we have is two clear messages:

1. The family is *diverse*: the simplistic idea that everyone lives in a nuclear family is very far removed from what is actually to be found. Single parenthood, single-person households, adults without children, gay couples and foster families mean that the reality is very different from the stereotype. When we also consider different cultural patterns in relation to the family in our multiethnic society, we can begin to appreciate just how diverse the family is.
2. The family is *changing*: what counts as the 'norm' for the family in one period of time will not necessarily be seen as the norm in another period of time.

If we do not bear in mind that the family is both diverse and changing, we can become rigid and judgemental in our expectations of families or of particular individuals from certain family backgrounds.

Problems in the family

The family has come to be seen as the bedrock of civilized society, with politicians of various parties praising the important role of 'family values'. There is no doubt, then, that family life is generally seen as a positive thing. However, while there is clearly much of a positive nature associated with the family, we have to recognize that there are also significant problems that need to be considered if we are to have a balanced and realistic view of the family. This is especially the case for professionals working with young children, as it is often where problems occur that so much professional input is called for.

The family is often presented as the solution to social problems, in the sense that the nurturing warmth and security that families can offer are seen as having the potential to prevent problems arising, for example crime and delinquency, and, to a certain extent, to act as a 'safe haven' to protect family members from outside stresses and strains. However, we have to be careful not to paint too rosy a picture of the family. While many people clearly have the benefits of a warm, nurturing family that provides a safe haven, many do not. Indeed, for a significant minority of people, the family is actually the primary source of their problems. Consider the following:

- *Abuse and violence:* It is unfortunately the case that many families are the site of violence and abuse. Significant numbers of children are abused in their families, whether physically, sexually, emotionally or through neglect. In addition, children can suffer as a result of domestic violence taking place within their home. The effects of abuse and violence in the home can be of major proportions, leading to a significant traumatic reaction (Tomlinson, 2004).
- *Separation and divorce:* Although separation and divorce do not necessarily cause problems, they can be painful experiences for children, involving a significant grief reaction that often goes unrecognized (Kroll, 2002). There can also be significant conflicts as a result of separation, and these, in turn, can be the source of great difficulties for the family concerned, especially for young children.
- *Mental health problems:* At one time, there was a school of thought that saw mental health problems, such as schizophrenia, as primarily, if not exclusively, the result of family dynamics (see Crossley, 2006). While this line of thinking is no longer given the credence it once was, it is still recognized by many thinkers that the family is highly significant in the development of mental health difficulties.
- *Homelessness:* Family tensions are a common cause of children and young people feeling the need to leave home and thus becoming homeless. Similarly, abuse and violence, as mentioned above, can often be a spur to a train of events that results in homelessness.
- *Crime:* For some families, crime and lawlessness can be a way of life, part of the family's normal patterns of behaviour, although it would be a significant mistake to assume that criminal behaviour necessarily reflects such a family culture. Crime can also be a response to family problems, for example theft in response to poverty or an assault as a result of family tensions being released outside the family setting.

It is also important to recognize that these problems are often interrelated. For example, a family member committing a crime may lead to family tensions that result in abuse or violence and this, in turn, may lead to homelessness and so on.

Implications for practice

One of the important lessons for practice we need to learn is that without an understanding of the complexities of 'the family' in its social context, we will be in a weak position to deal with the challenges that can arise in working with children and their families. To help you consider the implications for practice in more detail, we now move on to look at a short case study for you to explore.

PRACTICE STUDY

The Kerr family comprises David and his four-year-old son Scott from his first marriage, and Hansa and her three-year-old son Chandi. David had obtained custody of Scott after the divorce, as his mother had neglected him as a result of her drink problem. Chandi's father had been killed in a car crash only three months after he was born.

The family have been together for just over eight months. To begin with everything worked out very well, but for the past two or three months tensions have started to be quite a problem. Some people seem to disapprove of their relationship and keep their distance. David's approach is to ignore it, to get on with his life – the way his parents would have dealt with such a problem. Hansa's family would have dealt with it that way as well, but Hansa had always rebelled against that approach, believing instead that it is best to tackle problems, rather

than ignore them. This causes significant tensions between the two of them. The two children clearly sense the tension and are becoming unsettled. This makes David very worried, as he knows that Scott has already experienced neglect and does not want him to have further worries to deal with, especially at such a young age. Hansa, for her part, fears that the tensions will lead to the couple splitting up, leaving her with another loving relationship to grieve for.

The children attend a local children's centre where the staff have become aware of the tensions and the fact that the children are unsettled. One staff member expresses concern at a staff meeting. She says that this is a 'mixed-race', step-parent family, with one of the children having a history of abuse and with clear signs of tension developing. She feels the family should be referred for a social work assessment.

From what you have read, consider the following questions:

- Why might some people disapprove of this family setup? What does this tell us about attitudes towards, and understanding of, the family as a social institution?
- How does this family reflect the way society has changed in relation to families in general?

■ What factors about the diverse and changing nature of the family would you need to take into consideration in trying to help this family?

Conclusion

We often encounter a simplistic, stereotypical understanding of the family. This discussion of the family in its social context has shown just how far removed such an understanding is from the complex reality. Professionals working with children and their families therefore need to have a more sophisticated understanding of the fact that family life takes different forms in different settings and changes over time. A key part of that understanding needs to be a recognition of the dangers of being judgemental by assuming that 'nonstandard' families are in some way substandard. What constitutes a problem within a family is something that needs to be carefully assessed. It is quite dangerous to assume that families that do not fit the stereotypical picture of the family are in some way by their very nature problematic. Similarly, our more sophisticated understanding of the family will help us to avoid having a rose-tinted image of the family that fails to recognize the major problems that can and often do exist in families. Again, assessment of the circumstances is the key.

Sociology is an important academic discipline, because it helps us to look beneath the everyday understanding of aspects of society that we tend to take for granted and that therefore tend to go unquestioned. The family is part of society and, as such, will necessarily take diverse forms and will change over time. A sociological understanding of the family helps us to appreciate that there is a lot more to family life than people generally realize. In supporting children through family problems, we therefore have to make sure that we have a good understanding of the complexities involved.

REVIEW QUESTIONS

1. In what ways can the family be seen as diverse?
2. In what ways can the family be seen to have changed over time?
3. Why is it important to consider the problems associated with the family as well as the benefits?

Further Reading

Allan, G. (2007) Families, in M. Davies (ed.) *The Blackwell Companion to Social Work* (3rd edn), Oxford, Blackwell. Useful overall introduction.

Boylan, J. and Allan, G. (2007) Family disruption and relationship breakdown, in M. Davies (ed.) *The Blackwell Companion to Social Work* (3rd edn), Oxford, Blackwell. Good account of the issues associated with family breakdown.

Scott, J., Treas, J. and Richards, M. (eds) (2007) *The Blackwell Companion to the Sociology of Families*, Oxford, Blackwell. Not an easy read, but a good comprehensive study of social issues and the family.

Thompson, N. (2002) *Building the Future: Social Work with Children, Young People and their Families*, Lyme Regis, Russell House. Chapter 2 covers working with families.

The Influence of Parents, Siblings and Friends

Lesley Jessiman and Robert Adams

LEARNING OUTCOMES

By the end of this chapter, you should be able to:

- identify some key areas of influence on a child
- identify different parenting styles
- understand the role of siblings in a child's development
- understand the role of friends in a child's development

Childhood is a period of rapid development and as the child grows older, the balance between personality, family and environment changes. For example, as the child gets older, we can observe them interacting more and more with other children and adults beyond those of their own family. Thus, as the child engages in more formally structured settings such as nursery school, there are greater opportunities for formal as well as informal learning.

We can reasonably assume that by the end of infancy, the child will become increasingly shaped or influenced by the social world. The widening in social interaction comes about as the child gains in motor skills, language and confidence. The child becomes more aware of other children and adults, and also of themselves. As the child develops in these ways, there is greater curiosity in the world around them and, as such, adults need to balance tensions between safeguarding the child and allowing them to learn through exploration. Thus parents and professionals are required to set and maintain boundaries of acceptable and safe behaviour.

Family influences on child development

'Like little sponges' is something we often hear in reference to young children's minds. This description is, of course, very accurate; with every year of the child's development, we see them grow in every way possible as they systematically 'soak up' more and more of their distinct and varied 'social worlds', for example their home and family, their schools, teachers, peers and friends. We should note here that by focusing our attention on the role of the social world, we are by no means suggesting that biology and nature do not have a role to play. Indeed, dismissing the role biology plays in a child's development and advocating only the role of the social world is to provide you, the reader, with a somewhat singular, deterministic account of social influence. Thus, although our principal focus is social influence – as you will identify from the following discussion – there are other factors to consider such as those put forward by geneticists, biologists, behaviourists and neurocognitive scientists, to name but a few. We therefore recommend further reading in order that you consider and understand alternative explanations and approaches beyond that of social influence. Some of the alternative standpoints are discussed in this chapter, for example temperament theory, but a more comprehensive account will require some additional reading (see Further Reading at the end of the chapter).

Point for Reflection

Considering your own experiences, who do you consider the most influential on a child's development – parents, siblings or friends? Does this change through the life course?

We begin our discussion of the social world and its influences on the child's development by looking at how family factors influence and shape the child. As we shall see, the main aspects of family influence are the nature of parenting, culture and relationships with siblings. We end with a discussion on the influence of friends on a child's development.

Parents

Parenting styles

Do all parents want similar things for their children? That is, do all parents wish their child to be safe, happy, independent, friendly and competent individuals? In an ideal world, those are exactly the sort of things all parents would strive to achieve. Anthropologist Robert LeVine (1988) proposed that parents the world over share three common goals:

1. to provide safety
2. to provide the child with the skills to become economically productive adults
3. to ensure the child acquires the same cultural values as the parents.

It would be incredible if all parents worldwide believed these things to be important and adopted effective strategies for achieving them. Unfortunately, there is evidence to the contrary. Although some parents do indeed strive to achieve what LeVine suggests, parents the world over tend to hold different beliefs and desires about what they want from their child in terms of their child's behaviours, temperaments, personality and achievements. More importantly, how parents go about attaining what they deem to be the appropriate parent–child relationship can vary considerably.

In some countries, parents' beliefs about the appropriate parent–child relationship are motivated, as LeVine (1988) suggests, by the parents' culture and tradition. However, the nature of the parent–child relationship can also result from the parents' temperament/personality and/or the temperament/personality of the child. We would agree that, in the most part, parents would wish for their child to be safe, happy and competent, and it is really only in the most extreme cases, where the child is abused or neglected, that few or none of these things are achieved. Here we outline some of the differences in child-rearing ideologies and describe the different styles of parenting behaviours that can result from these different ideologies.

Baumrind (1967, 1971, 1989), a key figure in parenting style research, classified the different styles of parenting into three principal categories, authoritative, authoritarian (not to be confused with authoritative) and permissive, as shown in Table 9.1.

As you can see from Table 9.1, the different dimensions that Baumrind proposed were:

1. *expression of warmth or nurturance*, where the parent lay on the spectrum from cold to very affectionate
2. *discipline*, which ranged from punishment, coercion, persuasion and explanation
3. *communication*, for example the parent listening to the child or the parent demanding the child not to speak
4. *demands and expectations for maturity* ranging from an intolerance of immaturity or 'childlike' behaviour to an understanding of the child's developmental capabilities.

Table 9.1 Baumrind's classification of parenting style

Parenting style	Behaviours
Authoritative	Warm and responsive to the child
	Affectionate
	Grant autonomy (at the appropriate time)
	Engage in conversations with the child, for example explain to the child why they wish them to do certain things, such as: 'I would rather you didn't climb up the ladder because the ladder is unstable and I am afraid you will fall and hurt yourself, do you understand?'
	Unconditional love and support
Authoritarian	Score low on measures of warmth and affection
	Cold and punitive if the child fails to meet the parents' needs and demands
	Set high and often unrealistic demands
	'Victorian style' of child-rearing, for example 'children should be seen but not heard'
	Conditional love and support
Permissive	Vary on measures of warmth and affection
	Arbitrarily grant autonomy
	Some parents are overindulgent of their child
	Others lack interest in their child
	Set few demands on their child
	Concede to the child's demands, for example 'yes you can have those sweeties if it means you will stop talking'
	Some show love and support through overindulgence of the child's demands, while others show little love or support

So what effects does each of the parenting styles have on the child's development? In a series of longitudinal studies, Baumrind (1967, 1989) concluded that preschool children of authoritative parents are more likely to be successful and competent, and are also more likely to have high levels of self-esteem and empathy. Authoritarian parents, on the other hand, are more likely to produce children who are conscientious and respectful of authority but will also be reserved and score low on measures of self-esteem and happiness. Permissive parents are likely to raise children who lack self-control and empathy for others, are disrespectful of authority and score low on measures of self-esteem. When Baumrind tested these children again in middle childhood, she found the same significant associations between the child's social, emotional and cognitive development and the parenting style adopted. These findings suggest that the effects of specific parenting styles will often remain stable over time. More recent studies have also reported significant associations between the levels of parental control and rejection and anxiety disorders in children (Grüner et al., 1999). Divergent outcomes for the same parental style have also been found, such that high parental control and power resulted in obedience and passive behaviours in some children and aggressive, non-empathic behaviour in others (Maccoby, 1980).

The type of parenting someone adopts can often reflect their misunderstanding or ignorance of the child's cognitive development. For example, parents who expect a young child below 18 months old to be more empathic towards their needs, for example 'you are going to sit in the chair because you hurt my feelings', fail to grasp that children have yet to develop an understanding of self and therefore will also lack theory of mind (ToM). Understanding the concept of hurting another person's feelings is often beyond the cognitive capacity of the very young child. Likewise, a parent who expects a child of three – who is of limited linguistic ability – to understand the demand 'refrain from your self-indulgent behaviour' is also misguided in their beliefs about their child's level of comprehension. The child might very well understand the tone of both these directives but is unlikely to fully understand the content.

Parenting and temperament

There are also those who believe that the style of parenting is associated with the child's temperament, such that the type of parenting adopted directly results from the child's personality or temperament type (Braungart-Rieker et al., 1997; Bronfenbrenner and Morris, 1998; Thomas, 1984). The belief is therefore that authoritative parents are affectionate and warm to their child because the child has a temperament open to warmth and affection or that the parents' style of control manifests because the child is willing to comply with their rules (Lewis, 1981). The *transactional model* provides an alternative standpoint, proposing that the child and the parents' characteristics form a more reciprocal relationship (Rothbart and Bates, 1998; Sameroff, 1975, 1995). In other words, the child's temperament and respective behaviours influence the parents' responses and the parents' responses to the child influence and shape the child's temperament. More recent models of child development and adjustment thus propose bidirectional relationships or mutual influences of parents' and child's characteristics (see, for example, Lengua and Kovacs, 2005).

Parenting styles and culture

As noted earlier, one can also identify cultural differences in parenting styles. One cross-cultural survey (Hoffman, 1988), for example, found Indonesian parents rated obedience as a desired quality in their children significantly more than Korean and American parents. A large percentage of Korean parents wished their children to be independent, yet only a small percentage of Indonesian and

Turkish parents identified independence as important. The study also reported that in poorer rural areas, a premium is placed on obedience and family solidarity, whereas in more affluent urban areas, autonomy and personal virtues are more important. In countries like Japan, mothers of preschool children will use reasoning, empathy and expressions of disappointment to control their children, believing that before the age of six, the child is pure and should not be punished (Chen, 1996). Authoritarian parenting is also viewed less negatively in China than it is in the USA (Chao, 1994). In Palau, an island nation in the Pacific Ocean, physical punishment of children is seen as an acceptable part of the culture. The crossover from physical punishment to physical abuse is only determined by the severity and intentionality of the child's injuries. Palauan people also believe it is acceptable to leave a young child unsupervised if the parent has to work, and some parents would tie their two- to -three-year-old child's leg to a post when there was no one to supervise the child (Collier et al., 1999).

Siblings: their role in development

Another influence on the child's development is from close family members, in particular siblings. Schaffer and Emerson (1964), for example, found siblings could serve as effective attachment figures when the child's principal carer is absent or ineffective. Garner et al. (1994) found that older siblings – who scored higher on ToM measures (see Chapter 6) – were better at comforting their younger sibling during the Strange Situation experiment (see Chapter 4) compared to children who scored lower on measures of ToM. Thus older siblings can act as sources of comfort for younger siblings in situations of distress and as a secure base when the principal carer is not available.

A number of studies have also found significant associations between children's performance on ToM tasks and having older child-aged siblings to play and converse with (Lewis et al., 1996; Perner et al., 1994; Ruffman et al., 1998). McAlister and Peterson (2007, p. 269) suggested that one of the reasons sibling relationships facilitate ToM development is that children have more opportunities, not only to converse with their more linguistically competent sibling, but to also hear the 'negotiations, reminiscences, pretence, or disciplinary encounters between their siblings and parents'.

We also know that preschool siblings engage in both antagonistic and prosocial interactions. *Prosocial* refers to those attitudes and actions demonstrating concern for, and empathy with, the feelings and welfare of others. It is common for antagonistic and prosocial acts to be initiated by the older sibling and the younger sibling will simply engage in imitation of the older sibling (Abramovitch et al., 1982). Conflict provides the ideal opportunity for the younger child to see the point of view of their older sibling, thus facilitating the development of ToM. In addition to this, the imitation of the older sibling's prosocial acts, for example sharing a toy or helping to put away the toys for mummy, aids the development of the younger child's moral understanding. The older sibling benefits too, such that interacting with their younger brother or sister encourages nurturing and more prosocial behaviours.

So what about only children, are they at more, or less, of an advantage? We might assume from the above discussion that in the absence of sibling interaction, cognitive and social development will be somewhat encumbered. There is, however, evidence to the contrary. Only children and first-born children often score higher on tests of sentence comprehension, enunciation and communication (Moore, 1968). One suggestion for these findings is that only children are not competing with other siblings for parental attention. In addition, authoritative parenting styles are more common than authoritarian parenting styles in single-child families (Berger, 2001). The link between authoritative parenting style and single-child families perhaps reflects the parent's motivation for only having one child, for example in order to focus all their attention on the child and provide the best environment possible. An alternative explanation is that with more children, there is more conflict and therefore a greater need to adopt an authoritarian style of parenting.

Both suggestions are interesting, in that they highlight the need to consider the multiple determinants of the parenting style adopted and also the child's social, cognitive and linguistic abilities. Indeed, we might suggest that all developmental outcomes might be better understood in terms of the *ecological model* of parenting, which frames parenting within a multifactorial context. Thus, it is the multidirectional pathways that exist between the parent, the child and the environment, which best explain developmental outcomes. A more in-depth account of the ecological model is provided in Chapter 10.

Whatever the underpinning of the child's behaviours and cognitive and linguistic competences, it is clear that there are positive and negative outcomes of having siblings, in the same way that there are positive and negative outcomes of being an only child. The extent to which the only child or the child with siblings is affected by their more solitary or crowded environment will depend on a number of factors, such as the child's temperament/personality or the child-rearing practices adopted by the child's parents. Other factors to consider are birth order, socioeconomic status, social support, culture and religion.

Friends: their role in development

Another influence on the child's development is peers or friends. Researchers studying the social development of children have devoted much attention to the way in which children form friendships and also how friendships are important to the child's cognitive development. Social learning theorists, for example, suggest that social development results from *reciprocal determinism*, whereby a child's individual characteristics, such as temperament, cognitive skills and language ability, will influence their choices in the social world (Bandura, 1986). Thus, friendships result from the child's observation of other children and their subsequent acceptance or rejection of other children. Acceptance and rejection are, in part, the result of observing other children's personalities, their likes and dislikes, and their cognitive abilities (all of which have been exposed to environmental influence). For example, a child who has learned specific behavioural boundaries, that is, acceptable and unacceptable behaviours, will quickly reject a child who fails to behave within these boundaries and a friendship will not develop. Children will signal to other children when they find certain behaviours unacceptable, for example aggression or affection. The aggressive or overly affectionate child may therefore modify their behaviour in order to avoid rejection by their peers.

Cognitive theorists place greater emphasis on the cognitive skills involved in friendship formation. Thus, information-processing theorists would argue that in order for the aggressive child to respond to another child's unhappiness with their behaviour, they must be able to encode, interpret and respond to social cues, that is, they must have the necessary cognitive skills (Burgess et al., 2006; Crick and Dodge, 1994; Dodge and Price, 1994). If a child has not developed these skills, they will continue to be rejected from peer interactions, and the development of important social and cognitive skills will be affected, as we will shortly discuss.

It is therefore important to recognize that childhood is a process of development during which the child builds on earlier experiences and uses these as a basis for later learning. At the same time, the situations the child encounters broaden and become more social. Social encounters provide more social learning opportunities. In our discussion of play behaviour in Chapter 7, we identified the ways in which playing with other children during nursery facilitates the development of social behaviours and cognitive abilities in 18- to 36-month-old children. As the child grows older, the effects that friendships have on the child's development also increase.

Younger children's understanding of friendship is associated with specific times and social situations, for example the other children that the child sees at nursery or playgroup (Bigelow, 1977). By the time the child reaches school age, friendships result from the mutual agreement that such friendships are rewarding and interesting. Proximity is also a contributing factor, such that children who live close to each other often tend to form friendships because of convenience. Although proximity may contribute to the development of friendships, the friendship must also be rewarding in order for it to develop (Bigelow, 1977). Children will not make friends with the child next door if the child next door is a bully.

Preschool children also form friendships on the basis of similarity, for example same sex, same age and similar play interests (Selman, 1980). If you ask a preschool child 'why is he your friend?', he might say 'because he is a boy, same as me'. The young child who makes such social comparisons is also demonstrating their sense of self. Thus, in order for the child to make a social comparison, they must of course have an understanding of who they are in terms of their gender. Interacting with other children and forming friendships allows children to make important social comparisons and thus learn more about themselves and other people. A child with no friends will have less opportunity to reflect on the 'self' and 'other'.

The formation of meaningful preschool relationships is associated with an increase in social competence, which prepares the child for going to school and meeting new people (Lindsey, 2002). The child's preschool experiences are therefore extremely important for their psychological preparations for school. The type of friend the child becomes, that is, how other children rate them as a friend, also remains relatively stable over time (Cillessen and Bukowski, 2000; Cillessen et al., 2000; Coie et al., 1982). The formation of friendships in the preschool years has many positive social, emotional and cognitive outcomes (Hartup and Stevens, 1997; Newcomb and Bagwell, 1995). It is therefore extremely important for parents, and adults working with children, to ensure that preschool children have the opportunity to make friends and also learn what behaviours make for good and meaningful friendships.

Conclusion

The child's family and friends make a vital contribution to the child's cognitive, linguistic and social development. The particular style of parenting affects the development of the child, but other family members such as siblings also make an important contribution. Social factors such as the formation of friendships particularly help the child to acquire and practise social skills in interacting with other people, which enable the child to tackle a growing range of social situations. On a final note, we should say that the social world clearly has a role to play in the development of the child but it is also important to acknowledge that once the child develops language and a sense of who they are, they also begin to place themselves within their own social worlds; they are by no means passive agents in their own development.

REVIEW QUESTIONS

1. In what ways is the family important to the child's development?
2. What part does the development of friendships between children play in child development?
3. Do children play a passive role in their own development or does development depend on the interaction between the individual and their external worlds?

_____*Chapter Links*_____

For further discussion of parenting, see Chapter 10.
To understand more diverse 'family' settings, see Chapters 11–14.

_____*Further Reading*_____

Asher, S.R. and Coie, J.D. (1990) *Peer Rejection in Childhood: Cambridge Studies in Social and Emotional Development*, Cambridge, Cambridge University Press. Discusses the importance of friendships in school and examines the effects of peer rejections on the child's development. The stability of the effects is also discussed.

Damon, W., Lerner, R.M. and Eisenberg, N. (2006) *Handbook of Child Psychology*, vol. 3, *Social, Emotional and Personality Development*, New York, Wiley. Provides an excellent, in-depth account of the effects of socialization on development, focusing particularly on personality development, parent–child relationships and friendships.

Durkin, K. (1995) *Developmental Social Psychology*, Oxford, Blackwell. Provides a detailed and excellent review of how developmental and social psychology can 'join forces' to provide a comprehensive account of how infants, children and adolescents develop linguistically, cognitively and socially.

Herbert, M. (2003) *Typical and Atypical Development: From Conception to Adolescence*, Oxford, Blackwell. Balanced discussion of child development in children under six years.

Parenting and Family Relationships in Context

10

Terence O'Sullivan

LEARNING OUTCOMES

By the end of this chapter, you should be able to:

- explain the ecological model of parenting
- identify the roles of parental developmental history and psychological resources, child characteristics and contextual sources in shaping parenting
- explain how support in one domain can act as a buffer against stress in another
- explain some issues in supporting and strengthening parenting

Parenting can be considered to be the facilitation of child development (Woodcock, 2003) and it is generally recognized that the parenting a child receives is an important influence on their future development. It is commonly agreed that there are a number of factors that separate successful from unsuccessful parenting. These include the degrees of warmth/coldness, praise/criticism, consistency, sensitivity, responsiveness, availability and disciplinary control. Standard 2 of the *National Service Framework for Children, Young People and Maternity Services* (DH/DfES, 2004a) is that:

> Parents or carers are enabled to receive the information, services and support that will help them to care for their children and equip them with the skills they need to ensure that their children have optimum life chances and are healthy and safe.

If childcare professionals are to make an effective contribution to achieving this standard, they will, among other things, need to understand parenting in context, that is, they will need to know not only about parenting skills and qualities but the factors that influence the way parents parent their children.

The Common Assessment Framework (DfES, 2004b) considers three domains: a child's developmental needs, the parenting capacity of parents, and family and environmental factors. It has been argued that the third side of the triangle, 'family and environmental factors', has been relatively neglected (Jack and Gill, 2003) and what is needed is a more holistic, ecological and joined-up approach. Parents and children are embedded in ecological contexts, with parenting and child development being two sides of the same coin. This chapter will approach ecological contexts from the parenting side of the coin. An ecological model of parenting will be presented based on the work of Belsky (1984), a central feature of which is that parenting is multiply determined. Belsky's process model has been highly influential. Woodcock (2003) describes it as the currently favoured model, while Sheppard (2004) states that current theoretical thinking has been especially influenced by Belsky's work.

PRACTICE STUDY

Paul is a 7-year-old boy who attends school regularly; however, staff at his school have concerns about his behaviour. Duncan, Paul's father, is 24 years old and works full time for a local caravan manufacturer and frequently does overtime. Melissa, Paul's mother, is 27 years old and works part time in a local supermarket. The two adults and Paul live together in the same household. The maternal grandmother, who lives nearby, collects Paul from school when necessary and looks after him until Melissa returns home. At the request of Paul's teacher, the head of the school has spoken to Melissa about Paul's behaviour. Melissa feels that she has a constant battle with Paul about his behaviour and when his father is at home, he undermines her efforts.

Warmth and control

From the classic works of Baumrind (1967) and Maccoby and Martin (1983), two dimensions of parenting younger children can be identified – 'warmth' and 'control'.

Within this framework, Duncan's parenting could be classified as 'uninvolved', that is, low on 'warmth' and low on 'control', while Melissa's would be 'permissive', being high on 'warmth' and low on 'control'. The maternal grandmother's parenting of Paul would be 'authoritative', that is, high on 'warmth' and high on 'control'. None of them has an authoritarian style of parenting, which is low on 'warmth' and high on 'control'.

This family situation involves co-parenting between the mother, the father and the grandmother; however, the ecological model of parenting is equally applicable to single parents, same-sex parents and isolated two-parent families. When there are siblings, a complete analysis would include sibling relationships and how they interact with parenting. An analysis of the determinants of Duncan and Melissa's parenting needs to be put alongside a similar ecological analysis of Paul's development, which would include his family context, his school, peer group and the influences of the mass media.

An ecological model of parenting

The ecological model of parenting is a systems perspective in which parenting is embedded in an integrated whole system of influences, wherein the 'whole' is greater than the sum of its parts. An ecological model means that parenting is understood within in a multifactorial context, where many factors are operating and interacting with each other. The model concerns person–environment transactions in which parents and children are active participants; however, many of the contexts in which they act may not be within their direct influence or control. Central to the model is parent–child relations in their ecological contexts. The model sets out to explain individual differences in parenting and focuses on a range of influences. It is a general model that can be applied in all parenting situations and can be used as a framework for analysing the influences on a parent's parenting with the view of supporting and strengthening it if necessary. Belsky's process model (Table 10.1) identifies three broad domains of influence: the parents' developmental history and psychological resources; the characteristics of the child; and the contextual sources of stress and support. Each of these will be considered in turn.

Table 10.1 Belsky's model of parenting

Domain	Characteristics
The parent	Developmental history Psychological resources
The child	Characteristics of the child, for example their temperament
The contextual sources of stress and support	Co-parenting relations Social networks Work

Source: Based on Belsky (1984)

Point for Reflection

Write brief notes on what you think might be important influences on Melissa's and Duncan's parenting.

Developmental history and psychological resources

The developmental history and psychological resources of parents are often thought of as the most influential domains on parenting. As well as being a direct influence on parenting interactions with children, they are also recognized as having indirect influences on parenting by shaping the boarder context in which parent–child relations exist. For example, a parent's personality may influence their choice of and relationship with their partner, the willingness of their social network to offer help and their job satisfaction.

Developmental history

Belsky (1997) states that experiences in our family of origin influence our parental competence in important ways, although there is no simple one-to-one correspondence between experiences in childhood and adult functioning as a parent. For example, Main and Goldwyn (1990, cited in Belsky, 1997) found that what seems to determine whether developmental history negatively impacts on parenting was whether parents have psychologically resolved the issues from their past.

Duncan had an unhappy childhood with a very harsh father and has unresolved issues from his past, while Melissa feels she had a happy childhood with loving parents who looked out for her.

Psychological resources of parents

The psychological resources of parents include the enduring characteristics of the individual parent and their psychological wellbeing at a particular point in time. Belsky (1997) maintains that the psychological resources adults bring to their roles as parents influence the way in which they function as parents, and that parental psychological wellbeing and growth-facilitating parenting are positively related to each other. For example, a parent's mental health difficulties can, to varying degrees, impair their ability to parent. Smith (2004) identifies the self-preoccupation, unpredictable behaviour and lack of organization and planning, which are often associated with mental health difficulties, as being potentially disruptive to parenting.

Melissa has been feeling unhappy for a while, with problems at work and in her relationship with Duncan. She has become irritable with Paul, being intolerant of his behaviour and inconsistently chastising him. Duncan is rather content with his life at the moment, with the exception that he finds Melissa no fun anymore and increasingly spends time away from home.

The characteristics of the child

Children are actively involved in parent–child relations and, as Belsky (1997, p. 12) states: 'because the parent-child relationship involves two parties, it is not surprising that attributes of each participating member affect the nature of the interactions that transpire'. Most attention has been given to the role of a child's temperament in influencing parenting. Belsky (1984, p. 86) makes the important point that it is not a child's temperament per se, for example whether Paul has an 'easy' or 'difficult' temperament, but the 'goodness of fit' between the parents' and the child's characteristics. Another factor is parental perception of a child's temperament. For example, Melissa sees Paul as a difficult child, while Duncan sees his son as independent.

The contextual sources of stress and support

This domain consists of the contexts of parent–child relations and the degrees to which they act as sources of support and stress that directly or indirectly influence parenting. The amount and quality of the support available and the intensity of environmental stressors will have an important impact on a parent's parenting (Ghate and Hazel, 2002). Belsky's ecological model identifies three contextual sources, the co-parent relationship, social networks and work. Each source will be considered in turn and the degree of support and stress offered by each in the case study identified.

Co-parenting relations

The co-parenting relationship can be a source of stress and support in parenting. Of the three contextual sources, Belsky (1984) is of the opinion that the co-parent relationship has the greatest inherent potential for exerting the most positive and negative affect on parenting.

The relations between Duncan and Melissa will have an important influence on their parenting of Paul. It will be experienced as either a source of stress or support. At the moment, they are both experiencing their relationship as a source of stress. Duncan is spending increasing lengths of time away from home and Melissa is getting increasingly exasperated with him. She feels unsupported by him, while he feels she is always complaining about what he does and does not do. They are having problems in their relationship that are spilling over into their parenting, and Melissa feels that Duncan undermines her efforts to discipline Paul, while Duncan feels she is too lenient.

Social networks

Ghate and Hazel (2002, p. 217) state that social support is consistently cited as an important factor in parental functioning and 'is often described as one of the "key resources" on which individuals can draw when managing stress which may enhance natural coping skills and buffer against the deleterious effects of adverse circumstances'. However, they found that the experience in social networks was more complex and 'not always perceived in an entirely positive light', with a fine line between help and interference (Ghate and Hazel, 2002, p. 257). Cutrona (2000) specified different types of support, including concrete support, emotional support and advice support, and different qualities of support, including the degree of esteem the source is held in, the degree of emotional closeness, the degree of reciprocity, its reliability and intrusiveness. Even when a parent perceives social networks as supportive, they can have a negative impact on their parenting, for example when they are advised to physically punish their child (Belsky, 1997).

Duncan experiences his network of male friends as a source of support. Although this has a direct effect on his sense of wellbeing, it also has a negative impact on his parenting by taking him away from the family home. Melissa's social network largely consists of her wider family, which she generally experiences as sources of support in her parenting, although she sometimes experiences her mother as overcritical and interfering. She finds it extremely supportive that her mother looks after Paul but feels it comes at a price.

Work

The domain of work can be regarded as a major source of support and stress in relation to parenting. Whether a parent is in employment or not and if they are, their working conditions, including pay, working hours, type of work and degree of satisfaction with their work, are all factors that can either be supportive or stressful in relation to parenting. Mockford and Barlow (2004) found that the demands of work were a major impediment to parents implementing what they learned on a parenting programme.

Both Duncan and Melissa are in employment, the income from which is a direct source of support in their parenting. A direct negative impact on Duncan's parenting is the amount of overtime he does. Duncan generally enjoys his work and has recently been made foreman, which has contributed to his sense of wellbeing; indirectly, this could be a positive influence on his parenting if he was more involved. Melissa does not enjoy her work and is dissatisfied with her current job, feeling that her talents are not being fully utilized. This affects her current sense of wellbeing, which then influences her parenting, for example she sometimes takes her dissatisfaction out on Paul.

Point for Reflection

Taking Melissa and Duncan in turn, identify some sources of contextual stress and support in relation to their parenting.

Parenting as a buffered system

Parenting is regarded as a buffered system, in which support in one domain can act as a buffer against stress in another. This means that stress or weakness in one or two of the domains can be compensated for by support or strength in another. The strengths in Melissa's parenting system are her own developmental history, internal strength and determination, while a strength in Duncan's is his current sense of wellbeing. The buffering potential of the three domains are not thought to be equal. Belsky (1984) maintains that the personality and psychological wellbeing of the parent have the greatest buffeting effect and characteristics of the child the least. Hence, strengthening the different domains is not equally effective in buffering child–parent relations from stress. Belsky places the order of effectiveness as:

1. personal psychological sources of the parent
2. contextual sources of support
3. characteristics of the child.

How can parenting be supported and strengthened?

The ecological model suggests that supporting and strengthening Paul's parenting system can potentially be based on a detailed analysis of the determinants of his parents' parenting. This involves identifying sources of support and stress and the strengths and weaknesses of the different domains of his parents' lives. A systemic perspective can be brought to supporting and strengthening Duncan's and Melissa's parenting, in which changes in one domain either directly or indirectly impact on their parenting. A belief within a systemic perspective is that a change in one part of the system will have knock-on effects on other parts of the system, so that relatively small changes can bring about positive or negative system-wide change. The ecological approach enables the identification of components and aspects of the system that are most amenable or motivated to change, in contrast to those considered in most need of change. Melissa sees a notice in the school inviting interested parents to attend a parenting programme. When Melissa suggests to Duncan that they attend together, he refuses, so she decides to go on her own.

Point for Reflection

What impact do you feel Melissa attending the parenting programme will have on the parenting Paul receives? Think of ways it might or might not help.

It is uncertain whether attending a parenting programme in this situation will or will not help. The role of parenting programmes in improving parenting is a contested area. On the one hand, there is a good deal of evidence that parenting programmes are effective with a percentage of parents, while the same research shows they have limitations. Moran and Ghate (2005), in their research review of what is known about the effectiveness of parenting support, found that while many studies indicate parents are well satisfied with what they get out of their attendance, there remains a significant proportion of parents who either drop out or whose difficulties remain entrenched despite receiving help.

Much of current thinking sees the most effective way of strengthening parenting as enhancing a parent's sense of 'self-efficacy' and seeing themselves as the 'locus of control' (this refers to the extent to which individuals believe that they can control events that affect them). For example, Sanders (1999) sees the development of self-regulation as central in the development of parenting capacity. It is argued that through a developing belief in self-efficacy, other changes can ripple through the parenting system and other aspects of a parent's life. This would explain the common theme running through many evaluations of parenting programmes that attendance increases parental self-confidence, which then enables those who attend to bring about other changes in their lives. However, standard parenting programmes have limitations when parents have additional difficulties, such as parental conflict, mental health problems, substance misuse or high stress levels. Black and other minority ethnic group parents may wonder about the relevance of programmes when the child-rearing patterns of the course presenters and the majority of other participants are perceived to be different from their own (Smith and Pugh, 1996). Equally, the more members there are in a parenting system, the more difficult it will be to get all members to attend.

The case study provides a common situation, in which one parent of a two-parent family attends alone. Mockford and Barlow (2004) found that the attending member sometimes had a number of difficulties in implementing the new techniques learned, as well as other unintended consequences. Problems included difficulties in engaging their partner, changing their partner's practices, and finding time to parent together. They state that differences between parenting practices can increase, sometimes resulting in increased parental tensions and arguments. There has been limited research into fathers and parenting programmes, and one current challenge is that fathers are often reluctant to attend. Smith and Pugh (1996, p. 25) state that 'fathers may resist attending something which they may see as women's work'. Ghate et al.'s (2000) study of how family centres are working with fathers found that there was a complex network of barriers and enabling factors that prevent and promote fathers' use of the centres.

Currently, there are barriers to fathers attending parenting programmes and well-thought through efforts are needed to engage them. Parenting is still seen as a predominantly female domain, and Mockford and Barlow (2004) argue that governments and others will have to take further steps to enable fathers to have more time for family life and to feel confident and comfortable in the parenting role. They suggest that more male group leaders and 'fathers groups' that run in tandem with groups attended by mothers may help to promote male attendance.

The ecological model of parenting shows that there are complex interactive influences on parents' parenting, with two-parent and extended families having particularly complex parenting systems. There needs to be a critical awareness of the multiple influences on parenting, for example in two-parent families, ways need to be found to engage both parents in strengthening their co-parenting. Being aware of the multiple determinants of parenting can increase the chances that parents feel supported and their parenting is being strengthened so that their children's health, wellbeing and development are enhanced.

Conclusion

This chapter has surveyed some of the main conceptual and practice aspects of work with children and their parents. The undoubted complexities of the many factors affecting parenting and family life strengthen the need for practitioners to take parents and families into account at every stage of work with children.

REVIEW QUESTIONS

1. According to the ecological model of parenting, what are the determinants of parenting?
2. How can a person's parenting capacity be strengthened?
3. What can be done to engage fathers in the strengthening of their parenting?

Chapter Links

For discussion of parenting styles, see Chapter 9.
For discussion of parental mental ill health, see Chapter 22.

Further Reading

Moran, P. and Ghate, D. (2005) The effectiveness of parenting support, *Children and Society*, 19, 329–36. Gives a clear and succinct examination of what is known about the effectiveness of parenting support.

Sheppard, M. (2004) *Prevention and Coping in Child and Family Care: Mothers in Adversity Coping with Child Care*, London, Jessica Kingsley. Chapters 2 and 3 provide useful next steps in understanding parenting in context.

Mockford, C. and Barlow, J. (2004) Parenting programmes: some unintended consequences, *Primary Health Care Research and Development*, 5, 219–27. Considers some of the unintended consequences of attending parenting programmes.

Websites

http://www.practicalparent.org.uk/ Run by Dr Andy Gill, a resource for parents and professionals, which gives information and support on parenting, child behaviour and development, and family relationships

Working with Young Carers and their Families

11

Robert Adams

LEARNING OUTCOMES

By the end of this chapter, you should be able to:

- define young caring
- discuss the wider social policy and legal contexts of young caring
- understand how illness or impairment affects other family members
- appreciate the nature and implications of young carers' experiences in their families

Young caring is an often overlooked aspect of the lives of many children and young people. It forms an important strand of their experience, which is often invisible to those outside the family, including practitioners. This chapter examines what young caring is, how common it is, and how children are affected by it. It discusses some of the main implications of these realities for practitioners who work with children, young people and their families.

What is young caring?

The term *young carer* is used of a child or young person who takes on caring tasks for another person that would normally be carried out by a professional or another adult. The key feature of young caring is that the level of care the child or young person provides is inappropriately high for them. Becker (2003, p. 378) defines young carers as:

> children and young persons under 18 who provide, or intend to provide, care, assistance or support to another family member. They carry out, often

on a regular basis, significant or substantial caring tasks and assume a level of responsibility which would usually be associated with an adult. The person receiving care is often a parent but can be a sibling, grandparent or other relative who is disabled, has some chronic illness, mental health problem or other condition connected with a need for care, support or supervision.

Incidence of young caring

Informal caring by young people is distinguished by the fact that the traditional role of adults looking after children is reversed. Because it is informal, it tends to be invisible and underestimated. This may be because family members may prefer to cope without professional intervention or support. At the end of the 20th century, the government agency the Office for National Statistics estimated the total of young carers as 51,000 (Bibby and Becker, 2000).

The illness, impairment or incapacity of one or more parents through a medical condition or mental health problem can have an adverse effect on the upbringing of children. It can lead to children taking on caring roles in the household. The caring responsibilities shared with one or more children are even more pronounced when a lone parent heads the household; for example, more than half of young carers surveyed by the Young Carers Research Group were in lone-parent households (Dearden and Becker, 1998).

Additional responsibilities make children even more vulnerable (Becker, 1995). Research into the experiences of 60 young people caring for a parent who has a disability or long-term illness shows significant negative consequences for them, in terms of their own education, job prospects, social life and development towards an independent adulthood (Dearden and Becker, 2000).

The level and intensity of caring undertaken by young people may also be affected significantly by other factors, such as the disposition of roles between family members according to age and gender, cultural and faith factors, the incidence of poverty, and the extent to which support is available from agencies or sources of informal care.

Point for Reflection

Can you think of some reasons why young carers often remain 'invisible'?

Wider social, policy and legal context

The situation of young carers has not been helped in England by the policy change that separates the caring services for adults from services for children. This means that children and young people under 18 who care are not part of the provision for adult carers. There is a well-developed movement representing the interests of adult informal carers, but the same is not the case for young carers. Incidentally, in the healthcare and medical field, the term 'informal carer' is generally used to refer to the huge number – perhaps as many as 5 million – of adult carers who are not paid to act in a caring role. To make the situation of young carers even more marginal and, from the point of view of policy, less connected with the rest of the field of social care, the government agency Skills for Care does not deal with young carers; instead, its work lies closer to the responsibilities of the equivalent government body relating to children's services – Children's Workforce Development Council.

Until the late 1980s, caring by children under 18 was not recognized explicitly in law. Young carers and other family members had few if any incentives to reveal what was going on in the family. Perhaps adults were inhibited about the possible implications for benefits, and children were not encouraged to speak out about their caring role, on which adults depended. There were also issues of perception, in that many family members took for granted the support of other family members.

Since the early 1990s, the situation of young carers has improved, due to increasing professional and public awareness. This is one area of public policy where research has influenced legislation. Legislation empowers and requires local authorities to help young carers. The *Framework for the Assessment of Children in Need and their Families* (DH/DfEE/Home Office, 2000) offers guidance on the Children Act 1989 (s. 17), which specifies support for young carers (paras 3.61–3.63) (see Chapter 1). The Carers (Recognition and Services) Act 1995, Carers and Disabled Children Act 2001 and Carers (Equal Opportunities) Act 2004 grant young carers the right to an assessment of their needs and rights, including the rights to leisure, social life and education. Another improvement is the increased level of resources available to support young carers. An example is The Children's Society National Young Carers Initiative, part of the Include project. Some weblinks to other sources are given at the end of this chapter.

The realities of young caring

The largest survey of young carers in the UK to date was carried out by the Young Carers Research Group (YCRG) (Dearden and Becker, 1998), and it found that, overwhelmingly:

- these young carers were of school age
- they were mostly caring for the mother
- they were often caring for a person with a mental rather than a physical illness
- the average age of carers was 12 and some were as young as 5
- 43% of young carers were boys.

The kinds of care provided by children and young people cover a wide spectrum of responsibilities. Perhaps it is surprising that young carers do become involved in such a broad span of activities. The YCRG survey findings in this area are summarized in Table 11.1.

Table 11.1 Caring activities by young carers

Type of care	Examples	Percentage
Domestic	Cleaning	72
General	Giving medication; helping with mobility	57
Emotional	Support for person with mental health problems	43
Intimate	Personal washing and toileting	21
Other	Money management; translating; dealing with professionals; caring for other children	29

Point for Reflection

What kinds of difficulties are young carers likely to face?

It is important for practitioners to be sensitive to the experiences of young carers and to appreciate how the illness or impairment of one family member affects other members of the family.

Young carers' experiences

Aldridge and Becker (1993) conclude that the incidence of young carers, and the burden carried by them, has been underestimated in the past. According to their survey results announced in late 2010 (BBC Press Office, 2010), the previous estimate of about 170,000 young carers in the UK may be underestimated by at least four times, given the current survey's estimate of about 700,000.

Dearden and Becker (2000) conclude that caring often negatively affects the education and job prospects, as well as the social life and growth to independence of young carers. Dearden et al. (1998) conclude that young carers need recognition, an opportunity to air their problems, and the scope to fufil their potential through education, leisure and social activities. Research by Bibby and Becker (2000) into young carers' experiences suggests that factors outside the home contribute to the constraints on them. Some impression of the burden of caring and how it affects other aspects of the child's schooling, social life and leisure can be gained from the following two extracts from two different children, in the very moving collection of accounts in Bibby and Becker's book (2000, p. 46):

> In the morning I get up and if Mum's getting up I help her out of bed, if not I get ready for school and get her up when she's awake. When I arrive at school I'm fine until 11.00 am. Sometimes I'm okay and I just go to play but if I'm not I go to my head teacher and ask if I can phone my Mum. When I'm coming home I just go straight home unless my Mum asks me to go to the shop. When I get home I wash up, watch television some more and by 8.45 pm I get ready for bed, kiss Mum goodnight and I'm in bed by 9.00 pm. I read a book for 15 minutes and then it's another day in the morning. (girl, aged 10)

> He's getting worse now. I tend to do everything really, basically he is a kid and I'm the father. I do the shopping, I clean the place. I make the beds, I do the washing, I do the cooking, I do all that. I'm a good cook. I was only young, must have been about ten when it all started. (boy, aged 16)

Effects on the young carer of another family member's condition, illness or impairment

The effects on child carers of taking on caring responsibilities can be enormous. The reshaping of family responsibilities, following accidents or illnesses affecting family members who are cared for, is likely to affect child carers in different ways. The boundaries between what the adults and children are responsible for and do are shifted. The complexities of this can be challenging for all family members and for young carers in particular. There is no simple role reversal, where parents become like children and children play the parental role, rather, as Bancroft et al. (2005, p. 124) describe it, 'a complex of permeable, shifting boundaries between parents and children'. There may be many consequences, such as:

- Children may take on some parental roles
- Children take on some roles and responsibilities, including those of caring
- Children may become more at risk themselves from parental misuse of alcohol and drugs and other household members may be more at risk
- There could be enhanced risks from knowledge boundaries – such as those around what a child would normally know or not know at a particular age – being crossed or fractured
- Children could learn to use changed boundaries between settings and times as spaces for respite.

Children and young people often are pushed into caring roles because of the illness or impairment of another family member. The total of children and young people affected by family illness is not known. The total of young people, around 50,000, who are carers because of parental illness, is likely to be an underestimate of the actual total number affected (Bibby and Becker, 2000). A phobic condition such as agoraphobia (an anxiety condition where the adult has a panic attack at the thought that there is no escape from a situation such as, but not necessarily, an open space) may mean the adult is dependent on the child doing the shopping. The illness or other condition of the other family member may or may not affect the child. It is important to find out whether the person's condition affects the child. It may be that the child is relatively unaffected. The most likely circumstance where the child is affected is where family illness leads to the child taking on a caring responsibility for one or more other family members. At the same time, the child may suffer emotionally, when the illness first becomes apparent or is diagnosed and later when the parent has to go to hospital or undergo tests. These are likely to be stressful times for the children, partly due to the uncertainty.

Chronic illnesses or impairment of the cared-for person may lead the child carer to become depressed over a longer period. There may be symptoms of loss akin to those of a bereaved person. Chronic uncertainty about the outcome of the illness can severely affect the child. There may be a need for support and therapy in the family.

Some children have to adjust to family life with parental drug or alcohol misuse, as Bancroft et al. (2005) indicate in their review of research in this area.

Implications for practice

In the first place, young caring may be a hidden activity and practitioners with children and young people should work actively with families to encourage individuals to come forward and ask for help and support. It may be that the need for support emerges in different agencies and it is important that wherever it surfaces – be this in the nursery, school or social work setting – the response, in terms of expertise and services available to the young carer, should be the same. The nature and appropriateness of their caring responsibilities need to be assessed.

Since young caring invariably takes place in a family and household, work with the young carer should always be undertaken in the wider context of work with the family. A holistic approach to practice is appropriate, since invariably the situation will be complex. It is important for the practitioner to be able to recognize how the child is affected and what the needs of the child may be. The experience of the young carer is therefore paramount in reaching an assessment of their situation.

Young carers' needs should be the first consideration in work with them, which means that their experiences, wishes and preferences should be taken into account. It should be recognized by practitioners that young carers are experts by virtue of their experience as carers. Their rights are important as well, since, in the first place, they have a right to say whether or not they wish to undertake caring for other people.

Young carers, by definition, are still in the process of development and it is important for work with them to take into account their entitlement to a full and active life, in keeping with their developmental needs. Measures should be taken to ensure that, as required by legislation such as the Carers and Disabled Children Act 2001 and Carers (Equal Opportunities) Act 2004, they have equivalent access to education, career opportunities, leisure and social activities as other children of their age.

Young carers are at least as prone as other children to reacting emotionally to other family members' problems, including the kinds of mental, emotional and physical problems that increase the need for care. It is understandable that young carers may respond by withdrawing or becoming irritable and bad-tempered. Explosions of temper may be a way of releasing emotions, for the hurt being suffered, on a substitute target. Some children's behaviour and performance at school will be affected. Eating habits, sleep patterns and health problems may all be ways in which the child responds to stress.

The child may experience enforced growing up, as they take on responsibility for caring for younger children. The young boy may mimic the role of father and his young sister may begin to act like the mother. There are other consequences, as adults become dependent and children become independent. Undoubtedly, while the child or young person carer is coping, they are learning and growing through the experience of caring. However, this always has to be balanced against the costs of caring in personal terms, the opportunities for leisure, education and growing in other directions that are lost, the increased vulnerabilities and risks associated with the exercise of caring responsibilities. Caring remains a complex and demanding activity and, bearing in mind that much of this caring remains hidden, professionals and agencies should be alert to opportunities to find out where it is happening and, where possible, provide support and resources for young carers.

Conclusion

When children are in caring roles in the household, the extent of their responsibilities is often not apparent to outsiders. Consequently, they bear much of the caring burden without acknowledgement or support from outside the family. The priority is to assess the situation and to put in place sufficient support to enable individual family members and the family as a whole to manage the situation.

REVIEW QUESTIONS

1. What is young caring?
2. What is the difference between being a young carer and 'helping around the house' with household tasks?
3. What are the main provisions of the following legislation in respect of young carers: the Carers (Recognition and Services) Act 1995 and the Carers and Disabled Children Act 2001?

_____ Chapter Links _____

For discussion of how children deal with death and bereavement, see Chapter 15.

_____ Further Reading _____

Aldridge, J. and Becker, S. (2003) _Children Caring for Parents with Mental Illness: Perspectives of Young Carers, Parents and Professionals_, Bristol, Policy Press. Presents the implications of mental health problems experienced by the parents for the children caring for them.

Bibby, A. and Becker, S. (2000) _Young Carers in their Own Words_, London, Gulbenkian Calouste Foundation. Presents accounts by young carers of their caring experiences.

Dearden, S., Aldridge, J. and Dearden, S. (1998) _Young Carers and their Families_, Oxford, Blackwell. Relevant study of young carers in relation to their family circumstances.

_____ Websites _____

http://www.carers.org/ The Princess Royal Trust for Carers Provides information, advice, discussion and support for carers

www.lboro.ac.uk/departments/ss/centres/YCRG/ Information about activities related to research into young carers

www.shapingourlives.org.uk/ Shaping Our Lives National network promoting the interests of people who receive services and carers

www.carersuk.org/ Organization promoting the interests of carers

http://www.youngcarer.com/ Include project, part of the Young Carers Initiative

Working with Children through Family Break-up and Reconstitution

12

Robert Adams

LEARNING OUTCOMES

By the end of this chapter, you should be able to:

- understand family break-up in its wider demographic and policy contexts
- identify the changing patterns of marriage and divorce
- outline the key consequences and effects of family break-up on children

Families break up and are reconstituted for many reasons. Sometimes it is because the parents split up, one of the parents dies, or there is abuse of the child by one or more family members and the child is removed to a place of safety. Whatever the cause, the consequences for the child are often severe stress and disruption of the household.

This chapter deals with the consequences of family break-up, focusing particularly on how children experience this.

Demographic and policy contexts

Family structures and cultural characteristics differ markedly in the early 21st century from those a century ago. More families are forming and reforming, as parents break up as couples and form couples with new partners, and consequently 'serial' parenting is a feature, that is, where a couple each have children from the present relationship and from previous relationships, presenting step-parents with the role of caring for children from more than one previous set of partners. Five features are noteworthy, and are now discussed.

Declining marriage

Among all families, the incidence of marriage declined by almost 50% between 1970 and 2000, and the number of children born outside wedlock increased between 1979 and 1999 from about 10% to about 40% (ONS, 2002).

Increase in family break-up

There are two trends. The number of divorces in the UK fell from about 180,000 in 1993 to 159,000 in 1999, a total that needs to be seen in the context of the declining total of marriages. Despite this, about a quarter of children born in 1979 had personal experience of living in a divorced family by the time they were 16, in 1995. In the 30 years between 1971 and 2000, the number of children affected by divorce doubled to about 142,000 in 2000, and increased to 147,000 in 2001. About 25% of these were under five years and 70% were under ten years old (National Council for One Parent Families, 2001).

Changing patterns of lone parenting

Related to the above point about family break-up, there was an increase in the number of lone parents up to the 1980s, due to divorce, and a faster increase after the 1980s. Over the past century, however, the proportion of lone-parent families stayed almost constant, the difference being that in the 19th century most were widowed, whereas nowadays they are separated or divorced. About 22% of all families with dependent children in the UK in spring 2001 – 1.7 million families – were headed by lone parents, a threefold increase over the 30 years since 1971 (NCH, 2002). They care for about 20% of children in the UK – about 3 million children.

Increase in family reconstitution

Families do not just break up – they reconstitute. About 6% of families with dependent children in the UK in 1998–9 were stepfamilies with the head of the family under 60. Almost 90% of stepfamilies consisted of two adults and at least one child from the female partner's previous relationship (NCH, 2002).

Teenage parenthood

The UK had the highest teenage birth rate in the EU in 1996. Teenage parenthood increased during the 1980s and fell slightly during the 1990s. However, whereas the teenage pregnancy rate for under 18s improved slightly between 2002 and 2003 from 42.8 to 42.3 per 1,000, the teenage pregnancy rate for 13- to 15-year-olds increased from 7.9 to 8.0 per 1,000 (*Health Statistics Quarterly*, 2005). In terms of quantity, the total of under 18-year-olds pregnant in 1999 was 42,000 (NCH, 2002).

Positive and negative aspects of family life

Family life is changing and while some of these changes no doubt benefit some family members, some aspects have negative consequences. Some changes are not objective realities, but are experienced differently by different family members. Thus, a family break-up and reconstitution may be experienced as positive by one adult partner who has found another partner, but as negative by the other partner and by the children.

Economic factors may benefit all family members, where, for instance, one or more adults in the household obtains well-paid work. However, the continued gendered division of labour within the family (that is, tasks divided between males and females according to their gender) may be resented by a woman whose children are growing up, yet who feels pressurized to stay at home and undertake full-time housework, rather than to seek fulfilment in activities outside the household (McKie et al., 2005). At work, the labour market for some women continues to be gendered to their disadvantage. They are more likely than men to experience poverty and even more likely to in later life (Cabinet Office, 2000).

Families are more likely than ever to occupy more than one physical space (McKie et al., 2005). The fact that the children of parents and step-parents, for instance, may move between different households may be experienced either as positive or as negative, depending on whether particular benefits are available to the children in each household and whether these outweigh any negative consequences of this complexity and constant movement. 'Boundary ambiguity' is associated with the notion of the 'family boundary', an idea reflecting assumptions about what is, or should be, inside or outside the family. Boundary ambiguity may be experienced by family members who, at a time of family change, are not sure who is inside and who is outside the family boundary, who is responsible for what and who is doing what (Sweeting and Seaman, 2005).

Consequences of family break-up

Wallerstein and colleagues (Wallerstein and Blakeslee, 2004; Wallerstein and Kelly, 1980) have carried out long-term – extending to 25 years – follow-ups of the consequences of divorce for children. This makes their research classic in its field. Fundamentally, they question the illusion many adults retain that divorce is a transition to an improved state for children, a transient event with short-term consequences for children as well as parents (Wallerstein and Kelly, 1980). They conclude that for about half the adults in their study: 'the lost marriage was still alive with raw feelings and strong longings. These people were angry, bitter, and mired in conflict even fifteen years after the break-up' (Wallerstein and Blakeslee, 2004, p. xiii).

Wallerstein and Blakeslee (2004) conclude that the consequences of family break-up for children are twofold:

1. Many young people are hesitant about marrying for fear the marriage will break up as their parents' marriage did.
2. Many young people enter long-term relationships without marrying so as to avoid the drawbacks of later divorce.

Effects on children of family break-up

Research, unsurprisingly perhaps, illustrates the traumas of family life and the consequences for family members, and children in particular. However, research also demonstrates the resilience of family life, as emerges from the review of research on how children manage parental drug and alcohol misuse (Bancroft et al., 2005). According to Buchanan and Ten Brinke (1997, 1998), there are indications that working to equip children with the life skills to cope with interpersonal conflict has long-term benefits. Flouri and Buchanan (2003) conclude that work with fathers contributes to positive outcomes for children. Ford et al. (1995) conclude that many lone parents experience serious debt problems. Rowlinson and McKay (1998) conclude that poverty and lone parenthood correlate positively, that is, becoming a lone parent increases the person's proneness to poverty. Ford and Millar (1998) conclude that additional help is needed to enable some women to improve their earning prospects through training and education.

While adults may wish to believe that the effects of family break-up on children are short term, if handled correctly, there is evidence from research of children's experiences that, whether for good or ill, there are longer term consequences. One complex area is how the adults involved in the break-up behave towards the child. There is little doubt that when interacting with their children, some adults are anticipating how they may react. For instance, the guilt of one partner may cause them to be less assertive in disciplining the child. This is only one example, of course, in a complex matrix of anticipations and responses.

One of the main consequences for children – particularly infants and young children – of the patterns of child rearing by lone parents and young teenagers who become pregnant is that both parents and children suffer disproportionately from poverty and social exclusion.

Sweeting and Seaman (2005) have carried out qualitative research into children's experiences, in the young people's family life study. Two key themes, expressivity and discipline, emerged from this research. The theme of 'expressivity' is concerned with the parent being receptive to talking about how the child is feeling, while 'discipline' is concerned with setting boundaries to the child's behaviour. The child's experience is that both parents are available to play the expressive role in a listening capacity in respect of different aspects of what the child wishes to talk about, so in that sense, their contributions are complementary. On the other hand, in the area of discipline, the parental contribution is not only complementary but additive, in that 'two parents, even if one was non-resident, equalled twice the discipline' (Sweeting and Seaman, 2005, p. 103).

In order to gain a sense of the longer term impact on children of family break-up, it is worth referring to the classic research of Wallerstein and colleagues, carried out over a quarter of a century.

Eighteen months after family break-up

Wallerstein and Kelly (1980) found that during the first 18 months after family break-up, children's immediate shock and anger mellowed. The most widespread symptom was depression, which affected a quarter of the children and young people in the study. Similarly, while one-third of children had expressed anger at one or both parents during the early stages of family break-up, for some children the intensity of this anger decreased, although a year later, one-quarter of them continued to express intense anger at the marital failure. There was a greater increase in trust and respect for mothers than for fathers during the first 18 months after family break-up.

Five years after family break-up

Wallerstein and Kelly (1980) portray the complexity of children's responses five years after family break-up, noting the impossibility of isolating a single theme. They identify seven main factors as influencing these outcomes:

1. The extent of conciliation between the parents after divorce
2. The extent to which the parent with custody improves as a parent
3. The extent to which the child maintains a regular relationship with the non-custodial parent, matching the child's development

4. The extent to which the child is equipped in terms of personal resources and social maturity to deal with the break-up, alone and with other children and adults
5. The extent to which the child can turn to other people for support
6. The extent to which the child has overcome such feelings as anger and depression
7. The sex and age of the child.

Ten years after family break-up

Wallerstein and Blakeslee (2004) contacted 116 of the 131 children in the original study 10 years after the family break-up. Perhaps to a surprising extent, they still identify themselves as 'survivors of tragedy' (p. 23) and retain vivid memories of the traumas of the actual break-up. Children retain the traditional values of marriage and family life and still make judgements years later about who they see as betraying the marriage. At the same time, they show sympathy and empathy for their parents' feelings, often displaying 'a frankness, candor, gentleness and sweetness that does not reflect the way they feel they have been treated' (p. 26).

PRACTICE STUDY

Michael (13), Julie (11), Thomas (7) and Anna (4) have witnessed their parents going through a two-year process of family rows and an acrimonious divorce, followed quite soon by their mother bringing a new male partner to live in the household. Let us reflect on how the three themes help us to understand how each of the four children relates to these changing circumstances.

Anna may feel insecure about losing contact with her father at a time when she needs to depend on and trust her relationships with her parents. Thomas may feel panicky about losing his sense of stability. Julie may feel she is in competition with a new man in the house for the affections of her mother and has to depend more for emotional and social support on friends of her own age and an aunt who lives nearby. Michael may be pushed into staying away from the family home and relying more on friends at school, because it takes him a long time to adjust to life with his new stepfather.

In circumstances such as family break-up and reconstitution, adults' perceptions differ from those of their children. The children may seek support and guidance from other relatives, neighbours and friends, in the absence of access to appropriate services.

Family break-up where children are at risk of harm

While it is not the case that families break up because of child abuse, there are circumstances where professional intervention to safeguard children has the accompanying effect of breaking up the household. This may happen because an abusing adult or other carer is excluded from the family home, or it may come about because the child is removed to a place of safety or is looked after by the local authority.

While all children have needs, the practitioner must be able to assess, over and above this, which children need protection. The priority is to keep children safe and to minimize the risk of harm to them. This may entail removing them from people who have already harmed them or from those who may harm them. All too often, children who have been harmed want the harm to stop but do not want to be removed from the family home, even though it is all, or part, of the problem. They need to be given some support to enable them to make the transition between being at home and, for instance, being looked after by the local authority.

The immediate consequence of family break-up for the child is usually a period of insecurity, during which the trauma suffered previously is made more complex and less accessible by this enforced movement. Subsequently, after being taken into care, as a looked after child, there may be an immediate move to place the child with foster parents and longer term proceedings leading to adoption. This may be a lengthy process, taking several years to complete. Even after the adoption, the child may still suffer the consequences of all these changes, on top of the original traumas of the harm or abuse.

The consequences of abuse for the child and people immediately around the child can be profound. Even very young children can show signs of disturbance, manifested in extreme displays of anger and distress. Challenging behaviour can result from even quite minor upheavals such as a temporary move from the family home to live with a relative. Toddlers and young children may regress (go back) to infant behaviour, bed-wetting, soiling their clothes during the day, temper tantrums, screaming uncontrollably and refusing food and drink. Children who have been abused physically may become physically abusive, in a so-called symmetrical response to the violence they have experienced.

The task of enabling a young child subjected to abuse and subsequent family break-up to recover a sense of stability and resume a normal pattern of development is testing for practitioners and will often take a long period of time.

Conclusion

This chapter has provided a social context, in terms of demographic statistics, for the changing patterns of family life – in terms of families breaking up and reforming – that inform this discussion. There is a tension between these changes and transitions that families undergo and the needs of children for continuity and stability during their upbringing. There is also a need for practitioners to be able to assess the variety of family situations and ascertain which of these present risks to children, in terms of neglect or harm through physical or other forms of abuse.

REVIEW QUESTIONS

1. What is serial parenting?
2. What are the two themes of expressivity and discipline that emerged from the research study into young people's family life?
3. What does research indicate are the main long-term consequences for children, say, 10 years after family break-up?

Chapter Links

For discussion of how parenting contributes to the quality of family life, see Chapter 10. For further discussion of safeguarding (protection), see Chapter 23.

Further Reading

Butler, I., Scanlan, L., Robinson, M. et al. (2003) *Divorcing Children: Children's Experience of their Parents' Divorce*, London, Jessica Kingsley. Deals with the process, finding out, telling others, relationships through the process, contact and legal issues.

National Council for One Parent Families (2001) *One Parent Families Today*, London, National Council for One Parent Families. Provides factual information about families, divorce and children.

Stones, R. and Spoor, N. (2002) *Children Don't Divorce*, Bradfield, Happy Cat Books. A book to read through with young children.

Teyber, E. (2001) *Helping Children Cope with Divorce*, San Francisco, Jossey-Bass. A book intended for divorcing parents, to enable them to help their children cope.

Trinder, L., Beek, M. and Connolly, J. (2002) *Contact: How Parents and Children Negotiate and Experience Divorce*, York, Joseph Rowntree Foundation. A report on research into what factors make contact work or not work.

Utting, D. (1995) *Family and Parenthood: Supporting Families: Preventing Breakdown*, York, Joseph Rowntree Foundation. A useful study of parenting and families.

Wasoff, F. and Neale, B. (2006) *Private Arrangements for Contact with Children*, London, ESRC. A report of research stating that the quality of relationships contributes more to the quality of young people's family lives than the quantity of contact.

Websites

www.cwdcouncil.org.uk/social-work/remodelling/ Provides information on pilot schemes to enable social workers to spend more time doing effective work with children and families

www.divorceresource.co.uk/citizensadvicelawcentres.html Provides resources from Citizens Advice Bureaux and legal centres on the legal, financial and emotional aspects of separation and divorce

Working with Children through Adoption and Fostering

13

Robert Adams

LEARNING OUTCOMES

By the end of this chapter, you should be able to:

- locate fostering and adoption in the wider context of the 'care' system
- understand the nature and uses of fostering
- understand the nature of adoption and what the adoption process entails
- appreciate key factors affecting adoption and fostering
- compare the relative merits of adoption and fostering

Fostering and adoption

The three main 'care' options for children 'looked after' by the local authority are foster care, adoption and residential care (the latter is discussed in Chapter 14).

Fostering is the arrangement made for a child to be cared for and provided with accommodation, normally for more than 28 days, by a person other than a parent or other person with parental responsibility, sibling or close relative. Fostering is the most commonly used of the three placement option and most of these are 'emergency' placements. *Adoption* is the permanent placement of a child with adults who become parent figures and assume full parental responsibility. The adopted child takes on the family name of the adoptive parents and becomes as full a family member as a child born to them.

Fostering and adoption in the wider 'care' context

Since the late 1990s, there has been increased momentum in efforts by government, local authorities and independent childcare agencies to place looked after children, who formerly would have remained in the care of the local authority in children's homes, in families. *Looked after* is the term used to refer to children 'in the care' of the local authority. The aim of the incoming Labour government in 1997 was to increase the numbers of looked after children who were found a long-term placement and increase the speed at which this happened, once the decision had been made that being looked after was the best long-term option.

The government's *Quality Protects* (DH, 1998) policy initiative set the agenda for strategic and practice development. It reflected research lessons, which still apply more than a decade later, on the vital importance of the choice and stability of placements. At the same time, efforts were made to keep families together wherever possible, consistent with the goal of safeguarding children against harm. Despite this, the numbers of children being looked after by local authorities did not reduce in the next few years (Table 13.1), and in 2009, the figure was the same as 2005.

Table 13.1 Children looked after in England at 31 March 2001–5

	2001	2002	2003	2004	2005
All children	58,000	59,000	60,800	61,100	60,900

Source: Adapted from DfES (2005), Table 1

Despite the policy aim of reducing the number of placements of an individual child, only 10% of children have experienced only one placement and nearly 25% have had 11 or more placements (Shaw, 1998). There are problems in ascertaining whether this position has improved, but the indications are that, in England at any rate, it has not done so (DH, 2001).

The *Prime Minister's Review of Adoption* (DH, 2000a) was followed by the White Paper on adoption (DH, 2000b) and the Adoption and Children Act 2002 (see Box 13.1).

Box 13.1 Adoption and Children Act 2002

- Updates requirement for registrar general to register all adoptions
- Registrar general must give any applicant aged 18 or over a certified copy of their record of birth
- Local agencies must give counselling to any such applicant requesting it

One goal was to try to speed up the process of adoption and to ensure that, where appropriate, children were provided with the opportunity of permanent family placement. In 2000–1, there were about 5,000 adoptions in total, but this included a significant proportion of adoptions by step-parents, the net total of adoptions being about 3,000. In the following year, 2001–2, the number of adoptions increased to about 3,400. In the year 2004–5, 3,800 children were adopted in England, approximately the same total as the previous year and an increase of 38% on 2000–1. By 2008–9, this total had slipped by 13% to 3,200 (DCSF, 2009).

Whereas the total number of children in care increased only by 1% between 2001 and 2005, the increase in the number of infants under one year old was proportionately greater. The overall increase in numbers being looked after can be accounted for almost entirely by the increasing numbers of babies taken into care. The number of children under one year increased by nearly 20%. On the other hand, although the total number of young children aged one to five years was four times as great, this total declined by 400, more than 5%, during the same period.

The numbers of babies and very young children adopted are rising and the numbers of older children adopted are falling (DH, 2001). The aim of the adoption strategy was to increase the numbers of infants and very young children found adoptive placements as quickly as possible, in order to minimize disruption to their lives and offer them the opportunity of a permanent family placement. By 31 March 2005, 65% of the 23,100 children under 16 looked after for 2.5 or more years had been in the same placement for 2 years or more, or had been placed for adoption. The government target was to increase this to 80% by 2008 (DfES, 2005).

The number of babies released voluntarily for adoption in England each year is relatively small, at less than 300. Research indicates that even in these cases, the adoption process can be complex. Neil's study of 62 children under 12 months old placed for adoption found that more than a third were not straightforward voluntary adoptions and a little less than a third were adopted against parental wishes (Neil, 2000a, 2000b, referred to in Thoburn, 2002).

Many issues have arisen over the decades concerning contact between children and their birth parents. The Children Act 1989 introduced the right of adopted children, in some circumstances, to have contact with their biological parents. It is known from research that when adopted babies have no contact with members of their birth family, being in so-called 'closed adoptions', a proportion of them later suffer from teenage and adult emotional problems (Howe and Feast, 2000) and that these risks increase when placements involve children over six months old (Howe, 1992).

There is general professional and legal acceptance of the rights of adopted children to know about their biological parents and family background. The Adoption Act 1976 gave the adopted person the right to discover their identity, by obtaining a copy of their birth certificate. In some circumstances, professionals and other adults may raise barriers to this, where it would conflict with the interests of one or more parents. However, it is important that children are included in these discussions and that their rights to information are preserved (Cheng, 2009).

Fostering

Despite the fact that fostering is the most common way in which children are looked after by the local authority, it has traditionally been a less prominent childcare activity, in contrast with adoption. Since the 1990s, however, as the numbers of children in residential care have fallen, so the numbers in foster care have increased. On 31 March 2005, 68% of children were in foster care, an increase of 9% from 2001 (DfES, 2005).

Among important authoritative research into fostering and adoption are the large-scale and in-depth studies by Sinclair and colleagues (Sinclair, 2005; Sinclair et al., 2000, 2004, 2005) and research by Sellick and Connolly (2001). Research reveals that, since 2000, there is no indication of a change in the position that fostering is invariably the first and only choice of placement for about four-fifths of children (Waterhouse, 1997), which means that the government's goal of providing choice of placement is not being met and implies that insufficient high-quality placements are available. Sinclair's (2005) review of fostering research identifies three major changes since the 1990s. In the 21st century:

1. Fostering is less likely to take place because of parental misfortune and more likely through abuse to the child or because others find the child's behaviour too difficult.
2. Those who foster are more likely to be viewed as foster carers than foster parents.
3. There is an increased tendency for foster children to retain regular contact with their families.

Tapsfield and Collier (2005) use the findings of their research into the costs and benefits of fostering to conclude that foster carers should not be paid allowances, but should be trained and paid as other childcare practitioners. The government, while not accepting this argument in full, has published national rates of payment for foster carers (DfES, 2006).

Foster care can be through foster parents approved and paid by the local authority, or through a private arrangement between a parent and a person, other than a parent or relative, who is caring for the child. *Private fostering* is a little known term with a strict legal definition. It covers situations where a child who is not yet 16 – or not yet 18 if disabled – is put into the care of a person, who is not their parent, a close relative or a person who has parental responsibility, in a private arrangement. Children may be placed in foster care for many reasons, but most commonly because their normal family life and contact with their main parent or carer are interrupted or otherwise unsatisfactory.

While fostering is normally short term, such an arrangement may continue for many years. Although the precise number of children being privately fostered is not known, in 2000, it was estimated to be about 10,000 (Freeman, 2009).

While a child is in foster care, every effort should be made to retain the child's contact with the biological parent. If this is not possible, the effort should be directed to building attachment with another adult who can take on the parenting role. Sometimes this will involve preparing for adoption by another person or couple. As well as maintaining contact with biological family members, it is important, where possible, to maintain the child's sense of continuity and stability while in foster care.

Cleaver's research (2000) demonstrates that while accommodating children is used in general as a last resort, it can be used alongside family support to encourage a more creative attitude to contact, and better shared-care arrangements can be made between foster carers and parents. The assumption that a stable foster placement will be successful in these terms is not borne out by this research, which indicates that the child's return to the family is more likely to be successful when:

- there is a good relationship between the child and the parent
- parent(s) are well motivated
- the contact is purposeful and well resourced
- the child and the parent(s) experience the contact as positive
- the return of the child is part of a shared plan.

Foster care placements provide three benefits, over and above residential care:

- more intimate care
- continuity in caring
- predictability in care.

Sinclair (2005) recommends the development of four roles for foster care, as a way of tackling the reality that fostering cannot provide a child with a home for life, leaving many children with no option but eventually to return home to a situation they left previously because it was unsatisfactory. These four roles are:

- *Shared care and through care:* entails parents and carers each taking the child for short periods, as indicated by the child's needs
- *Treatment foster care:* foster care with therapeutic resources, to enable the child to change, a form of care that Sinclair argues should be routinely part of fostering and not regarded as separate or special

■ *Kinship care:* care by relatives
■ *Enhanced long-stay foster care:* a form of care which, Sinclair concludes from research, while it continues, is often indistinguishable from adoption.

Adoption

Government initiatives since 2000 have aimed to speed up the process of adoption (DH Adoption and Permanence Taskforce, 2001). The justification for this is that adoption is able to offer the benefits of stability and continuity to children and therefore potentially benefit the greatest number of children (Robinson, 2000).

Adoption normally begins with an initial inquiry by parents wishing to adopt a child, which comes to the family placement or adoption team in a social work agency or local authority children's department. This initial contact leads to the parents being invited to take part in a process of exchanging information about what adoption entails. During this, they are likely to discuss their wishes with a social worker and, perhaps, with other adoptive parents. Subsequently, they are likely to make a formal application of their 'expression of interest' and take part in a detailed process that considers their suitability to adopt. This involves a social worker carrying out an assessment with them and completing a prospective adopter's report. This then leads to an adoption panel, which takes into account the views and wishes of the adoptive parents and also the assessment by professional practitioners in adoption work. Assuming the applicants are successful, at this point the search begins for a suitable child for them to adopt. This is known as a 'matching process' and it needs to be handled with great care, because the three main parties to adoption – the original birth parents, the adoptive parents and the child – all have points of view and their respective rights have to be safeguarded. Legal proceedings in a family court are undertaken by the local authority and, perhaps, an adoption agency in the voluntary sector, such as Barnardo's. Different parties to the adoption receive independent advocacy and support throughout the process, through a reporting officer appointed by the independent body Cafcass (Children and Family Court Advisory and Support Service), which is responsible for looking after the interests of children involved in family proceedings. Whether or not the parents are in full agreement with the adoption without any conditions, the reporting officer ensures they understand what is happening as the process proceeds. Where they do not agree, this role is taken over by a children's guardian, who is appointed by the court, with the responsibility for safeguarding the interests of the child.

The above is an abbreviated procedural summary, but it is clear from this that the adoption process is necessarily complex and that a great deal of careful preparation precedes an adoption placement. It is extremely important for the right decision to be made, since adoptive parents assume parental rights and it would be emotionally disruptive for a child if an adoption broke down soon after the placement. Undoubtedly, this would be disturbing for adoptive parents as well, but the priority in such a situation would be minimizing the harm to the child, since, in such circumstances, the welfare of the child is paramount. Research indicates that about 5% of adoption placements of infants made at the request of the birth parents break down (Sellick et al., 2004).

Selwyn et al. (2003) have examined the circumstances, costs and outcomes of non-infant adoptions and conclude that it is vital for assessment, planning and intervention processes to be supported by adequate and clear documentation and for decisions regarding adoption to be speeded up. Also, they recommend that the incidence of children behaving in a distressed way at school makes it necessary that therapeutic and mental health services for children should be enhanced.

Relative merits of fostering and adoption

Although much remains to be explored through future research, we can identify many useful messages from research into the care system. Approximately one-fifth of placements from care to adoptive parents, or permanent foster parents whom the child has not known before, break down within five years of the child being placed, but only 5% of placements of infants placed at birth break down (Sellick et al., 2004). However, we should bear in mind that some children who are adopted or fostered have many needs that cannot easily be met and some placements can be difficult and demanding and can prove painful for adoptive and fostering parents, other children and relatives. Berridge and Cleaver (1987), Howe and Hinings (1989) and Howe (1996) have examined these difficulties, where placements have broken down. While some adults recover from the trauma, others suffer long-term hurt. On a more positive note, if we judge according to the criterion of service users' views, adoption is an effective service. About 80% of all adopters and adults who were adopted state that they are satisfied with their adoptive relationships (Sellick et al., 2004). What we do not know from research is how parents and professionals actually talk with children about the fostering and adoption, about their memories, about the traumas of their lives, and how adoptive parents and children cope with these traumas (Sellick et al., 2004).

Rowe et al. (1989) surveyed nearly 6,000 children and 10,000 placements and found that 53% of the foster care placements were judged successful and 20% unsuccessful. Residential care fared slightly worse, with 46% of placements being deemed successful, although only 16% were judged unsuccessful. Colton et al. (1995) compared 12 children's homes with 12 foster homes and found, in general, that:

- foster homes were more child oriented
- children in foster homes were better linked with the local community

■ the foster children were more positive about where they lived
■ and, interestingly, in view of the poor performance of children in residential care in contrast with those living at home, there were no statistical differences in children's behaviour and educational progress in children's homes and foster homes.

Aldgate and Tunstill (1995) carried out research aiming to complete a national view in England of approaches to implementing section 17 (preventive services for children 'at risk') of the Children Act 1989. In the mid-1990s, local authority resources were concentrated on meeting the needs of so-called 'high-risk' families at the expense of broader, preventive work using family support services. At the same time, there were problems in defining what was meant by children 'at risk'. Aldgate and Bradley (1999) carried out research focusing on 60 children receiving short-term fostering, available under section 20 of the Children Act 1989. This was generally regarded by families and children as positive, although parents and children with chronic needs were best helped by other forms of additional support. This research emphasizes the value of social work as a service to support families.

Research by Cleaver (2000) started with the presumption of the Children Act 1989 that reasonable contact takes place between separated children and families. This research found contact between fostered children and their families has increased. This contact was mainly with mothers, 11% of the children seeing their family on a weekly basis before the Children Act 1989. After the Act was implemented, on average this percentage increased fourfold. The findings of the research suggested that the more parental contact there was during the fostering period, the better the child's behaviour both during fostering and afterwards, when reunited with the parents. At the same time, foster carers were more likely to promote contact if trained, if they understood the purpose, if they got on well with the child and provided they felt they were supported.

Ward (1995) carried out research piloting early LAC (local authority circular) materials, examining issues involved in their implementation by local authorities between 1991 and 1995. The study involved 204 looked after children in five local authorities and a community group of 379 children in 'ordinary' families, as well as an in-depth study of implementation in one of the participating authorities. It was found that the children looked after by the local authority were less likely to receive adequate health and education services than those living with their families. More recently, and more optimistically, Macdonald (2001) concludes on the basis of research that most children benefit from residential as well as foster care. On balance, the evidence suggests that residential care should mainly be reserved for relatively short-term placements.

Key factors affecting outcomes in fostering and adoption

In their detailed research into the process and outcomes of fostering and adoption, Sinclair et al. (2005) identify five key factors:

1. *Permanence:* Despite the fact that foster care is for a limited period whereas adoption and a birth family is 'for life', fostering still needs to offer family care, and a feeling of permanence is part of that care. Sinclair et al. (2005) distinguish between:
   - *objective permanence:* being in a stable setting for a period
   - *subjective permanence:* whether or not the child feels secure
   - *enacted permanence:* whether the foster family treat the child as part of the family
   - *uncontested permanence:* whether there is pressure from relatives or others for the placement to end.
2. *Relationships with birth family:* It is important for the child to feel secure in the foster family, since this makes it possible to view relationships with the birth family more objectively and constructively.
3. *Attachment status:* Fostering is the setting where children explore, with greater or lesser success, issues of attachment in relation to their birth family and the foster family.
4. *School and work:* School is an important setting, outside the foster family, where the child can develop. Where children were happier at school, the research found that the foster placement went better for them.
5. *Working things out:* Foster children, like other children, have to find ways of working out their lives; however, foster care:

   confronts children with questions of blame. There is the question of why they are looked after. There are the related issues of whose fault this is and what this implies for the future and for the relationship with the birth family. Does it mean that the child has never been loved, or that he or she brought this about, or that he or she will never amount to much? Children's answers to such questions may inform their decisions about where they wish to be and what they want to do. (Sinclair et al., 2005, p. 244)

Point for Reflection

Why are the outcomes for fostered and adopted children likely to be different?

Apart from the five factors identified above, Sinclair et al. (2005) note that it is also important how disturbed children are by their experiences prior to being placed with fostering or adoptive parents. The skills of the fostering and adoptive parents matter too, as does their matching with the child being placed. Three particular factors affect the progress of the adoptive or fostering placement:

- The closeness of the relationship between the child and the adoptive or fostering parents
- The general quality of the relationship between the child and the adoptive or fostering parents
- The degree of maturity with which the child is able to reappraise their life, from the safety of a secure placement.

Conclusion

Fostering, adoption and residential care are forms of being looked after by the local authority, which should not be regarded as arranged in a hierarchy of 'goodness' and desirability. They are distinctive options, each with its own advantages and disadvantages, depending on the circumstances. Research can help to highlight the factors that contribute to our understanding of the child's experience of being looked after and set this against evaluations from the vantage point of professionals and other family members. There is a good case for arguing that the child's perceptions should be regarded as paramount.

REVIEW QUESTIONS

1. On the whole, would you reserve fostering or residential care for relatively short-term placements?
2. What is a 'closed' adoption?
3. What are the main advantages of fostering over residential care, from the vantage point of the child?

_____ *Chapter Links* _____

For further discussion of attachment and early development, see Chapter 4.
For discussion of residential care, see Chapter 14.

_____ *Further Reading* _____

Gilligan, R. (2009) *Promoting Resilience* (2nd edn), London, BAAF. Authoritative resource for working with children and young people.

Schofield, G. and Beck, M. (2006) *Attachment Handbook for Foster Care and Adoption*, London, BAAF. An encyclopedic reference book: Part 1 explores concepts and patterns of attachment; Part 2 discusses the components of building a secure, trustworthy, sensitive, accepting, cooperative and inclusive placement; Part 3 explores aspects of relevant theory and practice.

Sellick, C., Thoburn, J. and Philpot, T. (2004) *What Works in Adoption and Foster Care?* Ilford, Barnardo's. A critical review of the literature on the effectiveness of adoption and foster care.

Sinclair, I., Wilson, K. and Gibbs, I. (2004) *Foster Placements: Why They Succeed and Why They Fail*, London, Jessica Kingsley. One of a series of publications following the major study of the effectiveness or otherwise of foster care.

Sinclair, I., Baker, C., Wilson, K. and Gibbs, I. (2005) *Foster Children: Where They Go and How They Get On*, London, Jessica Kingsley. In-depth research into the nature and processes of fostering and adoption, which produces many insights into children's experiences.

Wilson, K., Sinclair, I., Taylor, C. et al. (2004) *Fostering Success: An Exploration of the Research Literature in Foster Care, Knowledge* Review 5, London, SCIE. Useful review of the research into fostering.

Websites

http://www.education.gov.uk/safeguarding/safeguardingchildren/a0068804/private-fostering/
A useful review of policy and practice in relation to private fostering

Working with Children through Residential Care

14

Robert Adams

LEARNING OUTCOMES

By the end of this chapter, you should be able to:

■ understand the nature of residential care
■ have a critical grasp of the strengths and weaknesses of residential care
■ appreciate the importance of messages from research into leaving care
■ discuss implications for family support, future care planning and independence

---

The nature of residential care

Formerly, children were taken 'into the care' of the local authority (see Chapter 1), whereas nowadays they are described as being 'looked after'. Looked after children most commonly are fostered and a small proportion are adopted (see Chapter 13). This chapter discusses a third group, those living in residential care establishments.

Residential childcare in the UK takes place in a range of different settings. In the 19th century, Dr Barnardo, Thomas Bowman Stephenson (1839–1912) and other founders of childcare charities began by setting up large orphanages, run on institutional lines, which catered for children in need. In parallel, there were reformatories, later Home Office approved schools, which, under the Children and Young Persons Act 1969, became community homes with education, which imposed quite structured and often regimented regimes (Millham et al., 1975). So, residential childcare has historically embraced these twin and quite different goals – providing a substitute home for children in need and resocializing children who have committed offences. This has one unfortunate consequence, in that, as Roy et al. (2009) observe, the vulnerability of all children is masked under the label of the few.

On 31 March 2005, there were 60,900 children being looked after by the local authority, 1% less than on 31 March 2004 but 3% more than on 31 March 2001 (DfES, 2005a). It costs a good deal to keep each looked after child. The legal costs associated with the child becoming looked after can run into tens of thousands of pounds. Each child has to be independently legally represented. The weekly cost of keeping a child in a children's home can range from £2,000 to £7,000 per week in some privately run, secure accommodation.

There are blurred boundaries between the uses of residential care for children, since, historically, children who offend have been placed in local authority-run, or paid-for, residential settings alongside children identified as 'in need'.

Point for Reflection

Are there ever circumstances which would justify a child or a young person being locked up in a prison?

A significant proportion – 29% of boys and 44% of girls – of the alarming total of about 3,000 children in prison custody at any one time between 2004 and 2006 have formerly been 'in care', that is, looked after by local author- ities (Worsley, 2007). A small proportion of these have been held in secure accommodation and since the 1970s, there has been increasing concern that secure provision by local authorities provides a less than ideal option (Millham et al., 1978). Campaigning organizations such as the Howard League for Penal Reform (n.d.) argue that the 85% of children and young people in custody, who were held in prison in 2006, tend to come from chaotic family backgrounds, have often experienced abuse and neglect, and cannot have their needs met in penal custody.

The Labour government advocated policy changes in a White Paper (DfES, 2007a), in the light of this continuing evidence of failures in the residential care system. The White Paper noted that during the period 2003–06, the rate of children in care cautioned or prosecuted for criminal offences was a constant 9.6% – three times the rate for other children (DfES, 2007a).

What 'good' residential care looks like

Residential homes vary enormously in their purposes and character, so in a real sense it is impossible to cover their range in this brief account. However, we can briefly describe the features of a 'good' residential home and how it works with children and young people.

A typical residential home for children and/or young people – perhaps aged 12–18 – is likely to be much smaller than the large institutions of previous generations. It probably will look and feel, outside and inside, like a large family home, with about half a dozen children or young people living in it. They might include children and young people with mental health problems, learning difficulties and autism, who may already have had several placements in different children's homes. Care staff in the home will be working as soon as a new child arrives to build relationships and reduce the likelihood of running away. There will need to be a sufficient core group of residents and staff to make the home viable as a family home. Too few young people will leave individuals more isolated from their peers, while too many will risk losing the intimacy and homeliness of the domestic setting. Staff in the home will ideally relate to children and young people as they would to their own families. They will seek to cultivate a family atmosphere in the normal, everyday activities they encourage. These will be both age appropriate and pleasurable, as well as serving the interests of the residential setting. The home will have a garden, perhaps with a play area, a pool with fish and a plot where the children can learn to tend plants and vegetables. There may be a sports area for ball games and a trampoline in fine weather and bicycles for outings in the locality.

Each child will have a personal space, including a single room with the freedom to choose the decoration, a bed, furniture for clothes and somewhere to display pictures, photographs and other items. There will be communal spaces as well, for them to enjoy activities such as computers, television, pool and table tennis, away from staff, as well as with staff. There will be quiet spaces as well as noisy areas. Children and young people will have the power to take part in meetings and other activities leading to decisions about how the home is run. They will have specified rights and, to balance these, responsibilities. There will be occasions when differences or disagreements arise and the staff will have the expertise, ideally, to defuse major aggression and violence and ensure that the children and young people have the experience of working through the inevitable difficulties of 'family' life together.

Younger children will expect the home to offer security and continuity; older children will be looking for growing freedom and responsibility and will be encouraged to take part in local programmes helping them to prepare for independence, a process that basically enables them to equip themselves with the knowledge, skills and resources they need when leaving residential care. Some may return to their former family home, others may seek semi-independence in another less restrictive home, while others may be living independently. Whatever their goals, young people will be encouraged to seek further education, training or work. They will be able to take part in visits to local libraries and sports facilities, including swimming pools. They will have regular outings to nearby towns for shopping and other activities and will be able to visit the seaside. They will have the opportunity of longer holidays, perhaps in other parts of the UK, and on an annual basis. They may be helped initially with preparations for work and given support with transport – perhaps to their destination or to the nearest bus or train. They will be encouraged to open a bank or savings account and will be given help with budgeting, shopping for clothes and food and with cooking for themselves and others in the home.

Children's actual experiences of residential care

Children's and young people's actual experiences of care are, as we would expect, positive as well as negative. Macdonald and Williamson (2002, pp. 275–6) gives a taste of these experiences, beginning with teachers' attitudes to children in care:

> They [teachers] automatically say 'oh you're in a children's home that's why you do that'.

> Schools think because you're in children's homes you're a problem tag not because of your proper family background.

In view of the negative press residential care often receives in the mass media, it is worth noting that children often report positive experiences:

> I mean I was really lucky and the staff that I had there, and I didn't want to leave, I mean I still keep in touch now, I phone them as often as I can. He was really, really funny, he cared…Most of the other staff were pretty much like him as well, but I don't know, there was just something about him because he was really like a father to me. I mean after I moved out he used to come down on the weekends, pick me up, take me out for a drink and I used to stay at his house with him and his wife and all that.

> [my social workers have] just treated me, like an individual, they don't treat me as if I'm someone in care and someone, that's, you know.

Evaluating residential care

The above snapshots of a children's home and children's experiences remind us of its positive qualities, but do not present a balanced evaluation of its contribution to childcare. A good way to think of the decision by the local authority to have a child looked after in residential care is that this comes about only in circumstances where the child's needs cannot be met at home and where, in many cases, the child is likely to be harmed by staying at home. The residential option is preferred where the child has additional needs that cannot be met in foster care or adoption. Thus, in some senses, there is a continuum of preferred options for the child, from the most preferred in the family home to the least preferred in residential care, and residential care should be the positive choice where all other choices are considered to be lacking in significant ways.

Point for Reflection

Is residential childcare necessarily 'bad' childcare?

Over the decades since the 1970s, residential childcare has acquired the reputation of possessing some inherently undesirable characteristics, not least through the succession of media-publicized inquiries into what later emerged as institutional physical abuse (Levy and Kahan, 1991) and sexual abuse (Waterhouse et al., 2000).

While children looked after by the local authority through foster care or residential care may have some very positive experiences, the evidence from research suggests that the experience of leaving the home neighbourhood for significant periods, or being moved from one care setting to another, is not generally positive. Despite the publication by the government in 2000 of principles for local authorities to follow in putting in place good corporate parenting and educational provision for children in care (DH/DfEE/Home Office, 2000), the outcomes for children did not improve. The care system still did not care for children adequately or enable them to reach their full potential. Being in care is a predictor of future social exclusion and anything from a quarter to a half of rough sleepers have previously been in care (SEU, 2003). Research by Sergeant (2006) found the following reasons for children being taken into care, that is, 'looked after' by the local authority:

- abuse or neglect (62%)
- dysfunction of the family (10%)
- one or more parents absent (8%)
- and only 3% through the child's behaviour causing concern.

In 2005, 18% of looked after children had not had a dental check, 20% had not had an annual health assessment and the immunizations of 23.5% were out of date (DfES, 2005b).

Research into the effectiveness of residential care has clear implications for practice. Parker (1988) surveyed different regimes and found that they affect children in different ways. Child-oriented regimes are more helpful to children than those that are institutionally oriented. Heads of home play a key role in shaping the character of the regime. Millham et al. (1978) found many weaknesses in the system of secure units for 'problem' children, not least the need for local authorities to clarify which children should be in them, what education and other treatment they should be offered, and how more focused help should be provided. Bullock et al. (1993) carried out a review of research into residential care, which suggested that regimes that benefit children more in terms of educational attainment and stability can still create secondary problems arising, for instance, from absconding and committing offences. The Audit Commission (2004) found that secure custody is expensive in absolute terms and (see next point below) its cost-effectiveness can be seriously questioned. The question is whether the expense is justified, or whether alternative ways of spending the money could be found. It costs about £165,000 to keep a child in a secure training unit and about £185,000 a year to keep a child in a local authority secure children's home. Overall, residential childcare provides a poor outlook for many children. Children who have been looked after by the local authority in residential care are three times more likely than other children to finish up in prison. About a half of young people in prison custody have been in care and about one in six admit to having been abused (NACRO, 2008).

Placement stability is viewed as secure attachment to a carer who can provide safe and effective care throughout childhood. Instability in placements, historically a problem in residential childcare, has improved. However, Rowe et al. (1989) followed up 2,000 children entering care and found that over the following two years, an encouraging half of these had no moves in care. Of the rest, those aged 14–17 were most prone to moves, with those entering care as offenders most likely to be moved. From this, it is clear that there is an issue concerning how well equipped staff are to manage challenging behaviour.

Children who have not had the benefit of continuity and stability of care throughout childhood are more likely to be excluded from achieving higher educational qualifications, maintaining friendships with their peers, and having access to good employment opportunities. Research by the National Foundation for Educational Research (Fletcher-Campbell and Archer, 2003) found that 47% of the total of care leavers were not entered for GCSE or GNVQ at Key Stage 4, in contrast with 3.6% of boys and 3.1% of girls in the general population. Currently, the percentage of young people leaving care with five GCSE passes is 11%, compared with over 60% of children as a whole. In research following up care leavers in the 21st century, Dixon et al. (2004) reported that more than half, 54%, left care with no educational qualifications of any kind and 47% finished up unemployed.

Educational performance of children in residential care

As indicated above, policy and practice continue to fail to abolish the gap between the education performance of children 'looked after' by the local authority and those living at home. Only 1% of young people leaving care progress to university (Jackson et al., 2003). A Social Exclusion Unit report (SEU, 2003, p. 2) recommended improving the life chances of children by 'substantially narrowing the gap between the educational attainment and participation of children in care and that of their peers by 2006', including improving the percentage of children in care in each local authority who achieved at least five GSCE passes at grades A* to C from 8% to at least 15%. This target was not met for five key reasons identified by the SEU (2003):

- too many children experience instability
- children spend too much time out of school
- children need more help with their education
- a lack of support and encouragement from carers
- the need for children to receive more help with their health and wellbeing.

The government initiated remedial policies to tackle these shortfalls in practice, including appointing a senior person in each local authority to track schools' progress with each child in care (DCSF, 2009b). Driscoll (2010) has researched children's perspectives on their experiences and confirms that many children have contact with too many professionals. She recommends that children would benefit more from a universal system providing a personal tutor to support each person through the educational process.

Lessons from research into leaving care

We have seen how research points to the crucial importance of what happens to children when they leave care; and when this transition is lacking, it tends to highlight shortcomings in their experience throughout their care and the preparations made when they leave care. Stein's report (2004) on children leaving the care system identifies the research messages on the nature and character of the system. About 9,000 children – including care leavers and children under 16 – in England and Wales leave custody every year and go into accommodation judged unsuitable, according to the Audit Commission (2004). Biehal et al. (1995) carried out a survey of specialist leaving care schemes aiming to determine which is most effective in helping young people to move on. This found that young people leave care at 16 and 17 and are still very vulnerable, but 75% of young people with access to a leaving care scheme had positive outcomes after two years, such as good accommodation, regular income, and a sense of purpose. All care leavers, however, had relatively low educational and employment outcomes. There was no ideal blueprint for a leaving care scheme; however, in general, to be effective, they did require a clear purpose, good management and adequate resources. It did not matter whether they were based in the statutory or voluntary sector. Since this research was carried out, the Children (Leaving Care) Act 2000 places new duties on local authorities to give increased support to young people while they are in care and when they leave care, especially as they face the tasks of seeking work, education and training. Local authorities are required to assess and meet the needs of care leavers, help and keep in touch with them.

Family support, future care planning and independence

Colton et al. (1995) carried out a study of services for children in need and their families, provided under Part III of the Children Act 1989, in England and Wales, before local authority reorganization in the eight local authorities in Wales. Interviews were conducted with over 100 social workers, 122 parents and 123 children, asking how far their needs were met and their views taken into account. It was found that there was a lack of guidance on the definition of what children needed. Social workers tended to fall back on child protection materials and rely on them in practice. Managers were not able to prioritize preventive work as they wished to. Some problems with interagency work remained. This research contributed to the broader definition of need, now incorporated into the *Framework for Assessment of Children in Need and their Families* (DH/DfEE/ Home Office, 2000). It also emphasizes the continuing necessity to include the views of children and parents in service planning and delivery.

Allen (2003) researched the transitions to independent living of young people leaving care, in order to identify the factors helping or hindering their progress. She found that, taking the adverse factors from their childhood into account, many young people showed remarkable resilience in overcoming problems, such as lack of a stable background and financial security, in establishing themselves. Support from professionals and through informal networks was important in enabling them to overcome barriers. Emotional support was particularly

---

PRACTICE STUDY: LEAVING CARE

Gemma has been in residential care since she was 10 years old. She will be leaving residential care when she is 18. Her social worker is in touch with the transitions coordinator who sets up a meeting in consultation with Gemma and the leaving care team. Gemma was given a personal adviser when she was 13, who will help her through the review process. The social worker and the personal adviser work with Gemma to complete the joint working document as the outcome of this stage of the process.

The review meeting, attended by Gemma, discusses Gemma's hopes and expectations and any support she needs and any arrangements that need to be made in order to enable her to make the transition from being looked after to supported living in the community. Particular priority is given to her needs – such as housing, education, training, work and leisure – in relation to the goal of her becoming progressively more independent.

valuable. Help with the transition from being 'looked after' to looking after themselves – such as with independent living, budgeting, running a household – was important. Young mothers faced similar problems to other young people making the transition to independence, but often demonstrated more maturity than their peers and made a more rapid transition.

PRACTICE STUDY: TRANSITIONAL PLANNING INTO ADULT SERVICES

Don was allocated a personal adviser from the youth and leaving care team at the age of 13, who has liaised with the social worker from the disabilities team. It is the policy of the local authority that every disabled young people will have a personal adviser. The role of the personal adviser is to ensure that the requirements of the Children (Leaving Care) Act 2000 are met. The social worker will retain responsibility as key worker, on behalf of Don, as he goes through the process of transition from being looked after to relating to adult services. It would have been possible for the social worker to be the personal adviser.

A pathway plan is completed with Don. This identifies opportunities for Don to engage in education and employment to meet his future needs. Particular attention is paid to ensuring that he will be able to attend on a flexible basis and will not be excluded from going through the process of application and entry to mainstream education, training and employment. Attention is paid also to Don's wish to explore the possible benefits to him of direct payments and individual budgets, as he becomes eligible for adult services. Marsh and Peel (1999) suggest that it would be helpful for practitioners doing life story work, for instance, to develop an extended family tree which could be added to the looked after children records, as a resource for this work with the wider family network.

Two of the main factors that matter to children and parents in working towards a high-quality journey of the child through care are reducing the stigma of being in care and enhancing the participation of children and parents in the decision-making process. Aldgate and Statham (2001) conclude from their review of relevant research that this situation would be improved if parents had more clarity about their rights and expectations and a better informed understanding about available services.

Conclusion

Residential care is a necessity for some children in some circumstances where the potential risks of harm through the available alternatives outweigh any other benefits. The relevant literature on the process of transition through care and through leaving care highlights the need for resources to support children and young people.

REVIEW QUESTIONS

1. What particular research findings into the educational performance of children in residential care would you highlight as important?
2. Which residential childcare features, would you suggest, mark it out as 'good' for a child?
3. Why do you think the transition from residential care of a child or young person leaving care is particularly important, for the child and for the practitioner working with the child?

_____ *Chapter Links* _____

For further discussion of looked after children who are fostered or adopted, see Chapter 13.

_____ *Further Reading* _____

Guishard-Pine, J., McCall, S. and Hamilton, L. (2007) *Understanding Looked After Children: An Introduction to Psychology for Foster Care*, London, Jessica Kingsley. A guide to mental health work with looked after children, relevant to those in residential care as well as those in foster care.

Stein, M. (2004) *What Works for Young People Leaving Care?*, Barkingside, Barnardo's. Invaluable and authoritative information in this updated review of the literature on children and young people leaving care.

Thomas, N. (2005) *Social Work with Young People in Care: Looking After Children in Theory and Practice*, Basingstoke, Palgrave Macmillan. Good basic introduction to work with young people in care.

Ward, H. (ed.) (1995) *Looking after Children, Research into Practice, The Second Report to the Department of Health on Assessing Outcomes in Childcare*, London, HMSO. A valuable collection of research papers.

_____ *Websites* _____

http://www.education.gov.uk/childrenandyoungpeople/families/childrenincare/a0065727/children-leaving-care/ Resource materials relating to children leaving care

Children, Grieving and Loss 15

Maggie Jackson

LEARNING OUTCOMES

By the end of this chapter, you should be able to:

- demonstrate theories of grief and grieving relevant to children
- grasp age-related understandings of loss
- understand how children grieve
- grasp ways of talking to children about loss

Loss can be seen as something that occurs naturally at each stage of life. Any change, positive or negative, involves a loss of some sort, but we do not consider all these changes to be losses as such. If you care about someone or something, when it is gone, you will feel the loss. We might call this a grief reaction. Often grief is defined as the emotional reaction to a loss – it is how you feel about it. Grief shows itself not just in emotional responses like crying and feeling sad but also in anger, low energy and lack of concentration or not wanting to be with other people. It might be shown in trying to put on a brave face or being responsible for others. Some children behave badly, others become incredibly well behaved. Some have lots of minor illnesses like colds. You can begin to see that there is a reaction to loss, but how it is shown is varied and it is important to listen and notice these changes so that a helpful response can be made.

This chapter will introduce the idea of children and loss by looking at their understanding of loss, particularly in relation to death; it will then consider how we can talk to children about loss and finally consider the range of situations where children may experience loss other than by a death.

A brief overview of theories of grief and grieving

There are many theories about grief and grieving and it is important to be aware that people grieve in different ways. The theories are helpful to us in order to make sense of the way someone is behaving so that we can help them if and when we need to. Being able to understand some of these theories can also help us to reassure parents and carers of children who are bereaved.

The first theory we will consider is that proposed by Bowlby and Parkes (1970; Bowlby, 1969). They had noticed that children who were separated from their parents or carers, even when this is a temporary separation, display signs of protest, which has three phases: protest, despair and detachment. It seemed apparent to Bowlby and Parkes (1970) that adults showed a similar response in reaction to the death of a partner and they described this as *phases of grief*. According to this, adults go through four phases in coping with the death:

1. Numbness (according to Bowlby and Parkes, 1970) or shock and denial (according to Bowlby, 1969)
2. Yearning and protest
3. Disorganization
4. Reorganization.

It is normal to find the news of the death of someone we love as overwhelming and we are unable to take this in at first, but soon we see that it is real and when we know that the person is not coming back, we long (or yearn) for them – this may even involve searching for them. The disorganization phase is a stage of helplessness and hopelessness and may include depression or extreme sadness and crying. The final phase is one in which, despite the loss, we can resume life in some way without the lost person. For children, it is suggested that they may go through these stages quickly and return to former stages depending on their level of cognitive development (which we will read about later in this chapter).

Another theory that has been proposed more recently is *meaning making* (Neimeyer, 2002). Neimeyer does not give us different stages or phases but says that when we lose someone we love, our 'assumptive world' is shaken and makes no sense any more. (The assumptive world is our taken-for-granted way of seeing the world, that is, that the people we love will be there and we cannot imagine a world without them in it.) So when someone dies, all the things we took for granted feel as if they are no longer true and we strive to make sense of why the person is no longer there. We might be angry or sad or depressed by this, but we still try to make sense of it in our heads. Neimeyer suggests that by being able to make sense of the loss (even if that means we understand the death to be a tragic accident or random act), we are then able to reconstruct a sense of the world in which we can cope in some way. This also fits well with the developmental stages seen below.

A third model that may be helpful to us in understanding the process of grief is the *dual process* model described by Stroebe and Schut (1999). Their model suggests that although we often think it is best for people to talk about their loss and to be emotional, sometimes this is not always how we see people behave. They suggest that people cope with their loss by moving between two orientations: loss orientation and restoration orientation. *Loss orientation* describes the very emotional state we feel – crying, feeling angry or avoiding people and so on; while the *restoration orientation* is getting on with life as best we can. This can look like we have 'got over the loss' or appear to be unfeeling, but Stroebe and Schut suggest that it can be a healthy coping mechanism to take time out from the extreme emotional pain of loss. Although this has not been specifically applied to children, we can recognize that children do move rapidly between these two states and we often can suggest that they have not been affected by a loss because they appear to be getting on with things.

It is clear from this brief overview that there is no one simple explanation that can apply to each person and it is important to understand that we should not try to fit someone into a model, because models are simply explanations of what we think might be happening and may not represent what another person experiences. There are suggestions in Further Reading that will give you a broader explanation of these theories.

How children understand loss

It had been thought for many years that children did not grieve (Corr, 2000). It is not uncommon to hear people say that a child has not really understood about the death of someone because they are too young, or that it was felt it might be too upsetting to tell them. People also sometimes comment that children are resilient and they expect them to cope if they are not told about losses. These things are not helpful and can indeed be harmful. Children do grieve (Dyregrov, 2008), but they may not do it in ways that adults anticipate. What is important is that adults understand the impact a loss might have on a child and consider how the child might be trying to come to terms with it so that we can find the best way of helping the child to make sense of it.

As with other aspects of children's development, they develop an understanding of loss as they grow and develop. This means that a very young child will not understand loss – or react to it – in the same way as an adolescent. It is important to realize that children have different understandings at different ages, so that our expectations of what they can make sense of are appropriate for their age. Piaget has defined this progression and it is seen to be a reasonable understanding of the development of how children understand loss at different ages. Here we will consider an overview of the different developmental stages. Jackson and Colwell (2001) give a fuller explanation of these.

How children under five years understand loss

Very young children do not realize that death is final and often ask questions which show this. They might, for example, ask: 'When will Grandpa come back from his grave?' They might think that the person might return after a holiday. Separations of any sort are difficult for a child to comprehend and so forever and two weeks may seem the same to them. For a young child, the idea that death is a different state from life makes no sense. Questions about whether grandpa will be cold in the ground make sense to them. They do not understand that death is universal, that it happens to everyone, and so may ask questions about who else might die. This can be distressing for the adults to hear, but is part of the process of the child trying to make sense of the world around them.

At this age, a child's thinking is dominated by what we call 'magical thinking'. This means that having bad thoughts or having been 'naughty' might have been the cause of something. For example, a child who had been angry with a parent who subsequently dies might think it was their fault for being angry and that they 'killed' the parent.

How children aged five to ten understand loss

Between five and ten children begin to understand that death is final and irreversible and that all functions cease. They tend to believe that death happens to other people and do not usually imagine it can happen to them. Often they will associate it with old age only. Magical thinking begins to subside, and children have an understanding that outside factors such as accidents and ill health can cause death. They may become interested in the concrete facts and ask questions that adults may find morbid. They may want to know details about the death or the grave. Children at this stage think in concrete terms and are preoccupied with how things work.

How children aged 10–16 understand loss

For most children over the age of 10, their thinking tends to become more abstract. They can understand possibilities and hypothetical situations. They begin to be able to see situations from a variety of viewpoints, not just their own. They will understand that death is not reversible and will know that it can happen at anytime and to anybody, including themselves. However, adolescents often have a feeling that they are invincible and so their behaviour can sometimes suggest that they imagine that only older people and sick people die. Although they can understand the world in a much fuller way at this stage, it is also considered to be an egocentric stage of development, where the search for personal identity is important.

Thinking about personal losses and reactions to them

Point for Reflection

You may not consciously remember when you first thought or heard about death but try to answer the questions in Table 15.1 below and complete the right-hand column, so as to help you think about what your early experiences of death might have been.

Table 15.1 Childhood memories linked with death

Age/stage	Situation	Memory
0–5	Can you remember playing games in which people 'died' and then came back to life?	
	Can you think of any nursery rhymes or songs about 'death'?	
	Did any one talk to you about death? What sort of words did they use?	
5–10	Think about pets or animals that may have died. How did you deal with this? What did you do?	
	Can you remember stories or TV programmes in which someone died – how did you feel/what did you think?	
10–18	Can you remember any incident that made you realize that you too could die?	
	Were there any books/TV programmes/films that made you think about death?	

Talking and communicating with children about loss

Having considered that children have a different understanding of loss at different ages, it is important to think about how we talk to children to help them understand. The way in which we talk to them has to take into account the level of understanding a child might have at any age and should allow for questions and comments that may at first appear to strange.

As we have seen, children understand death and loss in different ways depending on their age, so it is important that we consider the potential impact of the words we use when speaking to children about loss in order to help them understand as fully as possible. Before discussing this, it will be useful to tackle the Point for Reflection below, which concerns the words we use both when talking to children and generally when talking or avoiding talking about death.

Language of death

Point for Reflection
Consider the language used in connection with death, by making two lists under the following headings: Words used to mean 'dead' and Words used to explain to children when someone has died.

Many of the words you have used above will not have been about death, but instead you may have used a way of avoiding saying exactly what we are talking about. Sometimes we talk about 'going to sleep' or that we have 'lost' someone. It is important to be aware that children are mostly very literal in their thinking, so that by using expressions we may feel are more gentle and protective, we may, in fact, be causing them to feel more afraid. What could be more frightening than the thought that going to sleep and dying are the same thing? How scary might it be to think that your parents can lose your grandmother and not even bother to look for her!

The key to effective communication with children is to be open and honest (Jackson and Colwell, 2001). This means that we need to be prepared to answer questions we may find distressing. It is not about giving unnecessary detail, but about being able to listen to the child's questions and providing enough information in a clear way that tells the child it is alright to ask questions and to be unsure, because the adults around them will help them to make sense of it. For example, a fairly common question might be: 'What happens when you die?'

Answering this question from a child is not straightforward and it is important that we bear several things in mind before we give an answer. First, we need to understand what exactly is being asked. Does the child want to know what happens to the body in terms of decay? Do they mean where do you go and if so, are they asking for spiritual information or do they want to know where the grave will be? Perhaps they are asking about what will happen to them and who will look after them. We can see that giving a *right* answer is not going to be easy – but providing an easy, what might seem to be a more gentle answer can do a lot of harm.

As we have seen, children's ability to understand changes as they grow older and this is important to keep in mind, as we need to help children to achieve what is called 'cognitive mastery'. This means we need to help them make sense of things in the way they are able at the stage they are at. Often children will ask the same question many times. This is not an indication of lack of understanding as such, but rather is evidence that they are trying to make sense of it and to fit it into their current understanding of the world. For many adults, this can be distressing because having told a child some upsetting information, we may then be asked to go over the same thing frequently, but it is important that we are ready and able to do so. As the child develops in their understanding, they may well revisit old questions as they now are able to make sense of the information in a new way and have new insights into the meaning. We sometimes, mistakenly, take this to mean that a child did not understand earlier on or is in someway distressed, but this may not be the case. We know that children like to hear familiar stories over and again, and it is the same with difficult information. Children need time to process information and to fit it into their worldview.

It is important to bear in mind that when bereavement happens in childhood, often the world around the child changes as well. Parents may be too distressed to cope with the child in the same way, so there may be changes of home and school. Sometimes children are sent to live with other family members for a while, so that they suffer not one loss but multiple losses. This means that it is more important still to be clear and honest with the child about why changes have occurred. It can feel that suddenly everything they knew has disappeared and the world has become unpredictable and frightening. We all live our lives in a way that assumes that there are things we can rely on being the same from day to day. This is our assumptive world – we go to bed in the evening expecting that the kitchen will still be there when we get up, we expect that our clothes will still be in the wardrobe and so on. When major losses occur, this simple expectation of things staying the same and being predictable is damaged. We thought daddy would always be there. But if he is not and no one explains why, then what else could suddenly change? This is why it is crucial to help children make sense of loss.

Point for Reflection

It is useful to reflect on other experiences of loss. Try doing this by compiling the following two lists: all the things a child might experience as a loss, and things you remember as losses from your own childhood.

How children may cope with losses other than death

Having considered how children might cope with loss through death and what we need to bear in mind when talking with and trying to help them, we will now try to think about loss in a broader sense. In the lists you have made above, you will have considered a wide range of events. These may have included such things as being temporarily lost at the shops when very young, losing a favourite toy, moving house or changing schools. The lists will have been quite diverse and the impact of loss is dependant on how much it matters to you, that is, it is about how attached you are to it. Attachments help us to feel safe and secure, so the loss of something that makes us feel safe will inevitably make us feel unsafe, whatever the thing that is lost is. It is not just about people.

Losses can occur through divorce, as we know. Sometimes the impact of this on a child can be far more devastating than adults like to think. This is because the loss is often not just of one parent on a regular basis, but can include the loss of the family home, loss of school, loss of friends, loss of grandparents and loss of lifestyle. There is a tendency for us to focus on only the immediate and obvious loss and to minimize the real impact of such losses.

In adoption and fostering situations, the same issues can apply. Although we may focus on the benefits to the child, sometimes the sheer volume of the potential losses and the lack of predictability of the future because of those losses can make it hard for the child to use their normal coping abilities and so they may become difficult in their behaviour. They may become aggressive or silent and withdrawn; they may regress to earlier childish behaviour. In fact we may see all of the range of behaviours connected with bereavement, but if the adults consider only the positive aspects of the change, they may dismiss the child's real concerns.

Listening to the child is the key to helping them cope with change. Easy answers are not helpful and may cause the child to stop talking to adults because they will realize that they do not want to hear about the child's sadness or anger. As we saw earlier, honest communication, even when the only answer is that we do not know the answer, is more helpful to the child as they are trying to make sense of a puzzling, confusing and unpredictable world.

One way of helping us to talk to children about difficult and painful things is to use common or shared experiences. A good source of these is to refer to films, TV programmes or books that are familiar to the child. It can be a 'way in' to addressing difficult feelings by sharing a story or watching a film together. With older children, it may be possible just to refer to the film without sitting through it together. The benefit of this approach can be that the child can talk about the situation as if it was not about them. We call this 'projection'. It allows us to think about painful things but at a distance and then when we are able, we can see that some of those feeling may also apply to us. It is not avoidance; it can be a healthy way of coping.

Another benefit of using films and books is that the hard words we might have been trying to avoid saying have already been addressed in the film. The film *Toy Story 2* considers some sad and painful feelings about loss and separation, but does so within the context of a happy ending and at a safe distance, in that it is about the toys. The ending is, however, tinged with sadness as the toys realize that one day they will lose 'their child'. Consider the issues involved in *The Tigger Movie*. Tigger wants to belong. He has no family and so tries to be like the others. These are clearly things of concern to some children but because they are being talked about by familiar toys and cartoon creatures, they are at one remove, that is, the painful feelings they can stir up are at a distance, but we can talk about those feelings in relation to Tigger, knowing that the child will understand because they feel the same way too, even when they don't want to say so.

You may wish to make a list of the films and books that talk about painful subjects in a way that is accessible to children.

Conclusion

We have seen that children develop their understanding of loss over time and that this changes as their cognitive ability increases. The words we use to talk to them are important and can help them to understand and feel safe asking questions, or can cause distress by giving confusing information. Being honest and open, being prepared to repeat the same information many times and accepting that the child cannot be made better by easy words will help the child cope. This is sometimes the hardest thing for an adult to do, as we sometimes wish that children did not have to experience the horrible things in life. We think we are being kind by offering reassurance, but often this is really lying but is sugar coated. Honesty is hard when we feel we want to comfort the child, but is best because it helps the child to begin to make sense of the world and regain some sense of control and predictability again.

REVIEW QUESTIONS

1. What are some helpful models of understanding loss?
2. How might a child under five understand loss?
3. What issues are important in terms of the language used to talk to children about loss and death?

_____ *Chapter Links* _____

For discussion of the importance of attachment, see Chapter 4.
For discussion of fostering and adoption, see Chapter 14.

_____ *Further Reading* _____

Currer, C. (2007) *Loss and Social Work*, Maidstone, Learning Matters. Useful text that relates theories to practice.
Holland, J. (2001) *Understanding Children's Experiences of Parental Bereavement*, London, Jessica Kingsley. Helpful exploration of the experience of bereavement.

Ribbens-McCarthy, J. (2006) *Young People's Experiences of Loss and Bereavement*, Maidenhead, Open University Press. Relevant examination of how young people experience losses, including bereavement.

Websites

www.compassionbooks.com Books, DVDs and audios to help children and adults through serious illness, death and dying, grief, bereavement and losses of all kinds

www.leedsanimation.org.uk Leeds Animation Workshop was set up in 1976 to produce and distribute animated films on social issues

The following films and books are useful resources in talking to children.

Films

The Tigger Movie (2000) Disney. Tigger wants to belong and goes on a search to feel a sense of belonging in the wood. Issues about not feeling the same as others are considered here.

Toy Story 2 (2001) Disney Pixar. Woody is abandoned and forgotten about. Belonging and being loved, remembering and forgetting are the issues considered in this film.

Books

Brown, M. (1998) *When Dinosaurs Die: A Guide to Understanding Death*, Boston, Little, Brown. A friendly, colourful book to teach children about death. It covers what death means, feelings about death, customs and remembering life.

Holmes, M. (2000) *A Terrible Thing Happened: A Story for Children who Have Witnessed Violence or Trauma*, Atlanta, GA, Dalmatian Press. A gently told story that may be helpful to children who have witnessed a violent or traumatic incident. There are useful suggestions for carers at the end.

Moser, A., Thatch, N. and Melton, D. (1996) *Don't Despair on Thursday: The Children's Grief Management Book*, Kansas City, Landmark Editions. A good way of talking to 9- to 12-year-old children about grief.

Scrivania, M. (1996) *I Heard your Daddy Died*, Omaha, NE, Centering Corp. Written in a simple style for children between two and six, it is a helpful tool for families and carers.

Part 4

Ethics, Values and Professional Practice

Working Ethically with Children

16

Alison Cocks and Robert Adams

LEARNING OUTCOMES

By the end of this chapter, you should be able to:

- appreciate the meaning of 'values', 'ethics' and 'principles of practice'
- discuss the difficulty of arriving at a statement of values
- understand the values and ethical standards for those working with children
- set out the basis for ethical practice

Values, ethics and principles of practice

Point for Reflection

When considering work with children, what do the terms 'values', 'ethics' and 'principles of practice' mean to you?

It is difficult to explain ethics, values and principles of practice in a limited space, because there are a number of different angles from which ethics and values can be approached, such as philosophical, professional or political (Banks, 2008). In this chapter, our concern is with the professional perspective, looking at the definitions and guidelines that shape day-to-day practice with children.

Ethics tends to refer to our broader concerns with the morals and morality that exist within society (Banks, 2001). They can reflect the moral values of individuals, social groups or society as a whole, helping us to understand how we make moral judgements, for example how we know right from wrong. They also act as a reference point for us when making judgements and decisions, as they shape the moral norms and codes that we live by in the UK. For example, we believe that children should be protected from harm, so this guides our actions in relation to providing for them.

Values are difficult to define as they tend to be used in a variety of different ways according to the situation. Banks (2001, p. 6) states that in relation to social work, the term 'values' 'seems frequently to be used to mean a set of fundamental moral/ethical principles to which social workers are/should be committed'. It is often quite difficult to argue against values because they are so detached and generalized, but it is equally difficult to argue for them because they offer little in the way of hooks on which to hang particular pointers for practice. One such is 'social justice', which, when viewed simply, is a noun with an adjective attached, however, it can also be interpreted as the core of a value statement.

Principles of practice are statements about desirable ways of working, which usually relate explicitly or implicitly to statements of ethical standards and are rooted in values. For example, the Children's Workforce Development Council (CWDC, 2008a) has a statement of values in its corporate plan, setting out principles and ethics that will promote equality and diversity.

However, within all these terms, there is an overlap in the way they can be used, creating confusion about how we apply them. This is particularly the case as we view children within a range of moral frameworks that contradict each other, thus providing an unclear structure in which to work with children. This is not necessarily a negative thing as it encourages us to consider the issues in each situation, using reflexivity to find our way through the range of perspectives and guidelines. *Reflexivity* is the process by which we use our emotions and thoughts in the light of our own experience to help us to reflect on, and understand, people and situations external to ourselves.

Universal core values of practice are contested

It is difficult to visualize reaching a universally (internationally) agreed statement of core ethics, values and principles of practice for working with children, young people, parents and other family members. We live in a culturally diverse world. Children inhabit a particularly problematic situation in UK society. To all intents and purposes, childhood is marginalized as a temporary and transitional status (Wyness, 2006), the consequence being that children are excluded from occupying any real position within society. At the same time, adult attitudes to children are ambiguous. On the one hand, children – especially older children and adolescents – are regarded as inherently troublesome, perhaps because of the widespread perception that 'it's a phase they go through at this age' (Henderson et al., 2007). On the other hand, children are regarded as particularly vulnerable, partly due to their relative physical and emotional frailty in contrast with adults and partly because of their perceived immaturity in developmental terms (James and James, 2008).

The situation of children is made even more problematic when we consider their position within the social structure, which amounts to them being widely regarded as having 'needs' in one sense and 'interests' in another sense (Wyness, 2006, p. 46). These two sets of ideas lead in two quite different directions.

To take children's needs first, this notion relates to the common assumption that childhood is in some senses a period of 'deficit'. We can find the expression 'children in need' frequently during a casual reading of government policy documents and legislation, mass media publications, and academic and professional childcare literature about the personal, social and economic disadvantages experienced by many children. Thus childhood is defined by adults as a period of intrinsic 'need', justifying the intervention of adults in a range of roles (parents, professional, social workers, youth workers and so on) in children's lives. Adults are therefore seen to be acting as protectors and carers of children's lives until such time when children 'grow out of it' and become proper people, that is, adults (Archard, 2004). On close examination, this view of children 'in need' is evident throughout each of the outcomes aimed for within the Every Child Matters (ECM) agenda.

The focus on children's interests has increased significantly in the past decade, and views children as anything but deficit or dependent on adults. Here children are regarded as having 'interests' and 'rights' themselves, as able to exercise their voice directly, speak for themselves, articulate demands, contribute to shaping policies and services and hold agencies to account for shortcomings in those services (Goddard et al., 2005).

Since the late 1990s, the rights of children have been promoted, in the light of the UN Convention on the Rights of the Child (UNCRC) (UN, 1989) and the Human Rights Act 1998. This has been incorporated into UK policy such as *Every Child Matters* (DfES, 2003a) and the Children Act 2004, leading to the appointment of children's commissioners in the four countries of the UK, whose role it is to safeguard children's rights and 'give children and young people a voice in government and in public life' (DfES, 2003a).

In the ECM agenda, which is the key driver for how we are expected to work with children, there is a paradox, where those working with children are expected to meet children's 'needs', protecting their vulnerability, while also respecting their 'interests', in the shape of rights, ensuring that children's voices are heard. In this way, adults are then positioned as guardians or gatekeepers through which children's needs are met and their rights recognized. This is a complex balancing act, fraught with conflict and tensions, for those working with children, as decisions often need to prioritize 'needs' over 'rights' (or vice versa). Consider the issues within the case study below, identifying the conflicts that you might have to work with.

Identifying the complexities of a situation is only the beginning of ethical practice, as you then need to make decisions and find a balance within these tensions. To understand how those working with children can do this, it is useful to consider the role of professional bodies in shaping principles of practice that

PRACTICE STUDY

Sarah was 12 years old when her mother refused to allow her to remain living at home, stating that her violent outbursts were a threat to her younger step-siblings, one of whom had bruising to her upper arm as a result of being hit by her sister. Sarah was adamant that the only place she wished to be was at home. On arrival at a residential placement, her behaviour deteriorated significantly, causing material damage to the building.

1. To what extent was Sarah's problematic behaviour rooted in her feelings about home and how far was it a consequence of her placement in the residential setting?
2. How might you work with Sarah's views and opinions of her situation?

This family presented with multiple needs and risks that needed to be addressed by the professionals supporting them. Sarah was in need of acceptance from her family and was experiencing distress at their rejection of her – this carried with it the potential for more long-term psychological damage. However, the younger siblings were at immediate risk of further harm if Sarah lived at home. To return home was not a possibility, for three reasons:

1. the mother refused
2. the threat this posed to the younger siblings
3. relations between family members were at breaking point.

Sarah was allocated a key worker who spent a considerable amount of time listening to Sarah, building her self-esteem and helping her to reflect on her violent outbursts with a view to reducing their frequency and intensity. Three months later, Sarah was still living in a residential unit, but, with the support of workers and her mother, she began visits home at weekends, which were planned and carefully monitored.

guide everyday decision making. Hugman (2005, p. 28), drawing on the work of Banks (2001), explains:

> The way in which we should examine the fit between personal morality and public ethics is through a framework that the *person* takes on the role of the *profession* that in turn requires the performance of a *job or tasks*, all of which is set in the context of *social norms*.

Different professional bodies have developed their own statements of professional values, which translate into principles for practice. However, in the past decade, there has been a growing awareness of the need to work together to provide consistent and integrated services to children and their families. This has been led by the Children's Workforce Development Council (CWDC, 2010a), which has set out the 'one children's workforce framework'. This encapsulates the vision for an integrated workforce, incorporating all the professions, which has the following key features:

- Shared identity, purpose and vision
- Common values and language
- Behaviours focused on positive outcomes for children and young people

- Integrated working practices
- High-quality, appropriately trained workforce
- Complementary roles focused around children and young people
- Capacity to deliver and keep children and young people safe
- Outcomes focus.

The principles of a shared value base between the range of professions working with children is also carried forward in the 'common core of skills and knowledge', defined by the CWDC with the Department for Children, Schools and Families (CWDC, 2010b). In the introduction to the common core is the statement that:

> The common core reflects a set of common values for practitioners that promote equality, respect diversity and challenge stereotypes. It helps to improve life chances for all children and young people, including those who have disabilities and those who are most vulnerable. It provides more effective and integrated services. (CWDC, 2010b, p. 2)

So professionals have a number of guidelines, from their own professional body and the CWDC, to which they can turn when attempting to find a way to resolve the tensions caused by the complexity of ethics and values. In addition to this, there is an increasing pressure on professionals and practitioners to positively encourage the participation of children.

Participation by children

Participation has been identified as the 'new orthodoxy' (Badham, 2004) in working with children; indeed, it is given a central position within the ECM agenda, and refers to all aspects and levels of children's lives. However, when working with children, it is important to understand what participation really means to the children we are likely to be working with. The concern with participation has been informed by two changes in the way we understand childhood: sociologically and from a rights perspective. The sociology of childhood has promoted children's capacity, independence and ability to interact with the world around them, and thus their ability to voice those views and perceptions of their lives (see Chapter 3). At the same time, rights activists have argued that we move beyond advocacy through listening, respecting and responding to children's views.

At the national level, this is evident in groups such as Funky Dragon (http://www.funkydragon.org/), which is a well-established children and young people's consultation panel within the Welsh Parliament. At a more local level, decisions that impact on children's lives in schools, for example, are guided by school councils and youth councils. However, practitioners working directly with children on a day-to-day level are also expected to promote children's participation in the decisions that will affect their lives.

Example of participation

Participation Works (http://www.participationworks.org.uk/) has developed resources to guide practitioners working with children and young people within a range of settings. At the heart of its guidelines are the key principles that participation needs to be a positive, fun, inclusive and engaging experience for all children. The Children Now Participation Charter, drawn up in partnership with Participation Works, states that:

- Participation is a right
- Children and young people are the best authorities on their own lives
- Participation depends on respect and honesty
- Participation must be accessible and inclusive
- Participation is a dialogue to influence change
- Participation is built in
- Participation is everyone's responsibility
- Participation benefits everybody.

In order to ensure good practice in relation to participation, practitioners need to make a commitment to its practice. Kirby et al. (2003b) identify a number of key aspects in practice with children that encourage positive participation. Central is building positive relationships, which are reciprocal and where power imbalances are recognized. They recommend that this can be accomplished by achieving trust and respect between child and adult, respecting individuality by encouraging a child to talk about their own views and experiences rather than assuming that we, as adults, already know their thoughts. This comes about through dialogue between an adult and child – where there is openness and honesty, and where conversations are constructive. Where choices are raised and considered, children need to be provided with information that is appropriate to their age and ability. And once dialogue has happened, children also need to see action and receive feedback so that they know how their views are being implemented, and if not, why not.

Identifying your own values

So far, this chapter has established that the balance between professional frameworks and the legal imperative to include children in decision-making processes is difficult to achieve, especially when you consider the third dynamic, which is the impact of your own values and moral base, as touched upon in the earlier quote from Hugman (2005). This mix of personal and professional can pose challenges to even the most experienced practitioner.

A key starting point lies in being able to identify your own values and their origins, which might lie in your culture, gender, generation, experience, religion, sexuality, or social class (Banks, 2001). There might be values within you which will not resonate with the work you are doing. For example, if your religion does not condone homosexuality, you might find it difficult to work with parents who are in a civil partnership. This would challenge core beliefs within you, while professional values anticipate that you will treat these parents with respect, regardless of their sexuality. The first way to address this is through reflection and reflexive practice. The following activity illustrates one way in which you can begin to identify your own values.

Point for Reflection

Choose a story that has received wide media coverage, for example the reports about the death of Baby Peter in 2007. Read through five articles from newspapers (you can access all the daily papers online). Then consider which is the most informative, emotive, or political. Can you identify the value base of each of the authors by considering the language used?

Identifying personal values is an ongoing process for all practitioners working with children; as our own experiences and lives change, it is imperative that we are aware of their impact on our assessments, decisions and actions. When working in multiprofessional teams, this ability to be reflexive becomes an essential part of working alongside others who are informed by their own professional ethics and personal values (Hugman, 2005). If difficulties arise due to the different values held by team members, it is advisable to use supervision as the place to reflect on and address those differences.

'I have a secret'

An area that often causes difficulty for practitioners when working directly with children is that of confidentiality and knowing when to share information and with whom. While space precludes detailed consideration of information sharing among professionals, we feel that it is critical to explore the process of knowing what to do when a child wishes to share something 'in confidence' with you. No practitioner is in a position to promise to keep a child's secret. This is because secrets can contain information of abuse, tales of a child's vulnerability and vital information that might help others to piece together the experiences within a child's life. Thus there are limits of confidentiality (Cocker and Allain, 2008).

What practitioners can do, however, is listen to children, and explain to them that if they do disclose a worry or a concern, then it will be shared. The practitioner needs to explain to the child that information will only be shared after the child understands who will be informed, why it is of concern and what will happen next. In doing this, communication is kept open and honest, in order to maintain trust for any ongoing work that will be necessary. More often than not, the first person you will consider sharing information with will be your supervisor.

There are a range of situations that might arise when working directly with children where the role and input of supervision becomes an essential element of ensuring that you are working ethically and appropriately. For example, much information about what goes on in a disrupted or abusive situation will be sensitive. The child and other family members have the right to have the information treated confidentially. Normally, permission would be sought from the people concerned before confidentiality was broken. In situations involving very young children, those acting in the role of parents would be asked. There are, of course, exceptions, for example in situations when, in order to safeguard the child, information about the child has to be shared between professionals, whether or not consent is given by the child or family members. It is common practice for agencies to have a policy in relation to this, which will guide those directly working with children. It is also important to recognize the key role of supervision in deciding whether to share information.

Supervision is a central aspect of ensuring that the direct work of all people in contact with children – including managers, supervisors, senior staff and students – is ethically sound, adheres to the principles of practice of the profession, and reflects the policies and aims of the agency. It also provides an essential support for individual workers in reflecting upon the development of their day-to-day practice (Wilson et al., 2008).

Conclusion

In this chapter, we have considered the differences between ethics, values and the principles of practice, highlighting that there is no one answer to the dilemmas you may come across when working directly with children. We have looked at the professional bodies that offer practitioners guidelines on working ethically. In addition, we have highlighted the value of engaging with reflective and reflexive practice. To conclude, we have considered confidentiality and the important role supervision plays in guiding and supporting the ways in which you work.

REVIEW QUESTIONS

1. What tensions exist in meeting children's needs while also supporting their interests?
2. How could you promote the participation of children in decisions that affect their lives?
3. How might you explain the limits of confidentiality in talking with a child.

Further Reading

Alderson, P. and Morrow, V. (2002) *Ethics, Social Research and Consulting with Young People*, Barkingside, Barnardo's. Explains and explores how we can engage with children, and covers a number of central ethical principles, such as informed consent.

Ayre, P. and Preston-Shoot, M. (eds) (2010) *Children's Services at the Crossroads: A Critical Evaluation of Contemporary Policy for Practice*, Lyme Regis, Russell House. Stimulating series of chapters on key aspects of policy and practice.

Broadhurst, K., Grover, C. and Jamieson, J. (eds) (2009) *Safeguarding Children: Critical Perspectives on Safeguarding Children*, Oxford, Wiley-Blackwell. Collection of critical commentaries raising ethical issues and practice principles on aspects of practice including looked after children, health, refugees and asylum seekers, and youth justice.

Websites

http://www.participationworks.org.uk/ Participation Works Contains guidance notes for practitioners on how to work effectively when including children in decision-making processes

http://www.11million.org.uk/ The children's commissioner for England website outlines the aims of the commissioner and describes current projects relating to improving the lives of children in England

Participation by Children, Parents and Carers

17

Pat Watson and Wade Tovey

LEARNING OUTCOMES

By the end of this chapter, you should be able to:

■ understand the concept of participation
■ explore relevant research and the policy drivers for the participation of children and parents
■ appreciate ethical issues
■ examine issues raised by participation
■ appreciate the importance of engaging with groups as well as individuals
■ demonstrate awareness of the methods used to facilitate the active participation of children and parents

---

Point for Reflection

In what ways is participation by children important in different aspects of their lives?

There are two main reasons why it is important to include children in decisions made about their lives:

1. The UK government signed up to the UN Convention on the Rights of the Child (UNCRC) (UN, 1989) (see Chapter 1).
2. The government has made this a priority in, for example, *Every Child Matters* (DfES, 2003a) and the standards of the *National Service Framework for Children, Young People and Maternity Services* (DH/DfES, 2004a) (see Chapter 1).

Concept of participation

Participation and involvement are often used interchangeably, but they do mean different things. Adams (2008a, p. 31) defines these as:

Involvement refers to the entire continuum of taking part, from one-off consultation through equal partnership to taking control

Participation refers to that part of the continuum of involvement where people play a more active part, have a greater choice, exercising more power and contribute significantly to decision making and management.

Participation is multifaceted, not just in terms of who will or should participate but also within the many aspects of participation itself. When discussing participation, not only are there different acts of participation but also different levels of participation. Consultation tends to form the basis for much participation but in itself cannot be classified as true participation, as participants have little control over the methods of consultation or the topic area. Although having an opportunity to give views and opinions is a start on the ladder of participation, the road to more effective participation is not easy to achieve. For children, it is not just about a right to participate but also a key to child development.

Research is another area where the participation of key audiences, for example children and parents, is often essential. It is important to access the views of the target groups, and provide evidence of their views and perspectives, as opposed to the views of what either researchers or outsiders, or, in the case of children, what adults feel to be the case. Over the years, the participation of children and harder to reach groups has developed but has yet to become common practice, largely because of the challenges we shall discuss later.

Early work in this area evolved around the provision of preschool services and the emergence of the playgroup movement in the 1960s. Pugh et al. (1987) developed a framework of involvement for parents. This was mainly linked to empowerment and was based on the following stages:

- nonparticipation
- support
- participation
- partnership
- control.

This framework identified the progression from nonparticipation to absolute control. However, within each stage, there were a number of variables, for example choice, extent of involvement, contributions and partnerships. This framework has continued to be adapted and updated and many variations now exist. Earlier versions include the Arnstein model (1969), which was aimed at adults, and later Roger Hart's (1992) ladder of participation, which he developed and adapted for children and young people (Figure 17.1). These are still used as the benchmark to measure levels of participation today.

While the momentum of participation continues, progress to achieving the higher levels of participation appears slow. Greater headway has been achieved in developing countries, both in terms of research and informing policy and practice. There are many examples of participation of children and parents supported by research and carried out by nongovernmental organizations (NGOs) operating in the developing world, and there is much to be learned from their practice and methodologies and also in embedding participatory processes in policy. NGOs often lean towards a rights-based approach and they have done a lot of work involving parents and older children (quite often aged eight plus), focusing on their right to be heard rather than working within those institutions that have the greatest impact on younger children's lives, for example schools, healthcare and early years provision. Overseas work is often regarded as the foundation for developing the participatory culture in the UK and provides some interesting debates and methodologies that will help to increase understanding. However, participation of younger children, even in developing countries, still lags behind that of older children.

The Department of Health and the Department for Education and Skills – now the Department for Education – have also begun to promote participation. Kirby et al. (2003b) developed a handbook for the Department for Education

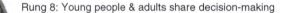

Rung 8: Young people & adults share decision-making

Rung 7: Young people lead & initiate action

Rung 6: Adult-initiated, shared decisions with young people

Rung 5: Young people consulted and informed

Rung 1: Young people assigned and informed

Rung 3: Young people tokenized*

Rung 2: Young people are decoration*

Rung 1: Young people are manipulated*

Note: Hart explains that the last three rungs are *non-participation*

Figure 17.1 Hart's ladder of young people's participation

Source: Adapted from Hart (1992). Reproduced with permission of UNICEF International Child Development Centre, Florence

and Skills (DfES) for building a culture of participation for involving children and young people in policy, service planning, delivery and evaluation.

The Healthy Care Programme, funded by the DfES, was developed by the National Children's Bureau. It grew out the National Health Care Standard, a national initiative to develop healthcare standards for looked after children, and incorporates the principle that looked after children and young people should participate throughout the entire process of healthy care – from initial audit and action through to reviewing and evaluating progress – with their carers and have their rights and responsibilities respected (Chambers, 2005). It illustrates that it is both possible and useful to consult with children.

There appears to be a perception that the lives of younger children (eight and under) should be controlled by parents, carers or professionals. To date, advocates of this view have been less proactive in the debates on children's rights, as there is a tendency for them to focus on promoting children's development rather than respecting and protecting their rights.

PRACTICE STUDY

A group of parents attend the local community centre on a regular basis. They are regularly involved in fundraising events and help to organize social events. They have now taken on a voluntary role to help out with the children's groups. Part of this new role will entail listening to the children's views and opinions and taking these on board.

1. How do you think they could do this and are there any issues that need to be addressed before they can actually start?

2. Looking at the ladder of participation above, what level of participation are they achieving now, explain why and say what needs to happen for them to move up to the next rung of the ladder.

Understanding relevant research

There is now a clear view that the participation of children and parents enables practitioners to gain new understandings about the priorities of children's lives. Participation in the shaping of services is another area of research. There is a lot of research showing the benefits of participation of children; however, this has again predominantly involved children aged eight and over. The involvement of children under eight is beginning to evolve, although not at the same pace as that of older children and youths.

There are an increasing number of projects that have now been evaluated using, as a priority, the participation of younger children and parents. Sure Start centres have developed a set of core principles for the involvement of children and young people and this is embedded in all their practice

(Lloyd et al., 2003) (see also Chapter 1). This also included research on the involvement of parents in local programmes and placed some emphasis on the involvement of fathers.

Children's rights

The reality of participation is very different. The right of children to have a say, be listened to and make decisions that affect their lives is no longer argued. Alderson (2001) maintains that children's rights remain an area of contention, and the idea that young children under eight years can think, comment and participate effectively is particularly seen as misguided but also as an attack on the rights of the family. Alderson challenges the lack of implementation of the UNCRC (UN, 1989). She demonstrates how infants and young children can actively be involved in choices and decision making and shows where their views have been incorporated into practice.

Ethical issues

Another common thread is the ethics of involving children in research. Morrow and Richardson (2002) focus on how children are positioned as 'vulnerable, incompetent and powerless' in society. Punch (2002) explores the differences in carrying out research with children as compared with adults and the dilemmas these differences create for adult researchers working with children. Cree et al. (2002) go on to argue that there are significant gaps between the principles of good practice in research with children and the practical realities of conducting the research.

What becomes very clear across the research is that involving younger children is challenging. It requires high levels of skills and creativity, and can be time-consuming and expensive. Ethical guidelines for the involvement of children and young people in research are also much stricter. It is, however, rewarding for staff to overcome these challenges, aids in children's development and is also of real benefit to service provision. Alderson has been and continues to be a key influence in researching the involvement of children, and challenges adult perceptions of children, the power base between adults and children, and also the capabilities of young children to participate.

Barriers to involvement continue to be a key area of research and even though participation continues to increase, the truth remains that for many individuals, organizations and institutions, there still needs to be a change in adult attitudes and often a major cultural shift or institutional change to adopt a truly participatory approach.

PRACTICE STUDY

A local authority is regenerating a housing estate. It has agreed that there is a need to ask children under eight what they feel is needed with regard to play space and equipment. It also wants parents to have a major input to these plans. Involving local children and parents in local authority planning is a major change in practice for this local authority.

1. Discuss the challenges and barriers local authority staff may face in involving children and parents and explore what needs to change to overcome these barriers and bring about effective participation.

Point for Reflection

What kinds of ethical issues does participation raise for the practitioner who wants to engage young children in their own right?

Contemporary issues of participation

Participation as a research topic has continued to grow and there is now clear evidence of such research feeding into and becoming part of new and emerging government policy. A key driver for participation of children was the UNCRC (UN 1989), which focuses on the rights and protection of children. Article 12 clearly states that:

> States Parties shall assure to the child who is capable of forming his or her own views the right to express those views freely in all matters affecting the child, the views of the child being given due weight in accordance with the age and maturity of the child.

Although ratified by governments around the world, implementation has been slow. However, it did form a baseline on which to build and develop a more active culture of participation. In addition to the UNCRC, more recent government legislation such as *Every Child Matters* (DfES, 2003a), *Every Parent Matters* (DfES, 2007b) and the Childcare Act 2006 all actively promote the participation of children and parents. Major government initiatives, such as the New Deal for Communities, Sure Start, the Children's Fund and Neighbourhood Renewal, all have an underlying philosophy of developing capacity and participation, to the extent that such participation must be evidenced throughout and is a strict requirement of funding.

The participation of parents and children remains high on the government agenda. Although agendas and policies actively promote and encourage the participation of parents and children, the challenges continue to be a barrier to effective participation. While there are growing examples of good practice on how to achieve participation, particularly in communities, many profession-als remain reluctant to integrate such an approach within their organizations. Participation is not just about getting people to take part and voice their opin-ions, it is about taking those views forward to action. This is often seen as a challenge to adult power and control and it requires a major shift in institutional practice to accept and value input from children and nonprofessional adults and for this input to inform practice, as opposed to the professionals taking control, making the decisions they feel need to be taken. There is certainly a lack of involvement of children under five, as this needs certain skills and an aptitude for working with this age group. It also challenges a long-term belief that under fives are unable to participate effectively.

Lansdown (2005) supports the view that the majority of this work focuses on children over eight. Many of the participatory approaches lean towards activi-ties promoting 'being heard' or 'being listened to', rather than working within those institutions that have the greatest impact on younger children's lives, such as family, school, healthcare and early years provision. The lack of focus on younger children's participation reflects the challenges it poses.

The new Early Years Foundation Stage (EYFS; DfE, 2008) brings together the *Curriculum Guidance for the Foundation Stage* (QCA, 2000), *Birth to Three Matters* (DfES, 2002) and the *National Standards for Under 8s Day Care and Childminding* (DfES, 2003b) and brings into policy a flexible approach to care and learning (see also Chapter 1). The EYFS framework dictates inclusive practice involving children and parents. It promotes good partnerships with parents in the care of children and also encourages and facilitates children to make their own decisions in accordance with their age and developmental stage.

In accordance with EYFS practice, a national network promoting the voices of young children has been established. The National Children's Bureau (NCB) is leading this initiative and local networks are being established across the country. The DCSF (now the Department for Education) has recently commis-sioned the NCB to consult with young children to find out about their experi-ences of the extended 15-hour flexible free entitlement to early years provision (Williams, 2010).

There are some examples of good practice. As part of the Middlesbrough Early Years Improvement Plan 2008–09, the Middlesbrough Young Children's Voices Network has been set up and is currently engaged in a number of local initiatives involving very young children in the decision-making processes (Middlesbrough Council, 2009).

Engaging with groups and individuals

Although research and more recently policy clearly advocate participation and the need to engage with groups and individuals, this has never been an easy thing to achieve in practice. Even with adults, facilitating meaningful participation can be difficult, not so much in engaging them in the first instance but in maintaining that engagement, in them feeling valued and listened to and, more importantly, seeing outcomes from the participation. The methods of engaging with adults can include traditional methods and more creative activities, and previous work has shown that their engagement with the use of participatory methods is much better than the more traditional methods of interviews and discussion groups (focus groups).

The way in which parents are involved is a key factor for successful participation. Gathering the views of parents is relatively easy, but it is much more difficult to obtain a representative cross-section of parents. Talking to a (focus) group can result in listening only to the more vocal, but many people whose views are invaluable because they are seldom heard are less able to take part. The problem is often engaging with the harder to reach groups, for example those living in deprived areas, those with differing abilities, the disabled, minority groups and so on. It remains essential that these parents become engaged.

PRACTICE STUDY

Parenting workers in Leeds took a long time to build up relationships with parents in one community. This community was socially deprived, had a high crime rate, high unemployment and adults generally did not participate in any community activities or forums. Parenting workers spent much time breaking down the barriers to encourage parents to set up a coffee morning in the school. As a result, parenting workers carried out a lot of work with the group looking at the problems in the area, their difficulties with their children, and linking them with other agencies who were providing valuable services that they were failing to access. Building up relationships through social and community events, the parents have now gone on to taking over the coffee morning, organizing events and also accessing parenting courses.

The key here is the time, resources and skill of the parenting worker to engage these parents, develop trust and help to break down the barriers between them and service providers.

A recent evaluation of this parenting programme in Leeds used a range of participatory methods to engage parents in the evaluation process. One example is *trust mapping*. This activity identifies who parents trust enough to go to for help, advice or support at times of crisis, that is, the individuals, organizations, community groups and so on that parents trust enough to approach for help, who are the most trusted and who is not trusted at all. Trust is vital to any active participation and this exercise can highlight difficult relationships and explore solutions to rebuilding those relationships (Watson, 2008). Parents can do this individually or as a group. You can work with them or let them do it on their own and use the map as a way of moving on the discussions.

Methods of facilitating active participation

Despite the growing literature on participation, in practice, the main method of involvement continues to be through consultation exercises. The fact that such consultation informs service development is encouraging but more needs to be done to facilitate the participation of parents and adults generally, at different levels, to gain real and additional benefits. For example, involvement in developing the consultation process and more input into the issues under consideration, as opposed to these being led by the service provider or organization, will rapidly instil more confidence in the process.

Involving children in decision making and service development is a more difficult prospect. The onus for children's participation tends to lie with adults. Any results of participation are fed back into the adult arena and therefore the responsibility to act on the results, either by immediate action or by understanding the value of such input and allowing it to inform future practice or development, lies with adults. This is a particularly pertinent issue when involving children under eight years. The power remains in the adult arena and the involvement of children continues to challenge that power base.

However, there are many examples in the literature of how children of this age can actively participate. Below are a number of case studies that illustrate good examples of participation and how this can be achieved.

PRACTICE STUDY

When a children's discovery centre was being set up in London, a forum of children aged 2–13 years was established to contribute to its design and development. The input of child-friendly, creative workshops with sculptors, poets, artists and storytellers provided ideas for the logo, exhibits, garden design, accessibility, opening times, age limits, crèche facilities and costs, and, in doing so, has ensured the attraction of the centre for other children (Lansdown, 2005).

Children have a capacity to share important perspectives through visual rather than verbal communication. Creativity in adopting methods to encourage participation is the key to achieving high levels of engagement.

PRACTICE STUDY

One project for four- and five-year-olds in the UK was designed to seek children's perspectives on public health issues. The children produced a mural depicting the local environment both as it was currently and as they wanted it to be. In their desired environment, play areas were concrete rather than grass, which was assumed by adults to be the most appropriate surfacing. When questioned, they were able to explain that concrete was preferable because grass hid broken glass, dog faeces and discarded needles used by addicts. The power of the pictures was more effective in confronting adults with the children's perspectives. Through visual images, these young children demonstrated that they were better able than adults in identifying what was needed for their own protection (Stepney & Wapping Community Health Project, cited in Lansdown, 2005).

Consultation with children forms the basis of children's involvement and participation. A multi-method approach tends to work best in these circumstances.

PRACTICE STUDY

Two local authorities were asked to nominate nurseries to take part in a consultation. The children, aged two to four years, were to give their views and perceptions of London and to do this they were taken on a 'sensory walk'. The children were encouraged to talk about what they saw, smelled, touched, tasted and heard as they walked along. Some of the children took photographs and drew pictures showing how things looked from their perspective. Their comments about the traffic, litter, noise and amenities were recorded, and demonstrated that even young children can give a useful insight into how much they already understand about the services provided by local and central governments ('It will be safe to cross at the traffic lights') and what they think needs improving ('I saw a lot of rubbish on the floor'). The children's views were fed into a Greater London Authority strategy (DfES, 2007c).

Providing young children with the opportunity to make decisions is vital to their development. Consulting with children can be a key part of this process. Many are surprised at the levels of understanding that children under five years can have. Miller (2003) illustrates well the developmental capacity, the types of decisions they can participate in and also the methods of that participation for children up to age seven. It is not only about gathering their views and opinions, some consultations can go deeper. They are also capable of negotiation and compromise in decision making.

There are numerous examples of good practice in involving younger children. However, the fact remains that many adults doubt the ability of these children to participate effectively and there is also the issue that working with this age group requires a higher skill set. There is a need to understand child development, have a knowledge of play therapy/activity, possess the ability to adapt methods to suit age and developmental needs, and have a rapport with the children that enables good participation.

The implementation of the EYFS has meant that staff working in nursery settings now have to adopt an inclusive practice approach in all the work with children and parents. Nursery staff providing care for under fours have adopted a *circle time* approach to engage the children, in line with the EYFS framework. Circle time or quality circle time is an approach that engages the child in a meeting of the whole group – often sitting down – and involves a range of activities including talking, so as to improve listening, morale and self-esteem among other things.

Participation means different things to different people, with its different levels and different methods. Being creative means we can engage children of a young age and get them to actively participate in making decisions on matters affecting them. Taking the time to build relationships with children and their families will increase participation. However, to ensure that all levels of participation are meaningful, two points are vitally important:

1. Feedback should be given to children and young people and parents on what they have said, with explanations of what will happen to that information and the results of their participation.
2. Children and young people should be told what has been done in response to what they have said.

Conclusion

In this chapter we have explored the concept of participation, examined some different perspectives on participation, discussed some of the main issues involved in implementing participation and illustrated a range of methods to aid the participation of young children.

REVIEW QUESTIONS

1. How would you distinguish between involvement and participation?
2. What are the main names on the eight rungs of Hart's ladder of participation?
3. What main points would you make about how to engage effectively with individuals and groups of children and their parents?

_____ *Chapter Links* _____

For further discussion of ethical issues in working with children and parents, see Chapter 16.

_____ *Further Reading* _____

Alderson, P. (2001) *Young Children's Rights*, London, Save the Children. Concentrates on children's rights and reflects the increasing knowledge and research activity in this area.

Brett, L. (2008) *Middlesbrough Early Years Involvement Action Plan 2008–2009*, Middlesbrough Partnership. Identifies ways of improving opportunities for children under five to get involved in developing and reviewing services.

DCSF (2008) *Working Together: Listening to the Voices of Children and Young People*, London, DCSF. Promotes the participation of children and young people, exploring the nature of this participation, the principles on which it is based and discussing its implementation in decision making in local authority services, schools and related settings.

Lansdown, G. (2005) *Can You Hear Me?: The Rights of Young Children to Participate in Decisions Affecting Them*, Working Paper 36, The Hague, Bernard van Leer Foundation. Argues the need for the active participation of children younger than eight years old in decisions that affect them and suggests ways of achieving this.

Miller, J. (2003) *Never Too Young*, London, Save the Children. Gives adults the opportunity to explore their own beliefs about children and childhood, looks at current practice and describes a range of methods on how to involve young children.

Morrow, V. and Richardson, M. (2002) Ethics of social research with children: an overview, *Children and Society*, 10, 90–105. Identifies the key ethical issues when involving children and young people.

Websites

http://www.ne-cf.org   National Evaluation of the Children's Fund   Includes a wide range of evaluation reports, literature reviews and, most importantly, a number of toolkits of methods used to involve children and young people in the evaluation process

www.earlychildhood.org.uk   Early Childhood Unit at the National Children's Bureau in England   Contains capsules of information on specific topics within early years care and education including work on consulting young children

www.ncb.org.uk   National Children's Bureau   Promotes the interests and wellbeing of all children and young people across every aspect of their lives; advocates the participation of children and young people in all matters affecting them; and challenges disadvantage in childhood

Inequality, Exclusion and Equality-based Practice

18

Robert Adams

LEARNING OUTCOMES

By the end of this chapter, you should be able to:

■ discuss the nature of social exclusion and understand how multiple problems contribute to social exclusion
■ discuss how a joined-up approach may be taken to tackle social exclusion
■ understand the inequalities of childcare, parenting and gender
■ appreciate the persistence of discrimination and anti-discriminatory practice
■ explore the relevance of constructing the good childhood
■ give details of anti-discriminatory and equality-based policies and legislation

This chapter examines how different aspects of social inequality and social exclusion affect the quality of the lives of children and how they operate cumulatively.

The UK is becoming an increasingly diverse society, in the sense that people's cultures and lifestyles vary. The term *diversity* refers to the variations or differences between different characteristics and factors. The term *inequalities* refers to differences that divide, separate and segregate people and lead to some lacking what others have in plenty. Social inequality is socially created or constructed, with better off people at the top and the worst off at the bottom. The factors that divide the children and families considered in this book, those inequalities that lead to their segregation into different groups, tend to be social factors. Additionally, society is stratified. *Social stratification* is the term used to refer to the structures in society that maintain social inequalities between people and their accompanying systems of hierarchy and social class. The main criteria by which social stratification, social inequality and social exclusion are judged include social class, gender, 'race' and ethnicity, and disability.

In 1997, the incoming Labour government (1997–2010) set up the Social Exclusion Unit (SEU) to tackle different aspects of social exclusion, abolish child poverty and transform services for children in need and their families. The Green Paper *Every Child Matters* (DfES, 2003a) (see Chapter 1) was devoted partly to reducing the social exclusion encountered by children, with numerous barriers preventing them achieving to the level of their capacity, in education, at work, and in their health and wellbeing. In 2006, the SEU was replaced by a smaller scale task force and the strategy was contracted, for two reasons:

1. To focus on the goal of abolishing child poverty
2. To concentrate on selected individuals and groups.

As the then Prime Minister Tony Blair wrote in the preface to the 2006 report, 'about 2.5 per cent of every generation seem to be stuck in a lifetime of disadvantage'. He proposed support for:

> very young children born into vulnerable circumstances … action to reduce teenage pregnancy … increasing educational attainment and ensuring greater stability and continuity in care [of looked after children] … a more personalised service for adults with multiple problems. (Cabinet Office, 2006, p. 3)

After 2006, there was therefore a narrower focus on more defined targets, such as families defined as particularly hard to reach. The focus was on encouraging lone unemployed parents and disabled people back to work by improving childcare benefits, a policy direction continued by the coalition government (2010 onwards).

Social exclusion

Social exclusion is difficult to define because of its multifaceted character. *Social exclusion* is the term generally used to refer to the ways in which people are barred from having an adequate share of resources and opportunities in society, whether through education, employment, housing, leisure or social inequality, or oppression. Social exclusion is the reverse side of social inclusion, which refers not only to having an adequate share in resources and opportunities, but also, as Stewart (2000) notes, being able to participate equally in shaping people's individual and collective life chances.

Cumulative impact of social exclusion on children and families

The impact of social exclusion on people, individually and socially, is not merely through the variety of its manifestations, but also because of their combined and cumulative negative effects. Governments have recognized the complex nature of the interacting factors contributing to social exclusion. Social exclusion is a complex concept, applied to the variety of circumstances people may experience through problems as various as poverty, poor housing, living in a crime-prone neighbourhood, bad health and family breakdown. Social exclusion can mean disconnection from, or an inability to access, facilities and resources in the local community. It can also refer to discrimination experienced through vulnerability, physical impairment or disability.

Social exclusion operates in a compound way, where more than one factor affects family members. For instance, a family of asylum seekers or refugees may have a disabled child or a parent who has an illness or chronic condition. The older family members may not speak English. The family members of working age may not have access to paid work, or adequately paid work. In these circumstances, they will experience exclusion on many fronts, for example not being able to afford sporting, leisure, social and educational activities. This is likely to adversely affect the children's experience of home life and being parented, as well as their schooling. In addition to contributing to parenting shortcomings, this also has psychological consequences for the emotional life of the parents and children.

The compound effects in such circumstances may not be immediately apparent. They may be reinforced through the very processes involved in applying resources and services. Children and parents may suffer double or triple jeopardy due to the combined operation of more than one area of inequality, such as social class, gender, ethnicity or disability. Children occupy a more marginal position in society than adults and are likely to suffer a disproportionately high level of exclusion. Those who suffer multiple social exclusions may have these reinforced by the ways in which so-called help is applied. Social exclusion may operate in a single dimension or in several dimensions, in the sense that one or more social problems may operate cumulatively to increase its impact.

The main aspects contributing to social exclusion and social inequality are poverty, gender inequalities, disability and inequality, ethnicity and inequality, health inequalities, poor housing and homelessness, and unemployment. Each of these areas are covered briefly below.

Poverty

Poverty rests at the core of social problems contributing to social exclusion. It is a persistent social problem in the UK, which affects a significant proportion of lone parents with children and adversely affects children's health, educational attainment, housing conditions and future prospects of better paid, rewarding work (Palmer et al., 2009). Approximately a third of children were living in poverty at the end of the 20th century, when the Labour government came to power.

The poverty of children and families tends to be associated with other problems such as living in a neighbourhood with significant environmental shortcomings, including a high incidence of vandalism and other crime and a lack of adequate free access leisure areas such as parks and safe play areas for children. Among poor people, there are those who are relatively poorer and who tend to suffer more of the consequences of these aspects than families with the financial means to travel out of the locality, whether by public transport or private car.

Poverty is a widespread and enduring experience of children in need, and more than nine-tenths of families with children who are at risk of neglect or emotional maltreatment suffer extreme poverty (Thoburn et al., 2000). Almost half of families with children in need are headed by a lone parent and have experienced recent changes in the structure of the family (Tunstill and Aldgate, 2000). The lack of material support with childcare is a major contributory factor, leading families to seek professional help, for instance, from childminders and nurseries (Statham et al., 2001).

Child and family poverty affects between 2.9 and 3.9 million children currently in the UK, depending on whether the government approach – of calculating before housing costs are deducted and producing the lower total – or that of the Child Poverty Action Group (CPAG, 2008) is used. Whichever total is used, more than 2 million children live in families receiving Income Support and also suffer from a lack of food and clothing, poor housing, and worsened educational opportunities and achievements (CPAG, 2000).

The government report *Reaching Out: An Action Plan on Social Exclusion* (Cabinet Office, 2006) identified early intervention as one of the five main principles for tackling social exclusion. The Labour government did not meet its target to halve child poverty by 2010 and the stance of the coalition government on the accompanying target of abolishing child poverty by 2020 is not clear. Hirsch (2006) estimates that to achieve this would require additional support through measures such as financial benefits and tax credits and would be very costly without recourse to wider educational and social methods. In the meantime, the cumulative effect of poverty on other aspects of social exclusion remains clear. The preliminary findings of research commissioned from Bristol

University by the Sutton Trust (Washbrook, 2010) indicate that children disadvantaged by poverty are twice as likely as other children to display behavioural problems.

Gender

Parenting and work with young children and families traditionally have been gendered activities in Western countries such as the UK, in that they have been associated with women. Inequalities between men and women in the workplace and at home tend to be closely linked – at work women tend to have the lower status, lower paid jobs and at home they tend to be the homemaker and carer for the children. Government support for childcare aimed to encourage flexible working tends to be taken up by women in poorer households, where there is a need to balance unpaid work in the home against the chance of lower paid, part-time work to supplement the household income.

The majority of the workforce in the UK who work with babies and young children are female. The small proportion of male nannies, childminders and children's nurses highlights the predominance of women in these occupations (Low Pay Commission, 2007). In theory, jobs in childcare are available and offered to applicants irrespective of their gender, but in practice, many people may have the expectation that babies and young children will be looked after by women. Historically, the fact that the financial rewards for childcare work have tended to be rather modest has made it a job for young women leaving school without higher education qualifications. Additionally, some young mothers have taken up childminding or playgroup work, because it enables them to look after their own young children at the same time as other people's. Further, in some ethnic groups and cultures, child rearing is associated primarily with the roles and responsibilities of women, which reinforces the assumption that the workforce in work with babies and young children will primarily consist of women.

There has been a tendency since the late 20th century for some blurring of this situation, notably through the convergence between the roles of men and women in relation to running the household and bringing up children. Societal, economic and social policy factors shape these trends and the geographical mobility of young people as they leave home and start families and the immigration of groups of people from different countries and cultures add to the complexity of the current situation.

Research indicates that women more than men are discriminated against in society, in terms of taking responsibility for childcare. Sometimes the only alternative for a woman, such as a lone parent, is to seek help from paid childminders or nurseries, a situation that multiplies the discrimination, because of segregation from political and economic power and poor or nonexistent access to equal opportunity in terms of financial rewards (New and David, 1985) New and David (1985) argue that childcare is too important to be associated with the sexual and financial relationship between adults. This goes much further than the equalizing of childcare benefits between men and women.

The overwhelming majority – over 90% – of lone parents with dependent children are women (National Statistics, 2001). There are longstanding problems of lone parents experiencing money problems, as research by Ford et al. (1995) indicates. They found that the common experience of many lone parents up to the mid-1990s was debt problems and the inability to fund basic living expenses. Research by Rowlinson and McKay (1998) found longstanding evidence that poorer women tend to become lone parents and at the same time lone mothers become poorer. Research by Ford and Millar (1998) found that while some women managed to improve their income through taking a training or education course, others could not and a more broad-based policy initiative was required to tackle this. This evidence that poverty is a particular feature of the lives of lone parents and their children led, in 1998, to the UK government introducing measures to tackle this, such as Working Families Tax Credit and the New Deal for Lone Parents. Five years later, research demonstrated that this had been very successful in helping lone parents to improve their prospects and living standards by doing paid work and improving their future employability (Evans et al., 2003).

Children and young people who are from poorer backgrounds – in terms of material poverty, poor housing and with parents who are unemployed or in lower paid jobs – are more likely to become teenage parents and lone parents as adults. Social exclusion resulting from social and economic deprivation is identified by research as a major cause of teenage pregnancy (McLeod, 2001). A young woman from an unskilled manual (low social class) background is almost 10 times as likely to become a teenage mother as a young women from a professional (highest social class) background (Berthoud et al., 2004). Research indicates that teenagers who become parents commonly experience greater health, educational, financial and social problems than those who are not parents (SCIE, 2004).

Disability and inequality

Disabled children are all too often subjected to discrimination and social exclusion. To be disabled, whether this takes the form of a learning disability or a physical impairment, is often to suffer stigma. Goffman (1963) wrote a pioneering text about stigma in which he referred to it as a visible or invisible characteristic associated with a person, which labels them as different or abnormal and leads to them being redefined as not a normal and whole person but as having a lesser and spoiled identity.

It is this notion of the disabled child as having a spoiled identity that contributes to their education and life chances being adversely affected as they grow up, partly because of the way other people regard and treat them and partly through societal barriers to being disabled. Disability affects the disabled child and other family members in many ways, inside and outside the home. A learning disability or physical impairment can affect not only a child's home life, but also can contribute to social exclusion – at school, in the playground, in the park, in leisure and sporting venues and in other places where informal play may occur. Disabled children have to surmount not only their impairment but also other people's stigmatizing and discriminatory responses to it (Davis, 2004). The Welfare Reform Act 2007 was based on the assumption that, with the exception of a small proportion of sick and disabled people, benefits will, increasingly, be made conditional on people showing an active commitment to seeking work.

Ethnicity and inequality

It is vital for practitioners to be aware not only of the diverse nature of the population in terms of language, religion, culture, cultural practices but also ethnicity and 'race'. This is because racism permeates society, in three major and mutually reinforcing ways, originally identified by Jones (1972), that ensure its pervasiveness – individual racism, institutional racism and cultural racism:

- *Individual racism* is described by Owusu-Bempah (2001) as individuals demonstrating prejudices against people, stereotyping and prejudging them.
- *Institutional racism* entails what Owusu-Bempah (2001, p. 43) describes as 'policies and practices of organizations that deny black and ethnic minority groups access to power and resources, often by construing them as being deficient in some way or holding them to blame for their low social and economic status or lack of power'.
- *Cultural racism* consists of 'the values, beliefs and ideas, usually embedded in our social representation or "common sense" that endorse or sanction the belief in the superiority of one "racial" group (white) and its culture or way of life over those of other groups' (Owusu-Bempah, 2001, p. 43).

The problems of social exclusion affect some ethnic groups in particular, notably people of Bangladeshi and Pakistani origin, as well as Travellers indigenous to the UK and Travellers from Ireland and Romany people from other European countries (see Chapter 29).

On the positive side, many black people do not regard themselves as totally cut off from the rest of the people of the UK. Research by Alam and Husband

(2006) into the perspectives of Pakistani-born men aged 16–38 in Bradford indicates that they identify themselves not as a segregated group, but as Muslim, British and of Pakistani heritage.

On the negative side, the poverty rate among ethnic minorities in the UK is about two-fifths – twice the rate for the white population. The rate of people on low incomes in working families is about 60% among Bangladeshi families, 45% among Pakistani families and 30% among black African families, in contrast with about 10% among white families. Nearly 50% of children from ethnic minorities live in low-income households, compared with about 25% of children in white low-income households (The Poverty Site, n.d.).

Children's wellbeing is not simply determined by their genes and their ability to pass certain child development milestones. They are affected by the health and wellbeing of their family, the immediate environment they live in and the wider locality. It may be that parents and carers find it straightforward to pro-vide the nurturing care needed during the early years. On the other hand, there may be barriers that affect some neighbourhoods, families and children more than others, in terms of the circumstances of their lives and the ease with which they can access support and the different services they need.

Some inequalities are correlated positively (increase proportionately) with ethnicity, which is not the same as referring to cultural diversity, although these two may overlap. The term *cultural diversity* refers to situations where people living in a community represent widely differing cultural beliefs and practices (Hardman, 2001) (see Chapter 7). People from some ethnic groups – notably Bangladeshi and Pakistani people – suffer multiple disadvantages, in that approximately 6 out of 10 live in households receiving less than half the national average income (Berthoud, 1997).

The urban disturbances in several parts of the north of England in the sum-mer of 2001 led to an inquiry, the final report of which identified a lack of community cohesion and a physical segregation and associated polarization between different communities, particularly in housing, employment and edu-cation (Cantle et al., 2006). The inquiry recommended ways of surmounting the ethnic and religious segregation that it found in the schools.

The European Commission against Racism and Intolerance (ECRI, 2005) draws attention to the need to improve the employment prospects of minority ethnic groups. It also identifies the need to prioritize housing policies, centrally and locally, regarding Traveller communities (ECRI, 2005). The children of refugee and asylum-seeking parents suffer difficulties, as they balance their own experiences and wishes with the differing expectations of those around them (Candappa and Egharevba, 2002). For instance, they may have to come to terms with learning a new language, grappling with unfamiliar cultural expec-tations and trying to make new friends, as well as coping with the wishes and standards of professionals in schooling and other adults.

Health and inequality

Health inequalities persistently affected children living in poorer families during the second half of the 20th century, as noted by the Black Report (Black, 1980) and the follow-up by Acheson (1998). In contrast, the health of better off children in the UK has improved. The Black Report confirmed that better off people and their children live longer and healthier lives. Acheson noted that inequalities of health and life expectancy vary according to the locality where people live, with a higher incidence of infectious diseases being a feature of living in a disadvantaged area.

Pickett and Dorling (2010) observe that despite the repeated publications since the early 1980s (Acheson, 1998; Black, 1980; Marmot, 2010) demonstrating the devastating consequences for adults of childhood inequalities in health, government policy has not prioritized tackling these inequalities. Pickett and Dorling (2010) suggest that in addition to establishing minimum incomes for healthy living, policy should impose a maximum income or a constraint on the ratio between the highest and lowest (what are called 'institutional') incomes. The Marmot Review (2010), meanwhile, notes that health inequalities in childhood have lasting effects for adults, in that the poorest and least healthy people suffer from less adequate educational achievement, poorer employment prospects, lower level and worse paid employment, poorer health in adulthood and later life and a foreshortened life course, with as much as 20 years between the longest lived better off and the least healthy worst off people in some parts of the UK.

Children living in poorer families are more likely to experience poor health, become ill, suffer injury in accidents or to die. About 10 million children across the globe are injured annually in road accidents and more than a quarter of a million die (Peden et al., 2008). According to benchmarks (that is, minimum standards) in early childcare and education, the UK now ranks a modest 11th among the richest countries in the world, in the extent to which it meets these standards (UNICEF, 2007).

The children of poor parents who are black are likely to be doubly discriminated against. Owusu-Bempah (2001) draws attention to discrimination in access and delivery of healthcare services that reflect racist attitudes and practices by staff, resulting in black and ethnic minority patients generally receiving substandard care and infant mortality being higher among black people in the community, as a consequence of their unequal access to healthcare services.

Poor housing and homelessness

Housing contributes to the quality of people's lives. Living in poverty and poor housing are inextricably linked. Housing problems may be a consequence of wider economic and social problems and the ability of the parents to rent or buy better housing may be restricted by unemployment and poverty. People in all ethnic minority groups are significantly more likely than others to be in poor living conditions or housing. For instance, about a third of Pakistani and Bangladeshi families – the most disadvantaged in housing terms – are likely to be in poor living conditions or housing (IRR, n.d.).

The consequences for children, particularly young children who have limited access to outdoors unaccompanied by adults or older children, can be very negative. They may have limited scope to play within the home. Living accommodation such as cooking and sitting areas may be small and shared by the entire family for long periods, such as when the weather is cold and wet. Washing may need to be dried indoors. Children may not have exclusive use of their own bedrooms. Bedroom spaces may contain beds or mattresses, but also other items of furniture and equipment such as computer games and TVs. Younger children may have the little territory they possess invaded by older children and adults who want space to use these items. Overcrowding exacerbates the difficulties of different generations engaging in their different interests and priorities.

Children living in poverty are twice as likely to be homeless or living in poor accommodation (www.endchildpoverty.org.uk). The Labour government set out to build 3 million new homes by 2020, 2 million of these by 2016, as part of its pledge to reduce the numbers of people living in overcrowded rented accommodation. Lack of privacy in overcrowded and otherwise substandard housing severely affects children's ability to thrive and reach their potential at school.

Employment and unemployment

The employment and unemployment patterns of parents have major consequences for their children, according to research by Ermisch and Francesconi (2001). The Marmot Review (Marmot, 2010) demonstrates that health inequalities in early childhood tend to be inextricably linked with other aspects of social deprivation, including poor employment and persistent unemployment of parents, continuing into the child's adulthood.

Thus, the personal and social costs of unemployment, for the adults and the children in their family, are manifold, including financial problems and social exclusion (Clasen and Gould, 1997), downgrading of housing, loss of confidence and self-esteem, depression and other mental health and health problems, social isolation and a loss of skills. The unemployment rate among adults in ethnic minority families with children is consistently about twice that for other adults (IRR, n.d.). The disparity between the numbers of economically active men and women is by far the highest among Pakistani and Bangladeshi groups, with a rate of about 70% among men and about 30% of women.

There is a higher chance of children involved in an accident suffering injury or death, where the parents are unemployed or have never worked. The human costs to families of accidents to children are high, leading to families having further reduced income and prospects of employment as well as increased caring responsibilities for other family members (Peden et al., 2008).

Persistence of discrimination

While progress has been made from the last quarter of the 20th century towards reducing discrimination on the grounds of ethnicity, disability, gender or culture, more remains to be done in the UK to bring about an equal society. This applies to children as much as to adults. The third report on the UK by the European Commission against Racism and Intolerance (ECRI, 2005, p. 7) notes that:

> the United Kingdom has not signed Protocol No. 12 to the European Convention on Human Rights (ECHR), which provides for a general prohibition of discrimination, [or] the Additional Protocol to the Convention on Cybercrime concerning the criminalization of acts of a racist and xenophobic nature committed through computer systems, and that it has no plans to do so for the moment.

Signing Protocol No. 12 would upgrade the Human Rights Act 1998 in the UK, which at present does not provide 'a general superseding guarantee against discrimination' (ECRI, 2005, p. 8). Although the UK Equality Act 2006 created the Commission for Equality and Human Rights, this 'will not be empowered to assist individuals in pursuing complaints of human rights violations' (ECRI, 2005, p. 8). Accordingly, the ECRI (2005, p. 8) recommends 'that the authorities of the United Kingdom consider ways of placing the right to be free from discrimination at a higher level in the domestic legal order'.

Anti-discriminatory and equality-based policies and legislation

---

Point for Reflection

Spend a few minutes considering how you would go about mitigating the effects of the different factors contributing to discrimination and social exclusion of children and young people and their families.

Policies concerning discrimination and social exclusion have shifted during the early 21st century from a concern with combating discrimination through 'anti-based' legislation to the promotion of people's rights through equality-based legislation. This reflects the view that the language of non-discriminatory practice should be positive, that is, talking about equality-based practice rather than inequalities. In this spirit, let us begin by exploring the notion of the good childhood.

Constructing the good childhood

Ideas about how childhood is socially constructed (see Chapter 3) contribute to our understanding of how practitioners, parents and carers together can construct the good childhood for and with infants and children, thereby challenging and, hopefully, transcending discrimination and inequalities.

Unfortunately, research indicates that in the early 21st century many children do not experience a good childhood. Layard and Dunn (2009), reporting on the Good Childhood Inquiry carried out by The Children's Society, point to the lack of positive experiences of many children. Children's interests are not being met by a society that does not make it easy, physically or financially, for parents and primary carers to devote the necessary time and resources to bringing up children. Children with lone parents and step-parents are particularly vulnerable to not having their needs met. Children's childhoods are too frequently more complex, difficult, anxious and troubled than in the past.

Policies and legislation

There is little doubt that infants and young children are among the most vulnerable members of society and are therefore in most need of protection against discrimination. Anti-discrimination, therefore, should lie at the heart of all practice. Discrimination and prejudice, unfortunately, are not only deeply rooted in society but exist in many different domains of life – interpersonally, in groups, organizations, the social institutions of family and school and in the social structure, where we see the stratification of classes and the operation of power and influence in society. Many of these are not visible and many of them are the subject of fierce debate, not least because inequalities between people and the question of how scarce resources are allocated to different individuals and social groups often arouse debate and controversy.

The four countries of the UK – England, Wales, Northern Ireland and Scotland – share some policies and legislation, while in other areas there are separate arrangements in each country. Varying levels of independence exist in the four countries. England has the greatest autonomy and to a great extent still provides the umbrella framework of laws and policies over the other three countries. However, Scotland has its own Parliament and elected members and Wales has the Welsh Assembly, with significantly fewer powers and independence than the Scottish Parliament.

Policies link with laws in different ways. Sometimes policies arise because politicians are under pressure from the mass media, at other times the pressure comes from professionals, through Parliament into policies and laws. Legislation and the official instructions – local authority circulars and procedures – that accompany them provide the legal powers to enable agencies and practitioners to carry out their responsibilities.

Some policies aim to reduce inequalities between people and lead to legislation with the same aim. For instance, legislation has existed since the early 1970s to reduce discrimination in various aspects of people's lives. Table 18.1 shows the major legislation in this field from 1970 to the present day.

Table 18.1 Anti-discrimination and equality legislation

Legislation	Main points
Equal Pay Act 1970	Provides that people of either sex should benefit from equal contractual arrangements and reimbursement for the same, or equivalent, work
Sex Discrimination Act 1975	Bans as illegal any form of discrimination on the grounds of gender or marriage. However, it does not make it unlawful to discriminate against a person because they are not married
Race Relations Act 1976	Forbids discrimination between people on the grounds of ethnic origin, nationality, citizenship, 'race' or 'colour'
Children Act 1989	The needs of the child should be considered, taking into account social class, religious, cultural, ideological and sexual diversity
Disability Discrimination Act 1995	Forbids discrimination against disabled people
Human Rights Act 1998	Protects people's rights and enables their rights to be protected in line with European and UN laws and conventions
Employment Equality (Sexual Orientation) Regulations 2003	Protects employed people and trainees from direct and indirect discrimination, victimization or harassment, on the grounds of their sexual orientation
Employment Equality (Religion or Belief) Regulations 2003	Protects people from direct or indirect discrimination, victimization or harassment, regarding their religious beliefs
Disability Discrimination Act 2005	Extends the anti-discriminatory provisions of the Disability Discrimination Act 1995 in relation to the human rights of disabled people, for example in the duty of public authorities to encourage participation by disabled people in public life (s. 3)
Equality Act 2006	Dissolved the Equal Opportunities Commission, the Commission for Racial Equality and the Disability Rights Commission, replacing them with the Commission for Equality and Human Rights (CEHR), which aims to eliminate prejudice based on age, disability, gender, ethnicity or 'race', sexual orientation, religion or beliefs
Equality Act 2010	Extends people's rights to equality of treatment under the law

Non-discriminatory practice with children

Having examined the broader field of anti-discriminatory policy and practice, how can we carry out anti-discriminatory practice with children? In the first place, it is helpful to clarify the nature of anti-discriminatory practice.

Defining anti-discriminatory practice

Anti-discriminatory practice is an important ingredient in equality-based policies. By its very nature, anti-discriminatory practice should be anti-oppressive. We use the term *discrimination* to indicate policy and practice that treat people unequally and differently and therefore unfairly. The term *racial discrimination* refers to treating a person unequally or unfairly on the basis of ethnic or national origins, colour or 'race'. Discrimination refers to the process of differentiating between people unfairly, while oppression has the additional connotation of the abuse of power. Discrimination and oppression operate in interconnected and mutually reinforcing ways. Burke and Harrison (2009, p. 210) state that in this definition of anti-oppression:

> there is a clear understanding of the use and abuse of power within relationships on personal, family, community, organizational and structural levels. These levels are not mutually exclusive – they are interconnected, shaping and determining social reality.

Discrimination operates in hidden ways and is often embedded in the structure of social settings. For instance, the ways in which the routine meetings in a children's centre are structured and run may, in effect, exclude parents or children with sight or hearing impairments, learning disabled children and adults, or carers who are not available before or after school hours. Discriminatory attitudes are also often embedded in people's assumptions about other people. Assumptions may be made about them simply because, in some way, they look or behave differently. Stereotyping may take place.

The challenging of discriminatory attitudes and practices begins with the person becoming more self-aware and more self-critical.

A joined-up approach to tackling social exclusion

It is true that health inequalities in childhood reinforce other social inequalities such as income, housing, education and employment, and the compound effects of these are profoundly important for later life, including health and life expectancy. However, these consequences are not inevitable. Marmot (2010) found that research in Canada indicates that half the deficit to the child's educational and social performance can be made up by reading to the child in young childhood. To be effective, work with children suffering the effects of multiple deprivation needs to be multiprofessional and geared to intervention in several domains simultaneously: individual, family, neighbourhood and policies. Family support has the capacity to engage with many aspects of the needs of the child, parents, other family members and carers. Family support engages physical, financial, social and emotional resources. Socially excluded parents of children may experience a lack of self-confidence and self-esteem and family support may enable them to tackle this.

PRACTICE STUDY: RAISING AWARENESS OF SOCIAL EXCLUSION

The staff in the children's centre in a small market town in a rural area work in teams with parents and children identified as experiencing multiple social exclusion.

Neighbourhood workers, community workers, social workers, youth and community workers and the centre staff work to contribute to a multifaceted strategy for raising awareness and, to a limited extent, attempting to tackle the main dimensions of social exclusion that affect the children and parents with whom they are working. This engages a number of agencies: children's services, health, housing, leisure and parks and recreation.

It is accepted by staff that their efforts alone cannot combat social inequalities and social exclusion. However, as an illustration of the small but significant part they play in the strategy, two community nursery assistants work with Tania, a lone mother of 17, and her two toddlers, one of whom has a physical impairment requiring some regular medical help. They get to know her at the centre and introduce her to ways of relaxing and enjoying herself with her children – which she says she has never experienced. They visit her flat and help her organize the children's room, putting up photographs and displaying personal items. They work with other staff at the centre to give her the confidence to walk to the shops, shop for fresh ingredients, prepare meals and visit the play area in the park with the children. With their encouragement, Tania enrols on a further education course, which she will take while her children are at nursery school. She also attends a regular group with other mothers in similar circumstances, shares experiences with them and they begin to organize meeting regularly together, at the park, in a local coffee shop and at the centre. Tania gains confidence and benefits from the continued support to her improved parenting skills. She helps her two toddlers with their reading on a daily basis. Their performance improves. Along with other mothers in the group, Tania is excited, whether realistically or not, at improving the prospects for their children.

Conclusion

This chapter has explored different dimensions of inequality and discrimination. It is apparent that discrimination needs to be challenged systemically, that is, at the policy, organizational and personal levels. It is clear that passing legislation does not of itself guarantee that discrimination will disappear.

Marmot (2010) concludes that we cannot improve these wider aspects of children's functioning and fulfilment without improving health services as well as encouraging improvements in the quality of early parenting, child development and learning. Marmot makes six main recommendations:

1. To give all children the best start in life
2. To enable all children to maximize control over their lives and their capabilities
3. To establish fair employment and acceptable work for everybody
4. To guarantee a healthy standard of life for everybody
5. To establish and maintain healthy and sustainable locations and communities
6. To ensure that health prevention is strengthened and more effective.

Social exclusion has implications far beyond the poverty that is the most likely social factor to trigger it. Poverty correlates not only with poorer diets but also with poorer housing and fewer opportunities for work, which is usually lower paid. Poor housing and poverty are contributory factors to health inequalities. Lone-parent poverty adversely affects children's health and wellbeing and, if it persists beyond the early years, their school performance as well. There may be long-term consequences for children because of social exclusion, which impacts adversely on their access to leisure opportunities and social and friendship groups. The consequences of social exclusion in the different dimensions of a child's life can affect childhood and growing up and have an impact on the next generation. To a large extent, the goals of Every Child Matters are likely to remain aspirations for the foreseeable future, since the problems of exclusion are deeply rooted and require broad, sustained and joined-up approaches in policy and practice.

Work with children and families needs to be multifaceted to try to prevent, or if necessary intervene to tackle, the different dimensions of social exclusion.

REVIEW QUESTIONS

1. What do the initials ECHR stand for?
2. What are the main differences between the ideas of 'diversity' and 'social inequalities'?
3. What major legislation would you identify as contributing significantly to developing non-discriminatory and equality-based practice with children, young people and their families?

Chapter Links

For further discussion of work with excluded groups such as Travellers, asylum seekers and refugees, see Chapter 29.

Further Reading

Alcock, P. (2006) *Understanding Poverty*, Basingstoke, Palgrave Macmillan. Rich source of ideas and facts about poverty.

Baldock, P. (2010) *Understanding Cultural Diversity in the Early Years*, London, Sage. Relevant book on cultural diversity.

Marmot, M. (2010) *Fair Society, Healthy Lives: A Strategic Review of Health Inequalities in England Post-2010* (The Marmot Review), www.marmotreview.org. Important and authoritative report on the wide-ranging consequences of health inequalities in childhood.

Siraj-Blatchford, J. (1998) *The Early Years: Laying the Foundations for Racial Equality*, London, Trentham Books. Useful text for practitioners.

Websites

www.equalityhumanrights.com   Equality and Human Rights Commission   Promotes and monitors human rights and protects, enforces and promotes equality

www.endchildpoverty.org.uk Provides information on child poverty

www.poverty.org.uk Provides general information on poverty

www.jrf.org.uk   Joseph Rowntree Foundation   Provides information on relevant research on social exclusion

www.cpag.org.uk Child Poverty Action Group Charity committed to ending child and family poverty in the UK through research, campaigning and publications

http://england.shelter.org.uk Campaigning housing and homelessness charity

Working with Challenging and Difficult Children

19

Robert Adams, Terry Thomas and David Thompson

LEARNING OUTCOMES

By the end of this chapter, you should be able to:

- understand what is meant by challenging and difficult behaviour
- appreciate the policy and legal context
- examine responses by professionals
- explore issues and tensions around labelling children

What do we mean by 'challenging and difficult behaviour'?

There is an inverse relationship between children's age and public tolerance of their minor and major misdemeanours. It is not too gross a generalization to say that in Western countries such as the UK there is a continuum from the very positive ways adults respond to infants in their prams and cots, to the intolerant and often punitive responses displayed to challenging behaviour by older children and young people. At the same time, difficult behaviour can become apparent at any time in the life course and is certainly not impossible even at a very young age in childhood. In Western countries, the dominant culture has tended to remain firmly unsympathetic towards children once they begin to assert their autonomy and test out their boundaries. To some extent, it is a subjective matter to judge what constitutes difficult behaviour. There is no objective standard, fixed for all time and for all cultures, of acceptable and non-acceptable behaviour. Historically in the UK, children were expected to be seen and not heard, or preferably not seen at all. In some ethnic groups and social classes, children are closely supervised by parents, whereas in others they have a good deal of freedom and there is much more tolerance of their behaviour. Whether behaviour is regarded as difficult is largely a function of cultural and social norms and boys may be granted more latitude than girls in some situations.

Policy and legal context

Children of all ages have to be worked with if challenging behaviour becomes problematic. Work with younger children below the teenage years is often in the context of general safeguarding work with families in need of help. The general legal marker that distinguishes the younger child from the older child considered old enough to be held responsible for their criminal actions is called the *age of criminal responsibility*. Despite the fact that the UK is in the European Union (EU) where many laws relating to human rights and responsibilities are broadly consistent, as is demonstrated in the Human Rights Act 1998, it remains the case that the age of criminal responsibility varies widely in different European countries. For instance, in Italy, and more generally the Nordic countries, after the age of 10, children are still largely dealt with outside the criminal justice system. In Italy, social workers have a role in assisting the court to identify particular social problems specific to the young person, while agents working within the justice system undergo specialized training (Scalia, 2005). It is only when children reach the age of 14 that they can be viewed as being criminally responsible, although even when dealing with those over the age of 14, it is the responsibility of the courts to ensure that 'the suspect has the full "capacity to understand and consciously act" (*capace di intendere e di volere*)' (Cavadino and Dignan, 2008, p. 261).

In much of the UK, once children pass the age of 10, a range of laws govern their behaviour and transform challenging and difficult behaviour into what we call 'crime' or 'antisocial behaviour'. The age of criminal responsibility in England and Wales was set at 10 in 1963 and is the lowest in Europe. In Scotland, the age is 8 but offenders go to a hearing rather than a court. In the Republic of Ireland, the age was 7 until 2001, when it was raised to 12. Children and young people may be brought before a youth court in England and Wales between the ages of 10 and 18. In other parts of Europe, the age of criminal responsibility is higher and the same sort of behaviour has to be dealt with in a different way rather than through the prism of criminality. The children are seen as in need of welfare rather than punishment.

UK policies for older children increasingly deal with this behaviour through the criminal justice system rather than any educational or welfare-oriented approaches. Over the past two decades, more children and young people than ever have come into contact with the UK youth justice system, to the extent that it is said we are unnecessarily criminalizing our children:

> Normal adolescent behaviour is being criminalised because of the 'over zealous' treatment of young people...incidents which used to be regarded as high-jinks or normal adolescent behaviour 15 to 20 years ago, are being seen as criminal activity now. (YMCA, 2006)

A former chair of the Youth Justice Board believes that children as young as 10 are being labelled with the 'mark of Cain on their foreheads because of a misplaced hysteria over teenage crime' and has cited examples of swearing in the playground and breaking windows as leading to court (quoted in Jones, 2006). Campaign groups have noted the same fears (NACRO, 2008) and chief constables have expressed their 'concerns about criminalising young people' and giving children criminal records for little more than a phase they are going through (House of Commons, 2008, Ev 79, Q489).

Responding to challenging behaviour

There is a continuum of responses to children who present challenging and difficult behaviour, which is graded according to the age of the child and the seriousness of the behaviour. This can, in turn, be broken down into two categories: prevention and intervention.

Informal approaches to preventing children and young people entering the youth justice system include curriculum-, behavioural- and relationship-based approaches. Older children who commit criminal offences are processed through the youth justice system.

Issues and tensions

Children and young people are entitled to the same basic rights as others of the same age regardless of their behaviour. We may need to contain and punish some children but they are still 'children first' rather than just offenders, who are too often put in custody (Chambers, 2009). In practice, there are arguments to be made that rights are being eroded when it comes to children, crime and antisocial behaviour in the UK. These rights include the United Nations Convention on the Rights of the Child (UN, 1989) and the Council of Europe's European Convention on Human Rights (1950). The UK is a signatory to both documents and in the case of the European Convention has brought it into the jurisdiction of the UK through the Human Rights Act 1998.

The UK government has to make periodic reports to the UN on how it thinks it is complying with the convention. These reports invariably try to put a positive gloss on events but many argue that the current levels of intervention in the lives of children and young people are leading to serial breaches of the convention. The interventions are seen as unhelpful and leading to the 'criminalization' of children and young people rather than offering help or even meaningful punishment. Such interventions can make behaviour worse and criminologists refer to 'deviancy amplification'. The UK's four commissioners for children, for example, have written:

> the [youth justice] system in England and Wales is dominated by a punitive approach...too many children are being criminalized and brought into the youth justice system at an increasingly young age. Between 2002 and 2006, crime committed by children fell, yet during the same period, it is estimated that there was a 26% increase in the number of children criminalized and prosecuted. (UK Children's Commissioners, 2008, para. 171)

The European Court of Human Rights has made regular comments on the youth justice system for England and Wales, most notably in its criticism of how insensitively the youth courts dealt with the young defendants in the case of the James Bulger killing (*T and V* v. *United Kingdom* (1999) 30 EHRR 121). In 2005, a Council of Europe (2005, para. 83) independent rapporteur commented that the use of antisocial behaviour orders:

> has been to bring a whole range of persons, predominantly the young, within the scope of the criminal justice system and, often enough, behind bars without necessarily having committed a recognisable criminal offence.

Difficulties arise in responding to the criminality of different groups of children and young people. While it may not be true that the law and the criminal justice system work in a crudely sexist way, it has been argued by criminologists that there is a gendered element in the processing of female offending, so that females are often dealt with on the basis of stereotypes (Heidensohn, 2006; Walklate, 2004).

Dilemmas may also arise in the very organization of services to children. Those working with families and children under 10 may not be alert to future behaviour becoming labelled 'criminal' and may not therefore focus on it. When it does arise and the child passes 10, they may be tempted to just pass 'the case' to the youth offending team, who may, in turn, work with the now 'criminalized' child without being fully aware of the child's earlier history and what work has been done with them.

Practice implications

The practice implications of working with children with challenging behaviour are numerous.

Challenging behaviour should not, for example, be taken at face value. Practitioners need a framework for practice to enable them to stand back and question what is going on behind this behaviour. Buchanan and Ritchie (2004) confirm the increasing number of children with these difficulties and note that children's services are often stretched in precisely those geographical inner city areas where there are many calls on their expertise. They argue that such children need social and educational resources in the context of improved support for their families, rather than medically based therapies. One of the most important features of childhood emerged from the National Child Development Study, from which Buchanan (2002) drew the finding that almost 50% of all children suffer from so-called 'difficult' behaviour at one time or another; half of these with problems at age 7 have grown out of it by age 11 and half of those with problems at age 11 have grown out of them by age 16. Very few of these have experienced any treatment at all. In fact, Buchanan (2002: 12) concludes that as children grow up 'most parents develop a range of strategies to help their son/daughter "come through" their difficult patch' and that in this way most of these difficulties are resolved in the natural process of growing up.

The above research is not a prescription for apathy by professionals, since it is imperative that measures are developed to be able to predict those children who will grow out of problems naturally and those who will not do so without professional help. Unfortunately, there is no hard and fast mechanism for developing predictive tests for such circumstances. All professionals can do is to turn to research such as that by Buchanan and Hudson (2000) identifying the risk and protective factors affecting children during growing up. Basically, they conclude that the emotional health and wellbeing of the child are improved if the number of risk factors is reduced and the number of protective factors is increased. The factors they identify include those in the person, in the family, in the school and community and in the wider world (Table 19.1).

The complexity of risk and protective factors and the difficulty of measuring them and establishing any causal relationship between these and the subsequent behaviour of a child is an inherently insoluble problem at the heart of predictive studies.

A perennial problem has been the ability to make early identifications of children who might turn into more serious offenders as they grow older. The idea has always been to try and intervene early and turn those children away from their evolving criminal behaviour. Preventive work can, however, have a self-fulfilling prophecy effect by labelling children and just confirming their delinquent career. There is a tension between developing positive preventive practice

	In the person	In the family	In the school and community	In the wider world
Table 19.1 Examples of risk and protective factors				
Risk factors	Biological vulnerability	Ill parents	Bullying	Poor housing
	Mental disability	Conflict with and between parents	Racial tension	Job insecurity
Protective factors	Biological resilience	Good family relationships	Supportive community	Inclusive policies
	Good health	Lack of domestic tensions	Opportunities for involvement and achievement	

Source: Adapted from Buchanan and Hudson (2000)

and identifying, and stigmatizing, misbehaving children who otherwise would have 'grown out of trouble' and matured without any statutory intervention and without presenting any significant problems.

Policy initiatives such as Youth Inclusion and Support Panels have sought to work with children as young as eight 'on the fringes of trouble' to make positive interventions and reduce poor behaviour. More controversial has been the attempt to 'spot' the future offender as early as three or four years old. This proposal had been made in the early 1990s (*Daily Mail*, 1991) and again in the mid-1990s (*Sunday Times*, 1995), but never followed through. The idea returned in 2005 and is still a topic of concern (Hurst, 2005).

In November 2006, the government announced the introduction of specialist clinical psychologists as 'parenting experts' in 77 local authorities to help parents make time for their children and to discipline them where necessary; the press soon called them 'supernannies' after the reality TV show of the same name (Ward and Wintour, 2006).

Challenging and difficult behaviour needs a clear framework for assessment (Chaplain and Freeman, 1998). We can see how learning theory is used as the basis for cognitive behavioural programmes designed to reward and reinforce socially approved behaviour. This avoids the classic 'mistake' of adults tending to take notice of the child when disobedient or naughty, thereby reinforcing 'bad' behaviour. There is also the issue of consistency. It is important to set clear boundaries, to give consistent responses, and not to give in under pressure. It is also important to avoid punitive aggression and to develop alternatives to physical punishment such as smacking. Newell campaigned for many years for the abolition of the corporal punishment of children in the UK and he argued that the punitive culture made it necessary that changes to legislation should be accompanied by a process of public education (Newell, 1989). Whereas corporal punishment is banned from professional settings, parents are still permitted to use physical means such as smacking to discipline their children, provided no bruises or other injuries are left. This remains a controversial area of debate (see www.kidsbehaviour.co.uk for further debate).

Oppositional conduct

Some commentators refer to *oppositional behaviour* as a conduct disorder, citing the fact that the child is temperamentally difficult or hyperactive. This is a way of locating the problem in the child, which deflects attention from other possible explanations of the difficulties, such as problems between the child and other children. It also rules out the possibility that there may be factors in the way activities are structured in the playgroup which contribute to the difficult behaviour displayed by some children.

When children reach the age of 10, they reach the age of criminal responsibility referred to near the start of this chapter, so the framework of criminal justice responses may be brought in. Since the 1990s, both the Conservative and Labour governments have responded to public concern about the threat posed by troublesome young people by developing a series of legislative measures aimed at curbing youth crime and antisocial behaviour, including:

- antisocial behaviour orders
- individual support orders
- dispersal powers
- local child curfews
- police anti-truancy powers
- secure training centres for 12- to 15-year-olds
- youth rehabilitation orders.

As we noted earlier in this chapter, while the 'challenging and difficult' behaviour of children in England and Wales is dealt with from a welfare-based perspective up until the age of 10, over the age of 10, actions are responded to from a criminal-based approach, whereas in Italy and other countries, the same or similar behaviours would tend to be addressed from a child welfare standpoint. Thus, what results from the low age of criminal responsibility, in England and Wales, is a making into adults, at an unnecessary age, of the children and young people in the justice system, leading to ineffective 'justice' solutions to resolve underlying social issues. In those countries with a higher age of responsibility, the welfare structures and framework allow a more flexible approach to dealing with difficult and challenging/antisocial behaviour.

While it would be naive to suppose that simply adopting a more welfare-based approach will resolve the problems of young people and potential criminality, there are still powerful arguments in support of integrating such an approach into policy being introduced in the UK (Cullen and Gilbert, 2003).

Conclusion

There is an element of normality about children pushing the limits of the boundaries they see containing them. It is part of establishing your own personality and place in the world. Sometimes these boundaries have been drawn too tightly and the result is seen as difficult or challenging behaviour. Sometimes these boundaries are not clear enough and the pushing again is seen as challenging and difficult because the boundaries are not there.

Practitioners need to stand back and assess the causes of difficult behaviour and reinstate appropriate boundaries for the children in question. Ultimately, the criminal justice system will do this for children and young people but resorting to that system to sort out problematic behaviour should be a last resort rather than a routine one.

REVIEW QUESTIONS

1. What particular issues are raised for practitioners by the fact that the age of criminal responsibility is not fixed across the EU but varies significantly from country to country?

2. What difficulties are raised for practitioners by the fact that legislation, agencies, professionals and members of the public tend to advocate a variety of often conflicting responses to children and young people who present challenging behaviour or actually commit criminal offences?

3. Do you believe that the principle of the welfare of the child or meting out justice to the child should be the prime basis for agency and practitioner work with children and on what basis do you justify your view?

_____ *Further Reading* _____

Green, C. (2003) *New Toddler Taming: A Parent's Guide to the First Four Years*, London, Vermilion. Contains many useful hints on managing behaviour.

Herbert, M. (1996) *Banishing Bad Behaviour* (PACTS), Leicester, British Psychological Society. A 48-page booklet covering conduct disorders, causation, assessment and intervention. PACTS stands for Parent, Adolescent and Child Training Skills.

Shriver, L. (2005) *We Need to Talk about Kevin*, London, Serpent's Tail Books. A novel that dramatically and sensitively highlights some of the frightening yet real issues faced by parents with children who demonstrate challenging behaviour.

Websites

www.barnardos.org.uk   One of the UK's leading charities, with plenty of information and resources on childcare matters

www.incredibleyears.com   Useful US website referring to research evidence-based strategies and tactics for managing children's difficult behaviour

http://www.neverhitachild.org/hitting1.html   EPOCH (End Physical Punishment of Children) provides advice on alternatives to corporal punishment

Part

5

Child Welfare

Promoting the Health, Safety and Wellbeing of Children

20

Robert Adams

LEARNING OUTCOMES

By the end of this chapter, you should be able to:

■ define what is meant by a child's health and wellbeing
■ understand that health is a social issue
■ appreciate the factors adversely affecting the health of children
■ examine the main factors protecting the health of children
■ describe the main approaches to promoting the wellbeing of children
■ discuss messages from research on health promotion

Defining children's health and wellbeing

Health is not merely the absence of disease or physical injury. A person's state of health was defined in the preamble to the Constitution of the World Health Organization in 1948 as 'a state of complete physical, social and mental wellbeing and not merely the absence of disease and infirmity'. Clearly, no person is completely healthy in these terms, but this concept of health focuses health on the positives in a person's life, rather than on the deficits. Thus, according to this holistic view, *good health* is the extent to which a person is able to make the most of their physical, emotional, mental, spiritual and social potential, satisfy their basic needs and achieve their aspirations. The best-known statement of the complexity and range of people's needs is by the psychologist Abraham Maslow (1908–70). His work is significant because it draws not only on psychological but also social and anthropological perspectives on people's needs and how to meet or fulfil them. The most widely known form of Maslow's five-level 'hierarchy of needs' originates in his early publication (Maslow, 1943), but he added to this over the following 20 years and this results in an eight-level pyramid of needs (Adams, 2008b), as shown in Figure 20.1.

It is clear from the above definitions of health that a child's health is central to all other aspects of that child's development. The five targets of the government's Green Paper *Every Child Matters* (DfES, 2003a) include health and wellbeing at the core of its goals. 'Be healthy' is the target that encapsulates promoting the health of children and young people, including their physical, emotional and mental health and living a healthy lifestyle.

Also, none of these aspects is separate from the others, in that a child's health and wellbeing are affected by, and affect, many other aspects of their day-to-day functioning. For instance, a child's progress at school is significantly affected by their mental, emotional and physical health (SEU, 2003).

8
Transcendence needs, enabling other people to achieve self-actualization

7 *Aesthetic needs*, to create or appreciate beauty and harmony

6 *Cognitive needs*, for knowledge and understanding

5 *Self-actualization needs*, for personal development and fulfilment

4 *Esteem needs*, for appreciation by others, status, reputation, and recognition of achievements

3 *Affection and belonging needs*, for loving relationships in the family and satisfaction at work

2 *Safety needs*, for protection and security boundaries

1 *Biological and physiological needs*, for air, food, drink, sleep, shelter, warmth and sex

Figure 20.1 Maslow's eight-level pyramid of needs
Source: Adapted from Adams (2008b)

Health promotion is not just a personal matter but a social issue

Underdown's classic text (2007, p. 1) on the health and wellbeing of young children states that 'in the twenty-first century children's health is still largely determined by social, environmental and economic factors'. It is important not to focus interventions to safeguard children on their immediate vulnerability as individuals, while neglecting the social factors that either reinforce health and social inequalities or contribute to the development of health, safety and wellbeing. Health services are unequally distributed. There are huge contrasts between the developed and developing countries in terms of the health of children. In developing countries, many children die in the first year of life and children are disabled or killed by many diseases whose effects are made worse by chronic poverty, poor housing, inadequate sanitation and malnutrition. In developed countries, vaccines have almost eliminated many serious diseases, such as poliomyelitis and more serious forms of meningitis, and there are widespread vaccinations to prevent rubella, mumps, chicken pox and measles. Within these broad comparisons, however, marked inequalities exist in the health of children in developed countries such as the UK. We acknowledge these in this chapter and also discuss different perspectives and initiatives on the health promotion of children.

Health and healthy living are socially constructed

Ideas about what constitutes a healthy life are socially constructed. This means that healthy living is not an objective fact but a matter of debate about a huge mass of research evidence, which accumulates continuously, concerning the cure and prevention of illnesses and the promotion of healthier lifestyles. The White Paper *Choosing Health: Making Healthy Choices Easier* (DH, 2004) promotes healthier lifestyles through creating smoke-free public and workspace areas – a reform that is expected to produce widespread health benefits in the longer term – and various reforms in the production and advertising of food, especially to children. The other side of the debate about illness and health is the notion of wellbeing, which is linked with questions of how people feel rather than objective standards of health.

Within the UK, the concept of health is socially constructed and the health of people worsens as we move down through society, from richer to poorer individual children and families. The better off you are in the UK, the better health you enjoy and the longer you are likely to live.

Clearly, although children need a variety of foods in order to develop healthily, their health and wellbeing may be affected adversely by eating and drinking unhealthily. The Hastings Report (Hastings et al., 2003) concludes that children's choices of what they eat and drink – including their consumption of sugary drinks and so-called 'junk foods' high in salt and fats – are shaped by advertising in the mass media, principally television.

Factors affecting the health of children

Health and wellbeing in society tend to be less studied than their absence, as reflected in the incidence of illness (morbidity) and death (mortality). As mentioned in Chapter 4, Uri Bronfenbrenner (1979) developed human ecology theory or ecological systems theory to explain the manifold influences on children's development, involving five levels of related and interacting systems:

- *microsystem:* the individual's immediate setting, such as home, playgroup and school
- *mesosystem:* interaction between microsystems, such as transitions from home to school or between schools
- *exosystem:* influences on a person from areas external to their own lives
- *macrosystem:* cultural factors influencing people
- *chronosystem:* how environmental factors affect people through their life course.

We can simplify the message from this: that children's health and wellbeing is a complex matter, shaped and contributed to by many mutually interacting social, psychological and physiological factors. Let us briefly consider these in turn.

Social factors

Major divisions in society separate people in terms of social class, gender, ethnicity and age. For instance, children brought up in lower social class households are less likely to experience a healthy lifestyle. The manual work of people in the lowest social class exposes them to greater occupational health risks, partly because they suffer greater environmental risks through poorer housing and living in more polluted areas and partly through lower income and greater poverty, with associated poorer diet. Poorer people are likely to have less access to the money, time and other resources to enable them to buy, cook and eat healthy foods. Death rates in the lowest social class are twice the rate of those in the highest social class. Also, there are consequences for the health of family members, including children, of different family lifestyles and cultures, for example the division of labour and rights between children and adults and between men and women, in terms of who carries out basic chores and what freedom family members have to engage in social, leisure and educational activities.

Underdown (2007, p. 1) identifies social factors such as 'the warmth of parenting, support from family, friends and neighbours, the type of housing and the safety of the environment' as having the greatest effect on children's health and wellbeing.

Preventable deaths of children

Local Safeguarding Children Boards in England reviewed 3,450 child deaths between 2008 and 2010 in England (on average about 5,000 children die each year in England) and concluded that 150 of these were preventable (DfE, 2010b). The largest number of these deaths – more than a quarter – are road traffic accidents. Research by the organization Road Safety Analysis (2010) demonstrates that children from poorer areas are much more at risk on the roads than those from better off areas.

Authoritative reviews of research into inequalities in health in 1980 (Black, 1980) and 1998 (Acheson, 1998) demonstrate that during the last quarter of the 20th century, the mortality, morbidity and accident rates remain stubbornly tied to people's economic wellbeing and social status in society. The findings of the Marmot Review (2010) of inequalities in health show that such inequalities persist into 2010.

Physical and physiological factors

The physical conditions in which people live – warmth, comfort and diet – contribute significantly to healthy development. Children, in particular, need to have space to play, run about and exercise, in order to help them to develop healthily. Exercise and good nutrition contribute to the prevention of illnesses, chronic conditions and obesity. Physiological factors such as genetic inheritance and physical robustness also contribute to the health and wellbeing of the child.

Psychological factors

A range of psychological factors contribute to the health and wellbeing of children, including those which maintain their emotional as well as their physical development. Children benefit from nurturing and secure relationships with caring adults and other family members. Howe (2005, p. 31) writes of the vital importance of secure attachments to children's development, which, he notes, develop where children 'find themselves in relationship with parents whose caregiving is sufficiently sensitive, loving, responsive, attuned, consistent, available and accepting'.

While it is true that some general factors adversely affect the health of children, particular factors affect them more at some ages than at others. For obvious reasons, perhaps, least is known about how different aspects of parents' behaviour and habits affect their unborn children. As children grow older, they display more overt signs of responses to different personal, familial and environmental factors and with growing independence and verbal ability are more in a position to describe their thoughts and feelings. The mental health problems of parents are likely to affect children significantly.

Promoting the health and wellbeing of children and families

Measures may be taken to minimize harmful effects on children's health and, where possible, to promote it. The health promotion goals of the World Health Organization are specified as 'the process of enabling people to increase control over and to improve their health' (Nutbeam, 1998, p. 12). The White Paper *Choosing Health* (DH, 2004):

■ sets out the government's strategy for encouraging people to live healthier lives by making better informed and healthier choices about their diet and lifestyle
■ signals a broad approach by encouraging individuals and shaping the commercial and cultural environment
■ puts health promotion in the foreground of national and local policy and practice.

Models of health promotion

We can group different models of health promotion into five main categories, according to their main focus and perspective (Table 20.1).

Point for Reflection

Which of the health promotion perspectives identified in Table 20.1 offers the most empowering opportunities for children and their parents or carers?

From the list of perspectives on health promotion given in Table 20.1, it is clear that health development and promotion are social and preventive rather than solely medical enterprises. The development of health and wellbeing is a social responsibility and not solely the responsibility of individuals. People may

Table 20.1 Health promotion perspectives and characteristics

Perspective	Dominant characteristics
Medical	Good health is the absence of disease or abnormality and medical healthcare is the way to achieve it
Social	Health interacts with the environment in which we live and people can be educated to live more healthily through understanding the social factors affecting their health
Empowerment	People may be empowered to take control of their own lifestyle in order to improve their health
Community action	Social action across the community is a prime means to bring about healthy living, for example through mass sponsored walks and runs, or opening a healthy living advice centre in a shopping precinct
Integrated	Health and wellbeing in the community is best achieved through a comprehensive strategy, employing all the above perspectives

be empowered through health development policies to take action to promote their health and wellbeing. Health and wellbeing can be achieved through a comprehensive and integrated strategy. A good example of a positive approach to health development is the National Healthy Schools Programme (NHSP) – a joint initiative, founded in 1999, between the Department of Health and the Department for Children, Schools and Families (now the Department for Education). It promotes a holistic approach both to the individual child's health and to the health of the whole school. The NHSP has four aims:

1. Improving health and reducing health inequalities
2. Improving the achievement of pupils
3. Increasing social inclusion
4. Promoting closer working between health promotion bodies and educational establishments.

Bodies such as the Health Education Trust also provide information on healthy eating in schools. Increasing attention is being paid to the links between children's eating habits and their health in later life.

Relevance of health promotion to children in need and their families

One illustration of the relevance of health promotion strategies is that of support in families where there is a risk of child maltreatment or neglect. This area brings together different perspectives on health and wellbeing.

Thoburn et al. (2000) surveyed children under eight in a sample of 122 families in three social services departments (two inner city and one rural) to investigate the nature and extent of preventive activity in services for children. They were particularly interested to find out whether children referred for child protection concerns, such as issues of emotional maltreatment or neglect, were filtered out of the system and received little or no protective support, that is, preventive services. Practitioners and managers were also interviewed to see how they reached their decisions and families were followed up 12–18 months later and the data were updated from social services records and health professionals. Just less than half the children had child protection issues. Most referrals for emotional maltreatment or neglect concerned children left alone by parents who said they couldn't afford childcare. The next most common referral was physical neglect, for example inadequate care or nourishment. The third was households where there was spouse abuse. Generally, families were struggling and not quite coping with serious practical problems rather than suffering from deeper and more serious protection issues. On the other hand, they were referred into a child protection system geared to assessing risks rather than supporting and bringing out the best in parents who were attempting to cope with adversity. This included a disproportionate number of refugee and recent immigrant families.

There was a small but significant number who kept returning to social services, which cost the authority and alienated the family. There was a question about whether short, intensive work or advocacy could have prevented problems later on. Other families could have had access over a longer time period to less intensive services, for instance a family centre, which provide support and might avoid the need for repeated referrals to social services. This highlights the expertise involved in gatekeeping and assessing and processing initial referrals by duty social workers.

Tunstill and Aldgate (2000) carried out research into families who approached social services or were referred under section 17 of the Children Act 1989 – under which services are provided for children in need – and not through child protection or disability. The researchers studied the circumstances and needs of the children from the respective points of view of children, parents and social workers. A significant proportion of 93 children sampled were under 6 years old, although more than half were aged 7–12. They found that the families were often struggling to cope before approaching social services. The families who were referred had a higher chance of services than self-referrals. A third of families received no services. The most requested help – social work support – was the least likely to be provided. Services anticipated and received were help with stress, child development, family relationships and practice problems. Children's main expressed needs were for support, help with schooling and the resolution of family conflicts.

This research shows how a range of problems overlap – social deprivation, parents' poor health, parenting problems and children's needs. It demonstrates the need to adopt a holistic view of family needs and for agencies to work together, possibly through joint commissioning. It also shows the need for more accessible services through, for instance, family centres and GP surgeries as well as social services area offices. There is a need, too, for services to be better tailored to meet the needs of children in mid-childhood and older children and young people.

Improving the health and wellbeing of children and families

In the light of the above discussion and taking into account the research findings summarized, it is appropriate to consider their implications for practice.

The Marmot Review (2010) of inequalities in health identifies six policy objectives that need to be tackled if health inequalities are to be reduced and the health and wellbeing of children correspondingly improved (see Chapter 18).

PRACTICE STUDY

In a local authority in the north of England, referred to here as the borough, the Children and Young People's Plan developed by the children's services department is a strategic plan for the provision of services to the children and young people of the borough, to enable them to meet the standards in *Every Child Matters* (DfES, 2003a) – to be healthy, stay safe, enjoy and achieve, make a positive contribution and achieve economic wellbeing.

Parents in the borough are participating in developing services to keep their children healthy and have helped professionals to design specific parenting programmes. When parents are consulted about health services in the borough, they identify four areas of particular concern, under the general banner of local publicity about preventive health and health promotion:

1. They want access to facilities, for example school playing fields at evenings and weekends and free access to leisure centres, to keep their children out of trouble and healthy
2. They want help in keeping their children free of alcohol and drug misuse
3. They want help with sex education and reducing teenage pregnancies

4. They want more support in coping with their children's behaviour during adolescence.

Seven particular areas of priority development are identified by parents in partnership with professionals:

1. Family support services to be delivered through the statutory and voluntary sectors
2. GP practices are all expected to offer child health surveillance services, with a particular focus on children under five having contact with health visitors
3. Health visitor and midwifery services will in future all be delivered from the new children's centres, one of which is sited in each district of the town
4. Expectant mothers have responded positively to the anti-smoking during pregnancy campaign and clinics at each children's centre for stopping smoking
5. The proportion of mothers breast feeding has risen
6. Young parents and all parents at risk of criminal violence in the home have access to supported accommodation
7. Families involved in substance abuse are monitored by integrated professional teams from health and children's services in the statutory, private and voluntary sectors.

Holistic promotion of children's health and wellbeing

It is important for agencies and practitioners to maintain approaches to promoting health and wellbeing that are consistent with policy goals and legal requirements. However, as we have seen, child health is not the sole prerogative of professionals. Parents have a crucial role to play as active participants in promoting their children's health and wellbeing, particularly in relation to primary and secondary prevention.

Primary prevention refers to the measures taken to avoid disease occurring in the first place. *Secondary prevention* refers to the measures such as screening taken in the detection and treatment of a particular disease. Physical examinations and screening – such as dietary screening in the prevention of obesity and other conditions – play an important role in monitoring children's development and growth and making it possible to intervene to promote their health and wellbeing. Screening also contributes to the assessment of visual, hearing and mobility problems and learning disabilities, as well as helping to improve measures to safeguard children.

While healthcare professionals and other practitioners working with them will have knowledge and expertise concerning primary and secondary prevention, it is vital that they work sensitively with parents and do not usurp their parental responsibilities. Issues of diversity, such as cultural and ethnic diversity, as well as the circumstances of refugees and Travellers, affect the health and life chances of children. In responding to diversity, practitioners need to balance their sensitivity to particular circumstances against their awareness of the consequences of social inequalities and social exclusion and attempt to tackle health and wellbeing with these in mind.

Conclusion

This chapter has examined some of the main areas needing consideration in any attempt to promote the health and wellbeing of children and their families. It is apparent from research that social as well as medical factors contribute to health and that any attempt to promote health must include tackling health inequalities in society.

REVIEW QUESTIONS

1. What factors would you identify as adversely affecting the health and wellbeing of children?
2. What are the main similarities and differences between medical, social and integrated models of health promotion?
3. What are the main proposals of the White Paper *Choosing Health* (DH, 2004)?

Further Reading

Barnes, M. and Prior, D. (eds) (2009) *Subversive Citizens: Power, Agency and Resistance in Public Services*, Bristol, Policy Press. Explores ways of understanding how citizens receiving services in the public sector develop their power. This is relevant when considering how partnerships develop between children and young people, their parents and the agencies and professionals providing health services.

Hall, D. and Elliman, D. (2002) *Health for all Children*, Oxford, Oxford University Press. Authoritative handbook of the main aspects of promoting children's health.

Nettleton, S. (2006) *The Sociology of Health and Illness* (2nd edn), Cambridge, Polity Press. Examination of inequalities in health.

Simmons, R., Powell, M. and Greener, I. (2009) *The Consumer in Public Services: Choice, Values and Difference*, Bristol, Policy Press. Useful source of ideas on working with children and thier parents, as service users and carers.

Websites

http://www.patient.co.uk/showdoc/16 Provides information about health promotion and lifestyles

http://www.healthedtrust.com The Health Education Trust Provides information about healthy living as a whole and topics such as healthy eating in schools in particular

http://resources.healthyschools.gov.uk Provides information about the National Healthy Schools Programme

Child Mental Wellbeing

Terence O'Sullivan

LEARNING OUTCOMES

By the end of this chapter, you should be able to:

■ take a critical and reflexive stance towards issues of child mental distress
■ explain different perspectives and models of child mental distress
■ understand the processes linking life difficulties, coping, stress and resilience
■ be aware of risk and protective factors of mental distress
■ explain how the mental health needs of children could be met

A child's mental wellbeing is as important as their physical wellbeing and childcare professionals have an important role in preventing and responding to child mental distress. The first of ten markers of good practice in Standard Nine of the *National Service Framework for Children, Young People and Maternity Services* (DH/DfES, 2004a, p. 4) is that:

> All staff working directly with children and young people have sufficient knowledge, training and support to promote the psychological well being of children, young people and their families and identify early indicators of difficulty.

This chapter will argue that childcare professionals need to have critical awareness of their role in relation to child mental wellbeing and think about and conceptualize child mental distress in a holistic, critical and reflexive manner. The stance taken is that our understanding of child mental distress, what causes it and what can be done about it stems from the models we hold.

PRACTICE STUDY

This chapter will consider the situation of Hannah, a seven-year-old girl, and the concerns of her teacher, who has observed that Hannah has recently gone from being a bright outgoing child to being emotionally flat, not wishing to engage with other children or adults and no longer taking pleasure in or concentrating on the activities she once found enjoyable. The teacher talks to both Hannah and her mother about how Hannah has not been herself lately. Hannah's mother explains how there have been many arguments between herself and Hannah's father recently.

Mental wellbeing and mental distress

The subject matter of this chapter is a contested field about which there are different discourses. Even though you have only been given a limited amount of information about Hannah and her situation, you will have started to interpret and construct Hannah's mental state. The domain of 'mental wellbeing' generally covers a child's thoughts, feelings and behaviours. There a number of different terms used in different ways to denote both the presence and absence of mental health. Terms for 'mental wellbeing' include mental health, positive mental health, being normal and having psychological wellbeing. Terms for the absence of 'mental wellbeing' include poor mental health, mental health difficulties, mental distress, mental disorder and mental ill health, to name but a few. This is not only a matter of terminology, as the words we use and the meanings behind them construct the sense we make of Hannah's situation. There is no neutral language and none of these terms can be considered ideal, each carrying its own connotation. For convenience and consistency, the terms 'mental wellbeing' and 'mental distress' will be used unless the context requires a more specific term.

Point for Reflection

In the light of the discussion so far, what do you understand by the terms mental wellbeing and mental distress?

Mental health can be seen as a continuum, with 'mental wellbeing' at one end and 'mental distress' at the other . Dogra et al. (2009, p. 18) state that, 'at one end of the spectrum [there is] complete mental health and at the other severe mental disorder'. In this chapter, the terms 'mental wellbeing' and 'mental distress' will be used to reflect a broad range of mental states. For example, the term 'mental wellbeing' will be used to denote a wide range of emotions and behaviours associated with everyday life, including being happy and being sad, while the term ' mental distress' will be used to denote mental states that range from 'mental health difficulties' through to what are regarded as 'mental disorders'. There remains the problem of at what point everyday emotions merge into mental heath difficulties and mental health difficulties become regarded as 'mental disorders'.

Point for Reflection

Where would you put Hannah's mental state along the continuum described above? Is it part of the ups and downs of everyday life, is she experiencing mental health difficulties or could it be categorized as a 'mood disorder'?

Different perspectives on child mental distress

The concepts of 'mental wellbeing' and 'mental distress' concern how children ought to feel, ought to think and ought to behave and, as such, reflect the values of different individuals, professions, cultures and societies. There are competing perspectives, models and discourses of child mental distress, some of which have achieved a dominant position in society. There can be considerable variation within and between professionals and nonprofessionals in relation to the meaning attached to different mental states. The perspectives and models used, and the discourses they engage in, will be important in considering Hannah's emotions, behaviours and beliefs, and the concerns of her mother and teacher. Two ways that professionals and family members may conceptualize Hannah's mental distress will be considered: descriptive approaches and ecological approaches.

Descriptive approaches

Descriptive approaches classify certain collections of signs and symptoms (particular emotions, thoughts and behaviours) as mental disorders. Not everybody takes this approach of classifying certain mental states as mental disorder; however, it is the dominant approach within many Western societies. Descriptive approaches require criteria by which a mental disorder is recognized. The criteria usually include signs and symptoms of the mental disorder and the degree of distress and interference with everyday living and psychosocial development. The two main classification systems of mental disorder in use today are the American Psychiatric Association's *Diagnostic and Statistical Manual of Mental Disorders* (DSM-IV) and the World Health Organization's *International Classification of Diseases* (ICD-10).

Having criteria to consistently classify symptoms as a disorder has the advantage of enabling certain types of research to be carried out and professionals to communicate with each other. For example, using the ICD-10, Meltzer et al. (2003, p. 186) carried out research on the prevalence of mental disorders among young people in the UK in 1999. They found that:

> 10% of children aged 5–15 years had a mental disorder: [of these] 5% had clinically significant conduct disorder: 4% were assessed as having emotional disorders – anxiety and depression – and 1% were rated as hyperactive... less common disorders (autistic disorders, tics and eating disorders) were attributed to half a percent of the sampled population.

Athough the descriptive approach provides a common language for professionals and researchers to communicate with each other, it has its critics (for example see Thakker et al., 1999). These critics consider the descriptive approach to be too narrow and inadequate, being biased towards a biomedical view of mental distress, with a tendency to medicalize problems of living. They argue that there is a tendency to ignore the causes of mental distress and solely define mental disorder as a dysfunction of psychological processes. The concept of 'disorder' itself is considered problematic in a number of ways, for example emotions, behaviour and beliefs that are regarded as a disorder in one society are not classified as such or do not occur in another, showing the 'culture-bound' nature of many disorders. For example, Thakker et al. (1999) state that anorexia nervosa is apparently rare or absent in nonindustrialized cultures.

Point for Reflection

Do you think it is appropriate to refer to Hannah's mental distress as a 'mood disorder? Give reasons for your answers.

Ecological approaches

Professionals within child mental health commonly take an ecological perspective on child mental wellbeing and distress (Dwivedi and Harper, 2004), sometimes alongside the descriptive approach. Within the ecological approaches, child mental distress is seen as multifactorial, that is, involving a number of interacting factors operating within and between a number of different domains. What ecological models have in common is the importance given to understanding Hannah's mental distress in the context of her everyday life and the systems she is a member of. Ecological models see Hannah as embedded in interacting human systems operating on a number of different levels. They focus on the relationship between Hannah and her interpersonal and social environments.

A common approach is to divide human life into three broad domains, the biological, the psychological and social, all three being seen as important and interacting with each other (see Thakker et al., 1999):

■ The *biological domain* focuses on the functioning of Hannah's physiology, the tissues and cells of her physical body and their interaction with her emotions, beliefs and behaviours, for example physiological responses to environmental hazards (Rutter, 2007).
■ The *psychological domain* focuses on the functioning of Hannah's psychological processes, including those involved in thinking, feeling, perceiving, reasoning and behaving, particularly any emotional, cognitive or behavioural patterns that developed as a result of her past and present experiences.
■ The *social domain* focuses on the functioning of social systems, including Hannah's family, her school, her peer group and the culture and society in which she lives.

Workers can use the ecological perspective as a conceptual framework, within which the causes, symptoms and treatment of mental distress can be understood. In practice, different nuances of the ecological perspective can be identified, including the psychosocial perspective, the biopsychosocial perspective and systemic perspective:

■ The *psychosocial* model focuses on the interaction between Hannah's psychological processes and her experience within various social systems. It pays less attention to the biological physical processes of the body. Within a particular situation, symptoms of mental distress may be thought of as having their primary origin within the child or outside the child.
■ The *biopsychosocial* model (see Pilgrim, 2002) is a whole system approach, involving the interaction between biological, psychological and social domains within interacting and integrated systems. Although many mental health professionals will state their preference for the biopsychosocial model, their actual practice may not necessarily reflect the model.
■ The *systemic* model is also an interacting whole systems model. It recognizes the nested nature of human systems; however, its focus is on the operation of relationships within human groups, for example family groups, professional networks and schools.

Life stressors and resilience

Resilience among children to cope with the range of life stressors is thought to vary considerably. Rutter (2007, p. 205) defines resilience as a 'relative resistance to environmental risk experiences or the overcoming of stress or adversity'.

Processes can be identified linking life stressors, the experience of stress and coping strategies, leading to either mental resilience or mental distress (Gore and Eckenrode, 1994). Some children cope with what others find difficult, for example going to school, whereas others successfully cope with extreme circumstances. The magnitude of adverse circumstances that children face can vary markedly. Most children cope with life transitions, events and difficulties without experiencing mental distress. However, for some children, changing school, moving house, parents getting divorced, a brother or sister being born, or a brother or sister leaving home can be difficult to cope with. Other children have to cope with the problems, emotions and behaviours of their parents, for example parental conflict, parental mental health problems and parental substance misuse. Children can witness their parents arguing, domestic violence and other violent acts. Children may be bullied, racially harassed or abused, live in poverty or be abused physically, sexually or emotionally. Others experience losses associated with the ending of a relationship, migration, dislocation, or a friend or relative becoming very ill or dying.

Risk and protective factors

Stress sets processes of coping in motion and professionals often think in terms of protective factors and risk factors. Protective factors give children a greater chance of resilience, whereas risk factors are thought to give children a greater chance of experiencing mental distress. The clustering of protective factors and risks factors in individual situations may reflect the influence of broader structural factors such as socioeconomic status and education (Gore and Eckenrode, 1994). Protective factors and risk factors are often the inverse of each other; for example positive peer relationships are generally regarded as a protective factor, whereas poor peer relationships are a risk factor. Iwaniec et al. (2006) divided the factors that determine resilience to emotional abuse into three categories: predisposing factors; factors intrinsic to the child; and environmental factors:

- *Predisposing factors* include the child's early care
- *Factors intrinsic to the child* include the child's attribution style, coping strategies and temperament
- *Environmental factors* include the support available, peer relationships and experiences at school.

Not only do children vary in terms of their resilience in the face of adverse circumstances but also in the way they cope with difficulties and experience mental distress. Mental distress is often thought of being manifested in one of two ways, with children either internalizing or externalizing their distress. Sometimes a distinction is drawn between externalizing disorders and internalizing disorders:

■ When children *internalize* their distress, they may display symptoms such as anxiety or depression
■ When they *externalize* their distress, they may display behavioural problems as they act out their suffering.

It is thought that girls tend to internalize their distress more than boys, who are thought to have a tendency to externalize their distress (Dogra et al., 2009).

Meeting the mental health needs of children

What unites those who advocate or use different models of child mental distress is the desire to meet the mental health needs of children. In the foreword to Dwivedi and Harper (2004, p. 9), Caroline Lindsey states that the fundamental principle is that 'children's mental health is everyone's business'. By this she means 'that all professionals who come into contact with children in their day-to-day work should be capable of taking action to promote their well being and prevent their mental ill health'. It is generally thought that the best way of meeting the mental health needs of children is to prevent mental distress occurring in the first place (Dwivedi and Harper, 2004). Key elements in this are promoting mental wellbeing, early intervention and supporting parents. Aspects highlighted by the Mental Health Foundation (2008) include attending a school that looks after the wellbeing of all its pupils and being part of a family that gets along well most of the time.

Caplan (1964) described a continuum of prevention – primary intervention, secondary intervention and tertiary intervention. There are different formulations but the different levels can be thought of as follows:

■ *Primary intervention* is aimed at the general population, for example public education programmes, and includes those programmes targeted at an entire population considered 'at risk', for example teenage mothers and their children.
■ *Secondary prevention* is early intervention timed for when the first signs of difficulty occur with the aim of preventing more serious problems.
■ *Tertiary intervention* is timed when more serious problems have developed and is aimed at limiting the damage done and providing effective treatment.

Point for Reflection

Which level(s) of prevention do you think is appropriate in Hannah's situation? Give reasons for your answer.

The above formulation of prevention is still influential today and is reflected in the 'four-tier strategic framework' for child and adolescent mental health services (CAMHS) (DH/DfES, 2004a, p. 8):

- *tier 1*, a primary level of care, provided by professionals, including GPs, health visitors, school nurses, teachers, social workers, youth justice workers and voluntary agencies
- *tier 2*, a service provided by CAMHS specialists to families and professionals in primary care, and includes primary mental health workers, psychologists and counsellors working in GP practices, paediatric clinics, schools and youth services
- *tier 3*, a specialist multidisciplinary service for more severe, complex or persistent disorders
- *tier 4*, tertiary level services, such as day units, highly specialized outpatient teams and inpatent units.

Hannah's teacher is a tier 1 worker and sees part of her role as promoting the psychological wellbeing of her pupils and liaising with their parents. She has been aware enough of changes in her children to identify early indicators of distress and to talk to Hannah's mother. Hannah is lucky enough to go to a school that has taken a whole school approach to mental health and actively promotes mental wellbeing among its pupils. In the past, her teacher has used some of the activities in the Mental Health Foundation publication *A Bright Future for All: Promoting Mental Health in Education* (Alexander, n.d.). Hannah's teacher, with the permission of Hannah's mother, has a word with the educational psychologist on one of her visits to the school. The educational psychologist suggests that the family is referred to the local CAMHS specialist (see Worrall-Davies et al., 2004), who, after an assessment, refers the couple for relationship counselling. During the assessment, the CAMHS worker witnesses, first hand, Hannah's parents arguing and explains what effect this is having on Hannah (see Sarrazin and Cyr, 2007). The parents agreed that they should not argue in front of Hannah and that, for her sake, they need to resolve their difficulties.

It is uncertain what the outcome of the intervention in Hannah's family situation will be. Barnes (2003), after reviewing evidence regarding interventions relevant to the prevention of mental health problems of infant and toddlers, identifies a number of factors associated with enhanced infant mental health outcomes. The general nature of these factors means that they are likely to have wider applicability than just to infants and toddlers. Among the primary factors were the quality of the relationship between parent and intervener, nonstigmatizing presentation of the intervention, cultural awareness and sensitivity. These primary factors were secondary to such things as choices of theoretical model, intervener, timing and location of intervention. Barnes (2003, p. 392) states: 'If the intervention is experienced as stigmatising/labelling or the family's cultural background is ignored then participation is unlikely to be maintained.'

Conclusion

This chapter has presented child mental wellbeing and mental distress as a contested field. Descriptive approaches that classify signs and symptoms as mental disorder are contrasted with ecological approaches in which child mental distress is seen in the context of the child's life and social contexts. The resilience to cope with life stressors varies, with some children coping with what others find difficult, and risk and protection factors can be identified that increase and decrease the chances of a child experiencing mental distress. Children have different coping patterns, with some internalizing and others externalizing their distress. It has been argued that the best approach is the prevention of distress in the first place, and that all professionals who come into contact with children have a contribution to make to the promotion of child mental wellbeing.

REVIEW QUESTIONS

1. What do you think about the way concerns about Hannah were handled?
2. What were the strengths and weaknesses of the actions of the teacher, educational psychologist, CAMHS worker and parents?
3. Are you left concerned or reassured that Hannah's mental distress has been taken seriously?

_____ *Chapter Links* _____

For discussion of mental health problems affecting parents, see Chapter 22.

_____ *Further Reading* _____

Aggleton, P., Hurry, J. and Warwick, I. (eds) (2000) *Young People and Mental Health*, Chichester, Wiley. Chapter 4 by John Pearce gives a good overview of the emotional difficulties that young people can experience.

Dwivedi, K.N. and Harper, P.B. (eds) (2004) *Promoting the Emotional Well-being of Children and Adolescents and Preventing their Mental Ill Health*, London, Jessica Kingsley. Chapter 4 by Kedar Nath Dwivedi considers the development of emotional competence in children.

Dogra, N., Parkin, A., Gale, F. and Frake, C. (2009) *A Multidisciplinary Handbook of Child and Adolescent Mental Health for Front-line Professionals* (2nd edn), London, Jessica Kingsley. Chapter 6 gives an overview of what causes mental health problems in young people.

Websites

http://www.camh.org.uk/ Child and Adolescent Mental Health A website for professionals, young people and parents that provides some useful information and resources

http://www.mentalhealth.org.uk/welcome/ Mental Health Foundation The UK's leading mental health research, policy and service improvement charity, it provides a number of download-able reports on child and adolescence mental health

http://www.mind.org.uk/ Mind An organization that campaigns for a society that promotes good mental health for everyone and where people who experience mental distress are treated positively and with respect. The site has a number of items relevant to child and adolescent mental health, for example a section on childhood distress

Parental Mental Health and Child Wellbeing

Jennifer Newton

LEARNING OUTCOMES

By the end of this chapter, you should be able to:

- explain how common mental health problems are in parents
- understand some of the circumstances that would cause particular concern in terms of the welfare of the children
- consider the main effects of parental mental ill health on the child
- suggest some ways in which a parent can be helped

It might be assumed that a parent with a psychiatric diagnosis will have difficulty providing the nurturing, supportive home life that a child needs for their own mental wellbeing. This can sometimes be the case, but it should not be assumed to be so. The impact of parental mental ill health should be judged by the parent's behaviour and the support available to that parent, not just their diagnosis. For instance, where additional problems like drug or alcohol misuse are evident, or the home circumstances seem very difficult, or family relationships are troubled, then a practitioner should expect that a good deal of support will be needed. Where the partner and other family members are providing good support, and the parent is receiving the treatment they need, there may be much less cause for concern.

Prevalence of mental ill health among adults

Mental ill health is very common. A survey of households in England, Scotland and Wales in 2000, in which over 8,900 adults age 16–74 participated (Singleton et al., 2003), found that over 1 in 6 of them were experiencing a common mental health problem, such as depression, anxiety or phobia. Serious mental ill health, which is both severe and longlasting and might include very severe depression or 'psychotic symptoms' such as hallucinations, delusions or paranoia, is much less common. These characteristics will often mean that the illness has been given a diagnostic label such as schizophrenia or manic depression, and the person will be under the care of a psychiatric service. These sorts of diagnoses were found to affect about 5 people in 1,000 (Singleton et al., 2003). Other mental health problems are also prevalent, such as those linked to alcohol misuse, drug dependency or personality disorder, and all these can, of course, affect how well a parent is able to focus on the needs of the child or children.

A substantial number of people with mental ill health are parents. Gould (2006) estimates that between a third and a half of people with a mental health problem have children. And in fact the 2000 British household survey mentioned above showed that couples who have children are actually more likely to experience a common mental health problem than couples without children, and single parents are nearly three times more likely to have mental health problems than couples with no children (Jenkins et al., 2003).

Some of this difficulty is no doubt linked to the other types of disadvantage suffered by a disproportionate number of single parents – low income and unemployment, and being separated, divorced or widowed, for instance, factors which are themselves linked to raised rates of mental ill health (Jenkins et al., 2003).

PRACTICE STUDY

Susan lives on a large estate, on an income derived from state benefits and occasional gifts from the father of her first child. She separated from her partner and father of her second child quite early in the pregnancy, and this child is now just a few weeks old. She has been depressed for more than a year, and is struggling to cope with the difficult behaviour of her three-year-old who seems to have many problems, including bed-wetting. Susan is quick to anger and the health visitor has been trying to help her learn better coping strategies. There is concern that she may also be misusing drugs.

Should we be concerned for Susan's children? Research indicates that children with a parent with mental ill health, taken as a group, have a statistically greater risk of impaired development, poor mental wellbeing, and poor educational attainment. But statistics are tricky – they lump people with a similar problem together and arrive at an average. Some of the children of a parent with a mental health problem will be resilient, showing few, if any adverse effects, and they will take this resilience into adulthood, showing a lower overall rate of ill health.

Cause for concern

At the other end of the spectrum, it is also true that a large proportion of con-firmed cases of serious child abuse are children of a parent with a mental health problem, and there have been some tragic cases where a child has featured in the parent's delusions and been killed. Friedman and Resnick (2007) have reported that mothers who murder their own child/children frequently have depression, psychosis, prior mental health treatment and suicidal thoughts. Their review (of studies published in English in peer reviewed journals from across the world in the last 25 years) showed that a child murder by a mother with severe mental health problems sometimes resulted from love, where she believed that she was saving the child from a fate worse than death, or wanting to kill herself and feel-ing that she could not leave the child behind without a mother.

A second common rationale for such killings resulted from voices featuring commands, together with powerful delusional beliefs. There was, for example, a widely reported and horrific case in Houston, USA in 2001 in which Andrea Yates drowned her five children in turn in the bath while experiencing a par-ticularly severe form of postnatal psychotic illness. Characteristics of mothers who have killed their child (and sometimes themselves immediately afterwards) include poverty, social isolation and full-time child caring role. Often, they are themselves victims of domestic violence or have other primary relationship problems. A child who cries a great deal, or is difficult to manage, can some-times be a triggering factor (Friedman and Resnick, 2007).

The death of a child of a parent with mental ill health may also result from maltreatment or battering, which may not have been intended to lead to death, and in these cases, there will usually have been several previous episodes of abuse. These deaths and the profile of the parents who have killed is somewhat differ-ent from that described above, and has more in common with child protection work with parents suspected of abuse (see Chapter 23), where the parent may or may not be known to have some mental health problems. But children are most vulnerable when mental ill health or problem alcohol or drug use coexist with domestic violence (Brandon et al., 2008; Cleaver et al., 1999). The latter analysis of all serious case reviews between 2003 and 2005 in England (two-thirds of these 161 children had died, and the remainder were seriously injured) strongly recommended that where parental mental illness coexisted with drug or alcohol misuse and domestic violence, this should be taken very seriously in informing assessment and intervention.

While the discussion in this chapter is primarily focusing on mothers, it needs to be said that fathers with mental health problems are just as likely (or rather, just as unlikely) as mothers to kill or deliberately harm their child. Procedures for safeguarding children should be followed in any cases of suspected abuse (see Chapter 23). Where there is any conflict of interest between the child's welfare and the parents' welfare, the Children Act 1989 makes it clear that the child's welfare is paramount, that is, the child's needs should take precedence over those of the parents.

One rare but well-publicized cause of child maltreatment is fabricated or induced illness, better known as Munchausen by proxy syndrome (MBPS), named after an 18th-century German baron famous for embellishing stories about his life or experience. In Munchausen syndrome, the person invents symptoms of physical or mental ill health, and may cause physical symptoms through deliberate *self-harm* in order to attract the attention and sympathy that goes with real illness. In MBPS, the person (typically a mother) misleads others into believing that *her child* is ill. She may exaggerate, fabricate or induce the symptoms, and the child may then be taken for numerous tests and hospital investigations and even surgery. The mother will appear very caring and attentive and have an ability to fool doctors repeatedly. MBPS is suspected when a child has multiple medical problems that do not respond to treatment, test results are inconsistent with the diagnosis, and symptoms reduce or disappear when the parent is not around. Mothers affected have marked emotional problems, and often a history of child abuse and/or a childhood where illness brought greater parental love. Vigilance is needed to check for MBPS in mothers with a diagnosis of Munchausen syndrome (Friedman and Resnick, 2007). UK policy sets out advice and procedures to follow where any worker suspects MBPS (DCSF, 2008).

Effects of parental mental ill health on the child

Mental ill health in a parent can affect a child in two main ways: through the genetic risks and personality characteristics they may inherit, and through the more unpredictable or difficult family environment that they may experience.

A third risk to bear in mind, however, is that which may result from the behaviour of the mother and those close to her during pregnancy. For instance, in severe cases, alcohol or drug misuse can cause abnormalities in the fetus, and domestic violence, such as physical assault, may result in other damage or miscarriage. Alcohol and drugs are a risk to the fetus while it is still developing – 4–12 weeks gestation – but also after the baby is fully formed, the effects may lead to the baby becoming addicted prior to birth, or may slow the growth of the fetus, leading to low birth weight. Cocaine and heroin can also cause placental detachment, and the injection of drugs risks both the fetus and the mother contracting HIV and/or the hepatitis C virus. Alcohol and drugs generally carry more risk the greater the quantity and frequency of consumption. And while most people with moderate and low intakes will give birth to healthy children (see Cleaver et al., 1999, part 4), the most likely ages (16–25) for drug misuse are also the woman's most fertile years. All kinds of drug or substance misuse in a pregnant woman should trigger a pre-birth conference of professionals following guidance set out in Working Together (DfES, 2006).

How much we inherit our good mental health from our parents and how far we our moulded by our environment, particularly our parenting, is at the centre of the 'nature/nurture' debate. There is no doubt that those of us with a parent with a severe mental health problem do have a slightly raised chance of inheriting some of the same susceptibilities and personality traits. For instance, the lifetime risk that any of us will develop problems of the type labelled 'schizophrenia' is less than 1 in 100, but for those with a parent with this diagnosis, the risk is higher, roughly 10 in 100, although the risk varies depending on the severity of the illness and the number of other relatives affected. This higher risk remains even if the children are adopted and raised in a different family. So genes play a role, although how much of a role is contested, and the figures mean that even with a relative with this diagnosis, there is a 90% chance of escaping it. For those with a parent or other relative with a less severe form of mental ill health, genetics appear to play a smaller role.

The ability of the parent to provide a supportive and vigilant oversight of their children will obviously vary depending on how unwell they are at any time. Mental ill health can be 'chronic' or 'acute', or intermittent, with long periods without much difficulty, alternating with periods of great difficulty. An 'acute' illness – what some people may call a complete mental breakdown – will invariably mean that the person is incapable of looking after themselves well, let alone a child, and they will need a great deal of help. Some problems of a less acute or severe nature will not trigger the same need for urgent intervention as the parent may be able to manage reasonably well; however, these problems can endure for long periods of time, in which case they are termed 'chronic illness'. A large proportion of mothers who are depressed have been depressed for more than a year.

But being depressed usually makes someone slow in everything they do, gloomy and impairs concentration, as well as appetite and sleep. This carries a potential risk if affecting the carer of a very young child, for whom a fast reaction and careful monitoring are often needed to keep them safe from accidents. A person can feel worthless, helpless and unable to manage even quite mundane everyday tasks, and may not be focused on their child's needs at all. If working with a parent with poor mental health and concerned for their abilities to supervise and support their children, a referral should be made to child and adolescent mental health services.

There is no doubt that parental mental illness, alcohol misuse, drug abuse and personality disorders can affect the parent's ability to concentrate, to pick up on signals from their child, and to respond as well as they would when well. These problems may, particularly if they persist, in turn affect the relationship between parent and child, interfering perhaps with the development of secure attachments in the very young child (see Chapter 4), affecting the child's confidence, behaviour and ability to learn, as well as making them more susceptible to accidents. Those working with parents with mental health difficulties should also look for other risk factors, such as delusions or obsessive behaviour that involves the child, absence of support, presence of unsupportive partner, suicidal thinking, violence in the home, lack of insight or empathy, or problems meeting the child's basic needs for physical care and safety.

Children are slightly less vulnerable, particularly older children, if they are of above-average intelligence, have an easy temperament, good support from another parent or parent figure, and good self-esteem from activities outside the home. They may, by contrast, have problems linked to their own role in caring for their parent. Living with a parent with mental health problems may lead to a child or children taking on a substantial proportion of work in the home or care for siblings, and as such they can be considered young carers (see Chapter 11). A survey by the NSPCC cited by Aldridge and Becker (2003) found that 4% of 18- to 24-year-olds reported having regularly cared for a sick or disabled family member through their childhood, and in one in three of such situations, the parents' problems relate to mental ill health, drug or alcohol problems (Aldridge and Becker, 2003).

These are not insignificant numbers, and these children do not all get the support they need to prevent adverse effects on their own lives, not just on their leisure time and friendships, but on their health, educational progress and emotional adjustment. They can also experience stigma and fear professional intervention, hence they may avoid seeking help. However, if the child is gaining support for themselves as well as helping a parent, it can, in some circumstances, lead to good coping skills and resilience. A priority for practitioners working with adults with mental health problems is to be alert to the needs of their children. Services in the UK specialize in child protection or adult mental health, and those practitioners in adult mental health services may not always think of the problems from the perspective of the children. Those working with an acutely ill parent, perhaps discussing admission to hospital, will need to remember to explain what is happening to the child or children, and consider what help and information the child might need, including what information and advice the child may be able to contribute.

Point for Reflection

Revisit the Practice Study. What more should we find out about Susan in order to inform our view of the risks to her children?

What help do parents need?

Where abuse is suspected, and the mother is known to have some mental health problems, professionals who took part in a large survey by Stanley and her colleagues (2003) most often identified a need for support with childcare (respite care, practical help, financial help, development of parenting skills), help for their mental ill health (although mothers themselves were more interested in talking treatments than medication) and emotional support. A fourth element of support was seen to be related to the attitude of the professional helping the mother, that is, that they are nonjudgemental, respectful and are 'there for them'. This was rated important by a minority of the professionals surveyed, but was of much greater importance in the responses gained in the survey from mothers themselves (Stanley et al., 2003).

In relation to emotional support and help with parenting, two types of intervention have been shown to be particularly helpful:

1. Strengthening informal sources of support – friendships, mother-to-mother support and befrienders, which all focus on helping the parent directly and indirectly, enable the parent to provide stronger support to the child
2. Focusing directly on the parenting of the child by teaching and developing parenting skills, perhaps through targeted home visiting programmes.

The parenting style judged best in terms of helping to create happy, well-adjusted children is 'authoritative parenting' (note this is not the same as authoritarian). An authoritative parent is warm and loving but not over-indulgent or too critical and overcontrolling. They set clear boundaries for permissible behaviour, are firm and clear about those boundaries, but tolerant within them (Martin, 2005).

Susan could be referred to a voluntary befriending project like Newpin or Homestart (the latter having a base in over 300 UK communities) through which she would receive regular visits from another mother. As well as her parenting experience, this volunteer will have received brief training to help her provide appropriate support – time to listen, chat, provide help and reassurance and, above all, friendship. Through their friendship, she will be able to introduce the mother to other local mums with children of the same age, and to local resources like playgroups.

Targeted home visiting schemes are also helpful. This approach, pioneered in the UK by Walter Barker from the Early Child Development Centre in Bristol in 1979, works with mothers to help them identify their own choice of development target for their baby or toddler, and provides resources, a toolkit or information sheets, for the mother to use, so they can gain self-esteem and satisfaction from seeing how they succeed in teaching skills to their young child, or improving their diet, behaviour, play or mobility, for instance. Barker trained home visitors in this approach, focusing on parents felt by the service to be struggling with their parenting role and sometimes also anxious or depressed. Projects since then have also used volunteer mothers given specific training – such as the Dublin Community Mothers programme.

Point for Reflection

Look up Homestart on the internet and read its home page. Search the site for details of one near you.

Box 22.1 Messages from research

- There is an increased risk of mental ill health and a range of other problems in the offspring of mothers with a diagnosed mental illness
- Insecure attachment is more likely when a mother has prolonged periods of mental ill health and/or substance misuse
- A combination of problems – symptoms of mental ill health, domestic violence, personality disorder, alcohol or drug misuse – can present particular risks to the young child

---

Box 22.2 Implications for practice

- A parent experiencing the symptoms of mental illness, or who is intoxicated with alcohol or illegal drugs will not be able to be fully tuned into signals from her child or to environmental hazards
- The same disorder in one mother may have quite different consequences for her child than for another mother with similar symptoms, who has a very different home environment and partner support, hence the context and support should be explored
- Parents will benefit from structured health visiting programmes and befriending projects, and being supported to engage with local support systems and services

Conclusion

This chapter has referred to the kinds of mental health problems that parents may experience and has described their prevalence. Family circumstances and support should be carefully explored, and where the mental health problems are combined with drug taking, alcohol abuse or domestic violence, should raise particular concerns regarding the welfare of the children. In such circumstances, it is important for practitioners to be able to offer appropriate help.

REVIEW QUESTIONS

1. How common is mental ill health in parents?
2. What support would help Susan?
3. What is authoritative, as opposed to authoritarian, parenting?

_____ *Chapter Links* _____

For discussion of different aspects of working with parents, see Chapter 9.

_____ *Further Reading* _____

Cleaver, H., Unell, I. and Aldgate, J. (1999) *Children's Needs – Parenting Capacity: The Impact of Parental Mental Illness, Problem Alcohol and Drug Use, and Domestic Violence on Children's Development*, London, TSO. Commissioned by the Department of Health, this report explores the numerous child protection studies and related research in order to inform social workers about how parental mental ill health, drug or alcohol misuse and domestic violence may affect the parent's capacity to respond to their children's needs.

Parrott, L., Jacobs, G. and Roberts, D. (2008) *Stress and Resilience Factors in Parents with Mental Health Problems and their Children:* SCIE Research Briefing 23. An overview commissioned by the Social Care Institute for Excellence of factors contributing to either stress or resilience in families where one or both parents have a mental illness. It does not examine interventions, as these are considered in other SCIE briefings (see below).

Williams, A.S. (2004) Infants with mothers with mental illness, in V. Cowling (ed.) *Children of Parents with Mental Illness 2: Personal and Clinical Perspectives*, Australian Council for Educational Research. Different types of mental ill health are examined, and how problems can mount if employment, support and income are affected. The mother's role as primary carer is examined, and then the effect of differing types of parental ill health (diagnoses) on a parent's behaviour are considered in turn, and what services, partners, others and policy makers may be able to do to help.

_____ *Websites* _____

www.mentalhealth.org.uk Information about the work of the Mental Health Foundation, which includes providing resources for people on understanding and dealing with mental health problems and issues

http://www.home-start.org.uk/ A charity providing family support, its website helps you find your nearest scheme, how to access its support and how to volunteer

www.fwa.org.uk All Newpin services in England, previously managed by National Newpin, have been transferred to the Family Welfare Association, a national charity providing a wide range of support services for some of England's most vulnerable families

http://www.scie.org.uk/publications/briefings/index.asp Provides access to a number of relevant SCIE reviews

Safeguarding Children

Liz Davies

LEARNING OUTCOMES

By the end of this chapter, you should be able to:

- understand what we mean by safeguarding
- distinguish between a child in need and a child in need of protection
- reflect critically on professional responses to the needs of abused children

This chapter aims to help you understand how you can safeguard children and how best to handle any suspicion of abuse or neglect. Because safeguarding children is the primary responsibility of social workers, the role of the social worker is also explained here. It is vital for all practitioners to understand the safeguarding roles carried out by social workers as well as by other professionals. Alongside reading this chapter, it is important for you to access your local child protection procedures. These will be available from your Local Safeguarding Children Board. You also need to become familiar with Chapter 5 of *Working Together to Safeguard Children* (DfE, 2010a), which is available from the DfE website.

What is meant by safeguarding?

Safeguarding is defined as:

- Protecting children from maltreatment
- Preventing impairment of children's health or development
- Ensuring that children are growing up in circumstances consistent with the provision of safe and effective care and undertaking that role so as to enable those children to have optimum life chances and to enter adulthood successfully.

Child protection is a part of safeguarding and promoting welfare. This refers to the activity that is undertaken to protect specific children who are suffering, or are at risk of suffering, significant harm (DfE, 2010a, 1.21)

All children's workers have prime responsibility for protecting children. Article 19 of the United Nations Convention on the Rights of the Child (UN, 1989) states that:

> States Parties shall take all appropriate legislative, administrative, social and educational measures to protect the child from all forms of physical or mental violence, injury or abuse, neglect or negligent treatment, maltreatment or exploitation, including sexual abuse, while in the care of parent(s), legal guardian(s) or any other person who has the care of the child.

The main principle of the Children Act 1989 is that the welfare of the child is paramount. Effective child protection practice requires practitioners to work together with other professionals in a range of agencies and to comply with and implement statutory procedures (DfE, 2010a).

Distinguishing between a child in need and a child in need of protection

It is important to recognize the difference between section 17 (Children Act 1989), which requires the local authority to safeguard and promote the welfare of children in need in their area, and section 47 (Children Act 1989), which requires the local authority to investigate where there is reasonable cause to suspect that a child is suffering, or is likely to suffer, significant harm. The investigation should include a multi-agency assessment of the child's need for protection and the ability of the family to meet these needs. There must also be a focus on investigation of the alleged or known perpetrators and seeking justice for abused children. Assessment protocols based on the *Framework of Assessment for Children in Need and their Families* (DH/DfEE/Home Office, 2000) apply to children in need but must never replace or delay section 47 inquiries. Victoria Climbié was defined by social workers as a child in need rather than a child in need of protection with tragic consequences and statutory procedures were not effectively implemented to protect her (Laming, 2003).

Messages from research

A study of 161 serious case reviews between 2003 and 2005 of children who died or were seriously injured as a result of child abuse and neglect has provided important insights into child protection practice (Brandon et al., 2008). It is, however, important to note that young children may also suffer sexual abuse and that children suffer abuse in every sector of society, within every religious and cultural group and by every gender and age of perpetrator. Brandon et al. (2008) discovered that:

- Two-thirds of the children in the study had died and a third had been seriously injured
- 47% of the children were under the age of one year, of which two-thirds were seriously harmed
- All but 7 were under six months old, with 21 under four weeks
- 25% were between one and five years old
- In 18 cases, siblings were also harmed and in a small number of cases parents were also victims of abuse.
- Fifty times more children were harmed in families where the carers were unrelated in comparison with those with two biological parents or a single parent.

Neglect cases

In neglect cases (Brandon et al., 2008), 21% of the total included children who had died or been harmed through house fires, accidents or poor living conditions. The key risk factors in neglect cases were:

- The mother had a history of emotional or physical neglect or child sexual abuse, suffered mental ill health, misused drugs and/or alcohol, had many house moves and was ambivalent or rejecting of professional help.
- The father often had similar histories to the mother but there was also evidence of criminality and violence towards the mother.
- Support for the family tended to be from family members who had their own physical and emotional problems.
- The child was often the last to be born in a long series of pregnancies, some of which had resulted in loss through miscarriages, adoption or terminations.
- Most of the neglected babies were of low birth weight and there was poor antenatal and postnatal care.
- Mothers would often discharge themselves from hospital despite their baby having difficulties.
- Many of the babies were left with inappropriate carers who were sometimes in an unfit state to care for a child.
- Babies tended to receive inappropriate physical care or discipline and/or be physically abused.

While it is clear that not all poor families are neglectful of their children, the majority of the families in this study were living in poverty even where an adult was in employment.

Physical abuse cases

In physical abuse cases (Brandon et al., 2008), half involved head and shaking injuries to very young babies. The key risk factors in physical abuse cases were:

- Commonly, there had been a history of previous injury, illness or admission to hospital. These families tended to have higher than usual contact with health services.
- Some of the babies developed problems which rendered them more difficult to care for, such as numerous infections, colic or persistent crying.
- The mothers had histories of witnessing domestic violence in childhood and of experiencing current violence, particularly during pregnancy, which they tended to minimize. Domestic violence was particularly present in the cases of babies who had suffered head/shaking injuries. Some mothers had illness during pregnancy, sometimes discharging themselves against medical advice, while others suffered mental ill health, had a known history of child sexual abuse or learning difficulties.
- The families often moved frequently and sometimes concealed their whereabouts.
- In some cases, the fathers or partners were adults who posed a risk to children and were known to probation and mental health services.
- In some extended families, there was violence and conflict, with the police being the agency often involved.
- While some families did have financial problems, there was not the long-standing poverty associated with the neglect cases.
- The families often had some contact with health and social care agencies and by no means all avoided contact with professionals.

Risk factors

There is often an interaction of risk factors. When a history of parental substance misuse, parental mental ill health or learning disability and parental violence are all evident in combination, the risk of harm to a child is particularly high. Also, parental noncooperation and avoidance should escalate the level of concern. Brandon et al. (2008) warn against the 'start again' syndrome when, despite a history of concerns, professionals believed that parents would care well for the child.

Only 12% of the cases had been defined as children in need of protection, although 63% had been known to children's services, and there was concern at the threshold for child protection intervention having been set too high. Instead of commencing multi-agency section 47 inquiries, most of the children were the subject of assessment processes (Brandon et al., 2008). In a study of 400 cases, Corby (2003) noted how conducting an initial assessment following a referral prior to safeguarding could lead to children not being adequately protected.

The NSPCC Inform website (www.nspcc.org.uk/Inform) has information about the extent of abuse of children within the four categories – physical, neglect, emotional and sexual. Children may also be abused through organized abuse such as child trafficking, sexual and domestic exploitation and online abuse when more than one child or adult is involved and, as with all types of abuse, a multi-agency response is required. Some forms of abuse are related to cultural practices such as female genital mutilation, forced marriage and children punished because they are thought to be possessed by spirits. Working Together (DfE, 2010a) provides guidance as to how to respond in a range of cases. Some children are known to be particularly vulnerable to abuse, such as children in custody, disabled children and asylum-seeking children, and protection systems may not be so effectively in place for them. To exclude some children from the protection procedures is a form of *childism* – discrimination against children. Every child has a right to protection.

Professional responses to the needs of abused children

It takes courage and determination to protect children and to hear the voice of the abused child. It is rare for a child to make up an allegation and their statements about abuse must lead to investigation. It is important to think about what might prevent you acting to break the cycle of abuse:

- *The rule of optimism* is when it is assumed that all is well for the child. There is a tendency to explain away indicators of abuse and convince yourself the child is safe. This form of professional denial is a common form of dangerous practice. It is essential to ask the question 'Is the child being abused' and to be prepared to think the unthinkable.
- *Stockholm syndrome* is when the adult's perspective is considered above that of the child. It is based on hostage situations where hostages begin to identify with the cause of their captors through fear and intimidation. This is a common response when professionals are frightened by dangerous adult behaviour and the child's needs become lost to view.
- When a *referral is from a neighbour or friend*, it may not be taken as seriously as when from a professional. Yet these are people close to the child, often with knowledge about the child's situation. It is important not to screen out allegations without full investigation whoever is the referrer.
- Abusive parents and carers can be very convincing and persuade professionals that they are working with them. This is called *false compliance* and it can distract from rigorous investigation, leaving the child unsafe.
- Sometimes professionals respond quickly with *concrete solutions*, by the provision of practical support such as finance, housing or furniture, leaving the

underlying causes of child abuse unaddressed. Families need practical support but not at the expense of protecting the child from harm.

■ *Assumptions* can be a way of avoiding confronting child abuse – such as presuming that another professional is dealing with the situation without checking this out or assuming that the abuse is a part of the family culture even though this can never be a reason to deny a child protection.

■ Sometimes *recent information* becomes a focus of the professional response and earlier facts and events known about the case are ignored. Chronologies of previous history are essential to forming a clear picture of what has taken place.

How to assess if this is a case of child abuse

Remember that a child protection investigation will screen cases out of as well as into child protection processes. To refer a case to children's services or the police requires 'reasonable cause to suspect' harm. At an initial stage, the evidence may not be very clear.

The first response must be to consider whether the child requires immediate protection and whether a referral to children's services and the police needs to be made. Does the child need to be made safe while an investigation takes place?

Here are some useful questions to ask when being alert to the possibility of child abuse:

■ What account does the child provide?

■ How does the child respond when asked about what happened?

■ If there are injuries or unexplained marks, are these in an unusual site where a child would not commonly receive an injury and does the injury match the explanation given by the child, parent or another person? It is the role of a child protection doctor to assess medical information about whether the harm to the child is consistent with child abuse.

■ Are there inconsistent accounts? Do some details not make sense or match with observable facts?

■ Is there corroboration of the child's account from a witness?

■ Is there a history of violence to adults, children or animals in the family?

■ Are there adults or children in the child's environment with criminal convictions for sexual or violent crime?

■ Is there evidence of neglect?

■ Is there evidence of emotional harm?

■ Are there gaps in the information provided or events which are unexplained? Consider factors that may not be obvious to view, such as an adult who visits the home, an adult who misuses drugs or alcohol or a child who is isolated from family activities.

It is not the role of the non-social worker practitioner to interview the child about abuse – that is a specialist task for police and social workers – but you can ask some initial exploratory open questions such as 'tell me what happened?' or 'how did this happen?' – questions which do not put words into the child's mouth. The practitioner needs to know just enough to make the referral.

It is also not the non-social worker practitioner's role to examine a child's injuries unless these are obvious to view. This is a specialist role and a child protection doctor will decide who is best qualified to examine a child.

PRACTICE STUDY: RISK INDICATORS FOR SAFEGUARDING WORK WITH CHILDREN AND FAMILIES

This case is derived from the executive summary of the *Serious Case Review* published by Swansea Local Safeguarding Children Board (2007) and media coverage of the criminal trial and professional response to the case.

On the 6 May 2005, in Swansea, Aaron Gilbert, aged 13 months, died as a result of brain damage. He had suffered over 50 injuries including a bite mark on his face. The injuries were caused by the mother's partner when she had briefly left the baby with him. His mother Rebecca Lewis, age 21 years, was convicted of familial homicide and sentenced to 6 years' imprisonment, as she failed to prevent the child's murder by her 23-year-old partner Andrew Lloyd. Mr Lloyd pleaded guilty to murder and was sentenced to 24 years' imprisonment for inflicting extreme abuse to the child, whom the judge said Lloyd had treated like a punch bag.

Events prior to Aaron's death

Mr Lloyd had moved into the household only eight weeks before Aaron died and after the birth father left the home. Until then, the baby was healthy and reaching all his developmental milestones. The mother had frequently taken Aaron to health services and there had been no concerns. No agency was aware that Andrew Lloyd was living in the household. Three weeks before Aaron's death, his mother took him to hospital with an arm injury but took him home before he was seen by a doctor. The hospital was concerned and contacted the GP but a follow-up visit by the health visitor did not take place because of staff sickness. Aaron was seen after this date at a Sure Start group where he attended with an unrelated carer. He was also examined by the GP because of a rash but no concerns were noted.

Referral to children's services

On 27 April, an anonymous call was made to children's services about bruising on the baby and alleging that Mr Lloyd misused drugs. The social worker did not trigger a child protection response. However, a letter was sent to the mother inviting her to come to the office on 5 May to discuss the allegations. It was sent to the wrong address and the mother had not received the letter. If a manager had reviewed the case and asked questions on the day, it is likely that the case would have been redefined as child protection. The anonymous caller rang again on 4 May and was told that an appointment had been made for the following day. On that same day, the health visitor called at the home and left her card.

Information provided at the trial

The anonymous caller, who was the mother's cousin, gave evidence saying that she had noticed Aaron with soiled clothes, smelling of urine and heard him screaming.

PRACTICE STUDY cont'd

A neighbour said she had noticed swelling on Aaron's head and bruising on his face, and another neighbour said Mr Lloyd had told them he wanted the boy to be hard and toughened up. The neighbours did not report their concerns and the anonymous caller did not provide the correct information. The mother had stated in her evidence that she had seen Lloyd mistreating Aaron but she feared for her own safety as he had threatened to kill her if she left him

Andrew Lloyd was known to probation, mental health services and the police

As a child, he had been the subject of physical abuse and neglect, had witnessed domestic violence and had been in care from the age of 11. He had two convictions for violence, including one for grievous bodily harm, but neither were for domestic violence or violence towards a child. On release from a prison sentence, he breached the conditions of a licence but was not arrested. For some reason, his details were not entered on the police national computer. He was known to adult psychiatric services following two suicide attempts and some domestic violence concerns in relation to a different partner. With regard to this previous relationship, there had been professional concerns about the safety of the child which were not referred to children's services. Police assessed the risk he posed but decided not to refer for multi-agency assessment. Mr Lloyd had a previous conviction for biting a man on the face.

Point for Reflection

Making reference to the research study above, what indicators do you think might have alerted the protective agencies to Aaron as a child at risk of significant harm? Remember to consider only what was known to professionals at the time.

Some lessons to be learned

The serious case review by Swansea Safeguarding Children Board concluded that there was a catalogue of warning signs in the case which had not been linked together.

Here is a list of signs which, if identified, could have led to further investigation.

Historical indicators:

- Possible impact on the family of the birth father leaving the household
- Andrew Lloyd's history of serious violence and domestic violence
- Mental health professionals' concerns about Andrew Lloyd's care of a child in a previous relationship
- Andrew Lloyd's noncompliance with probation services with regard to his licence conditions

■ Andrew Lloyd's childhood history in the context of his adult mental health and offending history.

Concerns relating to the eight weeks Andrew Lloyd lived in the household:

■ Mother's uncharacteristic avoidance of medical treatment for Aaron's arm injury
■ Concern that Aaron had an injury that had not been medically examined and might require treatment
■ The attendance at Sure Start with an unrelated carer should have been questioned by staff
■ Two anonymous calls reporting bruising on the child and problematic drug misuse by mother's partner.

Point for Reflection

Making reference to your local statutory child protection procedures, what action might have been undertaken by the agencies involved to protect Aaron from significant harm?

The risk Andrew Lloyd posed within the community to both adults and children had been previously identified by probation, the police and adult psychiatric services. These services focused on the adult but did not make a referral to children's services. If the information held by these agencies had been collated and analysed, in a multiagency strategy meeting, additional concerns would have been raised and further investigation and action might have taken place to assess the risk to the baby in his care. Instead, Andrew Lloyd was not currently identified as a significant risk to the public, his partner or children. The local Multi-agency Public Protection Panel should have reached a decision about the risk he posed to others, given that he was a known offender and perpetrator of domestic violence, with mental ill health issues.

The health service did not follow up the abandoned visit to the hospital when Aaron had an injured arm. If it had taken place, Aaron would have been monitored at a time when, it is now known, he was extremely vulnerable. The visit was planned but cancelled through staff sickness. Staff absences and the continued provision of services to children are a management responsibility.

Children's services should have received referrals from health, probation, police and mental health services. Instead the first referral was from an anonymous caller who provided the wrong address details. It was a clear allegation of abuse and neglect and should have triggered a child protection response under section 47 of the Children Act 1989, with managerial oversight of the social worker's compliance with procedures. It did not matter that the allegation was made anonymously as all such allegations must be thoroughly investigated.

Checks should have been made with all the relevant agencies and would have been likely to show the discrepancy in address and to have collated some prior concerns.

A strategy discussion with the police and subsequent strategy meeting with the other agencies would have brought together all available information, initiated child protection inquiries and planned an investigation. The social worker should have made a home visit, possibly jointly with the health visitor who knew the family. A letter of appointment was an inadequate response as the child must be seen preferably within the home environment. Aaron would have been seen and, given the nature of the referral, the mother would have been asked to take him for a medical examination. If she had refused, this would have escalated the concern and a court order such as an emergency protection order (Children Act, s. 44) could have been obtained to make sure Aaron was assessed by a paediatrician. Because of Andrew Lloyd's history, he would be asked to leave the household during the investigation. If he had nowhere to stay, then children's services would have provided him with alternative accommodation while the child protection investigation continued and the police made a decision about whether a crime had been committed and whether to pursue criminal proceedings.

When the mother was interviewed, either she would have disclosed what had been happening and would have gained professional support to keep Aaron safe or she might have wanted her partner to remain in the home and have been too frightened to speak. If her partner then refused to leave, Aaron would have been taken to a place of safety either with a trusted and vetted relative or in foster care until professionals were sure that he was safe. This might have been with the mother's agreement but if not then through gaining an emergency protection order or the police might have used their police powers of protection (Children Act, s. 46) to remove Aaron from his home for the duration of the investigation.

A child protection conference would have been convened within 15 days to enable full professional debate among all those who had historical knowledge of the family or information about current allegations. The mother would be present and the meeting would aim to reach agreement about the need for and implementation of a protection plan to keep Aaron safe. Decisions would be constantly reviewed at further strategy meetings and conferences until all professionals agreed that the child was safe.

Conclusion

Two main agencies have local responsibility for the protection of children. The Local Safeguarding Children Board has to make sure that professionals in its area train together, share common procedures, reach agreement on protocols and learn lessons from child abuse inquiries. The Multi-agency Public Protection Arrangements must be in place to protect children and families from dangerous adults in the community. It is important for all children's workers to know that they can report practice concerns to these organizations and seek advice from their agency safeguarding representatives on these panels.

It is very difficult for children to tell about abuse, particularly young children who may not have the means to communicate what is happening. Professionals who work with children must be the voice for vulnerable children and make sure their own voices are heard. Inquiries have repeatedly shown that staff working in unsafe environments make mistakes. This might mean poor management, a large workload, lack of supervision and training and flawed protocols. Legislation and policy now support whistle-blowing and confidential advice can always be sought from the group Public Concern at Work (see Websites below).

REVIEW QUESTIONS

1. What is the statutory duty of a children's worker under section 47 of the Children Act 1989?
2. What are the main statutory forums for multi-agency discussion and analysis of actual or suspected child abuse?
3. What should a practitioner working with children do if they do not think there has been an effective response to their reporting of child abuse?

_____ *Chapter Links* _____

For more information on the process of practice, see Chapter 24.

_____ *Further Reading* _____

Bray, M. (1997) *Poppies on the Rubbish Heap: Sexually Abused Children – The Child's Voice*, London, Jessica Kingsley. Through case studies, the author shows how abuse can affect the mental wellbeing of children, and how the repair of the child's trust in adults is crucial to healing.

Davies, L. (2009) *Protecting Children*, Gloucester, Lonely Scribe. Introductory text that describes child protection processes.

Davies, L. and Duckett, N. (2008) *Proactive Child Protection and Social Work*, Exeter, Learning Matters. The authors provide examples of how child protection works in practice and address all forms of child abuse, including organized abuse, and provide practical examples to support critical analysis within a context of research findings, legislation and policy.

Howe, D. (2005) *Child Abuse and Neglect*, Basingstoke, Palgrave Macmillan. Comprehensive overview of the subject with particular relevance to the protection of young children.

Keeble, H. (2010) *Baby X: Britain's Child Abusers Brought to Justice*, London, Pocket Books. A police officer working in the child abuse investigation team in London describes the complexities of his work to protect children.

Reder, P., Duncan, S. and Gray, M. (1993) *Beyond Blame: Child Abuse Tragedies Revisited*, London, Routledge. Through an examination of child abuse inquiries, the authors identify common themes in professional practice and explore issues of professional dangerousness.

Websites

www.napac.org National Association of People Abused in Childhood Helpline and support for adults abused as children

www.pcaw.co.uk Public Concern at Work An independent authority seeking to ensure that concerns about malpractice are properly raised and addressed in the workplace

www.stopitnow.org.uk Information and awareness campaign regarding the subject of child sexual abuse

www.childrenareunbeatable.org Coalition of organizations opposed to the physical punishment of children

Assessment and Intervention in Work with Children in Need

24

Robert Adams

LEARNING OUTCOMES

By the end of this chapter, you should be able to:

- appreciate what is entailed in initial and core assessment
- understand the social work process of planning, intervention, monitoring, reviewing and evaluating

In the previous chapter, we saw how the multiprofessional responsibilities of practitioners are exercised in safeguarding children. This chapter focuses on the core contribution of social work when a child is identified as in need or perhaps even in danger. Whichever area of working with children and families you are interested in, it is important for successful integrated working and a comprehensive knowledge base that you understand the process of assessing and potentially intervening when a child is in need.

Process of practice

A range of services are provided by local authorities to meet the needs of children, bearing in mind that children's needs are assessed in the wider context of their family background, the parenting they receive from parents and/or carers and their wider environment. Education and health services, for instance, are available to meet the full range of children's needs, whereas over and above this, more specialist childcare and education services are available to meet the additional needs of some children. For instance, some children have special educational needs and responses to meet these are undertaken as they proceed through their schooling. Other children have needs that require social work services. Social workers play a central role in working with children and families in such circumstances. Instances which come readily to most people's attention concern the risk of, or actual, neglect, harm or abuse of a child. In such circumstances, social workers go through a series of major stages of practice, as follows:

- Investigating
- Carrying out initial assessment
- Carrying out core assessment
- Planning services in consultation with children and their families
- Intervening and implementing services
- Reviewing and evaluating services.

In such situations, social work tends to be backed by legal powers, such as those conferred on local authorities by the Children Act 1989 (see Chapters 1 and 2). Different sections of this Act, in some circumstances in conjunction with other legislation, give local authorities and any partner childcare agencies with whom they are working – such as the NSPCC or Barnardo's – statutory powers to carry out various duties, including investigating situations, protecting children on an emergency basis where necessary, assessing children's needs and ensuring that they receive treatment to meet their needs.

Assessment

The Assessment Framework is a central component of the government's aspiration to deliver integrated services aimed at the goals of Every Child Matters (see Chapter 1) and to meet the needs of children and families. It is a standardized means of holistically assessing children's additional needs and determining how best these should be met, and is underpinned by the following principles. Assessments (DH/DfEE/Home Office, 2000, p. 10):

- are child centred
- are rooted in child development
- are ecological in their approach
- ensure equality of opportunity
- involve working with children and families
- build on strengths as well as identify difficulties
- are interagency in their approach to assessment and the provision of services
- are a continuing process, not a single event
- are carried out in parallel with other action and providing services
- are grounded in evidence-based knowledge.

The assessment of children and families is a complex matter, involving the integration of theories, methods and statutory guidance set out by central government and local authorities, an understanding of relevant research and practice wisdom.

This authoritative government guidance was published interdepartmentally (DH/DfEE/Home Office, 2000), and has been subjected to detailed critical scrutiny by Calder (2003). The requirement to safeguard children imposes additional responsibility on practitioners. Cleaver et al. (2004) use detailed interviews with practitioners and children, parents and carers to show that the emphasis on assessment affects the work done with children and families.

Assessments fall into two main categories: initial – preliminary and 'short'; and core – full and may take several weeks to complete.

Initial assessment

The purpose of initial assessment is to make a relatively brief judgement about whether there is a need for in-depth assessment and possibly significant intervention. Initial assessment often leads to the one of two conclusions – there is no need for the further involvement of children's services, or that there is, for example because there are grounds for suspecting significant harm to the child. The decision not to intervene would be backed up by the principle of the Children Act 1989, which is that where there are no indications to the contrary, the best action in the interests of the child is no action. In other words, parents and carers should normally be free to bring up their children without interference from the state or the local authority.

In the case where further action is indicated, immediate procedures may be followed to safeguard the child, including convening a child protection conference within a short period of time and bringing together a team of practitioners to carry out a core assessment. Normally, the team begins to carry out the assessment within days of the conference.

Core assessment

A core assessment is a major task – in which the social worker is central but a range of agencies and practitioners are likely to be involved – and may take as long as five working weeks – 35 days – to complete. Practitioners in the different agencies are drawing on a variety of sources and types of information and using what is commonly called an *ecological approach*. This entails a holistic assessment of the needs of the child, the parents or carers and other family members. The government guidance on this holistic assessment (DH/DfEE/Home Office, 2000) identifies three elements of the circumstances of the child: the child's developmental needs, the parenting capacity of parents and carers, and family and wider environmental factors.

Where the child is considered to need safeguarding from harm, the practitioner follows procedures prescribed by the Local Safeguarding Children Board (see Chapter 23).

The aim of these policies and procedures is to achieve *integrated assessment*. The assessment process involves practitioners reaching agreement, where possible, and applying an integrated approach to working with children and families towards agreeing the services they require. The core assessment, therefore, entails gathering information and reaching a judgement about the child's and the parents' or carers' wishes and incorporating these into a partnership agreement with them, and, where necessary, finding advocates to represent their interests, for example where civil court proceedings are taking place over whether the child should be looked after by the local authority.

Fahlberg (1991) argues that a complete assessment includes five components:

- the child's past history
- current adjustment
- direct observation of the child
- assessment using special procedures such as a paediatric or psychiatric consultation or a neurological examination
- the child's family history.

Fahlberg (1991) notes how essential it is to gather as comprehensive a picture as possible, since in the absence of this, there is less likelihood of producing an assessment based on the child's rather than the parents' needs. With this in mind, she states that it is important not only to draw on the written records from agencies and professionals having contact with the child, including schools, hospital, health clinic and health visitor, but also to interview widely. Interviews should include parents, relatives, previous carers and social workers, preschool and daycare practitioners, teachers, police officers and babysitters.

Three groups of children's needs and services are identified during the assessment process:

1. *Children with no identified additional needs:* they are eligible for universal services provided for all children and young people
2. *Children with additional needs:* they are identified as eligible for targeted supported, either through a single practitioner or an integrated approach
3. *Children with complex needs:* they are identified as eligible for integrated support from statutory or specialist services.

Children with complex needs include:

- those subject to a child protection plan
- looked after children
- children leaving care

- adopted children
- children with severe and complex special educational needs
- children and young people with severe and complex special health needs
- children with significant mental health problems
- young offenders.

The team around the child

The team around the child is the multiagency team of practitioners coordinated by a lead professional that works to deliver support to the child with additional and complex needs.

It is necessary to bear in mind the difficulties that can arise during assessments, where professionals can be biased when judging the level of risk to children (Macdonald, 2001). The Assessment Framework cannot eliminate such problems, neither can it obviate the necessity for a much more detailed assessment of children whose needs are more extensive due to more complex family circumstances.

It is easy to assert that assessment should be carried out *with* children and their parents or carers, rather than being superimposed *on* them. However, it is more difficult to achieve this in practice. McLeod (2008) provides detailed guidance on techniques for listening to children and young people.

Assessment is at best an inexact art, rather than a precise science. Procedures and checklists are no substitute for the sensitive and purposeful application of human qualities and professional expertise. Helm and Daniel (2010) provide practice-led guidance on how to appraise information and incorporate it into care planning. Horwath (2009) has produced clear and practical guidance on how to assess children and their families.

Planning

Planning entails working with children, parents and carers to translate the assessment into a feasible schedule, stating the goals and how they are to be tackled, what to do, who will do it and how and when people will be working together. The plan will ideally schedule a monthly, weekly and daily plan with desired outcomes for each part.

The plan should contain the following:

- the agreed needs of the parents and child
- the expectations of the parents and child
- the agreed plan of action for each need
- which professionals will be involved in meeting each need
- what services will be provided to meet each need
- what outcomes are anticipated once each need is met.

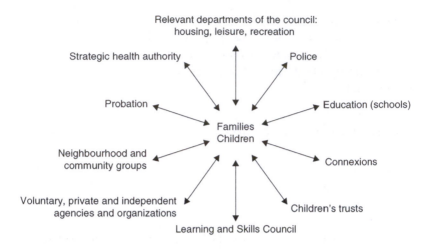

Figure 24.1 Contributors to the planning process

Planning is crucial in all work with children and other family members. All sessions involving contact with family members should be planned in advance. It is important to be able to rely on an adequate record as the basis for planning future work with the child and family.

Local authorities and professionals in different agencies work together to ensure the planning process is fully integrated. Interagency working (Figure 24.1) focuses on meeting the child's assessed needs.

Identifying specific goals and who will tackle each goal

It is no good making general statements in the plan. A good plan clearly specifies precise ways in which each goal identified in the assessment is going to be worked towards. There are three main types of goals, expressed in terms of expected outcomes:

1. Maintaining the person at the current level of activity
2. Bringing about change
3. Achieving results for the parents and/or child, such as improving their quality of life, feeling empowered, having a enhanced capacity to make decisions and take choices.

Where possible, the plan should identify the worker/s responsible for carrying out each piece of the practice. Quite commonly, there will be several people involved in different aspects of the work. The more lengthy the history and the more family members are involved, the more practitioners will be engaged in the coordinated planning of work to be done.

Negotiating the plan and modifying it

The planning process will not always be straightforward. Different parties to the situation may have different expectations. The different family members may have different views, which means there is no single 'answer' that will match people's expectations with the needs of the child, which should be paramount in all this.

The plan should be devised with the active participation of parents with, or on behalf of, the children and not simply devised by consulting them when it is decided. The planning process should keep their views, preferences and feelings at the centre. They should be given copies of the plan, and its later revisions, in writing or in other appropriate formats. It is important to keep updating the plan as fresh evidence accumulates and the work proceeds. Any details of the risk assessment should be reflected in the plan, especially if this involves a need for action under safeguarding children procedures.

Intervention and implementation

Intervention is an aspect of implementation, woven into the process of working with children. Intervention is integral to the stages of assessment and planning that precede it. There are tensions between the professionals intervening in the lives of parents and children and working in partnership with them. Sometimes practitioners have to exercise powers and use the law, rather than empowering children and families to take control of their lives.

There is a need for practitioners to appreciate the effects of not implementing plans, and changing plans already made, on the quality of life of children. There is a particular need for children to experience stability in their placements and secure attachments to adults responsible for their care, education and development (Jackson and Thomas, 1999). Research demonstrates the major consequences of the quality, or lack of quality, of the implementation of care plans on the future life chances of children (Harwin et al., 2003).

Intervention is extremely challenging and probably demands more of our knowledge, skills and commitment than any other stage of the process. Intervention in the lives of children and parents is part of the wider span of working with children and families, involving a multidisciplinary approach. The social work contribution to this tackles problems that are of a greater complexity and often require the use of legal powers. The most obvious examples of this are in the use of sections 17 and 47 of the Children Act 1989. Section 47 is used where the child is clearly in need of protection from harm and a response meets the immediate needs of the child and promotes the child's welfare. Under the Children Act 1989, a range of options is available, the first two being time-limited orders with limited powers:

- *an emergency protection order* (s. 44): used to ensure the child receives treatment where there is reasonable cause to believe that the child is likely to suffer significant harm (see Chapter 23)
- *a child assessment order* (s. 43): used to arrange an assessment if the social worker believes the child could be suffering significant harm
- *a supervision order* (s. 31): where the child is suffering, or is likely to suffer, significant harm and the harm is attributable to the care given to the child, or where the child is beyond parental control
- *an interim care order* (s. 38): a temporary arrangement made where the court is satisfied this should happen while decisions are made about the future
- *a care order*: can be granted where the child is suffering, or is likely to suffer, significant harm and the harm is attributable to the care given to the child, or where the child is beyond parental control
- *a residence order*.

Each of these entails a specified level of intervention by the local authority, which entails it exercising, through, for example, social workers, foster carers or residential care staff, a specified level of supervision, and legal authority, over aspects of the upbringing of the child. At the extreme, a child aged from birth to 18 may be taken from the birth family and, after careful and detailed consideration and planning, placed for adoption with another family, the parents of whom undertake full and permanent parental responsibilities for bringing up the child.

Perspectives on social work intervention

Brand et al. (2005) identify four perspectives on the need for social work intervention: service user and carer, frontline, national and international (Table 24.1).

According to the principle of person-centred services, parents and children should be central to the process of delivering services. These four perspectives all require an approach to working with children and families that is rooted in human rights and social justice. However, there may still be a tension between satisfying people's needs, prioritizing children requiring safeguarding, managing risks, and rationing resources. Tunnard (2002) specifies the services required to meet children's needs and from this we can derive the necessary interventions set out in Figure 24.2.

Table 24.1 Perspectives on the need for social work intervention

Perspective	Characteristics
Service user and carer	Needs arise from the support people require in order to maintain their independence, rather than from their inherent weakness
Front line	Practice is shaped by the face-to-face reality of practitioners meeting parents and children
National policy on wellbeing and regeneration	Practice is shaped by national health and wellbeing priorities and policies
International	International definition of social work shapes practice

Figure 24.2 Interventions required to meet variety of children's needs

Dealing with tensions and dilemmas

The circumstances of people's lives are often complex and uncertain, so it is not surprising that it is a feature of health and social care work. Despite our best efforts to plan and insure against accidents, risks and unforeseen circumstances, none of us is exempt from an unexpected incident, situation or illness.

Tensions arise where the worker has to make a choice between two or more equally problematic options. These tensions may amount to *dilemmas*, that is, two choices, each of which resolves one problem while creating another or leaving the original one unresolved. In practice, the practitioner may need to accept the reality that just as tensions have to be managed, dilemmas must be accommodated. By definition, a dilemma is a choice, where neither option provides a satisfactory outcome for everybody concerned.

Point for Reflection

What are the similarities and differences between implementation and intervention?

Monitoring, reviewing and evaluating

Review and evaluation can take place at different levels: central government, local authority, agency provider and practice. At the practice level, the people involved will be the child and parents as service users, the practitioners and other people who have a close knowledge of the child.

Monitoring and review are not one-off activities but part of continual processes, overlapping with planning, intervention and, where necessary, reassessment. Review is a form of reassessment 'on the job'. *Continuous review* is a constant, repeated process of appraising what we have achieved, adjusting our plans and restating what remains to be done. Reviewing is the stage where the practitioner asks how effective the work has been to date. It is a further stage of the process of the work. It feeds into evaluation, but it is just as likely to lead to further questions about the assessment. Modifications to this will require adjustments to the plan, in a continuing cycle. As an interim appraisal of the situation, a review is the opportunity for the people involved to reflect and discuss what has been achieved so far and discuss any issues that have arisen.

The review meeting contributes to the process of review, but is not the entire review. There are good reasons to involve the child and significant, usually parental, carers for the child in the review meeting. The precise way in which this is handled depends on the circumstances, including the feelings of those potentially taking part.

New goals may be proposed as an outcome of the review meeting, arising from changing circumstances, or the wishes and needs of the children and other family members.

Achieving joined-up practice

Monitoring and reviewing should be part of the continuous process of working with a child and their family. There should be no breaks in the continuity of the process, such that review meetings are seen as part of the process. Children, parents and other family members as appropriate should be empowered to participate actively in the entire process of planning services so as to meet their needs. Some children – those who are disabled, in need or in care – may need independent advocacy services to ensure that they can participate actively enough to enable their voices to be enhanced. The following questions are integral to the review:

- What have the practitioners done?
- How are the children, their parents and other family members feeling about this?
- What do the children, their parents and other family members regard as most effective?
- What do the children, their parents and other family members feel could have been done better?
- Were all the objectives in the plan met?
- If not, which objectives were not met?
- Were all the needs of the children, their parents and other family members met?
- If not, which needs were not met?
- Should new goals be set?
- What goals should be included in the revised plan?
- What should be done next?

What evaluating entails

Evaluating necessitates:

- taking an overall view of the work done
- making judgements about everything done to date and everything that remains to be done
- reaching a view about the strengths and weaknesses of the work done.

Evaluation is potentially a wide-ranging and comprehensive activity. It poses a number of questions:

- How useful was the work done?
- How well was it carried out?
- To what extent did it meet the targets?
- What shortcomings were there?

Children, their parents or carers and other family members as appropriate should take part in the evaluation. The evaluation should have at its centre their perceptions and experiences. These should form the heart of the evaluation and not be peripheral or carried out in a tokenistic way.

Practitioners draw on four main clusters of skills in carrying out evaluation:

1. Gathering information, especially concerning the feelings of children and their parents or carers
2. Recording information
3. Exchanging information
4. Reporting on information.

These skills depend on the expertise of the practitioners involved in gathering information and recording it in a systematic and accessible form, in line with the Data Protection Act 1998 and the procedures of the agency governing the gathering and storage of data about people.

Conclusion

The process described in this chapter should engage all professionals involved with the family, as well as children and family members. Assessment is the basis of all subsequent work and it is vital that it is carried out with the full involvement of children and other family members. Planning has a vital part to play in providing creative health and social care services, in negotiation with the person using services, rather than handing out traditional services to the person, in a way that reinforces dependence. Intervention is a crucial aspect of implementation of plans made in conjunction with children, their parents and carers. While implementation is a more neutral term covering the translation of any plan into practice, intervention is a term reserved for those situations where there is a compulsory element in the work the practitioner does with the person using services. Tensions exist in practice and some of these may be expressed in terms of practice dilemmas. Reviews and evaluations are different but they do overlap. Review is a more restricted activity, while evaluation covers the entire spectrum of the work done. Review and evaluation are among the most demanding tasks, because much information has to be collected from different people – work colleagues, children, parents and other family members – and require judgements that affect other people's lives.

REVIEW QUESTIONS

1. Name the main elements of the social work process.
2. How does a review differ from an evaluation?
3. What kinds of skills do you need to carry out an evaluation?

_____ *Chapter Links* _____

For further information about safeguarding the child, see Chapter 23.

_____ *Further Reading* _____

Calder, M. with Harold G. and Howarth E. (2004) *Children Living with Domestic Violence: Towards a Framework for Assessment and Intervention*, London, Jessica Kingsley. Detailed examination of research and practice issues, covering the process from assessment through to intervention.

Cleaver, H., Walker, S. and Meadows, P. (2004) *Assessing Children's Needs and Circumstances: The Impact of the Assessment Framework*, Lyme Regis, Russell House. An important critique of the Assessment Framework, in the light of practice.

Fahlberg, V. (1991) *A Child's Journey Through Placement,* London, BAAF. Authoritative reference book, giving detailed information at every stage of the process of working with children and families through the process of assessment, planning, intervention and review.

Macdonald, G. (2001) *Effective Interventions for Child Abuse and Neglect: An Evidence-based Approach to Planning and Evaluating Interventions*, Chichester, Wiley. Useful practice-oriented advice rooted in the evidence base.

Parker, J. and Bradley, G. (2003) *Social Work Practice: Assessment, Planning, Intervention and Review*, Exeter, Learning Matters. Chapter 3 contains some good illustrations of practical tools for planning.

_____ *Websites* _____

www.education.gov.uk/childrenandyoungpeople/strategy/integratedworking/a0068938/integrated-working/   Government website with guidance on key aspects of integrated working

Part 6

Diversity and Difference

Inclusive Practice and Diversity in Religious Family Life

25

Jan Horwath and Janet Lees

LEARNING OUTCOMES

By the end of this chapter, you should be able to:

- understand that religion can be defined in a variety of ways
- recognize ways in which religion can influence family life
- appreciate the knowledge and skills required to work inclusively with families where religion is significant to the family
- reflect critically on ways in which your own values and beliefs influence your practice

---

The Children Act 1989 (see Chapter 1) requires local authorities to 'give due consideration to the child's religious persuasion'. The Act is underpinned by a belief that children, young people and their parents should be treated as individuals. In order to achieve this, differences in child rearing, due to family structure, religion, culture and ethnic origins, should be respected and understood (DH/DfEE/Home Office, 2000). While some, such as Voas and Crockett (2005), argue that religion is losing its relevance in the 21st century, it is important to recognize that only 15% of the adult population in the UK (DWP/National Statistics, 2004) and 5% of married couples and parents in the USA identified themselves as having no religious affiliation (Mahoney et al., 2001). What appears to be happening is that the construction of religion is changing from one that included the institution and traditional practices, such as attending places of worship, to one that focuses more on human potential

(Pargament et al., 2005). This change is captured in the guidance to the *Framework for the Assessment of Children in Need and their Families:*

> Religion or spirituality is an issue for all families whether white or black. A family who do not practise a religion, or who are agnostic or atheists, may still have particular views about the spiritual upbringing and welfare of their children. For families where religion plays an important role in their lives, the significance of their religion will also be a vital part of their cultural traditions and beliefs. (DH/DfEE/Home Office, 2000, p. 49, s. 2.69)

Point for Reflection

Why do you think that, in the UK today, it is increasingly important for practitioners to understand how religious beliefs may affect children and their family life?

The importance of religion to family life has become increasingly topical as the UK becomes a progressively more multifaith society. Increased global mobility, resulting, for example, from the expansion of the European Union from 15 states in 1997 to 27 in 2007 and a significant number of refugee and asylum-seeking children and families (see Chapter 28) arriving in Britain, has resulted in people coming to the UK wishing to maintain a diverse range of religious beliefs and practices. The consequences are that a quarter of all babies born in Britain have at least one parent born outside the UK (Addley, 2007), and it is estimated that by 2017, 15% of the UK workforce will be Muslim (Ajegbo et al., 2007). For some, maintaining their religious beliefs and practices will be important.

What is religion?

If we are to understand the ways in which religious beliefs and practices affect children and families, it is necessary to explore what we mean by 'religion'. This is not easily achieved and would seem to mean different things to different people. In a recent study, Lees and Horwath (2009) asked young people aged 13–15 years from Muslim and Christian backgrounds who attended faith schools in a northern city in England to define religion. Their responses were varied and included activities like prayer (both private and public), reading holy books, discussing religious issues, giving to charity, and fasting. They also referred to taking part in the activities of the religious community, such as attending worship, taking part in pilgrimage and festivals. However, other young people considered that religion was more than just a set of behaviours but extended to all aspects of life and could best be summed up, in the words of one participant, as 'living religion basically'.

These findings indicate that religion can be defined in a number of different ways. With this in mind, practitioners are more likely to understand and validate the child and family's religious beliefs and practices if they allow family members to define religion for themselves (Sharpe, 1983). This is preferable to imposing a definition of religion on the family or drawing on the practitioner's own pre-conceived views about religion. However, it is also important that practitioners recognize that dominant religious beliefs within a society, such as Protestantism in the UK, will have a significant influence on structures and traditions that may marginalize members of other religious groups. For example, bank holidays in the UK are linked to Christian festivals such as Christmas and Easter.

Perceptions of 'religious families'

If religion is defined in different ways, it is inevitable that the ways in which religious families are perceived will vary. This is demonstrated through the examples provided by the young people referred to in Lees and Horwath's (2009) study:

> It's just a family that has religious values and beliefs and everyone in the family practises and everyone helps each other to practise it. (Muslim girl aged 14 years)

> They [the family] encourage each other and it's sort of high up in their priorities and what they do in life. (Roman Catholic boy aged 13 years)

> I think it would be a high priority in life, but I think they'd just be just the same as everyone else. I think they'd just do much the same as everyone else. (Roman Catholic boy aged 13 years)

> It's not that different from just being in an ordinary family. (Roman Catholic girl aged 13 years)

Definitions of 'religious families' included:

- Engaging in specific religious family behaviours. For example, praying together at different times of the day, week, month or year, reading holy books together, discussing religious issues together, holding similar religious family values.
- Taking part in the activities of the religious community. For example, attending worship together, taking part in other faith-based activities together, such as a sponsored walk for a religious charity.

The young people in the study also expressed views about 'what is not a religious family'. This was considered to be a family in which verbal adherence to a religion and behaviour did not match behaviours. In other words, the family did not practise what it preached in areas such as forgiveness or discipline.

Points for Reflection

What questions would you ask to establish what religion means to a particular child and members of their family? When framing your questions, consider the advantages and disadvantages of closed and open questions.

What different methods could you use to elicit information about religious beliefs and practices depending on the age of the child?

How does religion influence family life?

Drawing on the research literature on religion and family life, and the results of Lees and Horwath's (2009) study, religion appears to influence family life, parenting and child development in a number of ways. These are discussed in detail below.

Parenting styles

Two key dimensions of parenting behaviour are said to contribute to parenting style: parental responsiveness and parental demandingness. These have been developed further to describe four types of parenting style (Baumrind, 1966; Maccoby and Martin, 1983):

- *authoritative:* high demandingness, high responsiveness – the parent is warm but firm
- *authoritarian:* high demandingness, low responsiveness – the parent requires conformity to their expectations and standards
- *indulgent:* low demandingness, high responsiveness – the parent is permissive, passive and has few standards or expectations
- *indifferent:* low demandingness, low responsiveness – the parent is disengaged and neglectful.

Traditionally, most particularly in the USA, religious parents have tended to be perceived as authoritarian, demanding obedience from their children in line with the requirements of their particular faith. However, recent findings indicate that living within a religious family does not necessarily entail the low warmth/ high criticism environment associated with authoritarian homes (Gunnoe et al., 1999; Wilcox, 1998). Unfortunately, very little research about religion and parenting styles has been undertaken in the UK.

The development of identity

The importance of religious identity to families, young people and communities has recently attracted attention, particularly in multicultural contexts like the UK, where a problematic relationship between 'Britishness' and members of minority religious groups may exist (Saeed et al., 1999). Studies that have included explorations of religious identity are primarily from the USA and Europe. In a study of Muslim identities adopted by Pakistani youths in England, Jacobson (1998) found a range of identities from very devote individuals who practised their religion daily to those who never practised Islam but still called themselves Muslims. She concluded that because so much of British Pakistani Muslim young people's lives are open to question, the certainties contained in Islam are appealing.

In most faiths, there is an expectation that parents are responsible for raising their children as members of that particular faith community, with ceremonies to mark different levels of membership and commitment. The extent to which individuals internalize religious beliefs can have implications for their values, attitudes and approach to relationships. A child's religiosity tends to be similar to that of their parents and membership of a religious community encourages social conformity (Flor and Knapp, 2001; Gunnoe et al., 1999). The opportunity to develop a strong religious identity was just one of the reasons given by Muslim mothers for choosing Islamic schools for their daughters (Osler and Hussain, 2005). While they believed in the importance of academic achievements for their daughters, they also wanted the girls to develop strong and confident religious identities.

Responsibilities

One of the themes to emerge from data collected by Marks (2004) from highly religious families in the USA was the cost of family religious practices. Marks (2004) identified two aspects to this cost: financial costs associated with charitable giving and tithing practices, and the social costs associated with strict religious observance, such as not being able to attend social events organized by peers due to family religious commitments. Concluding that we need a greater understanding of what religious family life is like for the members, Marks also stated that we need to understand why families might shoulder such costs willingly and even view them as benefits. It is also worth recognizing the tensions this may create for some parents and children who are torn between their religious traditions and practices and the socioeconomic demands of a wider society.

Implications for practice

Lord Laming's (2003) inquiry into the death of Victoria Climbié highlighted the lack of knowledge and understanding of the role of religion in family life by professionals. Recent research has confirmed this (Gilligan and Furness, 2006). An understanding of religious beliefs and practices should inform the skills and knowledge required of practitioners when working with children and families. We describe some of the practice implications.

Communicating with and engaging with children and young people

While it is important for children and families to explain how they perceive religion influences their family life, this is most likely to occur if practitioners are open, listen and ask the right questions to elicit relevant information about the influence of religion on the family's life, particularly from children and young people. This may seem obvious yet religion is generally considered only when assessing the needs of families from minority ethnic groups where religion is perceived to be inextricably linked to culture. In terms of other families, practitioners may ignore religion because they do not know how to ask the right questions, feel it is irrelevant or are embarrassed (Crompton, 1996; O'Hagan, 2001). In addition, it is not enough to assume that the views of a religious parent and their child will be similar when it comes to religion. Some studies have shown that young people may be more or less religious than their parents. In Britain, the transmission of religious beliefs from parents to child is said to be only about 50% where both parents are religious and nil where neither is religious (Voas and Crockett, 2005). It is also worth noting that children and young people from nonreligious families may hold religious beliefs.

Meeting the developmental needs of children and young people

The moral development of children may be particularly important to religious families. This may have implications for the development of family and social relationships, with parents having views as to suitable family members, friends or community contacts. Some families choose a faith school because they believe it will support the religious values of the home rather than conflict with them, seeing this as important for the secure development of the child's religious identity.

If the developmental needs of the child are to be met, parents or carers must have the capacity to meet these needs. Parenting capacity consists of six different task or dimensions (DH/DfEE/Home Office, 2000). Religious beliefs and practices might influence the way in which parents approach the various parenting tasks:

- Religion may influence *basic care*, for example food, clothing.
- *Emotional warmth* in the parent–child relationship may be influenced by religion although not necessarily negatively. Warmth, encouragement and praise have been found to be an important part of religious parenting as much as discipline, guidance and boundary setting (Gunnoe et al., 1999; Wilcox, 1998). Not only does the development of individual autonomy need to be considered in a cultural context, but also in a religious context. Respect for parents and for the family and community as a whole may influence the way individual autonomy is expressed.
- The opportunities for *stimulation* a family provides may be influenced by religion. A religious family might think it is important that a child has access to the learning opportunities provided by the faith community, either after school or at weekends. These learning opportunities might be directly linked to religious beliefs and practices, for example learning the scriptures, or they may be social and provide a peer group of intergeneration community to which the child can relate.
- *Guidance and boundaries* are likely to be influenced by religious beliefs. These may include, for example, clear views about what it is appropriate for boys and girls to wear and do at different stages, guidance about sexuality and sexual relationships and standards of behaviour.
- Religion may influence the *stability* of a family. For example, when assessing relationships with the wider family through family history tasks, some religious families may include the involvement of family members who have died, and the ongoing relationship between living and dead family members may be of importance in the emotional life of a family.
- *Ensuring safety* is considered below.

Safeguarding and promoting the welfare of children and young people

Child maltreatment is not acceptable in any religion (DfES, 2007d; Zaman, 2006). However, there has been much recent publicity about child maltreatment in relation to members of faith communities. For example, physical abuse by mullahs, sexual abuse by Roman Catholic priests, and physical and emotional abuse by Roman Catholic nuns. In addition, the Laming Inquiry (2003) raised questions about abuse linked to beliefs in spirit possession. These concerns have been identified by members of the faith communities themselves, and in an attempt to address these situations, faith communities have introduced child maltreatment guidance and procedures and have appointed officers to raise awareness and address different forms of maltreatment in the faith community. In response, government guidance *Safeguarding Children from Abuse Linked to a Belief in Spirit Possession* (DfES, 2007d) has been developed to assist practitioners who are concerned that a child is being abused or neglected linked to a belief in spirit possession.

While practitioners should be aware of and recognize that these forms of abuse are taking place, they should also be aware that blanket negative assumptions about religion and maltreatment could lead to discriminatory practice. It is therefore important that practitioners are provided with opportunities to discuss their feelings, assumptions and values within supervision. They should also be aware that growing up in a religious family has been found to be a protective factor when it comes to young people engaging in risk behaviours, for example substance abuse (Bradby and Williams, 2006).

Supporting transitions

All children and young people pass through various stages and transitions. For a religious family this may include transitions within the faith community, which may have accompanying rites of passage (bar mizvah, confirmation, believers baptism and so on). Other transitions may be affected by religious beliefs and practices, including school to work transitions. Some types of work, for example in the military or the gambling industry, may not be acceptable to some religious families. Practitioners need to be aware of the relevant transitions, both religious and nonreligious, and be ready to provide support for children and young people considering these.

Multidisciplinary work

If practitioners are to meet the needs of children and their families, they will be required to work together with others. In the case of families who identify themselves as members of a faith community, this may mean working with members of faith communities and religious leaders. This can be particularly important in terms of identifying ways in which the faith community can support the child and their family.

When professionals work together, they might easily establish a fixed idea about a family (Reder et al., 1993; Munro, 2002). This can result in stereotyping or a shared view, which may not have been checked out with the family, as to how the family's particular religion is influencing their family life. It can also result in unintended collusion that religion is not important. For example, it is all too easy to presume that as the family have not mentioned religion and are not obviously members of a particular faith, it is not important to them.

Assessing the influence of religion on family life with children who are in need or have additional needs

The information about religion that is likely to be shared among practitioners will be influenced by the guidance provided to professionals undertaking assessments of children with additional needs using the Common Assessment Framework (CAF) (DfES, 2004b) and for children defined as in need under section 17 of the Children Act 1989, the *Framework for the Assessment of Children in Need and their Families*, known as the Assessment Framework (DH/DfEE/Home Office, 2000). Only one dimension of the Assessment Framework makes an explicit reference to religion: this is in terms of the developmental needs of the child and relates to the child's sense of identity. The CAF makes reference to religion under the dimension 'identity, including self-esteem, self-image and social presentation'. The only suggestion in the CAF guidance as to how these might impact on meeting the needs of children is in relation to bullying or discriminatory behaviour, which may occur because of religion, race and so on (DfES, 2004b). The emphasis is on oppression rather than recognizing that religion, or indeed the other factors, can be a source of empowerment and resilience and contribute to positive self-esteem and self-image. The only other reference in the frameworks is to attending places of worship. This fails to recognize that the faith community may be a possible community resource for the family. Furthermore, because a family state that they do not attend a place of worship, it does not necessarily mean they do not adhere to the beliefs and some of the practices of that faith. Also, practising at home is common in some religions.

Points for Reflection

Listed below are three situations one may encounter as a practitioner. Drawing on the content of this chapter, consider how you would respond.

1. A 12-year-old white girl from a Conservative Protestant family tells you 'What my dad says goes in our family'.
2. This family will make a particular journey to visit a specific place and carry out certain rituals, 12 months after the death of a family member. How do you ascertain how important this is to the 8-year-old child and the 14-year-old young person in the family?

> 3. A young person tells you that he is concerned about the aggressive attitude of an adult towards children in his faith community. This young person is from a large family and has several younger siblings who are also part of the same faith community. How do you proceed with the situation?

Conclusion

The diversity of religious belief and practice in 21st-century Britain requires that professionals working with children and families pay careful attention to including this aspect of family life in their understanding of any child, young person and family.

REVIEW QUESTIONS

1. What is currently known about the influence of religion on family life?
2. How can one begin to understand the meaning of religion to a child and their family?
3. How has your understanding of the influence of religion on family life changed since reading this chapter?

Chapter Links

For further discussion of aspects of discrimination, see Chapter 18.

Further Reading

Edwards, H. (n.d.) *Faith, Religion and Safeguarding: NSPCC Internal Briefing Paper*, http://www.nspcc.org.uk/inform/trainingandconsultancy/consultancy/helpandadvice/faithreligionandsafeguarding_wdf47840.pdf. An overview of safeguarding in faith communities from a nonreligious national voluntary organization.

Horwath, J., Lees, J., Sidebotham, P. et al. (2008) *Religious Parents Just Want What's Best for Their Children: Religion, Belief and Parenting Practices, A Descriptive Study*, London, Joseph Rowntree Foundation. Full report of the study of the perceptions of young people and parents describing the effects of religious beliefs on parenting practices in a multicultural, urban UK context.

Lees, J. and Horwath, J. (2009) Religious parents ... just want the best for their kids: young people's perspectives on the influence of religious beliefs on parenting, *Children and Society*, 23, 162–75. Article on part of the above UK study with young people aged 13–15 concerning religious beliefs and parenting.

Phoenix, A. and Husain, F. (2007) *Parenting and Ethnicity*, York, Joseph Rowntree Foundation. Summary of evidence from the parenting literature on the influences of ethnicity that points to the need for more research on the contribution of religion to everyday parenting practices.

Zaman, A. (ed.) (2006) *Child Protection in Faith-based Environments: A Guideline Report*, London: Muslim Parliament of Great Britain. Report on safeguarding from the perspectives of the main faith groups in the UK.

Websites

http://www.ccpas.co.uk/ Churches Child Protection Advisory Service Interdenominational agency used by the main Christian churches to advise about safeguarding issues

www.muslimaid.org Hosts the Muslim Aid Child Protection Policy, the safeguarding policy of the largest non-Christian religion in the UK

Working with Challenges to Children's Identities

Robert Adams

LEARNING OUTCOMES

By the end of this chapter, you should be able to:

- discuss what identity means in contemporary society
- explore different perspectives on identity
- examine the different aspects of identity relevant to working with children, young people and their families

---

This chapter explores some of the aspects of identity that are likely to impinge on work with children. It is important to be aware of the ways in which growing up and living in the contemporary Western world presents children and young people with challenges that were not part of the nonindustrial, traditional society, where the pathway from childhood to adulthood was clearly marked out and did not change from generation to generation. While it has always been true that children's identities are in transition throughout childhood, and certain developmental changes affect them physically, emotionally and socially, these transitions are more complex and demanding in the modern world.

One institution that has changed hugely over the past few decades is the family. For instance, many more children than formerly have to relate to and interact with other step-siblings, different adult partners of their main carers and different step-families. During childhood, they may encounter several new family forms and new carers in this way. These changes present children and young people with challenges, but they also represent opportunities. One of the transitions they are required to make is to construct a new sense of themselves, aspects of a new identity as a family member: as a stepbrother or sister, stepson or daughter, or stepgrandson or daughter.

Meanings of identity in contemporary society

What does identity mean to children and young people? The term *identity*, quite simply, refers to a person's sense of self. A child's identity develops from infancy through childhood and is often referred to by psychologists as the sense of 'self'. We can distinguish between an individual's *personal identity* – who they feel they are, a sense they have as individuals about themselves – and *social identity* – their sense of who they are in relation to the social groups with whom they identify and interact.

Children and young people are growing up not only in a rapidly changing world but in an increasingly globalized world where the dimensions of time and space are changing. These changes have a great impact on the lives of younger people in society, particularly as they are more networked than many older people, through the use of mobile phones and social network sites. Children and young people have their identities shaped by their birth, country and family of origin and place of growing up. However, it is also the case that they are freer than many of their older relatives were at their age to make choices, including making choices about their identities. Conventionally, the dimensions of social class, gender and ethnicity may be taken as a given in discussion of the constituents of identity. However, children and young people are better placed than former generations to superimpose their own definitions of their identity on these dimensions, in some cases ignoring or bypassing them.

The implications of these realities for children and young people may be expressed in a variety of ways. They may experience the benefits of enhanced opportunities, to explore, travel using virtual media and physically move to a new location. However, they may be vulnerable for one reason or another, marginalized or socially excluded. Their families may be poor, and poverty, illness and disability may be dominant features of their everyday lives. They may live daily with the consequences of these aspects of inequality. On the positive side, they may experience the benefits of opportunities for self-expression and creativity. On the negative side, they may experience insecurity, unhappiness, isolation and uncertainty. They may be in need, unhealthy, vulnerable and in need of protection.

What identity means in childhood

Identity has a different meaning to people, according to their age, social status, culture and environment. Psychologists have studied how the infant and young child develops a sense of identity and sociologists have examined the person's developing relationships with friends and social groups and classes, associated with notions of class identity or class consciousness. From a sociological perspective, identity refers to the different social and friendship groups to which the child relates. We can see that identities have different sides or faces, in that a child and young person develops multiple identities, in growing towards maturity, according to the different social aspects of their lives. They may relate to ideas and people in many different social groups. These different relationships will exist in different strengths. Some will be dominant and others much less important to them. The balance between these differences is likely to change through time. We need to be aware of the diversity of experience and perceptions but also of the fragmentation of the different facets of people's identities. These different facets may, on occasions, be in tension with, or actually incompatible with, each other.

Identity is not only a complex but also a contested concept, in the sense that there is no consensus among social theorists about its definition and therefore its relationship with other concepts and practice. Seidler (2010) authoritatively explains and illustrates a wealth of social theory, which it is important to mention here:

- *Structuralist* (for instance, Marxist) social theorists have emphasized class identity at the expense of, say, gender, sexuality or ethnic identity.
- *Postmodernist* theorists, in contrast, take account of social diversity and argue that people can assume multiple identities, reflecting the complexity of their life histories, and some of these can even conflict with each other. Thus, a child or adult may act in ways perceived by others as 'masculine' in some settings and as 'feminine' in others.
- *Modernist* understandings of identity inherit rationalist ideas from the18th-century Enlightenment. Theories of identity informed by modernist perspectives emphasize the distinction between reason and nature in human development: a dualism segregating people's 'higher' human qualities from aspects of their 'animal' nature such as sexuality.
- *Postmodernist* perspectives, in contrast, adopt the view that people's identities are not fixed by their inheritance, but can be developed and created.
- *Social constructionist* perspectives maintain that they are constructed historically and socially.

People's identities are not simple, one-dimensional, like a photograph, they are multidimensional – they may be perceived from different perspectives and those different perspectives may conflict with each other, so the meaning the person attaches to the term 'identity' will be multifaceted. It will reflect this complexity.

An illustration of the complexity of identities, expressed through the relationships between children's minds as well as their bodies, is impairment and disability. In a sense, this concerns children's images of themselves (their self-identity) and their experiences and perceptions of 'normality'.

Chapters 27 and 28 discuss different models of disability. In this chapter, we begin with the critics of the *medical model of disability*, which can be summarized as the view that your disability is another term for your individual, medically diagnosed physical or mental problem. Since the growth of the disability movement in Western countries from the late 1960s, many of these critics, such as Oliver (1990, 1996), have advocated the *social model of disability*, which argues that the body may have certain impairments but, on the whole, it is societal processes and pressures that, through stigmatizing and socially excluding people – including children – disable them. So, from this viewpoint, disability is the term used to refer to the ways in which non-impaired people act oppressively towards impaired people. At an extreme, the social model of disability argues that if these oppressive factors were eliminated, the disabling condition would disappear. The social constructionist perspective of sociology supports this view, in the sense that it appears to encourage the belief that the labelling and stigmatization of the disabled child is fundamentally a social process rather than a reflection of the bodily and mental differences between children. Critics of this from a materialist perspective, such as Thomas (2002), maintain that sociologists and professionals who work with disabled children should take account not only of the ways in which children's bodies and minds are understood and interpreted, but also of the real, material differences between different children. Shakespeare (2006) advocates this view, insisting that the person's impairment remains real no matter how it is represented. Physical impairment should not be denied and is part of the diversity of people.

This is relevant when we consider practice in a nursery, where the worker is expected to act in an accepting and non-discriminatory way when working with the diversity of young children. *Difference* is the term often used to refer to distinctive differences between social phenomena. Sociologists distinguish people in terms of gender, ethnicity or social class differences. This distinction is relevant here as a reminder of the variety of ways in which a child's identity is developed, according to the child's:

- *gender:* boys are often treated differently to girls by their parents, other family members, friends and professionals
- *ethnicity:* in different ethnic communities, children and adults are likely to treat each other distinctively and those in one ethnic group may be treated differently by those in another ethnic group

■ *social class:* a child in one social class where great wealth is the norm is likely to have a different experience of growing up and forming and developing an identity from a child brought up by a parent who is a labourer.

Difference: gender

Children begin to explore and develop their ideas about their identities – although, of course, not to arrive at a 'final' identity – when they begin to develop notions of who they are and to which friends and social groups they relate. Children's ideas about their gender emerge in this way as crucially linked with notions of identity. In part, this is because, in contrast with the biological features of their bodies, their gender is socially constructed. As children grow towards adulthood, their sense of their gender develops.

Thus, a person's sense of who they are includes their sense of gender and tensions or conflicts may exist between their personal and social identities in this respect. For instance, a child may come to feel that she is a female trapped inside a male body. Later, decisions may need to be made in response to her requests to change her physical body to conform to her inner sense of her identity.

These ideas enable us to question traditional notions of what 'male' and 'female' mean in society. We can take this further by selecting masculinity as the focus of this discussion, noting that femininity deserves an equivalent discussion.

Masculinity

The social world, by and large, tends to be shaped in most countries by ideas rooted in masculinity rather than femininity. Males are more privileged in most countries than women. In many societies, women occupy secondary positions in the social world and have less power than men to shape their lives. In some societies, male-dominated views and cultures support their assumptions and arguments by referring to tradition. In some countries, culture is interwoven with religious practices.

Some people believe that gender roles are shaped, even determined, by culture or biology. *Cultural determinism* is the term sometimes used to refer to such an approach. *Sociobiology* is another term used. Most social theorists, in contrast, emphasize perspectives that enable people to question dominant ways of shaping their lives, where these are in conflict with principles of social justice and equality. Such critical viewpoints may conflict with traditional, taken-for-granted views of society.

There is much scope for further theorization and debate and one area requiring further research is the relationship between ideas about masculinity, identity and the body. People's bodies play an important part in expressing their identities and this particularly applies as young children grow up.

Developing gendered identities

The settings where we work with children are locations where gendered roles and stereotypes may either be challenged or reinforced by staff and parents. It all depends on how these settings are led and how they run on a day-to-day, minute-by-minute basis.

According to psychoanalytic theory, infants undergo a process of forming a sense of who they are – the 'I', or as Freud puts it, the ego. Seidler (2010) illustrates how the development of gender identity is integral to this process. The fact that a baby's gender is not external is demonstrated by the cases he quotes of babies born at Great Ormond Street Hospital, London, where their gender identity is unclear. The doctor has to make a decision about which gender intersex children are by clarifying surgically the ambiguities in their external genitalia. Nursing staff are present and share in the delicate process of negotiating – with each other and with the parents – as this often denied and usually invisible process is dealt with by those present. Seidler (2010) notes that the wider societal context is typically widespread hesitance or even fear among the general public about sexual ambivalence and uncertainty, which can be resolved only through insisting on the dualism between male and female.

This is only part of the situation. Identity is not resolved at birth through an operation, but develops through the child's experience. Professionals share in this at every stage, whether as health visitors, nursery staff, infant teachers or social workers. So, when young children are very young, they may start to show an interest in their own bodies and curiosity about the bodies of other children and adults. It is important to perceive this curiosity for what it is and not to interpret it through the experience of an adult. Children, however, interact with each other and with adults, and through these interactions confirm that the physical differences between children can be attributed to gender. Conversations with them can help them to categorize different people – 'This is a boy. He is a man. She is a girl. She is a woman.' In these ways, the child's perception of gender will become richer as more points of questioning and discussion emerge – 'Girls wear skirts. Boys wear trousers. Some girls wear trousers. Some boys wear kilts.'

There are circumstances in which the natural process of children developing their awareness of sexuality is disrupted. For example, in some families, there may be disturbances to children's development such as those brought about either by witnessing or being subjected to sexual abuse. These may accelerate or distort the otherwise steady development of their sexuality. Thus, we can confidently predict that work with children will almost invariably need to take account of their developing gender and sexuality identities.

***

Point for Reflection

Consider what activities you would develop with young children so as to cross the boundaries of the traditional expectations of the roles of girls and boys.

***

Pointers for practice

Children are developing rapidly during the years of childhood and central to this process is their developing identities. As they develop, they first establish a sense of their identity as individuals and subsequently develop a sense of their identities, collectively – with other children, with adults, with their family members and with the communities of which they are members, such as nursery, primary school, secondary school and so on. During this lengthy process, children experience hurdles at key stages, such as the transition from being at home to attending a playgroup or nursery, or the transition from nursery to reception class in school. They experience tensions between the stage they have left and the next stage. They encounter different adults, working as professionals, at each stage – nursery staff, teachers, care workers, social workers and so on.

Embodiment

An important concept, referred to in Chapter 3 and which we need to acknowledge briefly here, is that of embodiment. *Embodiment* is the term used to refer to the bodily aspects of our human experience, that is, our subjective sense of experiencing ourselves as a person with a body, mind and emotions, rather than the distanced, external or objective view another person might have of our physical or psychological selves. So children's embodied view is of themselves experienced holistically rather than as observed. Rather than accepting a view of childhood defined by adults, professionals and social constructionists, children's own experiences and perceptions contribute to our understanding not only of their psychological and emotional development, but also of their journey towards independent identities as persons with rights in society. Seidler (2010) describes how, as people grow and change, they may move beyond simply accepting what others tell them is the way to behave and begin to make their own choices and develop their own opinions and tastes. They begin to accept themselves more holistically 'as embodied emotional and spiritual beings in the wider world' (p. 150). Children and young people become aware of the lack of certainty and risks in the world around them and of the ways in which people may be vulnerable to harm, abuse or violence. Part of this engagement with their circumstances entails an understanding of the complexity of their 'self' as 'made up of fragmented, multilayered, complex, fluid embodied identities' (Seidler, 2010, p. 150).

Practitioners need to be aware of the range, depth and intensity of children's experiences and perceptions and of the associated pressures children encounter as they grow and develop. They need to exercise skills in working with children. It is important to children that they grow in a positive way and that the experiences they have are positive.

PRACTICE STUDY

Cassie and Mick are the same age and go to the nursery five days a week. When Mick follows Cassie into the home corner and wants to help her set out the dolls to have a tea party and starts by washing the cups, Helen, the new staff member, leads Mick outside. She is overheard saying 'Boys don't do the washing up. Let's go and play with the other boys.'

The senior practitioner discusses with Helen how important it is to express the values of the nursery in her actions and words. One of the values they discussed during her induction was the belief in equality, expressed in non-sexist and non-gendered treatment of the children. The senior practitioner points out that the experiences of Cassie and Mick at the nursery are vital to their development. Children are not born with expectations that boys play with guns and fight, while girls play with dolls and make pretend cakes and bread out of play dough. They are socialized into, that is, they learn, these expectations.

Conclusion

This chapter has touched on important areas of children's development that are often neglected, since they raise difficult issues for practice. We can see that work with children and their parents and carers sometimes will broach matters of personal and social identity that are both private and sensitive for the individual and also display a social aspect. Indeed, sometimes the practitioner will have an opportunity to enable parents, children or young people separately or working together to challenge an aspect of their situation, perhaps using feminist theory about diet and eating habits as a reference point.

At the same time, the arguments discussed above do not have the character of biological facts or being proved scientifically. They are sociological theories, concerning aspects of social reality that are socially constructed. However, they are no less real, when the practitioner is working with the child and other family members.

REVIEW QUESTIONS

1. How would you define identity?
2. How do a child's social and personal identity differ from each other?
3. What particular insights does the notion of embodiment contribute to understanding children and childhood?

Chapter Links

For discussion of aspects of discrimination and equality-based practice, see Chapter 18.

Further Reading

Evans, M. and Lee, E. (eds) (2002) *Real Bodies: A Sociological Introduction*, Basingstoke, Palgrave – now Palgrave Macmillan. A series of theoretically based essays on sociological aspects of the body, many of which are important reference points for practice with children and families.

Seidler, V. (2010) *Embodying Identities: Culture, Differences and Social Theory*, Bristol, Policy Press. Thoroughly argued and stimulating, although quite theoretical, discussion of aspects of identity, which is relevant to work with children, young people and their families.

Websites

www.gender.bham.ac.uk A resource centre on gender and sexuality studies at the University of Birmingham

Young Children with Physical Impairments

27

Patricia Higham

LEARNING OUTCOMES

By the end of this chapter, you should be able to:

■ understand what is meant by 'disability' in young children
■ distinguish between disability and impairment
■ differentiate the social model of disability from the medical model of disability in relation to young children
■ reflect critically on social policy and service provision for young children with a physical impairment and their carers
■ identify appropriate knowledge and skills for intervention with young children and those who care for them

---

Working with children with physical impairments poses a challenge of recognizing the unique human qualities of an individual child, rather than seeing only the problems of the impairment. Because practitioners are used to problem solving, they instinctively look for problems in every situation – they may focus on physical impairment, and miss crucial developmental needs.

Recognizing the *child* along with the *impairment* is made more difficult by the fact that practitioners are accustomed to working in separate organizations and teams for children and families, mental health, learning disabilities, adults and physical disabilities, which, although administratively tidy and encouraging specialist practice, set up artificial boundaries. The needs of a child with a physical impairment will span disabilities, children and families, and, perhaps, mental health problems that might affect family members.

This chapter will encourage practitioners to think differently about young children with physical impairments as a precursor to improving their practice.

What is 'disability' in young children?

The Disability Discrimination Act 2005, which amended the 1995 Act, defines a disabled person as an individual with 'a physical or mental impairment which has a substantial and long term adverse effect on his ability to carry out normal day-to-day activities' (Secretary of State for Work and Pensions, 2006). The Act defines 'impairments' in relation to their effect on the ability to perform day-to-day activities (Sapey, 2008). Is it possible to substitute the word 'child' for 'adult' in this definition? Possibly not, because it is unclear whether practitioners can be certain that an infant or young child with a physical impairment will inevitably become 'disabled' in this sense (Pillai et al., 2007).

Another way of understanding disability in young children is to recognize the disadvantages a child with physical impairments will encounter because of physical and attitudinal barriers. Disability is linked to a person's relationship with their environment (Finkelstein, 1981; Thomas, 2003), therefore 'young disabled children' are children who are disadvantaged by environmental factors interacting with their particular impairment or long-term health condition (Pillai et al., 2007).

Disability and impairment

Point for Reflection

What kinds of physical impairments would you consider particularly affect children?

Specific physical impairments in children (Secretary of State for Work and Pensions, 2006) include the following:

- *Sensory*, affecting eyesight or hearing
- *Progressive,* such as muscular dystrophy, a group of hereditary progressive muscle diseases
- *Organ specific*, including respiratory conditions, such as asthma, a condition that affects the airways, making it difficult to breathe
- *Developmental,* such as autistic spectrum disorders, including autism and Asperger's syndrome, characterized by limited communication, restricted interests and repetitive behaviour, and dyspraxia, characterized by impairment of movement and sometimes language and perception
- *Prenatal or postnatal injury or lack of development to the body and/or brain,* including cerebral palsy, caused by damage to the brain's motor control centres mainly during pregnancy but also during childbirth and after; spina bifida, where the bones and nerves of the spine do not develop fully, sometimes resulting in bladder and bowel difficulties and problems with control of the lower parts of the body; and hydrocephaly, a condition to which spina

bifida children are prone, where the fluid surrounding the brain becomes blocked, and pressure builds up in the head.

These are some of the physical impairments that may affect young children. Another way of understanding the different impairments is to consider:

- ■ those that are progressive (worsening over time) and those that are not
- ■ those that are considered to pose more challenges to achieving independence and those that pose less
- ■ those that are 'invisible' physical impairments (loss of hearing) and those that are visible.

An additional consideration is when the impairment first reveals itself – before birth, at birth or later, and how the news of the impairment was communicated. An explanation of the full range of physical impairments is beyond the scope of this chapter, but the web pages of charities for particular impairments are informative.

Not a marginal issue

Pillai et al. (2007) argue that disability cannot be a marginal issue because it affects 1 in 5 adults and 1 in 15 children. Research findings differ on how many disabled adults and children live in the UK. According to the General Household Survey (ONS, 2002), there were around 11 million disabled adults and 770,000 disabled children in the UK (out of a total of 11.8 million children), while according to the Family Resources Survey (DWP/National Statistics, 2004), there were around 9.8 million disabled adults, and an estimated 700,000 disabled children.

Over the past 30 years, the numbers of disabled children have apparently risen, perhaps because of increased reporting (Mooney et al., 2008). More children are reported as having complex needs, autistic spectrum disorders and mental health issues. By 2020, the total number of children is likely to drop to 10.8 million, but disabled children's numbers may increase. The reasons for a predicted increase, although not completely understood, may be attributed to better diagnoses, the survival of very premature infants, more reporting of disability, and different definitions of disability.

Thinking differently: the social model of disability, citizenship and independence

Practitioners who aim to think differently about children with physical impairments must engage with the social model of disability (Oliver, 1983, 1990,

1996). The Union of the Physically Impaired Against Segregation (UPIAS, 1976, p. 3), which was formed in the UK in 1972, was the first user-led group to explain and advocate for a changed perspective of disability and impairment: 'Disability is something imposed on top of our impairments by the way we are unnecessarily isolated and excluded from full participation in society.'

The social model of disability, a major influence on contemporary practice, argues that the causes of impairment should not be located in the individual but in the structures of society. Society, rather than the young child with impairments, must change. The social model aims to remove the barriers impeding participation in everyday life – physical barriers that restrict access to buildings and transport and attitudinal barriers that restrict disabled people's acceptance by others as full members of society.

In contrast, the medical model of disability, in essence a 'professional model', individualizes the causes of disability and thus maintains the power of professionals over individuals with physical impairments.

Contemporary ideas about citizenship and independence are consonant with the social model's goals. For example, Pillai et al. (2007) evaluate current policy, health and demographic trends against a standard of full citizenship to paint a picture of the probable experiences of disabled people by 2020. The report *Improving the Life Chances of Disabled People* (PMSU et al., 2005) seeks to improve opportunities for independence in the 'opportunity society'.

The prime movers in UPIAS who began to develop the social model were (predominantly male) adults with physical impairments. Can young children with impairments, who are dependent on their carers, be helped by adult

PRACTICE STUDY

Josie Andrews, who is of African Caribbean ethnicity, was born six months premature, and is now two. She spent three months in hospital after birth, is partially sighted, has a heart problem, and is unlikely to be able to walk. Her mother, Dawn, is 18 years old and a single parent, having lost contact with Josie's father. Josie and Dawn live with Dawn's Jamaican-born parents and her three younger brothers in an overcrowded council house. Dawn's parents are in debt, their marriage is stormy, and Mr Andrews is an alcoholic. Their family life seems disorganized, but the family loves Josie and feel protective towards her. Dawn, who is shy and withdrawn, has asked the local authority for some help with Josie.

1. Think of the barriers that must be overcome to avoid Josie becoming 'disabled'.
2. Make two lists, one of the kinds of services consistent with the social model of disability, and one of services consistent with the medical model.

Here is a checklist of what to consider:

- Advice and information
- Health needs
- Developmental needs
- Family support.

Anti-discriminatory practice is an important consideration. You need to consider how to promote Josie's development and wellbeing, and provide support for Dawn and her family as Josie's carers.

concepts of the social model, citizenship and independence? The answer lies in the realization that today's young children with impairments will become disabled adults who are still dependent unless attitudes, policy and programmes begin to think differently about physical impairment and take appropriate action. With suitable support from parents and other carers, young children with physical impairments will be able to benefit from childcare and early education programmes and other life chances.

Social policy, young disabled children and their carers

Three social policies are particularly significant:

1. Providing suitable support for all children and young people, their families and carers to ensure their optimum development
2. Overcoming disability discrimination
3. Eradicating child poverty.

The success of these policies for young children with physical impairments will depend on integrating the policies and resourcing their implementation sufficiently.

In England, *Every Child Matters* (DfES, 2003a) promotes five priority outcomes for all children: be healthy, stay safe, enjoy and achieve, make a positive contribution, and achieve economic wellbeing. These are suitable outcomes for young children with physical impairments as long as it is recognized that they and their families will need extra support to achieve them. Two Audit Commission reports (2003a, 2003b) on services to children with physical impairments cited inadequate planning, confusing criteria to determine eligibility for support, long waits to gain support, and a lottery of service provision. Their educational attainment is 'unacceptably lower' than that of non-disabled children, their families experience high stress levels, and only 4% of these children are supported by social services. Clearly much remains to be done to ensure equitable provision.

An encouraging development is the positive duty laid on public authorities by the Disability Discrimination Act 2005 to promote equality for all disabled individuals, including young children with physical impairments (Pillai et al., 2007). This means supporting these children and their carers with better advice, integrated health and social care, housing, transport, education, and individual budgets that potentially provide more control and choice over service provision (PMSU et al., 2005). The UK social policy aim of eradicating child poverty must take note of the fact that children with physical impairments are more likely to live in poverty (PMSU et al., 2005), estimated at 29% (Pillai et al., 2007).

Services for disabled children and their carers

Oliver and Bailey (2002) conceptualized three models for delivering welfare, all of which are necessary:

■ *humanitarian:* based on goodwill towards those less fortunate
■ *compliance:* where policy and legislation determine services
■ *citizenship:* where disabled individuals are empowered to contribute to society.

Arguably, many traditional services for young children with physical impairments are founded on humanitarian and compliance models, but not citizenship. Historically, families of young children with severe physical impairments were offered residential care or residential education rather than community-based support (Audit Commission, 2003a; Morris, 1997). Service provision is now meant to provide more choice, and offer personalized services that enable young children with physical impairments to maximize their opportunities for development so that they can participate in society and contribute to it.

The Carers and Disabled Children Act 2000 made it possible for people with parental responsibility for children with physical impairments to receive direct payments and individual budgets, thus giving carers more control over selecting the kinds of personalized services they want, rather than being forced to slot into existing services or finding that no suitable services are available. Individual budgets will be applicable to children's services by 2012 (Pillai et al., 2007). However, the Daycare Trust (2005) found that 37% of families surveyed were unaware of direct payments and over 50% did not use them.

In 2007, the UK government published *Aiming High for Disabled Children: Better Support for Families* (HM Treasury/DfES, 2007), which announced funding of £340 million from 2008 to 2011 to provide short breaks, accessible childcare and more involvement for parents locally in shaping services, including parent forums.

Skills and knowledge for working with young disabled children and carers

Relevant knowledge and skills can build practitioners' confidence to assess situations appropriately and intervene effectively. The first step in building confidence, as the chapter introduction states, is to begin to think differently about young children with physical impairments – to see them as children not just 'disabled'. This, and all subsequent steps towards better practice, should accord with codes of ethics (BASW, 2003), codes of practice (GSCC, 2002), anti-discriminatory and anti-oppressive practice (Thompson, 2006) and social justice principles (Jones, 2003).

The *key worker* is a role that potentially draws on all the knowledge and skills listed below. A key worker is a named worker that a family can turn to for advice and practical help for issues about the young child with physical impairments. Key workers work collaboratively with other organizations, professionals and schools to gain appropriate support for children and their families. However, key workers need to be supported by management, receive training and supervision, and understand their role (Greco et al., 2005).

Knowledge

The practitioner should be aware of:

- child development milestones (Minnett, 2005)
- the foundation stage (DfEE, 2000)
- the impact of impairment on the child, parents, siblings, relatives and other carers (Morris and Wates, 2006)
- the social model of disability as applied to young children.

Attachment theory (Bowlby, 1969) (see Chapter 4), which transformed children's services over the last 60 years, is equally applicable to young children with physical impairments, and should be considered when planning respite care and short breaks.

When to invoke child protection processes constitutes essential knowledge (Morris, 1999). Theories of loss and mourning may be helpful for understanding some family emotions (Kübler-Ross, 1969; Parkes, 1998). Practitioners should be alert for evidence of mental health issues arising from stress and isolation (NI DHSSPS, 2004). Relevant social policies and the range of available multiprofessional support in a particular area (health, education, transport, housing, and social services) are core to effective practice.

Practitioners should be aware of debates around medical technology and 'geneticization' (Shakespeare, 2005; Pillai et al., 2007) that may pose new attitudinal barriers towards participation (Barnes et al., 2000). The concepts of genetic science may succeed in relinking disability with biology and abnormality, thus leading to more discrimination (Pillai et al., 2007; Shakespeare, 2005). For example, parents who refuse genetic screening and termination of an 'abnormal' fetus may be viewed as irresponsible. King (1998) warns of the possible emergence of an erroneous 'commonsense' view that a child with a physical impairment is incompetent and disadvantaged. The social model of disability argues back that if impairment is genetically determined, the person with the impairment cannot be held responsible.

Skills

Practitioner skills that are important for working with young children with physical impairments include:

- ▪ *Multiprofessional teamwork:* to gain more effective outcomes from collaboration across professional divides (Anning et al., 2006)
- ▪ *Effective communication:* to gain the confidence of the child and the family and establish trust for working together (Brock and Ranking, 2008)
- ▪ *Information giving:* to help children and families find out what kinds of services are available (Wessels and Bagnall, 2002; Working Families, 2008)
- ▪ *Advocacy:* to secure provision of missing essential services (The Children's Society, 2007)
- ▪ *Supporting choices:* by building confidence and the ability to negotiate difficult issues (HM Treasury/DEfS, 2007)
- ▪ *Family work:* to understand the interactions of strengths and needs (Goodley and Tregaskis, 2006)
- ▪ *Direct work with children:* to discover children's wants and needs by appropriate use of verbal and nonverbal communication, play therapy and other suitable methods (Marchant and Martyn, 1999; Morris, 1998)
- ▪ *Child protection:* to conduct an investigation (when indicated) to ensure safety (National Working Group on Child Protection and Disability, 2003).

PRACTICE STUDY

Darryl is a one-year-old child with cystic fibrosis, an inherited disease with an average life expectancy of 30–40 years that causes the lungs and digestive system to become clogged with mucus, making breathing difficult. Darryl is the first child born to Mary and Mike, who are university graduates in their late thirties, with professional jobs. They waited 10 years to have a child to enable them first to progress their careers. Darryl's cystic fibrosis came as a complete shock, as there was no previous incidence in their families. Since Darryl's birth, Mary has not been able to return to work and the couple's relationship has deteriorated. No relatives live nearby. Mary and Mike are protective of Darryl, are highly critical of health and social care services, feel isolated, and express little hope of getting any help.

Consider the issues faced by Darryl and his parents. What kind of support might they need?

A practitioner first has to gain the confidence of Darryl's parents before exploring different choices with them.

Conclusion

The life situations of young children with physical impairments differ, just as their physical impairments differ. Seeing the child, not merely the physical impairments, and using the social model of disability to guide practice are starting points for effective working.

REVIEW QUESTIONS

1. How does the social model of disability apply to young children with physical impairments?
2. What barriers do young children with physical impairments face?
3. How can these barriers be overcome?

Chapter Links

For discussion of learning disability, see Chapter 28.

Further Reading

Morris, J. and Wates, M. (2006) *Supporting Disabled Parents and Parents with Additional Support Needs*, London, SCIE. This report offers suggestions for support for parents and carers.

National Working Group on Child Protection and Disability (2003) *'It Doesn't Happen to Disabled Children': Child Protection and Disabled Children*, London, NSPCC. Highlights the importance of child protection in relation to children with disabilities.

Websites

http://www.ncb.org.uk/edcm/home.aspx   Every Disabled Child Matters   A campaign run by four leading organizations working with disabled children, it provides much relevant information

Working with Children with Learning Disabilities

Alison Cocks

LEARNING OUTCOMES

By the end of this chapter, you should be able to:

- understand the main theories that try to explain what life is like for a disabled child and their families
- have knowledge of the key policies that guide and shape the services provided for disabled children and their families
- form an understanding of best practice when working with disabled children and their families

---

One of the most challenging aspects in writing about children with learning disabilities is that the term itself is problematic and continues to be debated. Within this chapter, I base my discussion on the viewpoint of the British Institute of Learning Disabilities that *learning disability* is when intellectual impairment impacts on a person's overall functioning in life, limiting the opportunities available for them to fully participate in their lives. However, it needs to be clear that, first and foremost, children are children. As with all children, they will also carry a range of other characteristics and identities, such as race, religion, gender, personality and family.

The chapter also complements and links with Chapter 27, which explores the key issues in working particularly with younger children with physical impairments.

Life as a child with learning disabilities

It is uncertain exactly how many children in the UK are diagnosed as having a learning disability. This is because there is disagreement about what the term actually means and the ways of measuring the degree of someone's disability are so contentious (Emerson and Hatton, 2007). Figures commonly used suggest that there are approximately 570,000 disabled children in England (HM Treasury/DfES, 2007), and of this number, it is uncertain how many have learning disabilities.

There is also limited information about what life is actually like for children who have learning disabilities (Morris et al., 2002). From 1997 to 2000, there was a large programme of research sponsored by the Economic and Social Research Council, which explored 'Children 5–16: Growing into the 21st Century'. As part of this, there was a large-scale exploration of what was life was like for disabled children. One of the key findings was that disabled children are subject to higher levels of surveillance than their mainstream peers (Davis and Watson, 2002). This raised concern about how the structured and regulated environments that disabled children were finding themselves within were impacting on their experience of childhood.

In research where the lives of children with learning disabilities are considered, sometimes alongside those with physical impairments, there have been a number of key findings:

- Disabled children and their families feel that policies and subsequent service provision do not reflect their priorities and needs (Beresford et al., 2007)
- Disabled children are at high risk of experiencing poverty (EDCM, 2007; Emerson and Hatton, 2007; Preston, 2006) and issues of class, social capital and ethnic minority further compound this (Chamba et al., 1999; Gillies, 2005)
- Disabled children experience less access to leisure opportunities than their mainstream peers (Sharma, 2002)
- Children with learning disabilities experience high levels of specialist services such as short-term breaks and specialist play schemes, thus experiencing exclusion from mainstream activity away from their local community (Cocks, 2000)
- Children with learning disabilities tend to be excluded from participation due to a number of complex factors, such as a lack of resources to motivate and train adults to support the participation process (Badham, 2004; Franklin and Sloper, 2006).

From this evidence, it is reasonable to suggest that childhood for those with learning disabilities features exclusion, increased risk of harm and vulnerability.

Children with learning disabilities can have a number of professionals involved in their lives, assisting the family to support the child. While those professionals are trained from a range of perspectives, for example medical, social, occupational, educational and legal, there are a number of theories that can help to inform the decisions that are made relating to these children.

Theories

Within the key professions that work with children (education, health and social care), there are a number of different ways in which disability has been understood and thus approached. In order to begin to understand how to work directly with disabled children, it is important to appreciate these different views and their subsequent influence on practice.

As Higham explains (Chapter 27), the medical model of disability has been criticized for failing to adopt a holistic view of a person's life, focusing, as it does, on the problem, its cause and potential for a 'cure'. It was this criticism of the perceived narrow focus of the medical model that acted as a catalyst for the development of the social model of disability. However, some scholars in disability studies are keen to acknowledge that medical science has had a positive impact on many lives, and for some, it is a necessary, even essential, part of life (Swain et al., 2003). Key here is to recognize that medical intervention for a disabled child is only one part of a child's life and for many children with learning disabilities, they do not have any more ongoing medical needs than any other mainstream child.

In its most commonly understood form, the *social model of disability* differentiates between 'impairment' and 'disability'. As Barnes (1991, p. 2) explains:

> Impairment is the functional limitation within the individual caused by physical, mental or sensory impairment. Disability is the loss or limitation of opportunities to take part in the normal life of the community on an equal level with others due to physical and social barriers.

The social model has been the driver for legislative and policy change and also for a review of the way professionals are trained in working with people who experience disability. In working with children, the model has a positive impact on the inclusion of disabled children within legislation, for example the Children Act 1989.

However, as in all aspects of social care, ideas develop and change. The social model has been criticized for a number of reasons (Goodley et al., 2008), but primarily for focusing on the material nature of disablement, thus failing to acknowledge the complexity of life for those with impairments (Shakespeare,

2006). When reflecting on the social model from a child's perspective, particularly a disabled child's, the model has a number of flaws:

1. It prioritizes a focus on the systems and social factors that shape disabled children's lives, not their real experiences (Cocks, 2006).
2. It focuses on the material factors within life, such as employment and economics, which are not key considerations for disabled children (Connors and Stalker, 2007). A number of alternative models have been suggested, not least by sociologists and advocates of children's rights, that address this.

Using the perspective adopted within the sociology of childhood, Michael Wyness argues that our understanding of childhood can benefit from the study of the cultural and social realms, enhancing our insight into children's identities as relatively independent persons with rights as members of society (see Chapter 3). Thus, children are seen as active agents within their own lives, participating in and contributing to the environment around them. The focus changes from the oppressive factors that disable people to recognition that children with learning disabilities are not passive within their lives, rather they are actively involved in their lives, they have views and opinions, abilities and degrees of independence (Cocks, 2006; Davis and Watson, 2002). This viewpoint encourages adults to appreciate the contribution that children make to their own lives – even children with learning disabilities, complex needs and different forms of communication. This focus is also flawed, as it rests only on the interaction of children with their surroundings rather then viewing interaction as dynamic.

Shakespeare (2006) has suggested that by viewing disability as a complex interaction between individual and contextual factors, we are encouraged to recognize the dynamism between structures and social systems, and people who have impairments. As he states:

> I define disability as the outcome of the interaction between individual and contextual factors – which include impairment, personality, individual attitudes, environment, policy and culture. (Shakespeare, 2006, p. 58)

This model encourages professionals, researchers and society to recognize the multiple factors influencing the degrees to which, and ways in which, people experience disability. This approach requires professionals to seek out an understanding of how disability is not only related to the person or the society they live in, but also the relationship *between* the person and society.

Shakespeare (2006) and Goodley et al. (2008) also suggest that the social model of disability fails to recognize the complexities of care and associated dependencies between those cared for and those giving care. This is a particularly useful perspective as children with learning disabilities are subject to adult defined and delivered care, in their capacity both as children and as children with learning disabilities. The feminist *ethic of care* is useful here as it focuses on the relationships that exist between people, the nature of those relationships, the role of dependencies and interdependencies between them and the activity that occurs between people.

When considering the childhood experiences of children with learning disabilities, this perspective recognizes how caring relationships are played out on a day-to-day basis. As explained earlier, children with learning disabilities experience specialist services where there are high levels of adult supervision. Thus they are engaged in a two-way relationship with adults. While there are flaws within the feminist ethic of care, which I do not have space to engage with here, it can perhaps guide professionals in considering their role within the relationships they hold with children with learning disabilities.

Social policy

In appreciating the current shape of service provision and professional involvement in the lives of children with learning disabilities, it is worth pausing briefly to reflect on the past. The social ideology relating to children with learning disabilities parallels and reflects the development of services for groups perceived as socially destitute, such as those with mental health problems, unmarried mothers and 'deviants'. The response to these groups was one of institutionalization, first within poor houses and then separate provision in large buildings for the 'feeble-minded' (Jackson, 1996). Philanthropy was a key driving force for the development of supporting policies and government recognition of learning disability as a social issue.

The separation of children with learning disabilities from their local communities and mainstream peers became an accepted practice. Indeed, the Royal Commission on the Care and Control of the Feeble-minded 1904–08 believed that parents would be acting in the best interests of their children if they were to receive education and training at special 'colonies' (Oswin, 1998). While institutionalization has been criticized, Oswin (1998) reminds us that this was driven by a desire to improve children's lives. In 1971, King et al. forced recognition of the neglect experienced by children while in specialist residential settings, thus instigating a policy review. Latterly, the most significant policy shift for children with learning disabilities was their inclusion within the Children Act 1989 as 'in need'. This stated that local authorities have a duty to 'provide a range of services to those children's needs' (Children Act 1989, s. 17(1)).

Services provided include those which support children within their own homes, such as home care, and provisions within the wider community such as specialist play schemes and short break centres. The introduction of the *Every Child Matters* agenda (DfES, 2003a) stressed the need for multiprofessional and interdisciplinary working. The five outcomes (be healthy, stay safe, enjoy and achieve, make a positive contribution, achieve economic wellbeing) sparked controversy within the organizations that work with and for disabled children (both physical and learning impairment). Research shows that, for disabled children, the five outcomes do not accurately reflect their needs or aspirations (Beresford et al., 2007). The outcome of this has been the creation of Every Disabled Child Matters, a campaign run by four leading organizations working with disabled children, aimed at improving the inclusion of disabled children. It is this campaign that informed the *Aiming High for Disabled Children* programme, which committed a substantial sum of money into the provision of services within local authorities to be delivered between 2008 and 2011 (HM Treasury/DfES, 2007). The programme describes a framework of actions and proposals outlining government plans to improve services for disabled children and their families. It focused on three key areas:

- access and empowerment
- responsive services and timely support
- improving service quality and capacity.

Spending constraints introduced by the coalition government in the wake of the 2010 review of public sector finances are likely to ensure that services for children with learning disabilities remain troubled by economic difficulty and a lack of universal social commitment.

PRACTICE STUDY

Sean is a nine-year-old boy, who has been diagnosed by a paediatrician as having a moderate degree of unspecified learning disability. His parents feel that he would benefit from extra support at his local primary school as he is unable to keep up with his peers or establish friendships. They also worry that he does not have many friends outside home and school, and are increasingly concerned about his move to secondary school.

Points for Reflection

What types of support are available for children with learning disabilities? How might you address the risk of exclusion for each type of support?

In this situation, there are many possibilities of how support can be offered to Sean and his family, which might involve a range of childcare workers. For example, teaching assistants might be able to support him in the classroom, play workers may accompany him to Beavers, and social workers might become involved to assess his situation for the provision of a more complex package of care involving short-term breaks and specialist play schemes.

While the ECM and Aiming High agendas outline central policy object-ives, the *National Service Framework for Children, Young People and Maternity Services: Disabled Children and Young People and those with Complex Health Needs* (DH/DfES, 2004b) also influences the delivery of services. Reviewing the different policy guidelines, there are common themes that are essential for achieving good practice.

Communication is central to all aspects of working with children with learn-ing disabilities – with the children themselves, their families and professionals in their lives. Children with learning disabilities have their own views of their lives and impairments, hopes and fears (Kelly, 2005), which professionals need to hear and respond to. Komulainen (2005, 2007) suggests that professionals can address the way in which we understand 'communication difficulty' by rec-ognizing the influences of context, our own perception of what communication should be, and therefore how we hear 'voice'. Workers need to recognize that communication is channelled not only through voice, but through the body, facial expressions and action, in ways that are unique to each individual.

The *centrality of parents and carers* within the lives of children with learning impairments is another aspect of communication. Professionals must acknowl-edge and draw on parental expertise, recognizing the personal and emotional investment of parents and their emotions. In doing this, workers may find that, within families, there are different opinions that need to be respected and balanced.

Consideration about communication leads to another critical aspect of achieving best practice, and that is what you do with the information com-municated. One of the key principles within ECM and the UN Convention on the Rights of the Child (1989) relates to the *participation of all children* in decision making – in all aspects of a child's life. For disabled children, this outcome has been slow to emerge as we learn new ways of working. Kennedy and Wonnacott (2003) suggest a number of approaches, which when applied, improve the experience of intervention:

1. Keep the child at the centre of all the work you do, whether that be assess-ment, planning or actual intervention.
2. Child development theories can be useful, as they provide an understand-ing of the expectations adults have of children as they grow, which need to be refined to the uniqueness of each child according to their needs and life circumstances.
3. Workers need to recognize that those closest to the child, such as their families, will have a great degree of knowledge and expertise related to the child, which warrants respect. This applies in particular to the children themselves.

4. A strengths perspective focus on the whole child leads to the recognition of their strengths as well as difficulties.
5. Interprofessional working is critical in the provision of services for children with learning disabilities in order to effectively coordinate the delivery of services. The ECM agenda requires professionals to work together to support a child and their family.
6. Professionals need to recognize that work with disabled children is an ongoing process over time, during which life changes and new challenges arise while others are resolved, meaning that the provision of services needs to be flexible and adaptable to change.
7. Use evidence to support your assessments and decisions – evidence-based practice is essential in understanding how to provide the best services and knowing what works and what doesn't.

Conclusion

This chapter has provided a brief discussion of the issues relating to children with learning impairments. Research shows that these children do not experience childhood in the same way as their mainstream peers, instead, they are at higher risk of poverty and social exclusion. A brief historical reflection of service development gave a glimpse of how this has become accepted practice and how this is now being addressed through the development of policies, such as Aiming High, which is targeted at improving their inclusion. The chapter ended with a reflection on how practitioners can ensure that their practice is supportive and inclusive of children with learning disabilities and their families in day-to-day life.

REVIEW QUESTIONS

1. How do children with learning disabilities experience childhood?
2. Describe the key theories that help us to understand what life is like for children with learning disabilities.
3. What can practitioners do to improve the experiences that children with learning disabilities have of social care provision?

_____*Further Reading*_____

Burke, P.C. and Cigno, K. (eds) (1996) *Support for Families: Helping Children with Learning Disabilities*, Aldershot, Avebury. Useful collection of chapters on relevant aspects of practice.

Kennedy, M. and Wonnacott, J. (2003) Disabled children and the assessment framework, in M.C. Calder and S. Hackett (eds) *Assessment in Child Care: Using and Developing Frameworks for Practice*, Lyme Regis, Russell House. Useful guide for practitioners on the crucial stage of assessment.

Williams, P. (2006) *Working with People with Learning Disabilities*, Exeter, Learning Matters. Useful basic introduction to the practice of working with people with learning disabilities.

Refugees, Asylum Seekers and Travellers

Robert Adams

LEARNING OUTCOMES

By the end of this chapter, you should be able to:

- demonstrate awareness of the difficulties of defining refugees, asylum seekers and Travellers
- understand the main aspects of policy and practice regarding asylum seekers and refugees
- appreciate the key aspects of policy and practice regarding Travellers

This chapter brings together discussion of refugees, asylum seekers and Travellers, because they share certain features in their problematic legal status in society, their frequent experiences of discrimination and social exclusion, and the particular challenges posed in work with their children.

Problems of definition

The definitions of refugees, asylum seekers and Travellers are somewhat problematic. The definition of the refugee was shaped by the huge numbers of people who fled across national borders as a result of the Second World War (1939–45) and therefore refugee movements within national boundaries were somewhat neglected. According to the United Nations High Commission for Refugees' (UNHCR) Convention Relating to the Status of Refugees, a *refugee* is any person who has

> a well-founded fear of being persecuted for reasons of race, religion, nationality, membership of a particular social group or political opinion, is

outside the country of his nationality and is unable, or owing to such fear is unwilling, to avail himself of the protection of that country; or who, not having a nationality and being outside the country of his former habitual residence as a result of such events, is unable, or owing to such fear, is unwilling to return to it. (UNHCR, 1951, Article 1)

A quarter of a century later, the UN (1967) expanded this definition to include people who had fled from war or other violence in their own country. Even though the development of international human rights legislation (UN, 1948, 1989), as well the UK Human Rights Act 1998, in some ways makes these UN conventions somewhat dated conceptions, they still influence contemporary social policy. The office of the UNHCR still functions and in 2008, 144 member countries of the 192 member countries of the UN are still bound by the refugee conventions (Goodwin-Gill, 2008).

An *asylum seeker* is a person whose application for protection – which usually accompanies the granting of refugee status – has not yet been accepted by the host country. About 25,000 people a year apply for asylum in the UK. This statistic does not convey the human costs, and in particular the consequences for children, of uprooting from one country and culture and arriving in another country with a view to seeking a place of safety. Difficulties associated with discrimination and exclusion are often superimposed on these problems of transition. Despite the fact that it is nearly half a century since the Race Relations Act 1965 made racial discrimination 'in public' illegal, discrimination against travelling and migrating people on ethnic grounds still persists, as acknowledged by the government's Cabinet Office Strategy Unit (2003).

People known collectively in Europe as Roma, Romany, Gypsy or Gipsy (an offensive word to some) are referred to in this chapter by another widely used word – *Travellers*. The problematic status of such people is illustrated by the lack of consensus over their 'label'. The widely accepted expression 'Gypsy, Roma and Traveller' is often used – for example in research publications such as Wilkin et al. (2010) – to cover these groups; the term Roma is often used to refer to many different groups of Romani people in Central and Eastern Europe; however, some people find 'Gypsy' offensive. In this chapter, while the terms Gypsy, Roma and Traveller are sometimes used, on occasions the term Traveller is used to refer to all these groups. In UK law, the lower case of the term 'traveller' is required to be used, however, 'to avoid any presupposition as to the ethnicity of those who may be covered by the definition' (ODPM, 2006, p. 8). In the 1960s, Travellers, then more commonly called Gypsies, were defined in the Caravan Sites and Control of Development Act 1960 (Part 1, s. 4, footnote 8) as 'persons of nomadic habit of life, whatever their race or origin, but does not include members of a group of organised travelling showmen, or members of travelling circuses, or travelling together as such'. Definitions of Travellers vary, according to their circumstances and the social policies to which the definition relates.

The Housing Act 2004 requires local authorities to tackle the accommodation needs of Travellers and for planning purposes, the definition of Travellers was later modified by the Office of the Deputy Prime Minister, which stated that in planning cases, travelling should be for work (ODPM, 2006). For housing purposes, the definition recognizes the wider responsibilities of local authorities for the future needs and accommodation of nomadic people, accepting the need for them to be transitional between sites and bricks and mortar housing. It accepts the need to provide for people who, because of 'their own or their family's or dependants' educational or health needs or old age have ceased to travel temporarily or permanently' (ODPM, 2006, p. 9). The ODPM (2006) states that the needs of travelling showmen, circus people and New Age Travellers are not excluded from this broader definition. Despite the fact that New Age Travellers may have adopted their nomadic way of life relatively recently, the ODPM asserts that (2006, p. 9) 'their needs should be assessed alongside those of the more traditional gypsy and traveller groups. To do otherwise would be to neglect the needs of part of the community.'

Policy and practice regarding asylum seekers and refugees

Since the last decade of the 20th century, the numbers of people claiming asylum in the UK have increased significantly. Since the mid-1990s, there have been over 650,000 claims of asylum in the UK (Sriskandarajah, 2005). Since 1993, there have been an estimated 1.5 million new non-British immigrants (Sriskandarajah, 2005). In 2007, almost 23,500 people applied for asylum to the UK and of these, about 16% were successful. The field has become more complex, as the enlargement of the European Union (EU) has meant that people can migrate freely between the new member countries. The number of countries in the EU has increased from 6 in 1951 to 27 in 2009.

Refugees are people granted the status of refugee in the country where they have sought asylum. Asylum seekers can obtain residency in the UK only if they meet particular conditions:

- A well-founded fear of persecution
- Based on their ethnicity, nationality, religion, political opinions or their membership of a specific social group.

Humanitarian protection, formerly called exceptional leave to remain, may be given to them if, despite not meeting the above conditions, the Home Office judges that it would be dangerous for them to return to their country of origin. Discretionary leave to remain may be granted for up to three years in exceptional situations. This can be extended to six years and afterwards indefinite leave to remain can be applied for. Usually a person who applies for indefinite leave to remain is successful.

The United Nations High Commission for Refugees (UNHCR, 2001) estimates that over 169,000 refugees are living in the UK – less than 2% of the total refugees in the world. The UK ranks tenth among European countries providing resettlement for refugees. Under the Nationality, Immigration and Asylum Act 2002, asylum seekers are no longer are allowed to work in the UK.

Concern about community relations in the UK has grown since the 1990s, focused not on wider concerns but specifically on successive waves of immigration from other countries and the challenges they pose to indigenous people. The mass media have heightened public concern about the numbers of asylum seekers and refugees applying to stay in the UK and opposition to immigration has been increased by the recession from 2007 onwards. The main argument is that immigrants take the jobs of indigenous people and receive social benefits, including housing, on which people already living in a locality should have prior claim. Against this argument, it is argued that immigrants tend to take the lowest paid jobs which, in any case, indigenous people are unwilling and unlikely to take. Hayes (2005) points out that people wishing to migrate to the UK have had their right to enter progressively restricted since the mid-20th century, through legislation such as the Commonwealth Immigrants Act 1962, Commonwealth Immigrants Act 1968, Immigration Act 1971, British Nationality Act 1981 and Immigration and Asylum Act 1999. The outcome is that nowadays it is almost impossible to migrate simply to resettle, and only on the exceptional basis of seeking asylum from a catastrophe such as persecution, famine, war or similar crisis. Policy since 2000 has responded more to people's fears, fanned by the right-wing press, than to empirical evidence on any economic threat posed by immigrants.

Three main pieces of legislation further restricted immigration since the beginning of the 21st century: the Nationality, Immigration and Asylum Act 2002, Asylum and Immigration (Treatment of Claimants etc) Act 2004 and the Immigration, Asylum and Nationality Act 2006. The 2006 Act takes an even less sympathetic view than previous legislation of the cases of people applying to enter the UK as asylum seekers and refugees.

Many people who are successful in gaining asylum bring their problems as well as their families to the UK, including the psychological consequences of torture and imprisonment, post-traumatic stress syndrome, difficulties in mastering new languages, loss of career credibility and a lack of recognized qualifications to enable them to continue in equivalent professional employment.

These accumulated problems make it inevitable that the children of asylum seekers and refugees will be disproportionately likely to experience social exclusion in the UK. Often they suffer because their parents have to accept poorly paid work and live in poor housing and suffer associated health problems as well as poverty.

Consequences for children of asylum seekers and refugees

The conditions affecting the residence of asylum seekers have a potentially adverse effect on children. On arrival, they are likely to have no choice over their housing, initially being sent to one of 10 immigration detention centres in England and Wales, also referred to by the Inspectorate of Prisons as immigration removal centres. The Nationality, Immigration and Asylum Act 2002 also enables people to be housed in reception centres, normally for a maximum of six months. From initial reception, they may be detained further or may live in a house or flat selected by the National Asylum Support Service. Consequently, their children are likely to have restricted access to, or to be excluded altogether from, mainstream schooling.

A report from the Refugee Council (2001) concludes that children who apply for asylum need better treatment. In 2006, the Refugee Council, Save the Children and Bail for Immigration Detainees launched a campaign to ban the detention of the children of asylum seekers – reported by these organizations to be in excess of 2,000 children per year – in custodial institutions (Morris, 2006). The children's commissioner for England was reported by BBC Radio 4 and the press (*Daily Telegraph*) on 10 March 2009 as being very concerned that children as young as eight years were telling him that they were transported in caged conditions in locked vans, a claim denied by the head of the UK Border Agency. Dame Anne Owers, the chief inspector of prisons – responsible for inspecting the institutions where asylum seekers are detained – criticized the treatment of children in a report on an inspection of Yarl's Wood Immigration Removal Centre in November 2009 (HMIP, 2010). She noted that some babies and children were detained for longer periods than was desirable – 68 children for a month and one baby for 100 days, despite social workers expressing concerns for their welfare and their families' welfare. She expressed concern about force being used on families being deported and, on two occasions, force being used against children. She asked why it was necessary to detain these numbers of children and families, when half were eventually released into the community.

More importantly, the various risks of harm to children being held in detention, with or without their families, prior to removal led to the recommendation (Dorling, 2009) that they should not be repatriated in any circumstances against their wishes.

It is likely that, while adult refugees and asylum seekers suffer the indignity and uncertainty of their treatment, children are more vulnerable to suffering through the process of arrival in a strange country and its accompanying traumas.

Policy and practice regarding Travellers

Both Romany Travellers and Irish Travellers are given recognition as an ethnic group in their own right, under the Race Relations Act 1976 and the Race Relations (Amendment) Act 2000 respectively. Minority Rights Group International (n.d.) estimates that in 2009 there were 90,000–120,000 nomadic, that is, not living in a fixed home, but on the move, Travellers in the UK and about 200,000 Travellers living in permanent housing. While this seems paradoxical, it is important to recognize that the identity of a Traveller incorporates both a cultural and a material component. An individual or family may identify themselves culturally and in their physical lifestyle as Travellers, or they may identify themselves culturally as Travellers but for all or part of the year occupy fixed housing.

The Caravan Sites Act 1968 required local authorities to set aside sites for Travellers in their locality and it became a criminal offence for Travellers to live on unauthorized sites. Local authorities increasingly resorted to moving Travellers on so as to reduce their legal liability. This is despite the fact that local authorities have a duty to house homeless people under the Housing Act 1996 parts 6 and 7, as later amended by the Homelessness Act 2002. Romany Gypsies and Irish Travellers are referred to in the Housing Act 2004, which states that they should be included in the local authority's housing strategy.

The Criminal Justice and Public Order Act 1994, in response to an increasing population of New Age Travellers who aroused public resentment, removed the obligation of local authorities to provide sites. About a third of Travellers live on sites that are unauthorized. Crawley (2004) carried out research concluding that the provision of appropriate, officially endorsed sites for Travellers, known and treated as permanent housing, lies at the core of the inequalities of access to education, health and employment that they experience.

The irony is that just as Travellers have historically played an essential part in the rural economy of the UK by providing farmers with seasonal labour at harvest and other crucial times, so migrants to the UK fill many gaps in the workforce that would otherwise remain unfilled (Sriskandarajah et al., 2004).

While there is an obvious need to counter discrimination, prejudice and social exclusion against Travellers, it is difficult to arrive at simple prescriptions for policy and practice that would ensure better conditions for them. One measure that improves their ability to maintain control over their lives is the provision of permanent sites for Travellers. This measure has two potential benefits:

1. It helps to reduce the inequalities they experience
2. It contributes to resolving intercommunal tensions, racism and discrimination that they suffer.

In some local authorities, for instance, the provision of permanent sites enables children of school age to attend local schools for part or all of the year. Also, the appointment of liaison workers with Travellers can support them where necessary and advocate for their interests and promote the rights of their children and young people to health and wellbeing services and to education, training, leisure and employment opportunities.

Consequences for children of Travellers

The children of Travellers remain significantly disadvantaged, underachieving at school and in further and higher education and are less healthy than their peers in other ethnic groups in the UK. This issue of health is consistent with the broader reality that Travellers as a whole have the lowest life expectancy of any ethnic group in the UK and experience the highest rates of infant mortality.

The fact that Traveller children perform significantly less well in the school system is clearly due partly to the discontinuities brought about by their itinerant lifestyle, for example as the adults in the family move in response to the changing seasonal demand for agricultural labour. The scale of this issue is apparent when we consider that in 2007 there were more than 8,000 Traveller children in the school system in the UK. The mobility of Traveller children, however, is only one factor in the complex mix of factors contributing to their performance at school. In fact, such differences persist even when families settle in a caravan on a site or in a house. For instance, Gypsy, Roma and Traveller children have significantly higher levels of absence from school than other pupils (Wilkin et al., 2010). Wilkin et al. (2010) conclude from their review of the research literature that Gypsy, Roma and Traveller pupils perform less well at all key stages in school than their equivalent peers through three main barriers: lack of engagement, interrupted attendance and negative experiences of school.

The Department for Children Schools and Families (DCSF) (now the Department of Education) aims to significantly improve the levels of attendance and academic achievement of Traveller children, and Traveller children are included in the aims set out for children by *Every Child Matters* (DfES, 2003a) (see Chapter 1).

Wilkin et al. (2010) conclude from their literature review that the attendance of Gypsy, Roma and Traveller children at school is most likely to be improved where there are staff specifically responsible for attendance (such as the education welfare officer or the Traveller Education Services), where there is interaction with parents and where there is support through the curriculum. The Traveller Education Services coordinate most funding by local authorities. The Race Relations (Amendment) Act 2000 puts a duty on schools to comply with the duty to have a written ethnic equality policy and to monitor the policies and achievements of ethnic groups including Gypsy, Roma and Traveller children.

Measures to combat inequalities include the contributions made by teaching assistants, the Traveller Education Support Service and support through the curriculum. Gypsy, Roma and Traveller children have made most progress in situations where parents are encouraged to become more involved in a dialogue with schools and where staff value and celebrate Gypsy, Roma and Traveller culture (Wilkin et al., 2010).

In summary, it appears that Gypsy, Roma and Traveller children benefit most where they receive the support of specifically allocated practitioners, either in school (such as social workers) or in the community (such as social workers with particular responsibilities).

Point for Reflection

What do you think are likely to be the key social factors and problems affecting the situation of Gypsy, Roma and Traveller children in the UK?

Conclusion

Many Travellers in Europe and the UK remain largely excluded from many state services, not only as a result of their nomadic way of life but also because of racist responses to their ethnic identities. Travellers are often subjected to both systematic and ad hoc discrimination at all levels, by the EU, by the countries of the UK, by local authorities and by people in local communities. The generalization holds true that many bold statements are made by bodies such as the Council of Europe, global charities such as UNESCO and UNICEF, and by national governments, but the reality in practice is that the lives of Travellers such as the Roma (Romany) people are precarious in many countries, including the UK. It is important for practitioners to appreciate the consequences for children, their parents and carers of this situation and to be able to develop practice that contributes to policy efforts to challenge and, hopefully, eliminate it.

Prejudice and discrimination against Travellers and migrants to the UK, including asylum seekers and refugees, persist and there is still a gap between the rhetoric of acceptance and the barriers people have to face to acceptance and inclusion. The children of Travellers and migrants to the UK remain vulnerable and there is a need for services to be enhanced in order to lessen the discrimination and exclusion faced by many people. Practitioners need to be aware of the unsettling consequences for children of making the transition from life in one community to another, plus the additional trauma of the process of applying for refugee status.

The children of Travellers, asylum seekers and refugees are likely to share common vulnerabilities to being discriminated against and excluded and practitioners will need to take into account these factors when working with them. There is a need for practitioners to have the opportunity for specific staff development, to help them to understand the culture and social circumstances of children, interact with them and their families better and help them to overcome barriers to inclusion in the community and wider society.

REVIEW QUESTIONS

1. Under which two pieces of legislation did Romany Travellers and Irish Travellers achieve recognition as ethnic groups?
2. What particular problems affect the children of refugees and asylum seekers arriving in the UK?
3. What difficulties do Traveller children encounter in their schooling and how may practitioners help them to surmount these?

Chapter Links

For further material on discrimination and anti-discriminatory policy and practice, see Chapter 18.

Further Reading

Bhopal, K. and Myers, M. (2008) *Insiders, Outsiders and Others: Gypsies and Identity*, Hatfield, University of Hertfordshire. A critical book, locating attitudes to Travellers in the wider context of how strangers are recognized, misrecognized and misrepresented in white society.

DCSF (2008) *The Inclusion of Gypsy, Roma and Traveller Children and Young People*, London, DCSF. Useful publication, enabling the reader to identify the main strands of government policy.

Fell, P. and Hayes, D. (2007) *What are they Doing Here? A Critical Guide to Asylum and Immigration*, Birmingham, Venture Press. Source of critical commentary and guidance for professionals.

Witt, S. (2000) *Working with Travellers: A Practical Guide for Play, Youth and Community Groups*, National Playbus Association. Practice-based guide to working with Travellers.

Websites

http://www.grtleeds.co.uk/Education/links.html Gypsy Roma Traveller Leeds The permanent site of the Gypsy Roma Traveller communities, it provides information on local and national educational organizations, including the National Association of Teachers of Travellers and the Advisory Council for the Education of Romany and other Travellers

www.refugeecouncil.org.uk Refugee Council Provides information, advice and other help to refugees

http://www.minorityrights.org Minority Rights Group International Campaigning organization, working to secure the rights of minorities, including the Roma in Europe

www.irishtraveller.org.uk Irish Travellers Movement in Britain Seeks to raise the profile of Irish Travellers in Britain and increase their say in decision-making processes and forums

www.romasupportgroup.org.uk Roma Support Group Seeks to improve the quality of life for Roma refugees and migrants

www.gypsy-traveller.org Friends, Families and Travellers Seeks to end racism and discrimination against Gypsies and Travellers

http://www.justice.gov.uk/publications/ Provides details of reports by HM Inspectorate of Prisons of the inspections carried out in immigration removal centres

Concluding Comment
Prospects for Work with Children and Families

30

Robert Adams

The purpose of this book has been to identify and examine the major contexts for work with children and their families. This has entailed taking a broad view of childhood, children and the work of practitioners with children and their families. The field of policy and practice has changed significantly during the latter stages of preparing the book for publication and this chapter provides an indication of the implications of these for practice. We do this in two parts. The first identifies the main policy changes taking place during the past twelve months. The second pulls together the implications of this, together with the other material in the book, for practitioners in their work with children and families.

Policy changes affecting work with children and their families

In Butler and Drakeford's (2003, p. 243) study of scandals in social work services, they assert that social work nowadays is 'work in progress'. This is partly in the sense that work is currently being undertaken at central and local government levels to learn the lessons from the succession of scandals concerning failures of quality in childcare, both public and private, and partly because major changes in the structure, management and delivery of these public services are in prospect. Significant political and policy changes have affected children's services while this book was in final preparation for publication. Policy and practice in work with children are greatly affected by changes of government. In that sense, the coming to power of the Labour government in 1997 and the change to the coalition government in 2010 represent milestones, with major policy initiatives in the early life of each government.

Central to the future trajectory of public services under the coalition government (2010 onwards) is the announced intention to cut public services by up to 20% over four years from 2010. There are indications that the spending cuts are likely to affect, disproportionately heavily, the services for poorer children in poorer parts of the UK – early intervention services, Sure Start and children's centres, safeguarding children, specialist services for children and young people, youth pregnancy and addiction services. Neoliberalism is the term used to refer to approaches to economic and social policy based on a market approach, that is, with a range of public, private, voluntary and independent organizations and groups supplying and receiving goods and services. The coalition government is committed to extending the reliance on the market approach to supplying public services, which was emphasized by the Thatcher government (1979–97) and developed by the Labour government (1997–2010). The coalition government has initiated a shift from the state as the default provider of services to services provided by a variety of organizations and groups, for instance, in children's services, including groups of parents and children self-providing free schools, that is, developing, managing and delivering services for themselves.

We can see many of the debates and controversies that are likely to arise in the area of children's services as these new policy directions take shape being played out in the health sector. The first target of the coalition government within three months of being elected was the reform of the NHS, with a view to achieving both capping costs and improved quality by enhancing value for money spent on health. The White Paper (DH, 2010) setting out proposals for reorganizing the NHS to fulfil these goals was followed by proposed legislation (Health and Social Care Bill), comprising five themes:

- strengthening commissioning of NHS services
- increasing democratic accountability and public voice
- liberating provision of NHS services
- strengthening public health services
- reforming health and social care arm's-length bodies.

This early initiative took place within the context of achieving the more far-reaching goal of replacing the 'big state' with the 'big society'. Advocates of the health reforms point to the benefits of GPs, as practitioners, commissioning at least 80% of services, thereby putting the judgement of clinical practitioners close to decisions about patients' treatment, with the use of the tendering process for contracts increasing local competition to supply services. Critics tend to argue that the reforms are privatization of the health service by the back door, that they will lead to fragmentation and will encourage 'cherry-picking' by potential contractors wanting to provide services.

The 'big society' is the shorthand term coined by David Cameron, prime minister of the coalition government, to refer to the policy goal entailed in a major shift of resourcing, management and responsibility away from the state and towards people assuming these themselves. In this connection, the expression 'double devolution' has become widespread, referring to the two linked but distinct processes of devolving power from central to local government and from local government to the local community. There are debates about whether this shift will empower people at the same time as reducing the costs to the state of dealing with entrenched personal and social problems. Advocates of the big society argue that its principles of giving more freedom, more control and more choice will benefit people by reducing their dependence on centrally provided and controlled public services, decentralizing them and building responsibility and people's capacity to take control over their own lives. Critics argue that people with more resources can cope better with this shift, which affects poorer people more negatively, since it amounts to a reduction in available support and basic public services. Furthermore, they argue that the burden of people supporting themselves and caring for others will fall disproportionately on people who have the greatest problems and who are most vulnerable.

The Green Paper (Cabinet Office, 2010), under the banner of modernizing commissioning, builds on the government's outlined plans for developing the big society (HM Government, 2010), focusing on the creation of more equal opportunities for private, voluntary and independent groups and organizations in the third sector to bid to provide public services. This feeds into legislation outlined in the Public Services (Social Enterprise and Social Value) Bill 2011, reforming public services by moving away from the notion that central and local government is the default provider of public services and towards the notion that the decentralization of power will boost social action by members of the general public, encourage diversity and permit professionals to exercise greater independence in their practice.

At this stage in the life of the coalition government, it is too early to predict the precise nature of the consequences of these policy changes for children's services, beyond the general expectation that they are likely to be very significant. Having sketched these broad strategies, we turn now to consider the main implications for practice.

Implications for practice

The above discussion of policy takes place somewhat removed from the practice of work with children and their families, so arguably it is easier to prescribe what should happen in an ideal world. Realistically, however, there are some inherently problematic aspects of such work, which grow more apparent the closer we approach them. In this discussion, these aspects are illustrated in terms of the challenges – and in particular the tensions – they represent for practitioners.

The legacy of the Labour government included not achieving the policy objective set early in its administration of halving child poverty by 2010. However, the incoming coalition government announced its intention of maintaining the second goal of the Labour government – to abolish child poverty by 2020. Meanwhile, as we have seen (Chapter 18), a significant proportion of children in the UK and their families continue to live in poverty, and despite the resilience of children, early deprivation tends to affect their aspirations and achievements into adulthood and throughout their adult lives. Practitioners working with children and families have to manage the tension between the aspiration of supporting and empowering them and the boundaries on intervention imposed by these personal wants and structural and continuing social inequalities.

The workforce of children's services is extremely diverse in terms of its agency and professional base, qualifications and experience, reflecting the diversity of services provided. However, as Baldock et al. (2009) note, in the area of work with younger children, in several significant ways the workforce is not diverse: more than a third are under 25 years old, about 99% are women, very few are disabled or from ethnic minorities, and very few hold a qualification above Level 3, that is, the equivalent of the BTEC National Diploma. A repeated concern of inquiry reports into shortcomings in children's services has been the need for better trained practitioners. Given government aspirations to raise standards of services, this represents a considerable gap between these aspirations and reality.

Following on from the last point, there is a need for practitioners to engage in very challenging practice, especially when working with children and families in circumstances of significant complexity. For instance, the roles that children's services are required to carry out span the continuum between therapy and helping at one extreme and control and intervention in the lives of children and their families at the other extreme. Accompanying this broad span is the obvious tension that Dalrymple and Horan (2008) identify that practitioners must manage between, on the one hand, acting as advocates on behalf of children and their parents or carers, and, on the other hand, acting as practitioners intervening on behalf of the state to carry out what professionals regard as being in the best interests of the child.

One of the main messages from this book has been the need for practitioners to learn about children not only through what professionals are saying, but from the experiences of children themselves. Children's perspectives on the services with which they are engaged – often whether they like or choose to be or not – give cause for concern that it is easy to carry the letter of policy into practice than to implement it in reality. It is relatively easy in the enlightened 21st century to find examples of childcare practice where children are asked for their views about aspects of services. However, as Kjørholt (2005) discusses in a fascinating piece of research carried out in an early childhood centre in Denmark, it is important not simply to engage with children but to examine the space where that engagement takes place. Kjørholt points out that it is necessary to be aware that when adults create and construct the space where children can participate, this is not the same as children being able to construct that space themselves as fellow citizens and competent persons on an equivalent basis with the adult practitioners working with them. Practitioners need to be aware that any such space is an ideological and moral construction, which embodies certain ideas and assumptions about what is entailed in being – thinking and feeling – and acting as a child. That is, the spaces designed by adults for children have furniture and decorations, embedded in which are particular expectations of how and when people should use them, how far their actions are determined, shaped and conditioned by the social structure and nature represented by the spaces, and how far children are free to impose their own definitions on them. This represents a tension that practitioners working with children and their families need to manage.

Following on the previous point, practitioners need to be aware in their work of the gap that may exist between the procedures they follow and the reality for the children with whom they work. Children cannot be understood or assessed, or work with them undertaken, out of the context of their families and their wider environment. For instance, Rixon offers practical advice to practitioners on the assessment of children. According to Rixon (2008), assessments of children may follow government requirements that they should be child centred (DfES, 2004; DH/DfEE/Home Office, 2000; Scottish Executive, 2007), but this may not be achieved in practice. Rather than assessments being child centred, they may be dominated in practice by information obtained from dialogue with adults. Children, in practice, are treated as objects rather than as subjects. They are observed rather than the practitioner finding out what their perceptions are. Rixon notes that this problem is not confined to the UK, but is a negative feature of practice in Australia and Scandinavia as well. In addition, when the views of children are collected, practitioners may be uncertain as to how much weight to put on them.

It is easy to make the general argument that more training at a higher level is needed to equip practitioners for these challenges. It is true that basic and post-qualifying education, training and staff development should be strengthened to support the continued development of children's services. There is much that practitioners can do to equip themselves for the children's services workforce. Basic qualifications and continuing professional development (CPD) are both vital ingredients and agencies and practitioners share responsibility for these. Basic qualifications are needed so that the practitioner can enter the field of practice and CPD enables the dynamic process of reflection on practice and learning from it. CPD can be defined as 'the systematic process by which the complementary practitioner maintains and updates expertise, that is, knowledge, understanding and skills, thereby improving performance in practice' (Adams, 2009, p. 375).

However, education and training need to be focused on the specific themes and critical areas identified in this book as crucial contexts for better practice. A report published by Eileen Munro (2011) reinforces the main purpose of this book, which is to extend the understanding of the practitioner and to recognize that analysing what is going on in families is a complex activity. It requires not only a grasp of the child's needs within the family but also the ability to draw on knowledge from research and practice (Munro, 2011). Munro advocates that the practitioner should not be overwhelmed by the requirements of bureaucracy, however, nor pressurized by the need to carry out procedures to the extent that they neglect their professional responsibilities. The practitioner 'needs to be able to articulate their theoretical body of knowledge' (Munro, 2011, p. 114) informing practice, the manager needs to be clear about this and may need to 'guide and supportively and critically challenge the analytic determination of risk and need'. This indicates that practitioners should be critical, assertive and sceptical, rather than limiting their work to the slavish following of procedures. It is vital that the practitioner understands how to share understandings of what is happening with family members and is able to work ethically towards safeguarding the child, mitigating problems and maximizing health and wellbeing.

Conclusion

This final chapter has achieved two things. First, it has provided a bridge between the material in the rest of the book and current developments in the rapidly changing world of children's services. Second, it has demonstrated the essential need for the practitioner to become well acquainted with the ideas and areas of knowledge covered in the preceding chapters.

The final message of this process is that it is necessarily unfinished. The 'work in progress' referred to near the start of this chapter is the need for the practitioner to continue to study aspects of the world of the child, build knowledge of research and develop the habit of reflecting critically on further practice. Hopefully, these are all activities to which this book will make a contribution.

References

Abramovitch, R., Pepler, D. and Corter, C. (1982) Patterns of sibling interaction among preschool-aged children, in M.E. Lamb and B. Sutton-Smith (eds) *Sibling Relationships: Their Nature and Significance Across the Lifespan*, Hillsdale, NJ, Erlbaum.

Acheson, D. (1998) *Independent Inquiry into Inequalities in Health*, London, TSO.

Adams, R. (2008a) *Empowerment, Participation and Social Work*, Basingstoke, Palgrave Macmillan.

Adams, R. (2008b) Basic needs, in W.A. Darity (ed.) *International Encyclopedia of the Social Sciences*, Detroit, Macmillan Reference.

Adams, R. (2009) Working with children, young people and families, in R. Adams, L. Dominelli and M. Payne (eds) *Social Work: Themes, Issues and Critical Debates*, Basingstoke, Palgrave Macmillan.

Addley, E. (2007) Prince, Davina and the baby revolution, *The Guardian*, 25 July, p. 19.

Adey, P.S. and Shayer, M. (1994) *Really Raising Standards: Cognitive Intervention and Academic Achievement*, London, Routledge.

Adey, P., Robertson, A. and Venville, G. (2002) Effects of a cognitive acceleration programme on Year 1 pupils, *British Journal of Educational Psychology*, 72, 1–25.

Ainsworth, M.D. and Bowlby, J. (1991) An ethological approach to personality development, *American Psychologist*, 46, 331–41.

Ainsworth, M.D., Blehar, M.C., Waters, E. and Wall, S. (1978) *Patterns of Attachment*, Hillsdale, NJ, Erlbaum.

Ajegbo, K., Kiwan, D. and Sharma, S. (2007) *Diversity and Citizenship: Curriculum Review*, London, DfES.

Alam, M.Y. and Husband, C. (2006) *Reflections of Young British-Pakistani Men from Bradford*, York, Joseph Rowntree Foundation.

Alderson, P. (1994) Researching children's rights to integrity, in B. Mayall (ed.) *Children's Childhoods Observed and Experienced*, London, Falmer.

Alderson, P. (2001) *Young Children's Rights: Exploring Beliefs, Principles and Practice*, London, Save the Children.

Aldgate, J. and Bradley, M. (1999) *Supporting Families through Short-term Fostering*, London, TSO.

Aldgate, J. and Statham J. (2001) *The Children Act Now: Messages from Research*, London, TSO.

Aldgate, J. and Tunstill, J. (1995) *Making Sense of Section 17: Implementing Services for Children in Need within the 1989 Children Act*, London, HMSO.

Aldridge, J. and Becker, S. (1993) *Children who Care: Inside the World of Young Carers*, Department of Social Sciences, Loughborough University.

Aldridge, J. and Becker, S. (2003) *Children Caring for Parents with Mental Illness*, Bristol, Policy Press.

Alexander, T. (n.d.) *A Bright Future for All: Promoting Mental Health in Education*, Mental Health Foundation, available from http://www.mentalhealth.org.uk/publications/?EntryId5=43106, accessed 12 Feb. 2008.

Allen, G. (2007) Families, in M. Davies (ed.) *The Blackwell Companion to Social Work* (3rd edn), Oxford, Blackwell.

Allen, M. (2003) *Into the Mainstream: Care Leavers Entering Work, Education and Training*, York, Joseph Rowntree Foundation.

Anning, A., Cottrell, D., Frost, N. and Green, J. (2006) *Developing Multiprofessional Teamwork for Integrated Children's Services*, Maidenhead, Open University Press/McGraw Hill Education.

Archard, D. (2004) *Children: Rights and Childhood* (2nd edn), London, Routledge.

Aries, P. (1961) *Centuries of Childhood*, Harmondsworth, Penguin.

Arnstein, S. (1969) A ladder of citizen participation, *Journal of the American Planning Association*, 35(4): 216–24.

Audit Commission (2003a) *Too Little, Too Late: Services for Disabled Children and their Families*, London, Audit Commission.

Audit Commission (2003b) *Services for Disabled Children: A Review of Services for Disabled Children and their Families*, London, Audit Commission.

Audit Commission (2004) *Youth Justice 2004: A Review of the Reformed Youth Justice System*, London, Audit Commission.

Badham, B. (2004) Participation – for a change: disabled young people lead the way, *Children & Society*, 18(2): 143–54.

Baldock, P., Fitzgerald, D. and Kay, J. (2009) *Understanding Early Years Policy* (2nd edn), London, Sage.

Bancroft, A., Wilson, S., Cunningham-Burley, S. et al. (2005) Children managing parental drug and alcohol misuse: challenging parent-child boundaries, in I. McKie, S. Cunningham-Burley and J.H. McKendrick (eds) *Families in Society: Boundaries and Relationships*, Bristol, Policy Press.

Bandura, A. (1977) *Social Learning Theory*, Englewood Cliffs, NJ, Prentice Hall.

Bandura, A. (1986) *Social Foundations of Thought and Action: A Social Cognitive Theory*, Englewood Cliffs, NJ, Prentice Hall.

Banks, S. (2001) *Ethics and Values in Social Work* (2nd edn), Basingstoke, Palgrave – now Palgrave Macmillan.

Banks, S. (2008) Critical commentary: social work ethics, *British Journal of Social Work*, 38(6): 1238–49.

Barnes, C. (1991) *Disabled People in Britain and Discrimination: A Case for Anti-Discrimination Legislation*, London, Hurst & Co.

Barnes, C., Corker, M., Cunningham-Burley, S. et al. (2000) *Lives of Disabled Children: Children 5–16 ESRC Research Briefing 8*, London, ESRC.

Barnes, J. (2003) Interventions addressing infant mental health problems, *Children and Society*, 17(5): 386–95.

BASW (British Association of Social Workers) (2003) *A Code of Ethics for Social Workers*, Birmingham, BASW.

Baumrind, D. (1966) Effects of authoritative parental control on child behaviour, *Child Development*, 37, 887–907.

Baumrind, D. (1967) Child care practices anteceding three patterns of preschool behaviour, *Genetic Psychology Monographs*, 75, 43–88.

Baumrind, D. (1971) Current patterns of parental authority, *Developmental Psychology Monographs*, 4(1/pt 2): 1–103.

Baumrind, D. (1989) Rearing competent children, in W. Damon (ed.) *Child Development Today and Tomorrow*, San Francisco, Jossey-Bass.

BBC News (2008) Girl wins right to refuse heart, 11 November, www.bbc.co.uk.

BBC Press Office (2010) 'Hidden army' of young carers could be four times as high as official figures, http://www.bbc.co.uk/pressoffice/pressreleases/stories/2010/11_november/16/carers, accessed 11 May 2011.

Bean, P. and Melville, J. (1989) *Lost Children of the Empire*, London, Allen & Unwin.

Becker, S. (ed.) (1995) *Young Carers in Europe: An Exploratory Cross-national Study in Britain, France, Sweden and Germany*, Loughbourough University.

Becker, S. (2003) Young carers, in M. Davies (ed.) *The Blackwell Encyclopedia of Social Work*, Oxford, Blackwell.

Beckett, C. (2007) *Child Protection: An Introduction* (2nd edn), London, Sage.

Belsky, J. (1984) The determinants of parenting: a process model, *Child Development*, 55, 83–96.

Belsky, J. (1997) Determinants and consequences of parenting: illustrative findings and basic principles, in W. Hellinckx, M.J. Colton and M. Williams (eds) *International Perspectives in Family Support*, Aldershot, Arena.

Beresford, B., Rabiee, P. and Sloper, P. (2007) *Priorities and Perceptions of Disabled Children and Young People and their Parents Regarding Outcomes from Support Services*, Social Policy Research Unit, University of York.

Berger, K.S. (2001) *The Developing Person Through the Lifespan* (5th edn), New York, Worth.

Bernstein, D.A., Penner, L.A., Clarke-Stewart, A. and Roy, E.J. (2008) *Psychology* (7th edn), Boston, NY, Houghton Mifflin.

Berridge, D. and Cleaver, H. (1987) *Foster Home Breakdown*, Oxford, Blackwell.

Berthoud, R. (1997) *Work-rich and Work-poor: Three Decades of Change*, Bristol, Policy Press.

Berthoud, R., Ermisch, J., Fransesconi, M. et al. (2004) *Teenage Pregnancy Research Programme, Research Briefing: Long-term Consequences of Teenage Births for Parents and their Children*, London, DH.

Bibby, A. and Becker, S. (eds) (2000) *Young Carers in their Own Worlds*, London, Calouste Gulbenkian Foundation.

Bichard, M. (2004) *The Bichard Inquiry Report: A Public Inquiry Report on Child Protection Procedures*, HC 653, London, TSO.

Biehal, N., Clayden, J., Stein, M. and Wade, J. (1995) *Moving On: Young People and Leaving Care Schemes*, London, HMSO.

Bigelow, A.E. (1977) The development of self recognition in young children, *Dissertation Abstracts International*, 37(12B): 6360–1.

Bishop, J.C. and Curtis, M. (2001) *Play Today in the Primary School Playground: Life, Learning and Creativity*, Buckingham, Open University Press.

Bissell, S. (2003) The social construction of childhood: a perspective from Bangladesh, in N. Kabeer, G. Nambissan and R. Subrahmanian (eds) *Child Labour and the Right to Education in South Asia*, London, Sage.

Black, D. (1980) *Inequalities in Health* (The Black Report), London, DHSS.

Blasi, A. (1980) Bridging moral cognition and moral action: a critical review of the literature, *Psychological Bulletin*, 88, 1–45.

Blom-Cooper, L. (1985) *A Child in Trust: The Beckford Report*, London, London Borough of Brent and Brent Health Authority.

Bowlby, J. (1953) *Child Care and the Growth of Love*, Harmondsworth, Penguin.

Bowlby, J. (1969) *Attachment and Loss*, vol. 1, London, Hogarth Press.

Bowlby, J. (1973) *Attachment and Loss*, vol. 2, *Separation, Anxiety and Anger*, London, Hogarth Press.

Bowlby, J. and Parkes, C. (1970) Separation and loss within the family, in E.J. Anthony and C. Koupernik (eds) *The Child in his Family: International Yearbook of Child Psychiatry and Allied Professions*, New York, John Wiley.

Boyden, J. (1997) Childhood and policy makers: a comparative perspective on the globalization of childhood, in A. James and A. Prout (eds) *Constructing and Reconstructing Childhood*, Basingstoke, Falmer.

Bradby, H. and Williams, R. (2006) Is religion or culture the key feature in changes in substance use after leaving school?, *Ethnicity and Health*, 11, 307–24.

Brand, D., Reith, T. and Statham, D. (2005) *The Need for Social Work Intervention: A Discussion Paper for the Scottish 21st Century Social Work Review*, Edinburgh, Scottish Executive.

Brandon, M., Belderson, P., Warren, C. et al. (2008) *Analysing Child Deaths and Serious Injury Through Abuse and Neglect: What can we Learn: A Biennial Analysis of Serious Case Reviews 2003–2005*, London, DCSF.

Braungart-Rieker, J., Garwood, M.M. and Stifter, C.A. (1997) Compliance and noncompliance: the roles of maternal control and child temperament, *Journal of Applied Developmental Psychology*, 18, 411–28.

Broad, B., Hayes, R. and Rushforth, C. (2001) *Kith and Kin: Kinship Care for Vulnerable Young People*, London, NCB.

Brock, A. and Rankin, C. (2008) *Communication, Language and Literacy from Birth to Five*, London, Sage.

Bronfenbrenner, U. (1979) *The Ecology of Human Development: Experiments by Nature and Design*, Cambridge, MA, Harvard University Press.

Bronfenbrenner, U. (ed.) (2005) *Making Human Beings Human: Bioecological Perspectives On Human Development*, London, Sage.

Bronfenbrenner, U. and Morris, P.A. (1998) The ecology of developmental processes, in W. Damon and R.M. Lerner (eds) *Handbook of Child Psychology*, vol. 1, *Theoretical Models of Human Development*, New York, Wiley.

Brown, K. and White, K. (2006) *Exploring the Evidence Base for Integrated Children's Services*, www.scotland.gov.uk/Publications.

Bruce, T. (2005) Play matters, in L. Abbott and A. Langston (eds) *Birth to Three Matters: Supporting the Framework of Effective Practice*, Maidenhead, Open University Press.

Buchanan, A. (2002) Family support, in D. McNeish, T. Newman and H. Roberts (eds) *What Works for Children? Effective Services for Children and Families*, Buckingham, Open University Press.

Buchanan, A. and Hudson, B.L. (eds) (2000) *Promoting Children's Emotional Well-being*, Oxford, Oxford University Press.

Buchanan, A. and Ritchie, C. (2004) *What Works for Troubled Children,* Barkingside, Barnardo's.

Buchanan, A. and Ten Brinke, J.-A. (1997) *What Happened When They Were Grown Up? Outcomes from Parenting Experiences*, York, Joseph Rowntree Foundation.

Buchanan, A. and Ten Brinke, J.-A. (1998) *Recovery from Emotional and Behavioural Problems*, NHS/Oxford University.

Bullock, R., Little, M. and Millham, S. (1993) *Residential Care of Children: A Review of Research*, London, HMSO.

Burgess, K.B., Wojslawowicz, J.C., Rubin, K.H. et al. (2006) Social information processing and coping styles of shy/withdrawn and aggressive children: does friendship matter?, *Child Development*, 77, 371–83.

Burke, B. and Harrison, P. (2009) Anti-oppressive approaches, in R. Adams, L. Dominelli and M. Payne (eds) *Critical Practice in Social Work*, Basingstoke, Palgrave Macmillan.

Butler, I. and Drakeford, M. (2003) *Scandal, Social Policy and Social Welfare*, Bristol, Policy Press.

Cabinet Office (2000) *Adoption: Prime Minister's Review: Issues for Consultation*, A Performance and Innovation Unit Report, London, TSO.

Cabinet Office (2006) *Reaching Out: An Action Plan on Social Exclusion*, London, Cabinet Office.

Cabinet Office (2010) *Modernising Commissioning: Increasing the Role of Charities, Social Enterprises, Mutuals and Cooperatives in Public Service Delivery*, Green Paper, London, Cabinet Office.

Cabinet Office Strategy Unit (2003) *Ethnic Minorities and the Labour Market*, Final Report, London, Cabinet Office.

Calder, M. (2003) The assessment framework: a critique and reformulation, in M.C. Calder and S. Hackett (eds) *Assessment in Child Care: Using and Developing Frameworks for Practice*, Lyme Regis, Russell House.

Candappa, M. and Egharevba, I. (2002) Negotiating boundaries: tensions within home and school life for refugee children, in R. Edwards (ed.) *Children, Home and School: Autonomy, Connection or Regulation*, London, Falmer Press.

Cantle, T., Kaur, D., Athar, M. et al. (2006) *Challenging Local Communities to Change Oldham: Report of Institute of Community Cohesion*, Coventry University.

Caplan, G. (1964) *Principles of Preventive Psychiatry*, London, Tavistock.

Carmichael, K.D. (2006) *Play Therapy: An Introduction*, Upper Saddle River, NJ, Pearson Merrill Prentice Hall.

Cavadino, M. and Dignan, J. (2008) *Penal Systems: A Comparative Approach*, London, Sage.

Chamba, R., Ahmed, W., Hirst, M. et al. (1999) *On the Edge: Minority Ethnic Families Caring for a Severely Disabled Child*, Bristol, Policy Press/ Joseph Rowntree Foundation.

Chambers, H. (2005) *Healthy Care Programme Handbook*, London, NCB.

Chambers, M. (2009) *Arrested Development: Reducing the Number of Young People in Custody while Reducing Crime*, London, Policy Exchange.

Chao, R. (1994) Beyond parental control and authoritarian parenting style: understanding Chinese parenting through the cultural notion of training, *Child Development*, 65, 1111–19.

Chaplain, R. and Freeman, A. (1998) *Coping with Difficult Children*, Cambridge, Pearson.

Chen, S.-J. (1996) Positive childishness: images of childhood in Japan, in C.P. Hwang, M.E. Lamb and I. Sigell (eds) *Images of Childhood*, Mahwah, NJ, Erlbaum.

Cheng, W. (2009) Parental identity: a child's right to know, *Childright*, 254, 13.

Children's Society, The (2007) *Standing By Disabled Children: Policy Briefing*, London, The Children's Society.

Cillessen, A.H. and Bukowski, W. (2000) Conceptualizing and measuring peer acceptance and rejection, *New Directions for Child and Adolescent Development*, 88, 3–10.

Cillessen, A.H., Bukowski, W. and Haselager, G. (2000) Stability of sociometric categories, *New Directions for Child and Adolescent Development*, 88, 75–93.

Cillessen, A.H., Ijendoorn, H.W., van Lieshout, C.F. and Hartup, W.W. (1992) Heterogeneity among peer-rejected boys: subtypes and stabilities, *Child Development*, 63, 893–905.

Clasen, J. and Gould, A. (1997) *Long term Unemployment and the Threat of Social Exclusion*, York, Joseph Rowntree Foundation.

Cleaver, H. (2000) *Fostering Family Contact: A Study of Children, Parents and Foster Carers*, London, TSO.

Cleaver, H., Unell, I. and Aldgate, J. (1999) *Children's Needs – Parenting Capacity: The Impact of Parental Mental Illness. Problem Alcohol and Drug Use, and Domestic Violence on Children's Development*, London, TSO.

Cleaver, H., Walker, S. and Meadows, P. (2004) *Assessing Children's Needs and Circumstances: The Impact of the Assessment Framework*, Lyme Regis, Russell House.

Cocker, C. and Allain, L. (2008) *Social Work with Looked After Children*, Exeter, Learning Matters.

Cocks, A.J. (2000) Respite care for disabled children: micro and macro reflections, *Disability and Society*, 15(3): 507–19.

Cocks, A.J. (2006) The ethical maze: finding an inclusive path toward gaining children's agreement to research participation, *Childhood*, 13(2): 247–66.

Coie, J.D., Dodge, K.A. and Coppotelli, H. (1982) Dimensions and types of social status: a cross-age perspective, *Developmental Psychology*, 18, 557–70.

Collier, A.F., McClure, F.H., Collier, J. et al. (1999) Culture-specific views of child maltreatment and parenting styles in a Pacific-Islan community, *Child Abuse and Neglect*, 23, 229–44.

Colton, M., Drury, C. and Williams, M. (1995) *Children in Need: Family Support under the Children Act 1989*, Aldershot, Gower.

Connors, C. and Stalker, K. (2007) Children's experiences of disability: pointers to a social model of childhood disability, *Disability & Society*, 22(1): 19–33.

Corr, C. (2000) What do we know about grieving children and adolescents?, in K. Doka (ed.) *Living with Grief*, Washington, DC, Hospice Foundation of America.

Council of Europe (1950) European Convention on Human Rights, Strasbourg.

Council of Europe (2005) Report by Mr Alvaro Gil-Robles, Commissioner for Human Rights, on his visit to the United Kingdom 4–12 November 2004, CommDH (2005)6, 8 June, Strasbourg, Council of Europe.

CPAG (Child Poverty Action Group) (2000) *Tackling Child Poverty*, www.cpag.org.uk/info/sp_briefings/0200childpov.htm.

CPAG (2008) *Child Poverty: the Stats. Analysis of the Latest Poverty Statistics*, http://www.cpag.org.uk/info/briefings_policy/CPAG_poverty_the_stats_1008.pdf.

Crawley, H. (2004) *Moving Forward: The Provision of Accommodation for Travellers and Gypsies*, London, IPPR.

Cree, V.E., Kay, H. and Tidsall, K. (2002) Research with children: sharing the dilemmas, *Child & Family Social Work*, 7(1): 47–56.

Crick, N. and Dodge, K. (1994) A review and reformulation of social information processing mechanisms in children's social adjustment, *Psychological Bulletin*, 115, 74–101.

Crompton, M. (ed.) (1996) *Children, Spirituality and Religion*, London, CCETSW.

Crossley, N. (2006) *Contesting Psychiatry; Social Movements in Mental Health*, London, Routledge.

Crowe, B. (1977) *The Playgroup Movement* (3rd edn), London, Allen & Unwin.

Cullen, F.T. and Gilbert, K.E. (2003) The value of rehabilitation, in E. McLaughlin, J. Muncie and G. Hughes (eds) *Criminological Perspectives: Essential Readings* (2nd edn), London, Sage.

Cutrona, C.E. (2000) Social support principles for strengthening families: messages from America, in J. Canavan, P. Dolan and J. Pinkerton (eds) *Family Support: Direction from Diversity*, London, Jessica Kingsley.

CWDC (Children's Workforce Development Council) (2007) *The Lead Professional: Practitioners Guide: Integrated Working to Improve Outcomes for Children and Young People*, Leeds, CWDC.

CWDC (2008a) CWDC's commitment to equality and diversity, http://www.cwdcouncil.org.uk/about/diversity/cwdcs-commitment, accessed 17 Nov. 2008.

CWDC (2008b) Corporate plan, http://www.cwdcouncil.org.uk/assets/0000/1244/CWDC_Business_Plan_2008_-_2011.pdf, accessed 11 May 2011.

CWDC (2010a) *All Together, A Better Way Of Working: One Children's Workforce Framework*, Leeds, CWDC.

CWDC (2010b) *Common Core of Skills and Knowledge: At the Heart of What You Do*, Leeds, CWDC with DCSF.

Daily Mail (1991) The little tearaways, 15 February.

Dalrymple, J. and Horan, H. (2008) Best practice in child advocacy: Matty's story, in K. Jones, B. Cooper and H. Ferguson (eds) *Best Practice in Social Work: Critical Perspectives*, Basingstoke, Palgrave Macmillan.

Davis, J. and Watson, N. (2002) Challenging the stereotypes: disabled children and resistance, in M. Corker and T. Shakespeare (eds) *Postmodernity and Disability*, London, Cassell.

Davis, J.M. (2004) Disabled and childhood: deconstructing the stereotypes, in J. Swain, V. Finkelstein, S. French and M. Oliver (eds) *Disabling Barriers – Enabling Environments*, London, Sage.

Daycare Trust (2005) *Everyone Counts: Supporting the Daycare Needs of Disabled Children, Children with Special Educational Needs and their Families*, London, Daycare Trust.

DCSF (Department for Children, Schools and Families) (2008) *Safeguarding Children in whom Illness is Fabricated or Induced*, London, HM Government.

DCSF (2009a) *Children Looked After in England (including adoption and care leavers) year ending 31 March 2009*, http://www.education.gov.uk/rsgateway/DB/SFR/s000878/index.shtml, accessed 29 Oct. 2010.

DCSF (2009b) *Improving the Educational Attainment of Children in Care (Looked after Children)*, http://publicationseducation.gov.uk/eOrderingDownload/DCSF-00523–2009.pdf, accessed 29 Oct. 2010.

Dearden, C. and Becker, S. (2000) *Growing up Caring: Vulnerability and Transition to Adulthood – Young Carers' Experiences*, Leicester, National Youth Agency.

Dearden, S. and Becker, S. (1998) *Young Carers in the UK: A Profile*, London, Carers National Association.

Dearden, S., Aldridge, J. and Dearden, S. (1998) *Young Carers and their Families*, Oxford, Blackwell.

DES (Department of Education and Science) (1985) *Education for All: Committee of Inquiry into the Education of Children from Ethnic Minority Groups* (the Swann Report), London, HMSO.

DfE (Department for Education) (2008) *The Early Years Foundation Stage: Setting the Standards for Learning, Development and Care for Children from Birth to Five,* available at http://nationalstrategies.standards.dcsf.gov.uk/node/157774.

DfE (2010a) *Working Together to Safeguard Children: A Guide to Inter-agency Working to Safeguard and Promote the Welfare of Children,* London, TSO, available at http://publications.education.gov.uk/eOrderingDownload/00305-2010DOM-EN-v3.pdf.

DfE (2010b) *Preventable Child Deaths in England:* year ending 31 March 2010, available at www.dcsf.gov.uk/rsgateway/DB/STR/d000943/index.shtml.

DfEE (Department for Education and Employment) (1998) *Meeting the Childcare Challenge,* Green Paper, London, TSO.

DfEE (2000) *The Education (National Curriculum) (Foundation Stage Early Learning Goals) (England) Order 2003,* Norwich, TSO.

DfES (Department for Education and Skills) (2002) *Birth to Three Matters Framework,* London, TSO.

DfES (2003a) *Every Child Matters,* Green Paper, London, HMSO.

DfES (2003b) *National Standards for Under 8's Day Care and Childminding: Full Day Care,* London, DfES.

DfES (2003c) *Excellence and Enjoyment: A Strategy for Primary Schools,* London, DfES.

DfES (2004a) *Common Core of Skills, Knowledge and Competence for the Children's Workforce,* London, DfES.

DfES (2004b) *The Common Assessment Framework for Children and Young People,* now available from https://www.education.gov.uk/publications/eOrderingDownload/CAF-Practitioner-Guide.pdf.

DfES (2004c) *Children's Workforce Strategy,* London, TSO.

DfES (2005a) Children looked after in England (including adoption and care leavers): 2004–2005, SFR 51/2005, http://www.education.gov.uk/rsgateway/DB/SFR/s000615/index.shtml, accessed 14 Oct. 2010.

DfES (2005b) *Outcome Indicators for Looked After Children: Twelve Months to 30 September 2005,* London, DfES.

DfES (2006) *Working Together to Safeguard Children: A Guide to Inter-agency Working to Safeguard and Promote the Welfare of Children,* London, TSO.

DfES (2007a) *Care Matters: Time for Change,* White Paper, Cm 7137, London, TSO.

DfES (2007b) *Every Parent Matters,* London, DfES.

DfES (2007c) *Learning to Listen: Core Principles for the Involvement of Children and Young People,* London, DfES.

DfES (2007d) *Safeguarding Children from Abuse Linked to a Belief in Spirit Possession,* London, DfES.

DH (Department of Health) (1998) *Quality Protects: Transforming Children's Services: The Role and Responsibilities of Councillors,* London, TSO.

DH (2000a) *Prime Minister's Review of Adoption: Report from the Performance and Innovation Unit,* LAC (2000)16, London, TSO.

DH (2000b) *Adoption: A New Approach,* White Paper, Cm 5017, London, TSO.

DH (2000c) *Assessing Children in Need and their Families: Practice Guidance,* London, TSO.

DH (2001) *Children Adopted from Care in England,* London, TSO.

DH (2004) *Choosing Health: Making Healthy Choices Easier,* White Paper, Cm 6374, London, TSO.

DH (2010) *Equity and Excellence: Liberating the NHS,* White Paper, Cm 7881, London, TSO.

DH Adoption and Permanence Taskforce (2001) *Annual Report,* London, DH.

DH/DfEE/Home Office (2000) *Framework for the Assessment of Children in Need and their Families,* London, TSO.

DH/DfES (2004a) *National Service Framework for Children, Young People and Maternity Services: Executive Summary,* London, TSO, http://www.dh.gov.uk/en/Publicationsandstatistics/Publications/PublicationsPolicyAndGuidance/DH_4089100, accessed 10 March 2008.

DH/DfES (2004b) *National Service Framework for Children, Young People and Maternity Services: Disabled Children and Young People and Those with Complex Health Needs,* London, TSO, http://www.dh.gov.uk/en/Publicationsandstatistics/Publications/PublicationsPolicyAndGuidance/DH_4089112, accessed 17 May 2011.

DHSS (Department of Health and Social Security) (1974) *Report of the Committee of Inquiry into the Care and Supervision Provided in Relation to Maria Colwell,* London, HMSO.

Dixon, J., Wade, J., Byford, S. et al. (2004) *Young People Leaving Care: A Study of Outcomes and Costs,* University of York.

Dodge, K.A. and Price, J.M. (1994) On the relation between social information processing and socially competent behaviour in early school-aged children, *Child Development*, 65, 1385–97.

Dogra, N., Parkin, A., Gale, F. and Frake, C. (2009) *A Multidisciplinary Handbook of Child and Adolescent Mental Health for Front-line Professionals* (2nd edn), London, Jessica Kingsley.

Donaldson, M. (1986) *Children's Minds*, London, HarperCollins.

Dorling, K. (2009) Booted out: forced return of unaccompanied asylum seeking children, *Childright*, 253, 25.

Driscoll, J. (2010) *Making up Lost Ground: A Study of Young People Leaving Care with Disappointing School Qualifications*, www.beraconference.co.uk/downloads/abstracts/pdf/BERA2010_0188.pdf, accessed 11 May 2011.

Dwivedi, K.N. and Harper, P.B. (eds) (2004) *Promoting the Emotional Well-being of Children and Adolescents and Preventing Their Mental Ill Health*, London, Jessica Kingsley.

DWP (Department for Work and Pensions) (2006) *A New Deal for Welfare: Empowering People to Work*, Cm 6859, London, TSO.

DWP/National Statistics (2004) *Family Resources Survey, United Kingdom 2003–4*, London, DWP.

Dyregrov, A. (2008) *Grief in Children: A Handbook for Adults* (2nd edn), London, Jessica Kingsley.

ECRI (European Commission against Racism and Intolerance) (2005) *Third Report on the United Kingdom,* CRI (2005)27, Strasbourg, Council of Europe.

EDCM (Every Disabled Child Matters) (2007) *Disabled Children and Child Poverty*, http://www.ncb.org.uk/edcm/disabled_children_and_child_poverty.pdf, accessed 12 May 2011.

Eisenberg, N. and Fabes, R.A. (1990) Empathy: conceptualization, measurement and relation to prosocial behaviour, *Motivation and Emotion*, 14, 131–49.

Eisenberg, N. and Fabes, R.A. (1998) Prosocial development, in W. Damon and N. Eisenberg (eds) *Handbook of Child Psychology*, vol. 3, *Social, Emotional and Personality Development* (5th edn), New York, Wiley.

Emerson, E. and Hatton, C. (2007) The socio-economic circumstances of children at risk of disability in Britain, *Disability & Society*, 22(6): 563–80.

Erikson, E.H. (1968) Life cycle, in D.L. Sills (ed.) *International Encyclopaedia of the Social Sciences*, vol. 9, New York, Crowell, Collier.

Ermisch, J. and Fransesconi, M. (2001) *The Effects of Parents' Employment on Prospects for Children*, York, Joseph Rowntree Foundation.

Evans, M., Eyre, J., Millar, J. and Sarre, S. (2003) *New Deal for Lone Parents: Second Synthesis Report of the National Evaluation*, www.dwp.gov.uk/jad/2003/163_rep.pdf, accessed 11 May 2011.

Fahlberg, V. (1991) *A Child's Journey Through Placement*, London, BAAF.

Farrington, D.P. (1993) Understanding and preventing bullying, in M. Tonry and N. Morris (eds) *Crime and Justice: An Annual Review of Research*, Chicago, University of Chicago Press.

Finkelstein, V. (1981) To deny or not to deny disability, in A. Brechin, P. Liddiard and J. Swain (eds) *Handicap in a Social World*, London, Hodder & Stoughton.

Fletcher-Campbell, F. and Archer, T. (2003) *Achievement at Key Stage 4 of Young People in Public Care*, Slough, National Foundation for Educational Research.

Flor, D. and Knapp, N.F. (2001) Transmission and transaction: predicting adolescents' internalization of parental religious values, *Journal of Family Psychology*, 15, 627–45.

Flouri, E. and Buchanan, A. (2003) The role of father involvement in children's later mental health, *Journal of Adolescence*, 26, pp. 63–78.

Ford, R. and Millar, J. (eds) (1998) *Private Lives and Public Responses*, London, Grantham Books.

Ford, R., Marsh, A. and McKay, S. (1995) *Changes in Lone Parenthood 1989 to 1993, Department of Social Security Research Report No. 40*, London, HMSO.

Franklin, A. and Sloper, P. (2006) Participation of disabled children and young people in decision making within social services departments: a survey of current and recent activities in England, *British Journal of Social Work*, 36(5): 723–41.

Freeman, E. (2009) Somebody else's child: everybody's responsibility, *Childright*, 254, 19.

Friedman, S.H., and Resnick, P.J. (2007) Child murder by mothers: patterns and prevention *World Psychiatry*, 6(3): 137–41.

Garner, P.W., Jones, D.C. and Palmer, D.J. (1994) Social cognitive correlates of pre-school children's sibling caregiving behaviour, *Developmental Psychology*, 30, 905–11.

Geldard, K. and Geldard, D. (1997) *Counselling Children: A Practice Introduction*, London, Sage.

Ghate, D. and Hazel, N. (2002) *Parenting in Poor Environments: Stress, Support and Coping*, London, Jessica Kingsley.

Ghate, D., Shaw, C. and Hazel, N. (2000) *How Family Centres are Working with Fathers*, York, Joseph Rowntree Foundation.

Gil, E. (1991) *The Healing Power of Play: Working with Abused Children*, New York, Guilford Press.

Gil, E. (2006) *Helping Abused and Traumatized Children: Integrating Directive and Non-directive Approaches*, New York, Guilford Press.

Gillies, V. (2005) Raising the 'meritocracy': parenting and the individualisation of social class, *Sociology of Health and Illness*, 39(5): 835–53.

Gilligan, C. (1982) *In a Different Voice: Psychological Theory and Women's Development*, Cambridge, MA, Harvard University Press.

Gilligan, P. and Furness, S. (2006) The role of religion and spirituality in social work practice: views and experiences of social workers and students, *British Journal of Social Work*, 36, 617–37.

Gittins, D. (1998) *The Child in Question*, Basingstoke, Macmillan.

Goddard, J., McNamee, S., James, A. and James, A. (2005) *The Politics of Childhood: International Perspectives, Contemporary Developments*, Basingstoke, Palgrave Macmillan.

Goffman, E. (1963) *Stigma: Notes on the Management of Spoiled Identity*, Harmondsworth, Penguin.

Goodley, D. and Tregaskis, C. (2006) Parents of disabled babies: retrospective accounts of disabled family life and social theories of disability, *Qualitative Health Research*, 16(5): 630–46.

Goodwin-Gill, G. (2008) *Convention Relating to the Status of Refugees, United Nations, Geneva, 1951. Protocol Relating to the Status of Refugees, United Nations, New York*, Audiovisual Library of International Law, United Nations, http://untreaty.un.org/cod/avl/ha/prsr/prsr.html.

Gore, S. and Eckenrode, J. (1994) Context and process in research on risk and resilience, in R.J. Haggerty, L.R. Sherrod, N. Garmezy and M. Rutter (eds) *Stress, Risk and Resilience in Children and Adolescents: Process, Mechanisms and Interventions*, Cambridge, Cambridge University Press.

Gould, N. (2006) *Mental Health and Child Poverty*, York, Joseph Rowntree Foundation.

Greco, V., Sloper, P., Webb, R. and Beecham, J. (2005) *An Exploration of Different Models of Multi-Agency Partnerships in Key Worker Services for Disabled Children: Effectiveness and Costs and Skills*, London, HM Treasury Evidence Based Policy Fund and the Welsh Assembly Government in collaboration with Care Coordination Network UK.

Grüner, K., Muris, P. and Merckelbach, H. (1999) The relationship between anxious rearing behaviours and anxiety disorders symptomatology in normal children, *Journal of Behaviour Therapy and Experimental Psychiatry*, 30, 27–35.

GSCC (General Social Care Council) (2002) *Codes of Practice for Social Care Workers and Employers*, London, GSCC.

Gunnoe, M.L., Hetherington, E. M. and Reiss, D. (1999) Parental religiosity, parenting style, and adolescent social responsibility, *Journal of Early Adolescence*, 19, 199–225.

Hardman, C. (2001) Can there be an anthropology of children?, *Childhood*, 8(4): 501–17.

Harris, J.C. (2003) Social neuroscience, empathy, brain integration, and neurodevelopmental disorders, *Physiology & Behavior*, 79, 525–31.

Hart, R.A. (1992) *Children's Participation: From Tokenism to Citizenship*, Innocenti Essays No 4, Florence, UNICEF International Child Development Centre.

Hartshorne, H. and May, M.A. (1928) *Studies in the Nature of Character*, vol. 1, *Studies in Deceit*, New York, Macmillan.

Hartup, W.W. and Stevens, N. (1997) Friendships and adaptation in the life course, *Psychological Bulletin*, 121, 355–70.

Harwin, J., Owen, M., Locke, R. and Forrester, D. (2003) *Making Care Orders Work: A Study of Care Plans and their Implementation*, London, TSO.

Hastings, G., Stead, M., McDermott, L. et al. (2003) *Review of Research on the Effects of Food Promotion to Children* (Hastings Report), Glasgow, Centre for Social Marketing, University of Strathclyde.

Hayes, D. (2005) Social work with asylum seekers and others subject to immigration control, in R. Adams, L. Dominelli and M. Payne (eds) *Social Work Futures: Crossing Boundaries, Transforming Practice*, Basingstoke, Palgrave Macmillan.

Health Statistics Quarterly (2005) Summer, No. 26, pp. 58–61, http://www.statistics.gov.uk/downloads/theme_health/hsq26.pdf, accessed 14 May 2008.

Heidensohn, F. (2006) *Gender and Justice: New Concepts and Approaches*, London, Willan.

Helm, D. and Daniel, B. (2010) *Making Sense of Child and Family Assessment: How to Interpret Children's Needs*, London, Jessica Kingsley.

Henderson, S., Holland, J., McGrellis, S. et al. (2007) *Inventing Adulthoods: A Biographical Approach To Youth Transitions*, London, Sage.

Hendrick, H. (1997) Constructions and re-constructions of British childhood: an interpretive survey, 1800 to the present, in A. James and A. Prout (eds) *Constructing and Reconstructing Childhood* (2nd edn), London, Falmer.

Hendrick, H. (ed.) (2005) *Child Welfare and Social Policy: An Essential Reader*, Bristol, Policy Press.

Hirsch, D. (2006) *What Will it Take to End Child Poverty? Firing on All Cylinders*, York, Joseph Rowntree Foundation.

HM Government (2010) *Building a Stronger Civil Society: A Strategy for Voluntary and Community Groups, Charities and Social Enterprises*, London, TSO.

HMIP (Her Majesty's Inspectorate of Prisons) (2010) *Report of Inspection of Yarl's Wood Immigration Removal Centre*, London, HMIP.

HM Treasury/DfES (2007) *Aiming High for Disabled Children: Better Support for Families*, London, TSO.

Hoffman, L.W. (1988) Cross-cultural differences in child rearing goals, in R.A. LeVine, P.M. Miller and M.M. West (eds) *Parental Behaviour in Diverse Societies*, San Francisco, Jossey-Bass.

Horwath, J. (2009) *The Child's World: Comprehensive Guide to Assessing Children in Need*, London, Jessica Kingsley.

House of Commons (2008) *Policing in the 21st Century*, Home Affairs Committee 7th Report 2007–8, HC 364-II, TSO, London.

Howard League for Penal Reform (n.d.) *Growing Up, Shut Up Factsheet*, http://www.juvenilejusticepanel.org/resource/items/H/L/HLPRFactsheet%20on%20JJ08EN.pdf, accessed 19 May 2011.

Howe, D. (1992) Assessing adoptions in difficulty, *British Journal of Social Work*, 22(1): 1–15.

Howe, D. (1996) *Adopters on Adoption*, London, BAAF.

Howe, D. (2005) *Child Abuse and Neglect: Attachment, Development and Intervention*, Basingstoke, Palgrave Macmillan.

Howe, D. and Feast, J. (2000) *Adoption, Search and Reunion: The Long-term Experience of Adopted Adults*, London, The Children's Society.

Howe, D. and Hinings, D. (1989) *The Post Adoption Centre: The First Three Years*, Norwich, UEA.

Howes, C. and Matheson, C. (1992) Sequences in the development of competent play with peers: social and social pretend play, *Developmental Psychology*, 28, 961–74.

Hugman, R. (2005) *New Approaches in Ethics for the Caring Professions*, Basingstoke, Palgrave Macmillan.

Hurst, G. (2005) Disruptive infants to be treated as potential criminals, says report, *The Times*, 13 June.

Illgaz, H. and Aksu-Coç, A. (2005) Episodic development in preschool children's play-prompted and direct-elicited narratives, *Cognitive Development*, 20, 526–44.

International Labour Organization (1999) Convention No. 182, Worst Forms of Child Labour, http://www.ilo.org/ipec/facts/Worst Formsof ChildLabour/lang–en/index.htm, accessed 11 May 2011.

IRR (Institute of Race Relations) (n.d.) *Living in Bad Housing*, statistics, http://www.irr.org.uk/statistics/housing.html, accessed 1 Nov 2010.

IRR (Institute of Race Relations) (n.d.) *Employment Statistics in the UK*, http://www.irr.org.uk/statistics/employment.html, accessed 24 Oct 2010.

Iwaniec, D., Larkin, E. and Higgins, S. (2006) Research review: risk and resilience in cases of emotional abuse, *Child and Family Social Work*, 11(1): 73–82.

Jack, G. and Gill, O. (2003) *The Missing Side of the Triangle: Assessing the Importance of Family and Environmental Factors in the Lives of Children*, Ilford, Barnardo's.

Jackson, M. (1996) Institutional provision for the feeble-minded in Edwardian England: Sandlebridge and the scientific morality of permanent care, in D. Wright and A. Digby (eds) *From Idiocy to Mental Deficiency: Historical Perspectives on People with Learning Disabilities*, London, Routledge.

Jackson, M. and Colwell, J. (2001) *A Teacher's Handbook of Death*, London, Jessica Kingsley.

Jackson, S. and Thomas, N. (1999) *On the Move Again: What Works in Creating Stability for Looked After Children?*, Barkingside, Barnardo's.

Jackson, S., Ajayi, S. and Quigley, M. (2003) *By Degrees: The First Year*, London, NCB/The Frank Buttle Trust.

Jacobson, J. (1998) *Islam in Transition: Religion and Identity among British Pakistani Youth*, Routledge, London.

James, A. and Prout, A. (eds) (1997) *Constructing and Reconstructing Childhood* (2nd edn), London, Falmer.

James, A.L. and James, A. (2008) Changing childhood in the UK: reconstructing discourses of 'risk' and 'protection', in A. James and A.L. James (eds) *European Childhoods: Cultures,*

Politics and Childhoods in Europe, Basingstoke, Palgrave Macmillan.

Jenkins, R., Lewis, G., Bebbington, P. et al. (2003) The National Psychiatric Morbidity Surveys of Great Britain: initial findings from the Household Survey, *International Review of Psychiatry,* 15(1/2): 29–42

Jennings, S. (2010) Dance movement therapy, dramatherapy, art therapy, music therapy and play therapy, in R. Adams (ed.) *Foundations of Complementary Therapies and Alternative Medicine,* Basingstoke, Palgrave Macmillan.

Jones, C. (2003) *Social Work and Social Justice: A Manifesto for a New Engaged Practice,* University of Liverpool.

Jones, G. (2006) ASBOs put mark of Cain on children, *Daily Telegraph,* 24 April.

Jones, J. (1972) *Prejudice and Racism,* Reading, MA, Addison-Wesley.

Kavale, K.E. and Forness, S.R. (1996) Social skill deficits and learning disabilities: A meta-analysis, *Journal of Learning Disabilities,* 29, 226–38.

Kelly, B (2005) 'Chocolate...makes you autism': impairment, disability and childhood identities, *Disability and Society,* 20(3): 261–75.

Kennedy, M. and Wonnacott, J. (2003) Disabled children and the assessment framework, in M.C. Calder and S. Hackett (eds) *Assessement in Child Care: Using and Developing Frameworks for Practice,* Lyme Regis, Russell House.

King, D. (1998) The persistence of eugenics, *GenEthics News,* February/March, pp. 6–8.

King, R., Raynes, N. and Tizard, J. (1971) *Patterns of Residential Care: Sociological Studies in Institutions for Handicapped Children,* London, Routledge & Kegan Paul.

Kingsley, C. (1994) *The Water Babies: A Fairy Tale for a Land Baby,* London, Wordsworth Children's Classics.

Kirby, P., Lanyon, C., Cronin, K. and Sinclair, R. (2003a) *Building A Culture of Participation: Involving Children and Young People in Policy, Service Planning Delivery and Evaluation, Research Report,* London, DFES.

Kirby, P., Lanyon, C., Cronin, K. and Sinclair, R. (2003b) *Building A Culture of Participation: Involving Children and Young People in Policy, Service Planning Delivery and Evaluation, The Handbook,* London, DFES.

Kjørholt, A.-T. (2005) The competent child and 'the right to be oneself': reflections on children as fellow citizens in an early childhood centre, in A. Clark, A.-T. Kjørholt and P. Moss (eds) *Beyond Listening: Children's Perspectives on Early Childhood Services,* Bristol, Policy Press.

Kochanska, G., DeVet, K., Goldman, M. et al. (1994) Maternal reports of conscience development and temperament in young children, *Child Development,* 65, 852–68.

Kohlberg, L. (1963) The development of children's orientations toward a moral order: I, Sequence in the development of moral thought, *Human Development,* 6, 11–33.

Kohlberg, L. (1975) The cognitive-developmental approach to moral education, *Phi Delta Kappan,* June, 670–7.

Komulainen, S. (2005) The contextuality of children's communication difficulties in specialist practice: a sociological account, *Child Care in Practice,* 11(3): 357–74.

Komulainen, S. (2007) The ambiguity of the child's 'voice' in social research, *Childhood,* 14(1): 11–28.

Kroll, B. (2002) Children and divorce, in N. Thompson (ed.) *Loss and Grief: A Guide for Human Services Practitioners,* Basingstoke, Palgrave Macmillan.

Kübler-Ross, E. (1969) *On Death and Dying,* New York, Macmillan.

Kurtines, W. and Gewirtz, J.L. (eds) (1984) *Morality, Moral Behavior, and Moral Development,* New York, Wiley.

Lamb, M.E., Sternberg, K.J., Hwang, P. and Broberg, A. (eds) (1992) *Child Care in Context: Cross-cultural Perspectives,* New York, Erlbaum.

Laming, H. (2003) *The Victoria Climbié Inquiry Report,* Cm 5730, TSO, London.

Laming, H. (2009) *The Protection of Children in England: A Progress Report,* London, TSO.

Landreth, G. (2002) *Play Therapy: The Art of the Relationship* (2nd edn), Abingdon, Routledge.

Langston, A. and Abbott, L. (2005) Framework matters, in L. Abbott and A. Langston (eds) *Birth to Three Matters: Supporting the Framework of Effective Practice,* Maidenhead, Open University Press.

Lansdown, G. (1995) *Taking Part: Children's Participation in Decision Making,* London, IPPR.

Lansdown, G. (2005) *Can You Hear Me?: The Rights of Young Children to Participate in Decisions Affecting Them,* Working Paper 36, The Hague, Bernard van Leer Foundation.

Layard, R. and Dunn, J. (2009) *A Good Childhood: Searching for Values in a Competitive Age,* London, Penguin/The Children's Society.

Leblanc, M. and Ritchie, M. (2001) A meta-analysis of play therapy outcomes, *Counselling Psychology Quarterly,* 14, 149–63.

Lee, N. (2001) *Childhood and Society: Growing Up in an Age of Uncertainty*, Buckingham, Open University Press.

Lees, J. and Horwath, J. (2009) Religious parents: just want what's best for their kids; young people's perspectives on religious parenting, *Children & Society*, 23(3): 162–75.

Lengua, L.J. and Kovacs, E.A. (2005) Bidirectional associations between temperament and parenting, and the prediction of adjustment problems in middle childhood, *Journal of Applied Developmental Psychology*, 26, 21–38.

Leslie, A.M. (1994) Pretending and believing: issues in the theory of mind, *Cognition*, 50, 211–38.

LeVine, R.A. (1988) Human parental care: universal goals, cultural strategies, individual behaviour, in R.A. LeVine, P.M. Miller and M.M. West (eds) *Parental Behaviour in Diverse Societies. New Directions for Child Development*, No 40, San Francisco, CA, Jossey-Bass.

Levy, A. and Kahan, B. (1991) *The Pindown Experience and the Protection of Children: The Report of the Staffordshire Child Care Inquiry 1990*, Stafford, Staffordshire Social Services Department.

Lewis, C. (1981) The effects of parental firm control: a reinterpretation of findings, *Psychological Bulletin*, 90, 54 –63.

Lewis, C., Freeman, N.H., Kyriakidou, C. et al. (1996) Social influences on false belief access: specific sibling influences or general apprenticeship?, *Child Development*, 67, 2930–47.

Lewis, M. and Rosenblum, L. (eds) *Friendship and Peer Relations*, New York, Wiley.

Lindsey, E.W. (2002) Preschool children's friendships and peer acceptance: links to social competence, *Child Study Journal*, 32, 145–56.

Lloyd, N., O'Brien, M. and Lewis, C. (2003) *Fathers in Sure Start*, NESS, London, Birkbeck University.

London Borough of Greenwich (1987) *A Child in Mind*, London Borough of Greenwich.

London Borough of Lambeth (1987) *Whose Child? The Report of the Public Inquiry into the Death of Tyra Henry*, London Borough of Lambeth.

Low Pay Commission (2007) *Employment in Low Pay Child Care Occupations*, London, Low Pay Commission.

McAlister, A. and Peterson, C.C. (2007) A longitudinal study of child siblings and theory of mind development, *Cognitive Development*, 22, 258–70.

McCune-Nicholich, L. (1981) Toward symbolic functioning: structure of early pretend games

and potential parallels with language, *Child Development*, 52, 785–97.

Macdonald, G. (2001) *Effective Interventions for Child Abuse and Neglect: An Evidence-based Approach to Planning and Evaluating Interventions*, Chichester, Wiley.

Macdonald, G. and Williamson, E. (2002) *Against the Odds: An Evaluation of Child Support Centres*, London, NCB.

McKie, L., Cunningham-Burley, S. and McKendrick, J.H. (2005) Families and relationships: boundaries and bridges, in L. McKie, S. Cunningham-Burley and J.H. McKendrick (eds) *Families in Society: Boundaries and Relationships*, Bristol, Policy Press.

McLaughlin, J., Goodley, D., Clavering, E. and Fisher, P. (2008) *Families Raising Disabled Children: Enabling Care and Social Justice*, Basingstoke, Palgrave Macmillan.

McLean, A. (2003) *The Motivated School*, London, Paul Chapman.

McLeod, A. (2001) Changing patterns of teenage pregnancy: population based study of small areas, *British Medical Journal*, 323(7306): 199–203.

McLeod, A. (2008) *Listening to Children: A Practitioner's Guide*, London, Jessica Kingsley

McMillan, M. ([1911]2008) *The Child and the State*, London, William Press.

McMillan, M. ([1919]2009) *The Nursery School*, Delhi, Cosmo Publications.

Maccoby, E.E. and Martin, J.A. (1983) Socialisation in the context of the family: parent-child interaction, in E.M. Hetherington (ed.) *Handbook of Child Psychology*, vol. 4, *Socialisation, Personality and Personal Development*, New York, Wiley.

Mahoney, A., Pargament, K.L., Tarakeshwar, N. and Swank, A.B. (2001) Religion in the home in the 1980s and 1990s: a meat-analytic review and conceptual analysis of links between religion, marriage and parenting, *Journal of Family Psychology*, 15, 559–96.

Marchant, R. and Martyn, M. (1999) *Make it Happen: Communicating with Disabled Children: Communication Handbook*, Brighton, Triangle.

Marks, L. (2004) Sacred practices in highly religious families: Christian, Mormon and Muslim perspectives, *Family Process*, 43, 217–31.

Marmot, M. (2010) *Fair Society, Healthy Lives: A Strategic Review of Health Inequalities in England Post-2010* (The Marmot Review), www.marmotreview.org, accessed 23 Nov. 2010.

Martin, P. (2005) *Making Happy People: The Nature of Happiness and its Origins in Childhood*, London, HarperCollins.

Maslow, A. (1943) A theory of human motivation, *Psychological Review*, 50, 370–96.

Mason, D. and Frick, P. (1994) The heritability of antisocial behavior, *Journal of Psychopathology and Behavior Assessment*, 16, 237–246.

Mayall, B. (2002) *Towards a Sociology of Childhood: Thinking from Children's Lives*, Buckingham, Open University.

Meltzer, H., Gatward, R., Goodman, R. and Ford, T. (2003) Mental health of children and adolescents in Great Britain, *International Review of Psychiatry*, 15(1/2): 185–7.

Mental Health Foundation (2008) *Children and Young People*, http://www.mentalhealth.org.uk/information/mental-health-a-z/children-and-young-people/, accessed 10 March 2008.

Middlesbrough Council (2009) *Putting Children and Young People First: The Key to Middlesbrough's Future*, Middlesbrough Council.

Miller, J. (2003) *Never Too Young*, London, Save the Children.

Millham, S., Bullock, R. and Cherrett, P. (1975) *After Grace – Teeth: A Comparative Study of the Residential Experience of Boys in Approved Schools*, London, Human Context Books.

Millham, S., Bullock, R. and Hosie, K. (1978) *Locking Up Children: Secure Provision within the Child Care System*, Aldershot, Saxon House.

Minnett, P.M. (2005) *Child Care and Development* (5th edn), London, Hodder Education.

Minority Rights Group International (n.d.) Roma/Gypsies/Travellers, http://www.minorityrights.org/5421/united-kingdom/romagypsiestravellers.html, accessed 10 March 2008.

Mockford, C. and Barlow, J. (2004) Parenting programmes: some unintended consequences, *Primary Health Care Research and Development*, 5, 219–27.

Mooney, A., Owen, C. and Statham, J. (2008) *Disabled Children: Numbers, Characteristics and Local Service Provision (DCSF-RR042)*, London, DCSF.

Moore, N.V., Everston, C.M. and Brophy, J.E. (1974) Solitary play: some functional reconsiderations, *Developmental Psychology*, 10, 830–34.

Moore, T. (1968) Language and intelligence: a longitudinal study of the first 8 years, Part II: environmental correlates of mental growth, *Human Development*, 11, 1–24.

Moran, P. and Ghate, D. (2005) The effectiveness of parenting support, *Children & Society*, 19(4): 329–36.

Morris, J. (1997) Gone missing? Disabled children living away from their families, *Disability & Society*, 12(2): 241–58.

Morris, J. (1998) *Don't Leave Us Out: Involving Disabled Children and Young People with Communication Impairments*, York, Joseph Rowntree Foundation.

Morris, J. (1999) Disabled children, child protection systems and the Children Act 1989, *Child Abuse Review*, 8, 91–108.

Morris, J. and Wates, M. (2006) *Supporting Disabled Parents and Parents with Additional Support Needs*, London, SCIE.

Morris, J., Abbott, D. and Ward, L. (2002) At home or away? An exploration of policy and practice in the placement of disabled children in residential school, *Children & Society*, 16(1): 3–16.

Morris, N. (2006) More than 2,000 children of asylum seekers detained, *The Independent*, 28 March.

Morrow, V. and Richardson, M. (2002) Ethics of social research with children: an overview, in K.W. Fulford, D. Dickenson and T.H. Murray (eds) *Healthcare Ethics and Human Values*, Oxford University Press.

Moss, P. (1991) Day care policy and provision in Britain, in P. Moss and E. Melhuish (eds) *Current Issues in Day Care for Young Children*, London, HMSO.

Munro, E. (2002) *Effective Child Protection*, London, Sage.

Munro, E. (2011) *The Munro Review of Child Protection: Interim Report: The Child's Journey*, London, DfE.

NACRO (National Association for the Care and Resettlement of Offenders) (2008) *Some Facts about Children and Young People who Offend*, London, NACRO.

National Council for One Parent Families (2001) *One Parent Families Today: The Facts*, London, National Council for One Parent Families.

National Statistics (2001) *Census 2001 – Families of England and Wales*, http://www.statistics.gov.uk/census2001/profiles/commentaries/family.asp.

National Working Group on Child Protection and Disability (2003) *It Doesn't Happen to Disabled Children: Child Protection and Disabled Children*, London, NSPCC.

NCH (National Children's Homes) (2002) *FactFile 2002–3*, London, NCH.

Neil, E. (2000a) Contact with Birth Relatives After Adoption: A Study of Young, Recently Placed Children, unpublished PhD thesis, Norwich, UEA.

Neil, E. (2000b) The reasons young people are placed for adoption: findings from a recently placed sample and implications for future identity issues, *Child and Family Social Work*, 5(4): 303–16.

Neimeyer, R. (2002) Making sense of loss, in K. Doka (ed.) *Living with Grief: Loss in Later Life*, Washington, Hospice Foundation of America.

New, C. and David, M. (1985) *For the Children's Sake*, Harmondsworth, Penguin.

Newcomb, A.F. and Bagwell, C.L. (1995) Children's friendship relations: a meta-analytic review, *Psychological Bulletin*, 117, 306–47.

Newell, P. (1989) *Children are People Too: The Case Against Physical Punishment*, London, Bedford Square Press.

NI DHSSPS (Northern Ireland Department of Health, Social Services and Public Safety) (2004) *Inequalities and Unfair Access Issues Emerging from the DHSSPS Equality and Inequalities in Health and Social Care: A Statistical Overview Report*, Belfast, NI DHSSPS.

Nutbeam, D. (1998) *Health Promotion Glossary*, Geneva, WHO.

O'Donahue, W.T. and Ferguson, K.E. (2001) *The Psychology of B.F. Skinner*, Thousand Oaks, CA, Sage.

ODPM (Office of the Deputy Prime Minister) (2006) *Definition of the Terms 'Gypsies and Travellers' for the Purposes of the Housing Act 2004*, London, ODPM.

Ofsted (2005) *Framework for the Regulation of Childminding and Day Care*, London, Ofsted.

Ofsted (2008) *Children's Views on Advocacy: A Report by the Children's Rights Director for England*, London, Ofsted.

O'Hagan, K. (2001) *Cultural Competence in the Caring Professions*, London, Jessica Kingsley.

Oliver, M. (1983) *Social Work with Disabled People*, Basingstoke, Macmillan.

Oliver, M. (1990) *The Politics of Disablement*, Basingstoke, Macmillan – now Palgrave Macmillan.

Oliver, M. (1996) *Understanding Disability: From Theory to Practice*, Basingstoke, Macmillan – now Palgrave Macmillan.

Oliver, M. and Bailey, P. (2002) Report on the Application of the Social Model of Disability to the Services provided by Birmingham City Council, unpublished.

Olweus, D. (1993) *Bullying at School: What We Know and What We Can Do*, Oxford, Blackwell.

ONS (Office for National Statistics) (2002) *General Household Survey 2002*, Norwich, TSO.

Osler, A. and Hussain, Z. (2005) Educating Muslim girls: do mothers have faith in the state sector?, in T. Abbas (ed.) *Muslim Britain: Communities Under Pressure*, London, Zed Books.

Oswin, M. (1998) An historic perspective, in C. Robinson and K. Stalker (eds) *Growing Up with Disability*, London, Jessica Kingsley.

Owusu-Bempah, K. (2001) Racism: an important factor in practice with ethnic minority children and families, in P. Foley, J. Roche and S. Tucker (eds) *Children in Society: Contemporary Theory, Policy and Practice*, Basingstoke, Palgrave Macmillan/Open University.

Paley, V.G. (1990) *The Boy Who Would Be A Helicopter: The Uses of Storytelling in the Classroom*, Cambridge, MA, Harvard University Press.

Palmer, G., MacInnes, T. and Kenway, P. (2009) *Monitoring Poverty and Social Exclusion*, York, Joseph Rowntree Trust.

Pargament, K.L., Magyar-Russell, G.M. and Murray-Swank, N.A. (2005) The sacred and the search for significance: religion as a unique process, *Journal of Social Issues*, 61(4): 665–87.

Parker, R. (1988) Children, in I. Sinclair (ed.) *Residential Care: The Research Reviewed*, London, HMSO.

Parkes, C.M. (1998) *Bereavement: Studies of Grief in Adult Life* (3rd edn), London, Routledge.

Parten, M.B. (1932) Social participation among preschool children, *Journal of Abnormal and Social Psychology*, 27, 243–69.

Patterson, G.R., DeBaryshe, B.D. and Ramsey, E. (1989) A developmental perspective on antisocial behavior, *American Psychologist*, 44, 329–35.

Peden, M., Oyegbite, K., Ozanne-Smith, J. et al. (2008) *World Report on Child Injury Prevention*, Geneva, WHO/UNICEF.

Pellegrini, A.D., Dupuis, D. and Smith, P.K. (2007) Play in evolution and development, *Developmental Review*, 27, 261–76.

Perner, J., Ruffman, T. and Leekam, S.R. (1994) Theory of mind is contagious: you catch it from your sibs, *Child Development*, 65, 1228–38.

Piaget, J. (1932) *The Moral Judgement of the Child*, London, Routledge Kegan & Paul.

Piaget, J. (1954) *The Construction of Reality in the Child*, New York, Basic Books.

Pickett, K. and Dorling, D. (2010) Against the organisation of misery? The Marmot review of health inequalities, *Social Science and Medicine*, 71, 1231–3.

Pilgrim, D. (2002) The biopsychosocial model in Anglo-American psychiatry: past, present and future, *Journal of Mental Health*, 11(6): 585–94.

Pillai, R., Rankin, J., Stanley, K. et al. (2007) *Disability 2020: Opportunities for the Full and Equal Citizenship of Disabled People in Britain in 2020*, London, IPPR.

PMSU (Prime Minister's Strategy Unit)/DWP/DH/DfES/ODPM (2005) *Improving the Life Chances of Disabled People: Final Report*, London, PMSU.

Poverty Site, The (n.d.) *Key Facts, Summary*, http://www.poverty.org.uk/summary/key%20facts.shtml, accessed 28 Aug. 2009.

Preston, G. (2006) Families with disabled children, benefits and poverty, *Benefits*, 14(1): 39–43.

Prout, A. (2005) *The Future of Childhood*, London, Falmer Routledge.

Pugh, G., Aplin, G., De'Ath, E. and Moxon, M. (1987) *Partnership in Action*, vols 1 and 2, London, National Children's Bureau.

Punch, S. (2002) Research with children: the same or different from research with adults, *Childhood*, 9(3): 321–41.

QCA (Qualifications and Curriculum Authority) (2000) *Curriculum Guidance for the Foundation Stage*, London, TSO.

QCDA (Qualifications and Curriculum Development Agency) (n.d.) *National Curriculum*, http://curriculum.qcda.gov.uk/index.aspx, accessed 11 May 2011.

Qvortrup, J. (1994) Childhood matters: an introduction, in J. Qvortrup, M. Bardy, G. Sgritta and H. Wintersberger (eds) *Childhood Matters: Social Theory, Practice and Politics*, Aldershot, Avebury.

Qvortrup, J. (2008) Macro-analysis of childhood, in P. Christensen and A. James (eds) *Research with Children: Perspectives and Practices* (2nd edn), London, Falmer.

Qvortrup, J., Bardy, M., Sgritta, G. and Wintersberger, H. (eds) (1994) *Childhood Matters: Social Theory, Practice and Politics*, Aldershot, Avebury.

Reder, P., Duncan, S. and Gray, M. (1993) *Beyond Blame: Child Abuse Tragedies Revisited*, London, Routledge.

Refugee Council (2001) *Separated Children in the UK*, http://www.refugeecouncil.org.uk/policy/position/2001/separatedchildren, accessed 12 May 2011.

Ricaud-Droisy, H. and Zaouche-Gaudron, C. (2003) Interpersonal conflict resolution strategies in children: a father-child-construction, *European Journal of Psychology and Education*, 15, 157–69.

Riley, D. (1983) *War in the Nursery: Theories of the Child and Mother*, London, Virago.

Rixon, A. (2008) Positive practice relationships, in P. Foley and S. Leverett (eds) *Connecting with Children: Developing Working Relationships*, Basingstoke, Palgrave Macmillan.

Road Safety Analysis (2010) *Child Casualties 2010: A Study into Resident Risk of Children on Roads in Great Britain 2004–2008*, http://www.roadsafetanalysis.org/2010/child-casualties-2010/, accessed 17 Aug. 2010.

Robinson, E. (2000) *Adoption and Loss: The Hidden Grief*, New South Wales, Clova.

Rogers, S.J. and Pennington, B.F. (1991) A theoretical approach to the deficits in infantile autism, *Development and Psychopathology*, 107, 147–61.

Rothbart, M.K. and Bates, J.E. (1998) Temperament, in W. Damon (series ed.) and N. Eisenberg (vol. ed.) *Handbook of Child Psychology*, vol. 3, *Social, Emotional and Personality Development* (5th edn), New York, John Wiley.

Rowe, J., Hundleby, M. and Garnett, L. (1989) *Child Care Now: A Survey of Placement Patterns*, London, BAAF.

Rowlinson, K. and McKay, S. (1998) *The Growth of Lone Parenthood*, London, Grantham Books.

Roy, A., Young, F. and May-Chahal, C. (2009) Looked after children and young people in residential and foster care, in R. Adams, L. Dominelli and M. Payne (eds) *Critical Practice in Social Work*, Basingstoke, Palgrave Macmillan.

Rubin, K.H. (1982) Nonsocial play in preschoolers: necessarily evil?, *Child Development*, 53, 651–7.

Ruffman, T., Perner, J., Naito, M. et al. (1998) Older (but not younger) siblings facilitate false belief understanding, *Developmental Psychology*, 34, 161–74.

Rutter, M. (1981) *Maternal Deprivation Reassessed* (2nd edn), Harmondsworth, Penguin.

Rutter, M. (2005) *Families and the State: Two-way Support and Responsibilities: An Inquiry into the Relationship between the State and the Family in the Upbringing of Children, Commission on Families and the Wellbeing of Children*, Bristol, Policy Press.

Rutter, M. (2007) Resilience, competence and coping, *Child Abuse and Neglect*, 31(3): 205–9.

Saeed, A., Blain, N. and Forbes, D. (1999) New ethnic and national questions in Scotland: post-British identities among Glasgow Pakistani teenagers, *Ethnic and Racial Studies*, 22(5): 821–44.

Sameroff, A.J. (1975) Early influences on development: fact or fancy?, *Merrill-Palmer Quarterly*, 21(4): 267–94.

Sameroff, A.J. (1995) General systems theories and developmental psychopathology, in D. Cicchetti and D.J. Cohen (eds) *Developmental Psychopathology*, vol. 1, *Theory and Methods*, New York, John Wiley & Sons.

Sanders, M.R. (1999) Triple P-positive parenting program: towards an empirically validated multilevel parenting and family support strategy for the prevention of behavior and emotional problems in children, *Clinical Child and Family Psychology Review*, 2(2): 71–90.

Sapey, B. (2008) Engaging with the social model of disability, in P. Higham (ed.) *Understanding Post Qualifying Social Work Practice*, London, Sage.

Sarrazin, J. and Cyr, F. (2007) Parental conflicts and their damaging effects on children, *Journal of Divorce and Remarriage*, 47(1/2): 77–93.

Scalia, V. (2005) A lesson in tolerance? Juvenile justice in Italy, *Youth Justice*, 5(1): 33–43.

Schaffer, H.R. and Emerson, P.E. (1964) *The Development of Social Attachments in Infancy*, Monographs of the Society for Research on Child Development, no 29.

Schwartz, D., Dodge, K.A. and Coie, J.D. (1993) The emergence of chronic peer victimization in boys' play groups, *Child Development*, 64, 1755–72.

SCIE (Social Care Institute for Excellence) (2004) *Preventing Teenage Pregnancy in Looked After Children*, SCIE research briefing 9, www.scie. org.uk/publications/briefings/briefing09/index. asp, accessed 15 May 2008.

Scottish Executive (2007) *Getting it Right for Every Child: Guidance on the Child's or Young Person's Plan*, Edinburgh, Scottish Executive.

Scottish Government (2011) *Social Economy*, http:// www.scotland.gov.uk/Topics/Statistics/Browse/ Business/TrendSocialEconomy, accessed 11 May 2011.

Secretary of State for Work and Pensions (2006) *Disability Discrimination Act: Guidance on Matters to be Taken into Account in Determining Questions Relating to the Definition of Disability*, London, DWP.

Seebohm Report (1968) *Report of the Committee on Local Authority and Allied Personal Social Services*, London, HMSO.

Seidler, V. (2010) *Embodying Identities: Culture, Differences and Social Theory*, Bristol, Policy Press.

Sellick, C. and Connolly, J. (2001) *National Survey of Independent Fostering Agencies*, Norwich,

Centre for Research on the Child and Family, UEA.

Sellick, C., Thoburn, J. and Philpot, T. (2004) *What Works in Adoption and Foster Care?*, Barkingside, Barnardo's.

Selman, R.L. (1980) *The Growth of Interpersonal Understanding*, New York, Academic Press.

Selwyn, J., Sturgess, W., Quinton, D. and Baxter, C. (2003) *Costs and Outcomes of Non-infant Adoptions: Report to the Department for Education and Skills*, London, DfES.

Sergeant, H. (2006) *Handle with Care: An Investigation into the Care System*, London, Centre for Young Policy Studies.

SEU (Social Exclusion Unit) (2003) *A Better Education for Children in Care: Social Exclusion Unit Report*, London, ODMP.

Shaefer, C.E. and Kaduson, H.G. (2007) *Contemporary Play Therapy: Theory, Research and Practice*, New York, Guilford Press.

Shakespeare, T. (2005) Disability, genetics and global justice, *Social Policy and Society*, 4(1): 87–95.

Shakespeare, T. (2006) *Disability Rights and Wrongs*, Abingdon, Routledge.

Sharma, N. (2002) *Still Missing Out? Ending Poverty and Social Exclusion: Messages to Government from Families with Disabled Children*, Ilford, Barnardo's.

Sharpe, E.J. (1983) *Understanding Religion*, Duckworth, London.

Shaw, C. (1998) *Remember My Messages*, London, Who Cares? Trust.

Sheppard, M. (2004) *Prevention and Coping in Child and Family Care: Mothers in Adversity Coping with Child Care*, London, Jessica Kingsley.

Siegal, M. (1982) *Fairness in Children: A Social-Cognitive Approach to the Study of Moral Development*, London, Academic Press.

Sinclair, I. (2005) *Fostering Now: Messages from Research*, London, Jessica Kingsley.

Sinclair, I., Gibbs, I. and Wilson, K. (2004) *Foster Carers: Why They Stay and Why They Leave*, London, Jessica Kingsley.

Sinclair, I., Wilson, K. and Gibbs, I. (2000) *Supporting Foster Placements*, www.york. ac.uk/inst/spru/research/summs/fosterplace. php, accessed 21 Oct. 2010.

Sinclair, I., Baker, C., Wilson, K. and Gibbs, I. (2005) *Foster Children: Where They Go and How They Get On*, London, Jessica Kingsley.

Singleton, N., Bumpstead, R., O'Brien, M. et al. (2003) Psychiatric morbidity among adults living in private households, 2000, *International Review of Psychiatry*, 15(1/2): 65–73.

Smith, C. and Pugh, G. (1996) *Learning to be a Parent: A Survey of Group-based Parenting Programme*, London, Family Policy Studies Centre.

Smith, M. (2004) Parental mental health: disruptions to parenting and outcomes for children, *Child and Family Social Work*, 9(1): 3–11.

Smith, P.K. (1978) A longitudinal study of social participation in preschool children: solitary and parallel play re-examined, *Developmental Psychology*, 14, 517–23.

Smith, P.K. and Sharp, S. (eds) (1994) *School Bullying: Insights and Perspectives*, London, Routledge.

Snarey, J.R. (1985) Cross cultural universality of social-moral development: a critical review of Kohlbergian research, *Psychological Bulletin*, 97, 202–32.

Sriskandarajah, D. (2005) Outsiders on the inside: towards socially just migration policies, in N. Pearce and W. Paxton (eds) *Social Justice: Building a Fairer Britain*, London, Politico's/ Methuen.

Sriskandarajah, D. et al. (2004) *FactFile: Labour Migration to the UK*, IPPR, http://ippt.org/ research/files/team19/project158/FFLabMig FINAL/pdf, accessed 11 May 2011.

Stainton-Rogers, W. and Stainton-Rogers, R. (1992) *Stories of Childhood*, London, Harvester Wheatsheaf.

Stanley, N., Penhale, B., Riordan, D. et al. (2003) *Child Protection and Mental Health Services*, Bristol, Policy Press.

Statham, J., Dillon, J. and Moss, P. (2001) *Placed and Paid For: Supporting Families through Sponsored Day Care*, London, TSO.

Statham, J., Lloyd, E., Moss, P. et al. (1990) *Playgroups in a Changing World*, London, HMSO.

Steedman, C. (1990) *Childhood, Culture and Class in Britain, Margaret McMillan (1860–1931)*, London, Virago.

Stein, M. (2004) *What Works for Young People Leaving Care?*, Barkingside, Barnardo's.

Stewart, A. (2000) Social inclusion: an introduction, in P. Askonas and A. Stewart (eds) *Social Inclusion: Possibilities and Tensions*, Basingstoke, Palgrave – now Palgrave Macmillan.

Stroebe, M. and Schut, H. (1999) The dual process model of coping with bereavement: rationale and description, *Death Studies*, 23, 197–224.

Sunday Times (1995) Police computer to target six year olds, 15 October.

Sutton, J., Smith, P.K. and Swettenham, J. (1999) Bullying and 'theory of mind': a critique of the 'social skills deficit' view of anti-social behaviour, *Social Development*, 8, 117–27.

Swain, J., French, S. and Cameron, C. (2003) *Controversial Issues in a Disabling Society*, Buckingham, Open University Press.

Swansea Local Safeguarding Children Board (2007) *Serious Case Review*, Swansea, Swansea Borough Council.

Sweeting, H. and Seaman, P. (2005) Family within and beyond the household boundary: children's constructions of who they live with, in L. McKie, S. Cunningham-Burley and J.H. McKendrick (eds) *Families in Society: Boundaries and Relationships*, Bristol, Policy Press.

Symons, D. (2004) Mental state discourse, theory of mind, and the internalization of self-other understanding, *Developmental Review*, 24, 159–88.

Tapsfield, R. and Collier, F. (2005) *The Cost of Foster Care: Investing in our Children's Futures*, London, BAAF.

Tarry, H. and Emler, N. (2007) Attitudes, values and moral reasoning as predictors of delinquency, *British Journal of Developmental Psychology*, 25, 169–83.

Thakker, J., Ward, T. and Strongman, K.T. (1999) Mental disorder and cross-cultural psychology: a constructivist perspective, *Clinical Psychology Review*, 19(7): 843–74.

Thoburn, J. (2002) *Adoption and Permanence for Children Who Cannot Live Safely with Birth Parents or Relatives*, Quality Protects, Research Briefing 5, London.

Thoburn, J., Wilding, J. and Watson, J. (2000) *Family Support in Cases of Emotional Maltreatment and Neglect*, London, TSO.

Thomas, A. (1984) Temperament research: where we are, where we are going. *Merrill-Palmer Quarterly*, 30, 103–9.

Thomas, C. (2002) The 'disabled' body, in M. Evans and E. Lee (eds) *Real Bodies*, Basingstoke, Palgrave – now Palgrave Macmillan.

Thomas, C. (2003) Defining a theoretical agenda for disability studies, paper to the Disability Studies: Theory, Policy and Practice conference at Lancaster University.

Thorpe, D., Smith, D., Paley, J. and Green, C. (1980) *Out of Care: The Community Support of Young Offenders*, Harlow, Longman.

Tomlinson, P. (2004) *Therapeutic Approaches in Work with Traumatized Children and Young People*, London, Jessica Kingsley.

Tunnard, J. (2002) Matching needs and services: emerging themes from its application in different social care settings, in H. Ward and W. Rose (eds) *Approaches to Needs Assessment in Children's Services*, London, Jessica Kingsley.

Tunstill, J. and Aldgate, J. (2000) *Services for Children in Need: From Policy to Practice*, London, TSO.

Turiel, E. (1998) The development of morality, in W. Damon and N. Eisenberg (eds) *Handbook of Child Psychology*, vol. 3, *Social, Emotional and Personality Development* (5th edn), New York, Wiley.

UK Children's Commissioners (2008) *Report to the UN Committee on the Rights of the Child*, London.

UN (United Nations) (1948) *Universal Declaration of Human Rights*, Geneva, UN.

UN (1967) *Protocol Relating to the Status of Refugees*, New York, UN.

UN (1989) *Convention on the Rights of the Child*, New York, UN.

Underdown, A. (2007) *Young Children's Health and Well-being*, Maidenhead, Open University Press.

UNHCR (United Nations High Commission for Refugees) (1951) *Convention and Protocol Relating to the Status of Refugees*, Geneva, UN.

UNHCR (2001) *Number of Refugees Per Capita of Total Populations*, Geneva, UNHCR.

UNICEF (2007) *Child Poverty in Perspective: An Overview of Child Well-being in Rich Countries*, Innocenti Report Card 7, Florence, UNICEF Innocenti Research Centre.

UPIAS (Union of Physically Impaired Against Segregation) (1976) *Fundamental Principles of Disability*, London, UPIAS, www.leeds.ac.uk/disability-studies/archiveuk/index.html.

Voas, D. and Crockett, A. (2005) Religion in Britain: neither believing nor belonging, *Sociology*, 39(1): 11–28.

Vygotsky, L.S. (1962) *Thought and Language*, Cambridge, MA, MIT Press.

Vygotsky, L.S. (1978) *Mind in Society*, Cambridge, MA, Harvard University Press.

Vygotsky, L.S. (1986) *Thought and Language*, Cambridge, MA, MIT Press.

Walker, L.J., Pitts, R.C., Henning, K.H. and Matsuba, M.K. (1995) Reasoning about morality and real-life moral problems, in M. Keller and D. Hart (eds) *Morality in Everyday Life*, Cambridge, Developmental Perspectives.

Walklate, S. (2004) *Gender, Crime and Criminal Justice* (2nd edn), London, Willan.

Wallerstein, J. and Blakeslee, S. (2004) *Second Chances: Men, Women and Children a Decade after Divorce*, Boston, NY, Houghton Mifflin.

Wallerstein, J. and Kelly, J. (1980) *Surviving the Breakup*, New York, Basic Books.

Ward, L. and Wintour, P. (2006) State super-nannies to help struggling parents, *The Guardian*, 22 November.

Ward, H. (ed.) (1995a) *Looking After Children: Research into Practice*, London, HMSO.

Ward, H. (ed.) (1995b) *Looking after Children, Research into Practice, The Second Report to the Department of Health on Assessing Outcomes in Childcare*, London, HMSO.

Washbrook, L. (2010) *A Cross Cohort of Children's Behaviour Problems: Summary of Preliminary Findings from a Project for the Sutton Trust*, www.suttontrust.com/news/news/poorer-children-twice-as-likely-to/, accessed 2 Nov. 2010.

Waterhouse, R., Clough, M. and Le Fleming, M. (2000) *Lost in Care: Report of the Tribunal of Inquiry into the Abuse of Children in Care in the former county council areas of Gwynedd and Clwyd since 1974: Summary of Report with Conclusions and Recommendations in Full*, London, TSO.

Waterhouse, S. (1997) *The Organisation of Fostering Services: A Study of the Arrangements for Delivery of Fostering Services in England*, London, National Foster Care Association.

Watson, P. (2008) *Evaluation of the Leeds Prevention Programme*, London, Crime Concern.

Wessels, B. and Bagnall, V. (2002) *Information and Joining Up Services: The Case of an Information Guide for Parents of Disabled Children*, Bristol, Policy Press.

Whitney, I. and Smith, P.K. (1993) A survey of the nature and extent of bully/victim problems in junior/middle and secondary schools, *Educational Research*, 35, 3–25.

Wilcox, W.B. (1998) Conservative Protestant child-rearing: authoritarian or authoritative?, *American Sociological Review*, 63, 796–809.

Wilkin, A., Derrington, C., White, R. et al. (2010) *Research Report Improving the Outcomes for Gypsy, Roma and Traveller Pupils: Final Report*, London, DfE.

Williams, L. (2010) *Am I Staying for Lunch Today?*, London, DCSF.

Woodcock, J. (2003) The social work assessment of parenting: an exploration, *British Journal of Social Work*, 33(1): 87–106.

Working Families (2008) *Making it Work for You: New Guide for Working Parents of Disabled Children*, London, Working Families.

Worrall-Davies, A., Cottrell, D. and Benson, E. (2004) Evaluation of an early intervention tier 2 child and adolescent mental health service, *Health and Social Care in the Community*, 12(2): 119–25.

Worsley, R. (2007) *Children and Young People in Custody, 2004–2006: An Analysis of Children's Experiences of Prison*, London, Her Majesty's Inspectorate of Prisons/Youth Justice Board.

Wyness, M. (2006) *Childhood and Society: An Introduction to the Sociology of Childhood*, Basingstoke, Palgrave Macmillan.

YMCA (2006) Young people and children 'are being criminalised' says YMCA England, press release, 24 April.

Zaman, A. (2006) *Child Protection in Faith Based Environments: A Guideline Report*, London, Muslim Parliament of Great Britain, available at http://www.muslimparliament.org.uk/Documentation/ChildProtectionReport.pdf.

Author Index

Subject Index